PIVOTAL DECADES

Also by John Milton Cooper, Jr.

THE VANITY OF POWER: AMERICAN ISOLATIONISM AND
THE FIRST WORLD WAR

WALTER HINES PAGE: THE SOUTHERNER AS AMERICAN

THE WARRIOR AND THE PRIEST: WOODROW WILSON AND
THEODORE ROOSEVELT

PIVOTAL DECADES
The United States
1900 ⟋⟍ 1920

JOHN MILTON COOPER, JR.

W·W·NORTON & COMPANY·NEW YORK·LONDON

The text of this book is composed in Linotype Walbaum, with
display type set in Walbaum. Composition and
manufacturing by The Maple-Vail Book Manufacturing Group.
Book design by Antonina Krass.

First published as a Norton paperback 1990.

Library of Congress Cataloging-in-Publication Data
Cooper, John Milton.
  Pivotal decades : The United States, 1900–1920 / by John Milton
Cooper, Jr. — 1st ed.
    p.   cm.
  Includes index.
  1. United States—Politics and government—1901–1909. 2. United
States—Politics and government—1909–1913. 3. United States—
Politics and government—1913–1920. I. Title.
E756.C78   1990
973.91—dc20
                                                                    89-3397

ISBN 0-393-95655-5

W. W. Norton & Company, Inc.
500 Fifth Avenue, New York, N.Y. 10110
www.wwnorton.com

W. W. Norton & Company Ltd.
Castle House. 75/76 Wells Street, London W1T 3QT

9 0

FOR MY CHILDREN

Contents

List of Maps

Introduction

For the United States, the first two decades of the twentieth century marked a turning point. During these twenty years a political, economic, social, and cultural agenda was set that still dominates American life as we enter the century's final decade. To begin to grasp the pivotal character of this era, one need only recall certain salient facts about the United States in 1900. The airplane had not yet been invented, nor had radio, much less television. Automobiles were few and expensive, and there were no paved roads. In the development of nuclear energy, only the most basic discoveries had occurred and only the first tentative theories were being advanced. In 1900, women could vote in only four states. Throughout the entire period, black Americans suffered segregation, discrimination, disenfranchisement, racist political demagoguery, and racial violence that nearly always went unpunished and often won applause from whites. The United States Army in 1900 numbered fewer than 100,000 officers and enlisted men (and, except for nurses, who held separate and lower ranks, no women). The United States Navy in 1900, though modern in equipment, ranked far behind the navies of Great Britain and Germany in size and firepower.

Two decades later, the airplane had proven itself as a weapon of war and was about to be launched as a means of civilian transportation. As "wireless telegraphy," radio had long since become a major medium of communication and was now transmitting the sound of the human voice, making it a potential medium of information and entertainment as well. Automobile manufacturing had mushroomed into one of the nation's biggest businesses, and over a million cars and trucks traveled thousands of miles of asphalt and concrete roads through cities, towns, and even the countryside. Discoveries in electromagnetism and radiation, and theoretical advances concerning the atomic system and relativity, were unlocking the basic secrets of matter and energy. By 1920, four new amendments had been added to the Constitution: one stipulating that United States senators be elected by popular vote; one authorizing the federal government to levy income taxes; one prohibiting the manufacture, sale, and consumption of alcoholic beverages; and one extending the vote to women throughout the nation. Black Americans still suffered from virulent discrimination, and racial violence temporarily escalated around 1920. At the same time, however, blacks and whites had formed civil rights organizations to fight racism, and they had embarked on what would be a long campaign of legal and constitutional challenges to segregation and disenfranchisement. By 1920 hundreds of thousands of blacks had left the South and resettled in Northern cities in a mass migration that would continue for years to come. The United States had just fought a major war in Europe, during which the army had swelled to over four million men (there were still no women except in the nursing corps). The navy was expanding to become the largest in the world.

Optimism was the dominant mood of Americans at the beginning and again at the end of these two decades, and progressivism came to be the banner appropriated by the period's many groups of political and social reformers. Yet between the peaks of optimism and within the calls for progressive reform, fear, social conflict, and hatred flourished as well. Progress in science and technology itself bred discontent. Religious Americans, especially conservative evangelical Protestants, bridled at the public rejection of their beliefs in the supernatural origins of life and the universe, and they fought back through a fundamentalist movement that not only amplified their beliefs but also sought to limit or prevent the teaching of non-religious scientific views. America's industrial development during this period brought with it the rise of economic behemoths, huge trusts that spread fears about the corruption of public life and the stifling of economic opportunity. The major domestic political issues of these decades came increasingly to revolve around how to control private economic power. Regulation and "trust-busting" became the main items on the political agenda at the federal, state, and municipal levels of government. Earlier debates over tariff rates and currency reform were now subsumed under the overriding public concern with the concentration of wealth.

Economic fears fed racial and ethnic resentments as this "nation of immigrants" attracted growing influxes of people from Europe and Asia, particularly to cities in the North and West. With industrial jobs attracting blacks to the North at the same time, many whites felt besieged by the newcomers. Mob violence and movements to pass laws restricting immigration from abroad flourished between 1900 and 1920, while the conflict over the prohibition of alcohol assumed aspects of a clash among ethnic cultures. The labor movement absorbed these tensions as well, with conservative unions seeking to shut off immigration and the more radical unions becoming embroiled in violence and embracing socialist politics.

Gender relations altered significantly in this period as women sought new opportunities in politics, the workplace, the local community, and the world of arts and culture. Some middle-class women, frequently those with advanced educations, not only agitated for women's interests on the vote and other public issues, but also fought for women's interests in the private realm by organizing a movement for birth control. Other middle-class women broke into new fields of employment, such as office and sales work, while poorer women took jobs in the mills of the South and the factories of the North. Women reformers were prominent in the prohibition movement with its roiling social and cultural crosscurrents.

This turbulence inevitably forced its way into the political arena, most markedly at the state and local levels. At the federal level, the United States Supreme Court continued in the role of activist arbiter of economic and social issues that it had assumed earlier and has not yet relinquished. Beyond that the Court began to grapple with fundamental questions of civil rights—involving racial discrimination—and civil liberties—involving freedom of speech—that have likewise persisted as major public concerns. The presidency became the overweening branch of the federal government in these decades through the influence of forceful incumbents such as Theodore Roosevelt and Woodrow Wilson, as well as through the growth of bureaucracy and the prominence of national security issues. The two major political parties fortified their clearly opposing stands on economic issues, and the more ambiguous, overlapping positions on social issues, that they had begun to take just before 1900 and that they have retained with remarkable consistency since 1920. On issues of international activism or isolation for the United States, the parties began during these years to take the respective opposing stands that would largely separate them until the 1940s. With intervention in World War I in 1917, the nation moved to the center of the international stage and ambivalently assumed a role of world leadership.

In all, this was a second golden age of American politics—second only to the generation of the founders of the American republic. Like that earlier golden age, this one sported great leaders, with Theodore Roosevelt and Woodrow Wilson the most prominent among a group that included Jane Addams, William Jennings Bryan, Eugene V. Debs, W. E. B. Du Bois, Oliver Wendell Holmes, Jr., Robert M. La Follette, Henry Cabot Lodge, Elihu Root, and William Howard Taft. This political golden age likewise featured great commentators and analysts of public questions, such as Louis Brandeis, Herbert Croly, Walter Lippmann, and John Reed. These figures debated great questions about the meaning of liberty and equality in this century, as well as the balance of public and private economic power, the extension of rights and opportunities to the excluded, the elements of a national culture, and the proper role for the United States in world affairs—all questions that are today subject to continued, if less forceful, debate. This age encompassed extraordinary events, from the building of the Panama Canal and the impassioned election of 1912, to the vast destruction of World War I and the tragedy of the peace that failed. In all, it exalted a standard of public life that later generations have rarely attained.

As vital as America's political culture during these decades was its popular culture, which took distinctive and lasting shape between 1900 and 1920. Major league professional sports, particularly baseball, produced new popular heroes, such as Ty Cobb and Babe Ruth. Motion pictures, even before the advent of sound, created "stars" in such men as Charlie Chaplin and Douglas Fairbanks and such women as Lillian Gish and Mary Pickford. Movies and radio—still embryonic—foreshadowed the long heyday of electronic "mass media." Mass journalism, already established in large-circulation newspapers, made a great leap ahead with the rise of popular magazines in this era. These magazines established the first truly national medium of information and entertainment, and in their avid pursuit of critical exposure and analysis—dubbed "muckraking"—they fixed the canons of investigative reporting and set the posture of the press that have endured ever since.

This book offers various interpretations of political, economic, social, and diplomatic developments in the United States between 1900 and 1920. My aim has been to construct a comprehensive narrative and not to argue an overarching interpretation of the period. Many observers have noted that the major fields of history have wandered far apart from each other in recent years. Social, economic, and political histories of this period have often had so little reference to each other that one critic noted not long ago that they seem to have been describing different countries. But, for all its diversity, the United States is one nation, and I have taken it as my task to gather together again the diverse departments of life during these decades and the rich characters who filled them.

ACKNOWLEDGMENTS

Writers can be a complaining lot: When it comes to the loneliness of their craft, they let everybody know about it. Less sung is the cooperative aspect of writing books, and for me that aspect has loomed much larger than the solitary acts of filling blank pages or revising ones already cluttered with additions, deletions, and corrections. A number of people have helped me generously and intelligently with advice and criticism. John Braeman (University of Nebraska) and Michael McGerr (Indiana University) each read a draft of the manuscript, made many suggestions, and saved me from errors. Charles Eagles (University of Mississippi) read the manuscript with great care and critical insight, offered extended comments on the entire work, and gave advice on approaches to several areas. John M. Blum (Yale University), whose work I had long known and admired, became a friend and advisor in the course of discussing the book and reading two drafts with consummate critical skill and unsurpassed knowledge of this era. Steven Forman encouraged and aided me greatly along the way, and read the drafts with the eye for structure, arguments, balance, and style that mark the editor at his very best. Margie Brassil applied her considerable talents as manuscript editor with patience, care, and efficiency. Eric Crawford provided essential cartographic information at a critical time. Ruth Mandel did wonderful picture research. The staff of the Department of History of the University of Wisconsin-Madison cheerfully and efficiently filled my repeated requests for "word processing." Anita Olson and Karen Delwiche did singular service in this department. To all of these folks, and to my family for living with me through this project—deepest thanks.

John Milton Cooper, Jr.
Madison, Wisconsin
May, 1989

PIVOTAL DECADES

1

The United States in 1900

The beginning of a century leads nearly everyone to think about where they and their nations have come from and where they are going. For the United States of America, 1900 was only 124 years since thirteen modest-sized, thinly populated, mostly unsettled colonies along the Atlantic seaboard of North America had declared themselves independent from Great Britain; 111 years since those newly independent states had joined together in a federal union under a constitution; 97 years since the fledgling republic had extended its territory beyond the Mississippi River; and 52 years since its boundaries had reached the Pacific Ocean. Further, 1900 was just 35 years since the country had assured its survival as a united nation with the victory of the Union in the Civil War.

Yet, as many Americans publicly proclaimed, look where their country stood in 1900. Not only had the United States grown to continental size, but its population had swelled to seventy-six million, spread from coast to coast in forty-five states, and concentrated in thirty-eight cities of more than one hundred thousand people. In 1900, no aspect of American life was more striking than this rapid, fantastic growth. The ballooning numbers of people sprang in part from a high, but now declining, annual birth rate: 32.3 live births per thousand of population (down from 55 in 1800 and 43.3 in 1850). Greater growth resulted from lowered infant mortality and lengthened life span, which had reduced the annual death rate to 16.5 per thousand, the lowest in the world. But by far the greatest numbers of new Americans came with the waves of immigration from overseas. Nearly 425,000 Europeans arrived on the nation's shores in 1900 alone.

Americans were proud of the drawing power of their political and religious freedoms, which had long since made them a "nation of immigrants." From the beginning of the nineteenth century, European migration to the United States had steadily mounted and had become more diverse than in the colonial period, when most settlers had been English and Scottish Protestants. Starting in the 1840s, thousands of Irish immigrants, most of whom were Roman Catholics, as well as Germans of various religious persuasions, flocked across the ocean. After the Civil War, the sources of European immigration broadened still further to encompass growing numbers from Scandinavia, Italy, Greece, and Eastern Europe. These newcomers, like their predecessors, felt the magnetic attraction of freedom drawing them away from Europe's aristocratic, inegalitarian traditions; they sought escape from the poverty, religious prejudices, and forced military service that had made the "Old World" seem, to many of its inhabitants, a vast prison. But they were also seeking jobs, land, and advancement in the nation that boasted the greatest agricultural and industrial economy on the face of the planet. In 1900, the rate of immigration was

Hopeful newcomers at Ellis Island in New York harbor.

still accelerating. During the first decade of the twentieth century, over eight million more immigrants would come to the United States—the largest number in any decade before or since. These newest arrivals would account for more than 10 percent of the entire American population.

Size, population, wealth—each marked how far the United States had come in such a short time from its raw, humble beginnings. Only two countries, Russia and Canada, occupied larger land areas. Among the Western nations—those with predominantly European ethnic origins, languages, and cultures—only Russia had a larger population. No country anywhere enjoyed so large and dynamic an economy. American commerce, transportation, industry, and agriculture were wonders of the world. By almost any measure of economic performance, the United States excelled. Steel production in 1900 amounted to over ten million tons, more than a third higher than Germany's, the closest competitor. Railroad trackage stretched to 167,000 miles, or one-third of the world's total. Per-capita income was estimated at $569, far above the nearest rival, Britain. Literacy rates stood at nearly 90 percent of the populace. The country had over 2,200 newspapers and nearly one thousand colleges and universities, with a combined student body of nearly 240,000. School enrollment amounted to over sixteen million pupils—the world's largest in both numbers and percentage of the population. Of those students, nearly one hundred thousand would graduate from secondary schools in 1900, also ahead of every other nation in numbers and percentages, and nearly double the total in 1890. Its physical expanse, and its economic and social dynamism, made the United States one of the biggest, richest, and potentially strongest nations in the world in 1900.

Advances and Social Divisions

For most Americans in 1900, optimism ran rampant. The scientific and technological revolutions of the nineteenth century had begun to fulfill age-old dreams of human mastery over nature. Thanks to steam and internal combustion engines, sea transportation had grown much less subject to wind and wave, while river traffic could defy the currents. Even more spectacularly, the railroad had transformed land travel. For the first time in history, people and goods could move more swiftly and easily over land than over water. More amazingly still, through applications of electricity to communications, the telegraph could transmit information faster than a person could carry it, and during the previous twenty-five years, the telephone had projected voices virtually instantaneously over any distance. Horizons often seemed unlimited in 1900 because—compared with all previous human experience—they were.

But some Americans' horizons extended much further than others'. Technology gave nearly everybody access to better and cheaper products, but rich Americans benefited much more from this bounty. In cities, prosperous businesses and wealthier homes received electricity, but gas remained the main source of energy for home appliances and street lighting until after 1910. In the countryside, two-thirds of farm families would not get either electricity or indoor plumbing until the late 1930s. There were 1,356 telephones in 1900, but only government and business establishments and the residences of the rich had them. The United States counted 8,000 automobiles in 1900, all of them costly curiosity pieces at a time when less than one mile of smooth paved road existed in the country.

The horizons of many Americans were further limited by the uneven distribution of political and social benefits in the United States. Not all

Telephone office, Dorrance, Kansas, 1910.

of its citizens shared equally in the heritage of American democracy. In theory, the right to vote belonged to slightly less than half the adult population; in practice, it belonged to fewer than that. Over 95 percent of American women could not vote. Only four sparsely populated western states—Wyoming, Idaho, Colorado, and Utah—had extended the franchise to both sexes. The Fifteenth Amendment to the Constitution legally barred racial discrimination in voting, but only a small fraction of adult black males actually voted. Whites, who controlled state governments in the South, where 90 percent of blacks lived in 1900, had barred them from the ballot box through poll taxes, limitations on registration, and literacy tests. Whether by accident or design, those restrictions took the vote away from large numbers of poor southern white males as well. Newly arrived immigrants faced naturalization and registration restrictions, while non-English speaking newcomers suffered from both the language barrier and their unfamiliarity with democratic participation in government. The United States boasted of being the "land of the free," but some Americans enjoyed more freedoms than the majority of their compatriots.

The distribution of resources was uneven not only among the nation's citizens, but among its regions as well. Economically, America was not one country, but three. Less than one-sixth of the continental land area, the regions north of the Potomac and Ohio Rivers and east of the Mississippi, contained 45 percent of the population. This area—the Northeast and Midwest—held an even larger share of the cities and towns, money and banking institutions, schools and libraries, offices and commercial concerns, and factories and railroads. These two regions formed the nation's industrial, financial, and cultural heartland.

The remaining five-sixths of the country was divided into two outlying regions, each culturally and economically dependent on the heartland. The older, less extensive of these sections was the South, which had not overcome the legacy of its defeat in the Civil War thirty-five years before. White Southerners had sustained huge financial losses from widespread battlefield destruction and from uncompensated emancipation of their slaves. Those losses had combined with the retarding effects of cash-crop agriculture to leave the South the least urban, the least industrial, and thereby the poorest region of the country in 1900.

The other outlying section was the West. Although the West sprawled over more than half the continental United States, most of the region struggled with the burdens of sparse population, rugged terrain, and arid climate. Its economy suffered from dependence on quasi-nomadic grazing, agriculture, and the ever-chancy extraction of raw materials for industry. Cowboys made colorful figures for popular literature, but cattle and sheep ranching required vast spreads to produce even modest profits. Miners and lumberjacks also inspired romantic legends, but their work was dangerous, poorly paid, and sporadic. Ranching, lumbering, and mining all failed to foster population growth, high-wage and high-skill jobs, and substantial investment—the necessary conditions for economic development. Only a few parts of the West provided exceptions to this pattern of economic retardation. Ambitious publicly and privately funded irrigation projects transformed extensive areas of California into fertile farmland. Cities such as Los Angeles and San Francisco began to grow too, generating wealth and denser settlement, but California's dependence on scarce water supplies created special problems. Already in 1900, movements had arisen for "conservation" of natural resources and had clashed with westerners who wanted wide-open exploitation of land, timber, minerals, and water.

The comparative poverty and lagging development of the South and West, as compared with the heartland, had already bound these regions in a political alliance in the 1896 presidential election. Together, the South and West had rallied behind two measures—monetary inflation through the coinage of silver and lowered tariffs on industrial products—which they believed would relieve their economic distresses. These two regions had likewise rallied behind both William Jennings Bryan and the Democrats, the champions of those causes. By contrast, the Northeast and Midwest in 1896 had lined up even more solidly behind monetary deflation through a single gold standard, and a protective tariff on industrial products, which they believed would maintain their economic prosperity. The heartland regions had joined to support William McKinley and the Republicans, who had passionately espoused those causes. The same issues, candidates, and regional alignments would shape the 1900 presidential election.

Race and ethnicity also contributed to these regional differences. The nine million former slaves and their descendants who lived in the South constituted the bottom rung of society there in every way. They were the poorest in the region: black per-capita income was variously estimated at between a quarter and third of that of whites in the south. They were the least educated: the black illiteracy rate in 1900 stood at 48 percent in the South as a whole, and over 50 percent in the four states of Louisiana, Alabama, South Carolina, and Georgia. Many white Southerners did not fare a great deal better. Southern whites' income averaged around half the national per-capita figure. Their illiteracy

Hauling a bale of cotton to market, 1910.

rate was over 11 percent, more than double the nationwide rate for native-born whites. New immigrants also occupied low rungs on the social and economic ladder. Because most of them settled in the Northeast and Midwest, they could often get factory work, but their lack of skills and unfamiliarity with English forced them to take the lowest-paying jobs. Because schools were scarce in the parts of Europe from which more and more immigrants were coming in 1900, large numbers were badly educated. Of all the foreign born, nearly 13 percent were illiterate in 1900.

Racial, regional, and ethnic disparities were not new to the United States in 1900, but a heightened sense of alarm about them was novel. Earlier, the nation's least settled areas had provided, in belief if not necessarily in fact, a "safety valve" for social discontent in the older, more densely populated areas. The existence of the frontier was supposed to relieve America of the overcrowding, scarcity, and inequality that plagued Europe. But in 1890 the Census Bureau had declared the frontier "closed." Parts of the South and nearly all the West remained underpopulated, but the great tracts of unoccupied public lands previously marked on the maps by the frontier line no longer existed. That news had immediately aroused fears that something distinct and precious in American life had been lost. Scholars and writers mourned the closing of the frontier by arguing that the availability of vast expanses of open land and pioneering opportunities had been essential to the development of political democracy and individual self-reliance. The need to reclaim an adventurous heritage in the face of new industrial conditions formed the link between domestic concerns and foreign policy issues for political leaders. For many of them, America's greatest need was a new frontier, which they meant in the most literal way.

Nothing aroused more ambivalent attitudes in Americans in 1900 than the cities, especially such metropolises as New York and Chicago. For some, they held out promises of opportunity, glamor, and excitement. Young middle-class men and women from farms, small towns, and the outlying regions were flocking to the cities in pursuit of ambitions to become doctors, lawyers, teachers, journalists, and businessmen. Enough of them had found success to add a new wrinkle to traditional American beliefs in the self-made man and, more recently, woman. The highest-paid corporation lawyer of the 1890s, Elihu Root, was the son of a professor at Hamilton College in upstate New York. The most successful magazine editor of the late 1890s and early 1900s, Samuel Sidney ("S.S.") McClure, had grown up as a fatherless immigrant boy from Northern Ireland on small farms in Indiana and Illinois. The pioneering social worker, Jane Addams, hailed from a medium-sized Illinois town, where her father had been a moderately prominent lawyer.

Yet cities also stirred apprehension. They appeared to threaten the established way of life of white Protestant middle-class groups from both below and above. The threat from below lay in the mounting influx of immigrants, particularly from southern and eastern Europe. In 1900, the foreign born in America numbered about eleven million, or 14 percent of the total population. It was the highest proportion of immigrants to "natives" since the 1850s. The newcomers were arriving as part of a massive overseas dispersal of surplus population from all over Europe. They came from many different backgrounds. Some were wealthy and well-educated. Many were Protestants from Britain, the original source of the nation's white population. Large numbers of Germans and Scandinavians went to rural areas, particularly in the upper Midwest and on the Great Plains, where they either bought established farms, worked as agricultural laborers, or brought new land under cultivation as "sodbusters." Increasingly, however, the immigrants settled in the cities of the Northeast and Midwest, in distinct neighborhoods with saloons, stores, and restaurants that catered to their old-country tastes, and with clubs and churches that spoke their own

Bohemian cigar makers at work in a tenement.

languages. Their exotic languages, unfamiliar customs, different religions, and evidently darker complexions, bred uneasiness in the native
white middle class about the country's changing social character.

At first the only institutions that welcomed the immigrants or tried
to ease their adjustment to a new culture and environment were the
city political machines. In the eyes of many white Protestants, immigrant voting therefore seemed to heighten the nefarious influences of
those reputedly corrupt, undemocratic organizations. In the early 1890s
organizations were formed to agitate for the restriction of European
immigration, just as Asian immigration had been largely shut off in
1881. The restrictionists favored requiring adult immigrants to pass
literacy tests in their native language. The intended result of such tests
would be to bar the new immigrants from southern and eastern Europe,
and admit the predominantly Protestant Nordics from Germany,
Scandinavia, and the British Isles. Similarly, the long-standing crusade against alcoholic beverages, allied with certain Protestant churches,
was assuming an increasingly anti-immigrant slant. Prohibitionists now
denounced saloons and beer halls as threats to morality and arms of
corrupt city political machines.

If the alien and debased urban masses seemed menacing to middle-class white Protestants, so did the relatively few at the opposite end of the social and economic spectrum. Ever since the advent of the industrial revolution in the 1820s and 1830s, some observers had voiced misgivings about the resulting vast accumulations of private wealth and their consequences for political freedom and for equality of economic opportunity. Particularly haunting for many Americans was the specter of European society with its entrenched privileges and degraded commoners. Warnings against monopoly and the inordinate influence of wealth had been heard as early as the 1830s, and they had grown more insistent with the nation's fantastic economic growth since the Civil War. The underlying fears had found a classic statement in Henry George's widely read book, *Progress and Poverty,* published in 1879. Despite the "prodigious increase in wealth-producing power," George had declared, ". . . it becomes no easier for the masses of our people to make a living. On the contrary, it is becoming harder. The gulf between the employed and employer is becoming wider; social contrasts are becoming sharper; as liveried carriages appear, so do barefooted children."

The Vanderbilt mansion on New York City's Fifth Avenue.

Cries like George's and others' against the social dangers of great wealth had attracted attention without making many converts to the varied remedies offered. The federal government did, however, act to regulate combinations of great wealth and power. In 1887 Congress had established the Interstate Commerce Commission, which marked the first step toward federal regulation of commercial transportation. In 1890, Congress had passed the Sherman Antitrust Act, which had affirmed the legal principle of prohibiting unfair restraints in economic activity. A number of states, particularly in the South and West, had gone further in attempting to assert public supervision and discourage economic concentration.

Apprehension over the dangers of wealth revived as the nineteenth century ended. An enormous wave of business consolidation had gathered during the mid-1890s, and in the six years between 1897 and 1903 this wave broke over the United States, fundamentally altering the shape of the American economy. During those years, over three hundred consolidations took place, totaling $7.5 billion in capitalization and encompassing an estimated 40 percent of the country's industrial output. These consolidations became a vast horizontal integration that brought large segments of an industry, and sometimes the whole industry, under the control of a handful of firms. Railroads led the way, with 95 percent of all trackage controlled by six lines in 1899. Steel soon followed suit; the formation of the United States Steel Corporation in 1901 brought about 80 percent of production under one company. U.S. Steel, whose formation was announced on March 4, 1901, the same day as the inauguration of the president, was the first business in the world to be capitalized at $1 billion. Other fields, most notably aluminum, tobacco, and life insurance, soon underwent consolidations that left them comparably concentrated. These business behemoths, popularly dubbed "trusts," raised fresh fears about where the United States was heading economically in 1900.

Popular fears focused not just on impersonal organizations but on flesh-and-blood tycoons. Some of these tycoons had risen to dominance in manufacturing. They included the puckish, philanthropic, Scottish-born steelmaker, Andrew Carnegie, who had forseen the huge demand for steel to build railroads and cities and had become the largest producer in the industry. When Carnegie sold out to U.S. Steel in 1901—at an outrageously inflated price, critics charged—his profit was over $300 million. The most notable tycoon to arise in manufacturing was the man who singlehandedly ruled an entire industry, the devoutly religious but ruthlessly domineering petroleum magnate, John D.

John D. Rockefeller, 1905.

Rockefeller. In the early 1900s, Rockefeller reportedly became the first American to amass a personal fortune worth $1 billion.

The chief initiative for business consolidation sprang, however, not from the manufacturers themselves but from the financiers who sought to eliminate wasteful competition and impose order on the market-place. The greatest financier and prime mover behind the trusts after 1897 was the New York investment banker, J. Pierpont Morgan. A masterful and coldly rational man, Morgan set out to organize and control virtually every basic American industry, and by the early 1900s, he had largely succeeded. He controlled U.S. Steel, held sway over more than half the nation's railroad trackage, and dominated the elec-trical, merchant marine, farm machinery, and insurance fields as well. In 1912 a congressional investigating committee found that Morgan and his partners controlled $22 billion in capital, which made them the largest single factor in American economy, not excepting the United States government.

Even the source of all the fantastic technological and industrial progress—scientific discovery—created ambivalence in Americans. In no previous period of human history had science more dramatically unlocked great secrets of the natural world, in physics, chemistry, geology, and biology, than during the nineteenth century. Americans had not led in those scientific advances. The birth of modern biology, chemistry, and physics owed most to the discoveries and theories of Britons, Frenchmen, and increasingly Germans. Not until the third and fourth decades of the twentieth century would American laboratories and universities harbor great contributors to basic science. But Americans unquestionably led the world in technological innovation— the applications of these new discoveries to industry and to everyday life. The Ohio-born, self-taught inventor, Thomas Alva Edison, had made his name synonymous with electrical wizardry, while the Scottish immigrant, Alexander Graham Bell, had developed the telephone. Henry Ford, the Michigan mechanic-turned-manufacturer, had begun, even before 1900, to lay the groundwork for mass production of automobiles, and in December 1903, a pair of brothers who were bicycle mechanics from Dayton, Ohio, Orville and Wilbur Wright, would construct and fly the first heavier-than-air flying machine at Kitty Hawk, North Carolina.

Thrilling as these advances were, they had profoundly unsettling

J. Pierpont Morgan.

"A tenement-house alley gang. Candidates for crime." An illustration from Crane's Maggie: A Girl of the Streets.

implications. Protestant and Catholic clergymen alike denounced materialism, by which they meant non-spiritual explanations of life and natural phenomena, and decried the growth of religious skepticism—to little apparent effect. Skepticism about religion was not new to the United States in 1900, but materialistic explanations of the natural world had understandably grown in popularity in the late nineteenth century because science and technology could explain and control so much in the world. It had also become fashionable to apply the objectivism of science to art and literature through realism and naturalism, which affected to remove spiritual and morally refined elements in favor of the re-creation of "real life."

Two gifted American novelists typified this new spirit. Stephen Crane, a New York journalist, unsentimentally chronicled the seamy side of urban life in *Maggie: A Girl of the Streets* (1893), and produced a graphically harrowing depiction of military combat in *The Red Badge of Courage* (1895), before his death from tuberculosis in 1900 at the age of twenty-eight. Frank Norris, a Californian who became a New York magazine writer and book editor, likewise depicted degeneracy in city life in *McTeague* (1899). He then began a trilogy about exploitation by rapacious railroad managers and financiers, but only the first volume, *The Octopus* (1901), appeared before Norris's death in 1902, when he was thirty-two; the second volume, *The Pit*, was published posthumously. Both Crane and Norris came from middle-class backgrounds and neither was a political or social radical, but their writings revealed a growing middle-class identification with life among the lowly, and alienation from the rich and respectable.

Society and politics were likewise subjected to "scientific" studies that purported to yield hard, predictable explanations that stressed the effects of physical and economic forces. These efforts had begun as early as the 1870s with the English sociologist Herbert Spencer's application of concepts borrowed from the sciences—especially his reading of Charles Darwin's theories of biological evolution—to human behavior and institutions. Spencer argued that human society had evolved through the same processes as biological species—through a "struggle for existence" characterized by "survival of the fittest." In the higher stages of this evolution, Spencer believed, governmental controls had given way to unfettered economic competition, which ensured progress through the triumph of the strongest, or "fittest," competitors. Spencer's writings enjoyed a great vogue in the United States, thanks in part to the patronage of Andrew Carnegie.

Such applications of science to literature and society provoked resistance and counterattack from critics. Conflicts over artistic and literary standards were simmering among cultured Americans at the turn of the twentieth century. In both the visual arts and literature, conserva-

George Bellows's The Street, *1917.*

tives spurned realism and naturalism as debased and animalistic. Established magazine and book publishers usually, but not always, leaned in conservative directions. Short stories and serialized fiction in periodicals and popular novels featured mainly sentimental, romantic tales, although both Crane and Norris reached a broad reading public. Among painters, the more gentle and visually pleasing realism of Winslow Homer and Thomas Eakins gave way after 1900 to the Ashcan School. Realists of this school, including John Sloan, Robert Henri, and George Bellows, employed more somber colors, arranged less contrived compositions, and depicted such unrefined subject matter as factories, prize fighting, and city slums.

Scientific approaches to public life, especially Spencer's Social Darwinism, aroused Protestant clergymen in particular to reassert spiritual values. The most significant religious strife lay in the relation between science and the Bible. The major Protestant denominations were already reeling from repeated controversies over the extension of Darwin's theories of evolution to the origin of the human species. These tensions set the stage for a cultural and religious conflict that would last through the first quarter of the twentieth century and beyond.

THE POLITICAL ARENA

At the end of the nineteenth century this young republic had reached an ironic turning point. In 1898 the United States had won a quick, easy victory in a war with Spain, an aged colonial power, and had snapped up nearly all of Spain's remaining overseas colonial possessions. The sympathies of large numbers of Americans toward Cubans who were fighting for independence from the Spaniards had played a major part in precipitating the war. Cuba emerged from the war formally independent, the latest in a long list of former colonies in the Western Hemisphere to emulate the United States in becoming an autonomous republic. In fact, however, Cuba became a protectorate of the United States. American troops remained as occupying forces for over four years, and the United States retained the power to intervene if Cuban political conditions did not meet with American approval. Three other former Spanish possessions became outright colonies of the United States—Puerto Rico in the Caribbean Sea, and Guam and the Philippine Islands on the far side of the Pacific Ocean. In addition, the United States annexed the formerly independent mid-Pacific country of Hawaii in a separate action during the Spanish-American

"Well, I Hardly Know Which to Take First." Uncle Sam ponders the spoils of the Spanish-American War as President McKinley looks on.

War. Within the space of a few months, the nation born of the first colonial revolution in modern history had itself become a colonial ruler. The country that had long ago renounced Old World power politics and scorned international rivalries had now staked out commitments halfway around the globe. The irony was not lost on observers in this year of taking stock, of looking to the past and gauging the future.

Among those who were assessing the future, their nation's and their own, were America's politicians. The presidential and congressional elections of 1900 were agitated by issues arising out of the Spanish-American War—colonial rule and overseas commitments. These issues of imperialism mixed domestic concerns with questions of foreign policy, and they divided American political opinion in 1900.

On one side of the foreign-policy issue stood a small band of ardent imperialists, which included some of the most dynamic characters in public life. Their chief political spokesmen were two wealthy, socially prominent men in their forties. One was the slender, reserved Republican senator from Massachusetts, Henry Cabot Lodge. A Harvard-educated historian and member of one of Boston's most distinguished "Brahmin" families, Lodge urged the United States "not [to] be a hermit nation hiding a defenseless, feeble body within a huge shell. . . . shut up and kept from its share of the world's commerce until it was smothered by a power hostile to it in every conception of justice and liberty." The other leading imperialist political spokesman was Lodge's closest friend, the ebullient war hero and newly elected governor of New York, Theodore Roosevelt. Likewise an historian and Harvard man, as well as a former rancher, hunter, and New York City police commissioner, Roosevelt had already broadcast the phrase "the strenuous life" as his prescription for personal and national life. "Greatness means strife for nation and man alike," he avowed. "The guns of our war-ships in the tropic seas of the west and the remote east have awakened us to the knowledge of new duties. Our flag is a proud flag and it stands for liberty and civilization."

But the imperialists' view of America's future was deeply ambivalent. Although they thrilled to the glories of military victory and far-flung expansion, and exulted in the nation's industrial might, they also expressed fears about what might become of the United States if it failed to assert itself in the world both politically and economically. Privately, Lodge, Roosevelt, and other imperialists harbored misgivings about the changes that were being wrought by the burgeoning of cities and large-scale industry, the mounting influx of immigrants, and the closing of the frontier. Imperialism was their antidote to those influences. They wanted the United States to follow the examples of leading European nations in subjugating and ruling backward peoples and in playing the role of a major power on the international stage. By being a republic and an empire, the United States could, they believed, become the greatest nation in the whole world, and save its own soul.

On the other side of these foreign-policy issues, a collection of impassioned anti-imperialists included equally colorful figures. Their two principal spokesmen were William Jennings Bryan and Carl Schurz, a prominent European immigrant. As the Democratic party's presidential candidate in 1896, Bryan had championed the honest toilers of the "great crescent"—the South and West—against the financial moguls of the "enemy's country," the Northeast. Although he had agitated for and served in the war with Spain, Bryan scorned the acquisition of colonies as a false construction "upon the foundation stones quarried by revolutionary patriots from the mountains of eternal truth." Far better to remain, warned Bryan, "a republic standing erect while empires are bowed beneath the weight of their own armaments . . . a republic whose flag is loved where other flags are only feared." German-born Carl Schurz epitomized the American dream of freedom and success

Carl Schurz, senator from Missouri.

for the immigrant. A youthful revolutionary and political exile from his native land, Schurz had served successively as a Union general in the Civil War, as a senator from Missouri, as secretary of the interior under Rutherford B. Hayes, and as editor of several respected newspapers and magazines. Schurz argued that colonialism did "ruthless violence to the spirit of our Constitution and to all the fundamental principles of democratic government. Nor would such a repudiation of the government of, by, and for the people fail to produce a crop of demoralization and corruption beyond what this country has ever seen."

As Bryan and Schurz made clear, the anti-imperialists harked back to hallowed principles that had made the United States different from other countries, especially the aristocratic and monarchical regimes of Europe. They cited not only the affirmations of self-government in the Declaration of Independence and the Constitution, but they also echoed the warnings against involvement in European power politics in George Washington's Farewell Address and Thomas Jefferson's first inaugural address. Popular government and the avoidance of entangling alliances were for them the best guarantees against the destruction and despotism that plagued the Old World. The anti-imperialists worried as much as the imperialists about the ill effects of industrial consolidation, urban growth, and immigration, but they believed that aping European examples would only make those conditions immeasurably worse. Although Bryan advocated domestic reforms to address those problems, Schurz and other more conservative anti-imperialists did not. But they all agreed that instead of curing those ills, the imperialist position would bring on an even graver disease. Paraphrasing Abraham Lincoln, Bryan summed up the anti-imperialists' case with the declaration, "this nation cannot endure half-republic and half-colony—half free and half vassal."

THE ELECTION OF 1900

The man who would play the largest role in all the public conflicts of the coming two-and-a-half decades was already at center stage. This was forty-year-old William Jennings Bryan. Born and educated in Illinois, Bryan had moved to Nebraska in 1887 and risen quickly in politics there. As a young man he had possessed the good looks then more often associated with stage actors than with politicians, and throughout his life he possessed a powerful, mellifluous voice which he had first used in college as an orator. Politically, Bryan had combined loyalty to the Democratic party with advocacy of many of the concerns of the farmers' protest movements that had arisen in the late 1880s. Elected as a congressman from Nebraska in 1890 and 1892, Bryan had distinguished himself as an eloquent spokesman for the interests and grievances of Southerners and Westerners.

The one issue that had catapulted Bryan to political prominence was the expansion of the currency through the unlimited coinage of silver, a reform intended to relieve the burdens of debt for people in the outlying regions of the country. In a speech at the 1896 Democratic convention, Bryan had thundered at the northeastern advocates of a single gold standard, "You shall not press down upon the brow of labor this crown of thorns. You shall not crucify mankind upon a cross of gold." Bryan had electrified the delegates and won the presidential nomination. His whirlwind personal campaigning by train and his tireless oratory had not won the election in 1896, but they had made him the undisputed spokesman for the South and West and a national figure to be reckoned with for the rest of his life.

By 1900, the premature effects of middle age had begun to soften Bryan's handsome features, while familiarity was dimming his aura of zealotry. Yet no leading politician spoke more directly to many of the strongest doubts and misgivings that assailed Americans. Bryan's anti-imperialist arguments reflected anxieties about America's emerging role in the world. His denunciations of the trusts bespoke fears of the influence of wealth. Many of the economic reform measures that he advocated would become staples of public-policy debate for the next twenty

William Jennings Bryan.

years. Bryan's championship of cultural and religious causes still lay in the future, but his distinctive political style, which he borrowed from evangelical preaching, and his well-publicized stress on personal morality already foreshadowed those involvements. Taken together, Bryan's persistent and varied roles during the first quarter of the twentieth century would rank him alongside such political giants from the nation's past as Alexander Hamilton, Henry Clay, Daniel Webster, and John C. Calhoun. Like those illustrious predecessors, Bryan would become one of the most important American politicians who never became president. Unlike them, he would achieve his stature almost entirely apart from holding any major office.

The presidential contest of 1900 did not have a big impact on the course of American history. It did not alter the alignment of voters behind the two major parties nor, with one exception, did it broach significant new political concerns. The election of 1900 did not do those things mainly because it was a rerun of the 1896 contest, which had accomplished both those results. In McKinley and Bryan, the two parties' standard bearers were the same, and despite the intervening war with Spain, domestic issues once more predominated in the campaign.

The Democrats reverted to their tried-and-true issues of 1896, making free silver again their centerpiece. The free-silver proposal advocated that the United States Treasury would buy all silver offered and convert it into coins at a ratio of sixteen ounces of silver to one ounce

"Take Your Choice of the Two Bills!" A cartoon critical of "Bill" Bryan's support of free silver, 1900.

of gold. Because gold's market value was over $35 an ounce and silver's was less than a dollar, coinage at sixteen to one would have, in effect, cut the value of the already existing gold-backed United States currency in half. That was the point behind the free-silver movement: inflation. Currency-short and debt-ridden interests—farmers and businessmen alike—favored inflation in order to borrow more easily and repay their debts in cheaper dollars. Since the great majority of people in the South and West were either short of money or in debt, they rallied fervently to Bryan and free silver in 1896, and again in 1900. Creditors and non-debtors, who made up the great majorities of people in the Northeast and Midwest, opposed free silver and clung to the gold standard. Fittingly in 1900, the Republicans reiterated their 1896 arguments in favor of "honest money" in the form of a gold standard, with silver coinage to be governed by the market value of less than one dollar per ounce and, hence, no inflation.

Only one other issue so sharply pitted the industrial and financial heartland against the less-developed regions of the country. That issue was the tariff, which the two parties had been contesting since the 1880s. The Democrats advocated low tariffs on most imported goods, but chiefly on industrial products from abroad. By making those products cheaper, low tariffs would benefit the sections that consumed them—the South and West. The Republicans championed protective tariffs, mainly on industrial products. High tariffs aided the producing sections—the Northeast and Midwest—by shielding them against lower-cost foreign competition. The tariff issue undercut the Democrats' efforts to portray themselves as the champions of, in Bryan's words, "the toiling masses everywhere." The Republicans appealed to industrial workers on the ground that the protective tariff spared their jobs and upheld their wage levels against underpaid foreign workers. The Democrats tried to counter this Republican appeal to labor by adopting a friendlier stance toward unions. Although that unionist appeal would later help the Democrats to gain substantial support among industrial workers, it did not cut much ice in 1896 or 1900.

The Democrats and, to a lesser extent, the Republicans also repeated broader themes from 1896. Bryan and his supporters decried anew the influence of big business and reaffirmed their advocacy of stronger antitrust laws, stricter governmental regulation of railroads and telegraphs, and the adoption of federal income and inheritance taxes. The Republicans once more remained chary about broader arguments, although many of them continued to scoff at radical ideas about government interference with private business and economic activity.

Not since before the Civil War—when first Thomas Jefferson's Republicans and then Andrew Jackson's Democrats had battled with opponents whom they tagged as the socially and economically privileged—had American politics witnessed so stark a contrast of leaders and parties as between Bryan's Democrats and McKinley's Republicans. Their countervailing slurs on Democratic "radicalism" and Republican "plutocracy" were exaggerated, however. Both parties subscribed to the same fundamental beliefs in popular government and private property. Both parties numbered among their adherents people of all degrees of wealth and education and with myriad racial, religious, and ethnic identities. And for both parties, the tariff issue made ideological purity impossible. As protectionists, the Republicans found themselves advocating a larger governmental role in the economy, whereas the Democrats, as low-tariff stalwarts, championed a smaller role. Still, as the 1896 contest had revealed, the candidates and parties had become highly polarized in their styles, emotional colorations, and followings. In 1900 Bryan again hammered away at social and economic privilege. Yet, despite his favorite nickname, "the Commoner," Bryan did not speak for less-advantaged classes or occupation groups so much as for less-advantaged sections of the country.

By contrast, William McKinley stood in 1900, as in 1896, preeminently as the champion of the Northeastern and Midwestern heartland. McKinley was a fine speaker and good mixer, but he continued to reject his opponent's whirlwind personal stumping in favor of the supposedly more dignified and certainly more cleverly designed "front-porch campaign." In 1896 McKinley had received delegations of visitors at his home in Canton, Ohio, and in 1900 he received them at the presidential mansion in Washington. This technique allowed the candidate to target his appeal to the visitors' chief concerns in remarks that had been printed in advance for distribution as leaflets and newspaper accounts, sometimes in several languages. McKinley could present himself genuinely as a paragon of respectability and caution. Fifty-seven years old in 1900, he had been, like all but two of the presidents since the Civil War, an officer in the Union army. He had served seven terms in the House of Representatives, where he had helped shape the Republicans' protectionist tariff policy, and four years as governor of Ohio. Throughout his long official career, he had shown himself to be a careful organizer and shrewd manager.

More than imagery and technique made McKinley and his party attractive to big majorities in the Northeast and Midwest. McKinley had originally been known best as a protectionist. The Republicans had in fact devoted more spoken and written words in 1896 to the tariff than to the currency issue. Protectionism was an appealingly embracing issue because it drew support from workers and industrialists, both of whom feared the threats posed by cheap foreign competition to wages and profits. Still, it was the currency issue, the "battle of the standards," that had given the Republicans' appeal a passionate edge. Their defense of "honest money" had tapped deep wells of interest and emotion among Northeasterners and Midwesterners whose savings, investments, salaries, and property values would have been slashed by tampering with the gold standard. When Bryan resurrected free silver in 1900, a leading Republican chortled, "Now we've got him where we want him. Silver, silver, silver, that's our target."

If the candidates, campaigns, and issues were the same in 1896 and 1900, so were the elections' outcomes. McKinley increased his majority in the popular margin by slightly over 100,000 votes and almost one percentage point, to nearly 52 percent. He carried five Western states and twenty-one electoral votes which had been Bryan's in 1896, for a

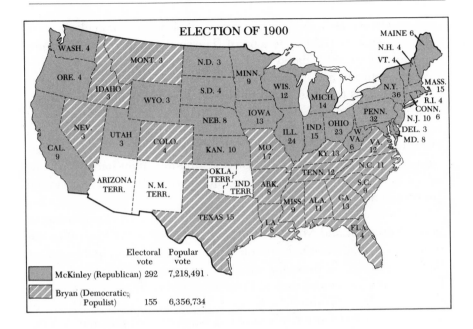

ELECTION OF 1900

	Electoral vote	Popular vote
McKinley (Republican)	292	7,218,491
Bryan (Democratic; Populist)	155	6,356,734

margin of 292 to 155. The only noticeable minor-party vote belonged to the Prohibitionists, who drew over 200,000 votes, about 1.5 percent of the total. The Republican gains reflected some success in wooing back Western silverites who had defected earlier, and in claiming credit for the prevailing satisfaction with national economic prosperity. Such differences notwithstanding, the dominant feature of the election returns in 1900 was the same as four years earlier: sectionalism. The Democrats, aided somewhat by local white drives to disenfranchise black voters, had solidified their hold in the South and had won back two Border States temporarily lost in 1896, while they continued at least to break even in the West. The Republicans again based their victory on sweeping the Northeast and Midwest, including fringe states along the Atlantic seaboard and just across the Mississippi. Their gains in the West were merely frosting on the cake. By confirming Republican domination of the heartland, the election of 1900 ratified the majority position that the party would enjoy, with one interruption, for nearly the first third of the twentieth century.

The sharpness of the contrast in the parties' imagery and sectional allegiances prompted both winners and losers to charge foul play. Republicans felt galled by their dismal performance in the South, where their share of the vote had been 34 percent in 1896 and had risen only to 40 percent in 1900. They did so poorly in the South, they believed, because Democrats were disenfranchising their voters, particularly black voters. They were right up to a point. The sectional polarities of American politics in 1900 dated back to the issues of the Civil War and Reconstruction. The Democrats did owe their sway in the South partly to their appeals to white racial solidarity, which they now increasingly buttressed by purging the electorate of blacks and dissident poorer whites. Yet racial solidarity and disenfranchisement merely enhanced Democratic dominance in the South. By embracing silver currency, antitrust laws, and stricter business regulation, they had put themselves in tune with the overriding economic concerns of their sectional constituency.

The Democrats likewise sought to explain their dismal performance in the Northeast and Midwest and their slippage in the West through some form of disenfranchisment. They accused the Republicans of buying votes by encouraging creditors to coerce farmers and small businessmen, and employers to threaten workers. They also had some basis for their suspicions. The Republicans outspent them in 1896 and 1900 by margins variously estimated between five and ten to one. Likewise, dire predictions of economic disaster had undoubtedly convinced many people not to vote for Bryan. Yet the use of money had merely added to the Republicans' hold on the nation's heartland. By standing for a protective tariff and the gold standard, they spoke to the overriding economic concerns of their sectional constituency. A greater number of voters lived in those parts of the country—the Northeast and Midwest—that had profited from the fantastic industrial growth; voters in those sections therefore rejected programs and ideas that they feared might threaten their prosperity. This identification of interests, which was at once conservative and optimistic, lay at the heart of the Republicans' majority party standing.

Those alignments of voters and sentiments did not mean that Northeasterners, Midwesterners, Southerners, and Westerners were immune to each others' misgivings. Both the Democrats and the Republicans harbored potentially dissident elements that sympathized with their opponents on some issues. Democrats in the Northeast often opposed Bryan and his followers over free silver and the trusts, although they supported him on the tariff and foreign policy. Republicans in the Midwest and West had already expressed fears of wealth and apprehensions about the erosion of American democracy. In New York, Governor Theodore Roosevelt had voiced concern over the political influence of corporations and had gingerly suggested new programs for business taxation and regulation. Roosevelt's programs, though mild and tentative, had sufficiently disturbed the state's Republican boss, Thomas C. Platt, to impel him to plot Roosevelt's removal by getting him nominated for vice-president in 1900. In the Midwest, several Republican and Democratic city reform movements had arisen to denounce corrupt ties between business and political machines and to advocate municipal ownership of utilities. In Wisconsin Robert M. La Follette, a dynamic Republican insurgent—an intra-party rebel against the dominant conservative party organization—won the governorship on a platform that called for popular primaries for party nominations and more equitable railroad taxation. In Iowa another group of insurgent, reformist Republicans led by Albert B. Cummins, who would be elected governor in 1901, was demanding removal of tariff protection from products made by the trusts. Beneath the apparently placid surface of Republican dominance flowed potentially disturbing currents.

At least two noticeable aspects of the 1900 election also indicated important changes since 1896. One of these was a new issue that excited the presidential campaign at the outset. Bryan entered the race bent on making imperialism the dominant campaign issue, but when he began his whistle-stop campaign with denunciations of the United States occupation of the Philippines and of America's suppression of the native uprising there, the issue fell flat. According to one story, a Kansas farmer listened to Bryan's exhortations about the dangers of imperialism and then said to his neighbor, "Price of hogs is 60 cents a pound. Guess we can stand it." Some conservative anti-imperialists among the Democrats availed themselves of the candidate's subsequent switch to denunciations of the trusts, and renewed advocacy of free silver, as excuses to desert him. Republican anti-imperialists, however, gener-

"Unmasked." Bryan abandoned the issue of imperialism for an emphasis on free silver in the 1900 campaign.

ally stayed loyal to their party in spite of intramural foreign-policy differences.

If nothing else, the 1900 election demonstrated the primacy of domestic concerns to American voters. Yet the attempt to broach foreign policy as a major issue did have consequences. Some colorful Republican campaigners, most notably vice-presidential nominee Roosevelt and Wisconsin gubernatorial candidate La Follette, waved the flag frenetically and scorned calls to pull out of the Philippines as cowardly and unpatriotic. Still, even they denied that Republican policies contemplated any departure from the nation's traditional avoidance of international alliances and overseas power politics. If the election results could be read as a mandate against withdrawal from the Philippines, they could be read even more clearly as an indication of overwhelming popular unconcern about great power politics. The 1900 campaign climaxed what had been for the United States a brief imperialist fling; it did not mark the beginning of the long-term imperial involvement practiced by European powers. Imperialism retreated from American popular consciousness as suddenly as it had intruded, although territory, commitments, and residual attitudes remained for future encounters with world affairs.

The other notable change between the elections of 1896 and 1900 involved the vice-presidential candidates. In a gesture intended to offset Bryan's youth and reputed radicalism, the Democrats reached back to renominate their last vice-president, sixty-five-year-old Adlai E. Stevenson of Illinois. In a move fraught with far greater future significance, the Republicans went the other way by nominating forty-one-year-old Theodore Roosevelt, whose widely publicized war heroism and vivid personality had created vast reservoirs of popularity. Although only three men who had served as vice-president had gone on to be elected to the top office, four others had succeeded when presidents had died. As McKinley's close associate, Senator Mark Hanna of Ohio, suggested privately, "Don't any of you realize that there's only one life between this madman and the White House?"

Future presidential prospects aside, Roosevelt's nomination for vice-president in 1900 offered another example of a broader trend toward direct, personal campaigning in American politics. Since the mid-1890s, a succession of "boy orators," as Bryan had been dubbed, had seized nominations and offices largely on the strength of their speaking skills and dynamic public appearances. In the cases of Bryan at the national level, and Robert La Follette and Albert Cummins in their respective states, these newcomers hitched their political wagons to a variety of new issues. But common to these ambitious younger politicians in both parties was the drive to gain speedier preferment at the expense of older leaders steeped in patient service to their organizations. No wonder the direct primary for party nominations became their favorite political reform. The primary not only promised to broaden popular participation and to break the power of machines, but it would also create an arena in which aspiring campaigners could practice their barn-storming talents earlier and to greater effect. Such impulses crossed party lines and transcended dominant issues. Ironically, the nation's first party primary law would not be enacted in Wisconsin by the Republican reformer La Follette, but in Mississippi, where the flamboyant editor-orator James K. Vardaman bested the Democratic leadership by appealing to racist sentiments in an all-white electorate.

Roosevelt's vice-presidential nomination by the Republicans in 1900 most clearly epitomized this political popularization. The party that had reaped so much success by applying organizational techniques was conceding that something was missing from its campaign arsenal. By choosing a socially prominent war hero with nearly two decades of adoring press coverage behind him, the Republicans were betting on glamor for its own sake. Not an accomplished orator, Roosevelt balked at looking like "a second-class Bryan," but he soon found that he did not need to match the Commoner's verbal skills on the hustings. The sheer fascination of his presence among people who had already read or heard about him, together with the pungency of his personality,

Republican vice-presidential candidate Theodore Roosevelt over-shadowing his running mate, President McKinley, 1900.

made him the sensation of the 1900 campaign. Although the Republicans did not need such assets to win, they were delighted at having discovered a whistle-stop performer who could match Bryan's energies in eighteen-hour campaign days and outdraw him in crowds and applause. American politics would never be the same again. The day of personality and publicity had come to stay. So, ironically, had the decline in popular participation. The percentage of eligible voters who participated in 1900 had declined nearly six points from 1896, to just under 74 percent. Colorful or at least skillfully packaged public personalities, greater reliance on the mass communications media, and fewer eligible voters going to the polls—those three factors would persist and become increasingly important in American electoral politics.

Despite their differences in background, party allegiance, and stands on major issues, Roosevelt and Bryan were similar harbingers of political change. Each man was already well along toward assuming his position as one of the three most important political figures of the next twenty years. Between them and joined by others, they would help to inaugurate another golden age of American politics, second only in significance and depth to the time of the founding of the republic. In foreign policy, Roosevelt's and Bryan's debate over imperialism, though temporarily muted, would later resurface to establish the poles of thought about America's role in the world for the next fifty years. In domestic affairs, their differing expressions of disquiet over the growth of big business and its political influence would point the way to the major political debates and policy initiatives of the succeeding four decades. In their persons, their attractiveness in public forums, and their ages, they highlighted transformations that were sweeping through America. Rapid transportation and widespread reporting of events had invested individual personalities with a larger public role than ever before. For the first time the two leading parties had filled half of their top tickets with men too young to have fought in the Civil War. As the new century approached, the United States was poised to see a new political generation take hold.

2

"That Damned Cowboy"

On September 6, 1901, a thin young man with a bandaged right hand approached President McKinley in a receiving line at the Pan-American Exposition in Buffalo, New York. The bandage concealed a revolver, and the man, an anarchist named Leon Czolgosz, shot the president twice in the abdomen. McKinley died eight days later from the internal bleeding and infection caused by the gunshot wounds. The president's death saddened the nation, but there was less shock and outrage than had greeted the two previous presidential assassinations, of Abraham Lincoln in 1865 and of James A. Garfield in 1881. The subdued mood stemmed in part from McKinley's having been a remote figure and in part from curiosity about his successor.

CHANGING THE GUARD

Succeeding to the presidency at the age of forty-two, Theodore Roosevelt became the youngest man to hold the office before or since. His succession swiftly brought great change, at least to the surface of American public life. In practically every outward circumstance he seemed the opposite of his predecessor. Not only was he sixteen years younger than McKinley, but he was physically vigorous and personally expansive where the fallen president had been ponderous and reserved. Both men were decorated war veterans who liked to be addressed by their military ranks: "Major" McKinley and "Colonel" Roosevelt. But Roosevelt had earned his distinction just three years before in the

Spanish-American War, while McKinley had done so three decades before in the Civil War. Even their Republican party allegiance sprang from different social roots. Roosevelt's were in the cosmopolitan upper classes of the Northeast, while McKinley had belonged to the stay-at-home middle classes of the Midwest.

So much seemed fresh and new from the moment the new president took office. His family was large, exuberant, and appealing. Roosevelt's six children ranged from his seventeen-year-old daughter Alice, the only child of his first marriage, through the children of his second marriage, another daughter and four sons, the youngest of whom was not yet four when their father became president. These offspring hit the somewhat stodgy executive mansion like a miniature tornado. The adolescent Alice assumed the stature of a social idol as she hobnobbed in swanky society and inspired fashions with her "Alice blue gown." Her strong, athletic good looks and slightly outrageous boldness personified the new social ideal of adventurous young womanhood depicted in the popular stories of Richard Harding Davis and the drawings of Charles Dana Gibson. Her still more athletic and energetic younger

President Theodore Roosevelt and Mrs. Roosevelt (second from right), surrounded by their family. Alice is standing, at center.

half-brothers kept ponies on the White House lawn and broke windows batting baseballs at the presidential domicile.

These images of the Roosevelts may have been superficial, but they were not trivial. In his person and background, the new president brought unfamiliar qualities to the office. The show and stir that he and his family fomented, often in spite of themselves, highlighted the new public dimension of the office. The presidential family, especially the elder daughter, attracted attention from the press and public not just because they were lively and attractive but even more because they belonged to the highest social circles, the nearest equivalent in the United States to an aristocracy.

Born in New York in 1858 to a moderately wealthy family descended from some of the city's earliest Dutch settlers, young "Teedie" had enjoyed extensive family travels in Europe and North Africa, an education by private tutors, and membership in the fashionable circles at Harvard University. Only poor health had marred his golden childhood, but he had overcome his weaknesses through strenuous physical exercise and rugged outdoor living. Boyhood interests in nature study developed into a passion for hunting and exploration, leading to his three-year sojourn as a part-time rancher in the Dakota Territory during the 1880s. His retentive mind and ability to read at astonishing speeds had earned him a Phi Beta Kappa key at Harvard and enabled him to write ten books before he became president, all while pursuing his time-consuming political career and outdoor hobbies.

Roosevelt's choice of politics as a vocation had seemed odd for an educated upper-class youth, and for nearly two decades he had bounced among stints in the New York Legislature, an unsuccessful race for mayor of New York, service as one of the city's three police commissioners, and assistant secretary of the Navy. In 1898 the Spanish-American War suddenly transformed his life. His raising of the cavalry regiment composed of cowboys and Ivy Leaguers, dubbed the "Rough Riders," and their charge—on foot—up Cuba's San Juan Hill had made him a national hero.

Roosevelt was curiously ambivalent about his background. As his popularity and fame grew, so did quasi-legendary accounts of his early years, which he took a hand in shaping. Roosevelt consistently downplayed his inborn advantages of wealth, status, and intellect; instead he helped foster exemplary tales about how he had developed modest gifts of mind and body into the highest forms of achievement and service through hard work and unstinting application. In one sense Roosevelt was obscuring his privileged background in order to get ahead

Charge of the Rough Riders at San Juan Hill, *by Frederic Remington.*

in a political culture that had long prized humble origins and self-improvement in its leaders. His two strongest public identifications, with the West and with his Rough Rider regiment, portrayed him as a man of the people who could hold his own with rough folk in dangerous, physically demanding environments.

Those images also reflected Roosevelt's impatience with his upper-class social peers. Twenty years before, when he had first entered politics, his friends had sniffed that he would be rubbing elbows with such riffraff as grooms and saloon-keepers. "Then, if that is so," Roosevelt had shot back, "the groom and the saloon-keeper are the governing class and you confess weakness. You have all the chances, the education, the position, and you let them rule you. They must be better men." Roosevelt had devoted much of his life before he became president to proving that his birth and upbringing had not unfitted him for membership in that "governing class." He had likewise devoted himself to the fulfillment of the principle of stewardship—that those favored by wealth, social position, and education in turn owed their less fortunate fellows service, inspiration, and guidance.

Still, Roosevelt never tried to deny his exalted social status. Had he done so, his manner, dress, and accent would have kept him from passing as a genuine commoner. He also implicitly recognized that his social origins were in reality a political asset. The one condition he never knew as a politician was obscurity. Since his first days as a fledgling

New York state legislator in the 1880s, he had moved in the limelight of publicity, basking in the fascination of newspaper and magazine readers with the doings of members of the upper crust.

Roosevelt's exploits as a rancher, hunter, and soldier made him a real-life embodiment of the gentleman-adventurer heroes featured in popular magazines and dime novels. He resembled no one as much as that most popular fictional paragon, the blue-blooded superathlete of Yale, Frank Merriwell. Much about social change in America during the next three decades would be epitomized in the shifting mores of these fictional characters, from the clean-living Frank Merriwell, through Owen Johnson's hard-drinking Yale athlete Dink Stover, to the "beautiful and damned" Princeton creations of F. Scott Fitzgerald. On the female side, the "Gibson Girl" incarnated a long-limbed, elegantly dressed, beautiful adventuress, who rode horses, drove automobiles, played tennis, and generally indulged in freer behavior than her middle-class sisters, even, it was rumored, privately smoking cigarettes and occasionally drinking whiskey.

In his aristocratic background and sense of stewardship, Roosevelt recalled the status and spirit of the earliest presidents and leaders of

"Accident to a Young Man with a Weak Heart," 1900. The "Gibson Girl" represented changes in social mores for some American women.

the American republic. The resemblance was no accident. The new president was a historian, and he identified himself with the example of George Washington and the governmental views and approaches of Alexander Hamilton. This historical consciousness underscored another quality rare in presidents since the 1820s, but common among such early leaders as Hamilton, Thomas Jefferson, James Madison, and the two Adamses. Roosevelt was, by almost any definition of term, an intellectual. His ten books included five substantial volumes of history. He spoke three foreign languages with ease, if not total fluency, and he could read four others. He had read widely in the histories of many times and nations, and in literature, art, economics, politics, and especially the natural sciences. As an outdoorsman, he was an accomplished naturalist, and thanks to his reading and friendships, he was the most scientifically literate president since Jefferson a hundred years before.

It was ironic that Roosevelt resembled Jefferson in his intellectual range and depth. There was no predecessor whose legacy and influence, particularly on states' rights and the support of limited governmental responsibilities, the new president disliked more. As a self-proclaimed Hamiltonian, Roosevelt meant to exalt the power and prestige of the federal government. As a self-anointed heir of Lincoln and Civil War Republicanism, he yearned to preserve his party's fidelity to nationalism and centralization. But the resemblance to Jefferson was more than intellectual. Roosevelt likewise quickly became a patron of science, scholarship, art, and literature. Prominent among the Roosevelts' frequent and well-publicized guests were the painters John La Farge and Frederic Remington, the sculptor Augustus Saint-Gaudens, the historian James Ford Rhodes, and the Western novelist Owen Wister. The president promoted scientific research through the Smithsonian Institution, which had been founded in 1846, and boosted public art by commissioning Saint-Gaudens to redesign the nation's coins. In all, through his public pronouncements, associations, and private encouragement and criticism, Roosevelt made himself a cultural arbiter such as the United States had rarely seen before in a president.

The new president's upper-crust social background and intellectual leanings had instilled in him some strongly held, deep-seated views on history and public affairs. Although these views were never categorized as liberal, later in his presidency, and more frequently afterward, Roosevelt's positions became associated with reform movements in part through his own efforts. But the term Roosevelt used most often over the years to define his politics was "conservative." He knew his own mind, and his later "progressive" self-designation always occurred within a carefully defined conservative framework.

Roosevelt's blustery manner and reputation for hotheadedness belied a high regard for caution. Far from being impulsive, he was a crafty political professional who had made it to the top through shrewd calculation and clever manipulation. Moreover, Roosevelt's social vision for the United States tempered any impulse toward one-sided action. Roosevelt was convinced that America faced the same internal peril as other advanced industrial nations, a peril he derisively dubbed "materialism." To Roosevelt, materialism meant primarily the social and political impact of huge concentrations of wealth. Bryan, the Democrats, and some Republican insurgents likewise decried the trusts and the interests, but Roosevelt gave these views a special twist that made his viewpoint highly unusual among his countrymen.

By the time he became president, Roosevelt had long worried about a pair of evils related to materialism. One was the vulnerability of what he called "the great fighting features of our race" to the combined effects of physical softening through material comfort and spiritual coarsening through frenetic moneygrubbing. By those "fighting features," he meant strength, courage, and the willingness to subordinate and sacrifice self in service to noble causes. As early as 1886, he had bemoaned that a man "in a bourgeois state of development" was only too apt "to be a miracle of timid and short-sighted selfishness." The other evil that Roosevelt feared was the undermining of community ties and devotion to the common good by economic classes bent on gaining narrow material ends. The greed of the rich and the envy of the poor repelled him equally, and during the 1890s he had repeatedly feared incipient social revolution. Roosevelt had then stood unhesitat-

Theodore Roosevelt on the stump, 1903.

ingly with pro-business Republicans against radicals and Bryanite Democrats, whom he had luridly likened to the zealots of the French Revolution. Yet he had never believed that the cure for ills caused by the growth of big business and industry lay in choosing sides. In 1894, Roosevelt had told his friend Henry Cabot Lodge that to control mobs he would send troops who were "not over-scrupulous about bloodshed; but I know the banker, the merchant and the railroad king well too, and *they* also need education and sound chastisement."

Roosevelt's broad social vision gave him a perspective on public issues—domestic and international—that was virtually unique among the front rank of American leaders in the early 1900s. His friend and fellow aristocrat Senator Lodge felt the same disdain for commercialism, but Lodge feared the lower orders too much to share the new president's double-edged social concern. In fact, Lodge and only a few others were exceptional in coming as close as they did to Roosevelt's position. Not only did the president differ profoundly from the Democrats and their aggrieved Southern and Western constituency, but he also stood apart from the main factions in his own party: the small but growing band of Midwestern insurgents who viewed the basic division in America as "the People" versus "the Interests" and who sought to break up big businesses and the broad phalanx of conservatives with ties to big business.

Political calculations as well as a broad social vision commended caution and circumspection to the new president. Since McKinley's successive victories had solidified a national majority behind the Republicans, the Democrats posed no serious threat as long as Republican ranks held reasonably firm. But maintaining their majority status and party unity presented special difficulties. Drawing together as they did the Northeast and Midwest, along with outposts in the West, the Republicans represented diverse, far from completely compatible constituencies. The Midwestern municipal reform drives and the intraparty insurgencies in Wisconsin and Iowa had already revealed strains within the broad Republican coalition. Although those movements remained relatively weak during Roosevelt's first term, their presence portended future trouble for the party. Even if the new president had been more sincerely in sympathy with either the nascent insurgents or the more powerfully entrenched pro-business conservative leaders, the national perspective of his office would have dictated caution, just as it had done for McKinley.

Roosevelt also faced a special problem because he had assumed the presidency without being elected to it. Historical precedent gave him scant comfort: Before 1901 no vice-president who had succeeded a fallen president had yet gone on to win in his own right. Elements in Roosevelt's particular position did not look good, either. He had disturbed his party's conservative bosses when, as governor of New York, he had launched reform initiatives to tax and regulate big businesses. Moreover, there was the possibility that McKinley loyalists and pro-business Republicans would put forward a potential rival for party leadership in Senator Mark Hanna of Ohio. In short, political survival in the White House demanded a circumspect approach to major domestic issues, no matter what the new occupant's views might have been.

Actually, Roosevelt's political fears were exaggerated. His vivid personality and well-developed talent for reaching the public were great political assets, and he exploited them to immense profit. Unlike every previous vice-president who had ascended to the presidency, he owed his succession to the personal strength he had brought to the ticket. Roosevelt's vice-presidential nomination had been an acknowledgment of the new popular dimensions of politics. As long as he committed no grave blunders, the same qualities that had gotten him second place in 1900 could assure him the top spot in 1904.

Roosevelt's expansion of the public dimensions of the presidency accelerated the changes that he, Bryan, and others had already begun to make in American politics. Early in his first term, Roosevelt coined another memorable phrase when he called his new office a "bully pulpit." He made tireless use of that pulpit to preach three main sermons to Americans. First and foremost came international duty, which meant the development of a strong army and navy and the pursuit of a vigorous, alert diplomacy as one of the world's great powers. Two domestic prescriptions stood just behind this internationalism and were connected with it. One was the avoidance of class divisions. "No republic can permanently exist when it becomes a republic of classes," Roosevelt warned in 1904, "where the man feels not the interest of the whole people, but the interest of the class to which he belongs, or fancies he belongs, as being of prime importance." His other domestic prescription was the transcendence of materialism. Inveighing equally against the greed of the rich and the envy of the poor, Roosevelt in 1902 urged his countrymen to remember, "Material prosperity without the moral lift toward righteousness means a diminished capacity for happiness and a debased character. The worth of a civilization is the worth of the man at its centre."

During his first term, Roosevelt backed these prescriptions mainly with administrative action. Though reluctant to introduce new legislation that might disturb Republican solidarity in Congress, the president was much bolder within his own branch of government. Roosevelt followed this course out of a penchant for exercising executive power, and because he was acquainted with the views of advanced European and American political analysts, who de-emphasized legislative remedies and commended administrative methods in dealing with problems of industrial societies. Politicians at the state and local levels were reaching similar conclusions. In Wisconsin, Robert La Follette's reform movement was starting to experiment with expert commissions to regulate railroads, utilities, and agriculture. In the nation's cities, municipal reformers were devising administrative approaches to the management of sanitation, transportation, land use, and construction. The intellectual dovetailed with the activist in Roosevelt to place him in the vanguard of a new breed of devotees of administrative government.

One avenue for administrative action was through appointments. The new president appointed a higher caliber of people to federal offices than the capital had seen in a long time. Roosevelt's appointees tended to be men like himself, educated in the nation's oldest colleges and best universities and, if not from his own upper-crust circles, still possessing cultivated tastes and cosmopolitan outlooks. Two of his earliest appointments epitomized Roosevelt's choices. In 1902 he made his first change in the cabinet, naming as secretary of the navy a Massachusetts congressman and fellow Harvard man, William H. Moody. Two years later Roosevelt transferred Moody to the Justice Department, appointing him attorney general and making Moody his chief advisor on domestic policy. In 1906 the president moved Moody again, this time to a seat on the Supreme Court.

In his first choice to fill a Supreme Court vacancy, the president in 1902 picked yet another Harvard man, who was also one of the country's most formidable thinkers and an heir to a great nineteenth-century New England intellectual tradition: Oliver Wendell Holmes, Jr. The new justice possessed more than a widely regarded legal and literary name. He was one of the most important new thinkers about public affairs. For over twenty years, Holmes had waged war against prevailing conservative views on government intervention in economic and social affairs. He rejected arguments that the framers of the Constitution had laid down a set of immutable principles and that later amendments had extended those principles into a nearly absolute ban on the regulation of private economic activity by local, state, and fed-

Oliver Wendell Holmes, Jr.

eral governments. Instead, Holmes argued, the Constitution and its amendments were a flexible, adaptable charter of government that legislatures and judges must interpret broadly to meet ever-changing circumstances and popular desires. These views did not, however, make Holmes a reformer by any stretch of the imagination. A profound cynic about human nature and society, he flayed liberal as well as conservative ideas and actions. To Roosevelt's chagrin, the new justice's first opinion on the Supreme Court went against the Roosevelt administration in its first antitrust prosecution, the Northern Securities case. The president reputedly snorted, "I could carve a better justice out of a banana." Holmes soon partially redeemed himself, however, in Roosevelt's eyes with attacks on anti-regulatory interpretations of the "due process" clause of the Fourteenth Amendment.

More broadly, Roosevelt carried out his philosophy of government by imbuing public service with a prestige unknown since the early days of the American Republic. Besides appointing such able and attractive men as Moody and Holmes, he retained distinguished McKinley appointees such as Secretary of War Elihu Root, and promoted others such as the head of the Forest Bureau of the Department of Agriculture, Gifford Pinchot, and William Howard Taft, the civil governor of the Philippines. In these ways the new president advertised the seriousness with which he regarded governmental enterprise. For too long, in his view, public office had been regarded as merely a reward for party work, inferior to private pursuits. The superiority of public service to private profit formed a major sub-theme in Roosevelt's preachments against materialism. "Napoleon said that in war the moral was to the material as ten to one," he observed in a speech early in his presidency; "and it is just as exactly as true [sic] in civil and social life." In 1905 he lauded a group of Civil War veterans for having "the qualities which made you put material gain, material well-being, not merely below, but immeasurably below devotion to an ideal, when the crisis called for showing your manhood." To instill such devotion in peacetime public service was one of Roosevelt's main objectives as president.

The president also supplied a personal ingredient that imbued his administration with a special spirit. Roosevelt gathered about him an inner circle that took on the air of a jolly but exclusive fraternity. With these intimates he mixed the political and non-political aspects of his life. Learned public figures such as Holmes, Moody, Root, and Lodge and their wives mixed with the writers, artists, scientists, and scholars who frequented White House social gatherings. "Distinguished civilized men and charming civilized women came as a habit to the White House while Roosevelt was there," recalled his old Harvard friend, the novelist Owen Wister. "For that once in our history, we had an American *salon.*" The president also shared his outdoor interests—riding, hiking, hunting, and camping—with younger members of his circle. Two with whom Roosevelt became especially intimate on rides and rambles were Gifford Pinchot, whom he elevated to the position of chief forester when the Forest Service became a separate agency in 1905, and James R. Garfield, whom he appointed to head the newly created Bureau of Corporations in 1903 and later named secretary of interior. Roosevelt's inner circle came to be called the "Tennis Cabinet," a sobriquet that, though inaccurate, did capture the glamor and excitement, and the unmistakable upper-class tinge, that Roosevelt lent to the higher reaches of his administration.

CONTINUITY AT HOME

With Roosevelt's accession to the presidency, the tempo of public life accelerated. Politics had always formed the staple of journalism, but now newspapers and, even more so, magazines transferred to their treatment of public affairs much of the lighter tone and technique they employed in covering society and "human interest" subjects. Not all of this change was due to Roosevelt; a larger journalistic movement was already afoot. This movement would soon burst on the scene with the sensational, deep-delving investigations that Roosevelt himself later dubbed "muckraking." But the lively, glamorous president and first family unquestionably made the political scene more interesting and more personal to ordinary citizens. Roosevelt and his strong-minded wife Edith brought an unpretentious elegance to their new residence, whose official title he changed from the Presidential Mansion to "the White House," and whose dowdy, worn interior she redecorated in the most tastefully restrained style. This well-publicized cultivation of taste, together with their cultural patronage, enhanced their fascination in the public eye.

With Roosevelt at the helm, the pace of public debate and legislation measurably increased, particularly as questions involving business consolidation and regulation came more insistently to the fore. In 1902 he allowed the Justice Department to initiate a series of prosecutions under the Sherman Antitrust Act. These prosecutions, which had been planned and approved by McKinley, were aimed in some degree at curbing business consolidation.

The first target had special significance: it was the Northern Securities Company, a mammoth merger of transcontinental railroads engi-

Uncle Sam looks on as Roosevelt wrestles with the railroads.

neered by J. P. Morgan. It was a shrewd prosecution from the legal standpoint, because interstate transportation was one area indisputably left open to governmental action by the Supreme Court's earlier, narrowly restrictive interpretations of the Sherman Act. Symbolically, the target could hardly have been more appropriate. Morgan had joined with two widely known railroad barons, James J. Hill and E. H. Harriman, and with the Rockefeller interests, to form a gigantic holding company that would control nearly all the long-distince rail lines from Chicago to the Pacific Coast. Moreover, the railroads had long been objects of popular agitation and concern. Still, the Northern Securities case was not an airtight one for the government. The defense argued that as a holding company, rather than a primary carrier, the railroad combine was not subject to regulation under interstate commerce, nor was it covered by the Sherman Act. Justice Holmes agreed in the dissenting opinion that so infuriated Roosevelt. Nevertheless the government won the case all the way through a challenge before the Supreme Court in 1903, and those legal victories began to establish Roosevelt's reputation as a trust-buster.

Roosevelt went on to win more acclaim during the summer and fall of 1902 when he mediated a miners' strike in the anthracite coal industry. Although federal intervention in strikes was not new, it was a departure for the government to act in a way that did not at least tacitly favor management. The miners had gained public sympathy for several reasons. Their grievances stemmed from low wages, long hours, and dangerous working conditions. Their union's leader, John Mitchell, was conciliatory, demanding only pay raises, better hours for shifts below ground, and some safety provisions. Mitchell demonstrated his flexibility by ultimately abandoning the effort to have the union recognized as a bargaining agent. The mine owners, in contrast, were intransigent. Their leader, George F. Baer, earned widespread opprobrium when he declared that "God in His Infinite Wisdom has given control of the property interests of the country" to such people as himself. Roosevelt's response was to issue public calls for conciliation and to conduct a series of White House bargaining sessions. He also brought private pressures to bear on the mine owners, including financial threats by Morgan and others on Wall Street. At length, Roosevelt secured a settlement of the strike which met the miners' demands for better pay, shorter hours, and safer working conditions, but not recognition of their union. The settlement also included a 10 percent price increase for all coal, which was soon felt by manufacturers and homeowners. Never-

*"The Real Object of the Operators Is to Crush It." A cartoon
from the* Ohio State Journal *critical of the mine owners during
the 1902 strike.*

theless, the public hailed Roosevelt as a champion of workers and consumers.

The acclaim for the president was slightly misplaced, however. Before
his assassination, President McKinley had worried about the rampage
of trust formations, and he had given the go-ahead for the initial antitrust prosecutions. The government attorneys who brought the suits
were McKinley appointees whom Roosevelt had retained. Overall
direction of the campaign came from Attorney General Philander C.
Knox, a corporate lawyer appointed by McKinley and kept on by Roosevelt. Presidential intervention in a coal strike was not unprecedented, either. Two years earlier, McKinley had quietly but forcefully
bent the mine owners to meet a few union demands. Much of the owners' intransigence in 1902 stemmed from resentment at the earlier
presidential pressure. The main difference between McKinley's and
Roosevelt's actions on these issues was that Roosevelt acted partly in
public and thereby gained open acclaim. This was neither the first nor

the last time he would reap where others had sown—a fate that would ultimately befall him, too.

Roosevelt's wariness about ruffling the sensibilities of Republican congressional leaders did not prevent him from sponsoring three pieces of important legislation in 1903, in part because two of the new laws were uncontroversial. The Expedition Act expanded Justice Department personnel by adding two assistant attorneys general and other staff, and changed court procedures to facilitate litigation under the Sherman Act. The new law speeded up the Roosevelt administration's antitrust prosecutions and further enhanced the president's "trust-buster" reputation. The Elkins Act forbade railroads from granting rebates on rates to big shippers, such as Rockefeller's Standard Oil and Carnegie's steel firms. Not only did this reform draw support from politicians of all persuasions, but it also enjoyed the active backing of railroad executives, who were happy to relinquish this costly means of competition. One Democratic senator alleged that the Elkins Act had been drawn up by railroad lawyers. His claim was incorrect, but the law did represent a major legislative victory for the railroads.

The only one of the three new laws of 1903 that aroused opposition was Roosevelt's proposal to establish the Department of Commerce. The measure initially won support from conservative Republicans on Capitol Hill, but their support cooled when an amendment was passed to establish a Bureau of Corporations with powers to investigate—with subpoenas if necessary—interstate business operations. A number of Wall Street leaders and big manufacturers openly opposed the measure, while others lobbied secretly against it. For a time, it looked as if the whole bill would not be allowed to come to a vote in either house, but Roosevelt broke the deadklock by once more bringing public pressure to bear. He charged that John D. Rockefeller had sent telegrams to key senators denouncing the Department of Commerce bill as "antitrust legislation. . . . It must be stopped." No senator owned up to receiving a telegram from Rockefeller, although it was later revealed that Rockefeller's chief attorney had indeed sent such messages. In any event, the tactic worked splendidly. Both houses speedily passed the Department of Commerce bill by large margins. "I got the bill through by publishing those telegrams and concentrating the public interest on the bill," Roosevelt later boasted.

Like every vice-president who had succeeded a fallen predecessor, Roosevelt had publicly pledged to maintain the previous administration's personnel and policies, and during the first term, he tried hard to honor his pledge. No member of McKinley's cabinet departed until

Secretary of State Elihu Root.

well into 1902; four remained until after the 1904 election; and one stayed in the same post throughout Roosevelt's presidency. Moreover, when Secretary of State John M. Hay, whom McKinley had appointed and Roosevelt had retained, died in 1905, his replacement was another McKinley appointment who had stayed through most of Roosevelt's first term, former Secretary of War Elihu Root. Remaining secretary of state until shortly before Roosevelt left office in March 1909, Root became the president's single most valued advisor. Continuity between the two administrations was maintained as well in domestic policy. The antitrust prosecutions, intervention in the coal strike, and the 1903 legislation were the only actions that Roosevelt took during his first term on the problems of concentration of economic power and relations between capital and labor, and these initiatives had strong roots in the McKinley administration.

Just one area of domestic policy presented an exception to Roosevelt's inaction during his first term. From his background as an amateur scientist, naturalist, and outdoorsman, he had gained a deep feeling for the natural environment. He had grown disgusted at the ways

Americans despoiled forests, prairies, and streams. He worried about the future availability of resources and about preserving the beauty and challenge of the wilderness. As governor of New York, Roosevelt had created forest reserves and appointed commissions to study water and woodland resources. As president, Roosevelt felt none of the hesitation about pressing for conservation measures that he sometimes showed in other domestic fields. He devoted the longest section of his first message to Congress in December 1901 to a call for new laws to protect forests, game, and watersheds on the vast tracts of federally owned land in the West. In 1902, he backed a bill drafted by Congressman Francis G. Newlands, Democrat of Nevada, which would set aside money from sales of public lands for irrigation and reclamation projects in the West. Because the measure favored agricultural development as much as conservation, both Democrats and Republicans from the West favored it, while the main opposition came from conservative Republicans from the Northeast and Midwest. Roosevelt's strenuous efforts to secure passage of the Newlands Reclamation Act in the summer of 1902 caused his first clash with the leaders of his party on Capitol Hill.

The president later convened White House conferences to bring business and academic experts together with state and federal officials to discuss irrigation, grazing, timberland, and waterway problems. Despite skepticism and mounting opposition from development-minded Westerners, Roosevelt repeatedly spoke out for stronger action. "I ask with all the intensity that I am capable," he declared just after the 1904 election, "that the men of the West will remember [to distinguish] . . . between the man who skins the land and the man who develops the country. I am going to work with, and only with, the man who develops the country." His strong words had already found their match in action. Roosevelt repeatedly availed himself of presidential authority to expand forest reserves on the federal lands in the West. During his first term over thirty million acres were added to the reserves, increasing their size by nearly half.

Conservation became a critical element in Roosevelt's domestic politics largely through the influence of Gifford Pinchot. Roosevelt was governor of New York when he first met Pinchot, who was another denizen of upper-crust New York society and a Yale graduate with European training in forestry. Pinchot did not share Roosevelt's intellectual curiosity and grounding in science, but he was an equally ardent outdoorsman and naturalist. Unlike most of Roosevelt's other intimate friends, Pinchot had a zealot's temperament, strong policy commitments, and ambitions as a bureaucratic empire-builder. He and Roosevelt tended to reinforce each other's sense of urgency about their common concerns.

Roosevelt's advocacy of conservation and abetting of Pinchot's ambitions led to the greatest domestic accomplishment of his first term. Ever since Pinchot had entered the federal government in 1898, he had been laboring to upgrade his tiny Forest Bureau into a larger, more powerful agency. He also sought to gain control of the federal government's forest reserves, which were under the jurisdiction of the Department of Interior. Roosevelt helped achieve those aims by stirring up public concern over conservation and through persistent lobbying on Capitol Hill. Pinchot's bureau grew steadily during Roosevelt's first term, and his crowning achievement came three months after the 1904 election. In February 1905, Congress transferred management of the much enlarged forest reserves to Pinchot's agency, which was further expanded and renamed the United States Forest Service. Pinchot's own title became Chief Forester, and he remained under the loose authority of the Department of Agriculture. In order to manage the reserves, Pinchot was authorized to recruit a new force of men, whom he called Forest Rangers, whose distinctive badges and uniforms he designed, and in whom he instilled his, and Roosevelt's, spirit of exciting public service. The Forest Service and Forest Rangers would stand as Roosevelt's finest and most lasting contribution to American life.

Foresters at work in the Coronado National Forest, Arizona, 1905.

BIG STICK ABROAD

In contrast to his restraint in domestic policy, Theodore Roosevelt conducted a vigorous, assertive foreign policy during his first three years as president. Many contemporary observers and later historians have judged these years the high-water mark of American imperialism. Roosevelt frequently proclaimed himself an unabashed, unapologetic imperialist. The baldest statement of his convictions came in his December 1904 message to Congress, in which he enunciated what he had repeatedly said privately and in secret diplomatic messages. This was his Roosevelt Corollary to the Monroe Doctrine. "Chronic wrongdoing," he announced, "or an impotence which results in the general loosening of the ties of civilized society may in [North and South] America, as elsewhere, ultimately require intervention by some civilized nation, and in the western hemisphere the adherence of the United States to the Monroe Doctrine may force the United States, however reluctantly, in flagrant cases of such wrong-doing or impotence, to the exercise of an international police power." Even before becoming president, Roosevelt had repeatedly offered the motto of a West African tribe, "Speak softly and carry a big stick and you will go far," as the

Roosevelt wielding the "big stick" in the Caribbean.

best guide to foreign policy. The "big stick" quickly became the emblem of his diplomacy.

Within a year of taking office, Roosevelt intervened in a major way in Latin American affairs. For several months during 1902, the president engaged in elaborate diplomatic maneuvers, partly public but mostly private, to block Germany from intervening in Venezuela to collect debts owed to German banks. Similar problems of large debts to European lenders later prompted him to exert pressures on Haiti and, starting in 1904, to establish an American financial protectorate over the Dominican Republic. Later in 1906, Roosevelt confirmed the purely formal character of Cuban independence by sending in troops to begin a three-year occupation. These actions lent substance to boasts in the United States that the Caribbean was an "American lake."

Nor did Roosevelt's settled beliefs in Anglo-American cooperation prevent him from asserting United States primacy on the North American continent. For at least a decade, Roosevelt had been convinced that Britain and the United States had no serious conflicts of national interest and instead shared a great mission as the chief representatives of the "English-speaking races." Such solidarity, however, did not stop him from pushing around the British and their former colonial dependents, the Canadians. In 1902 a long simmering dispute with Canada over the southeastern boundary of Alaska, which had been an American territory since its purchase from Russia in 1867, heated up again when new gold discoveries were reported in Alaska. The president sent additional troops to patrol the border areas claimed by the United States. The disputed lands were not rich or extensive—only a few hundred square miles of wilderness—but they seemed essential to both countries because they controlled access to the sea. Roosevelt meanwhile engaged in another bit of complicated public and private maneuvering to gain permanent cession of the territory to the United States. After repeatedly refusing arbitration, Roosevelt relented during the summer of 1903 and, with a great show of reluctance, agreed to permit an international tribunal settle the dispute. This allowed the Canadians apparently to save face, although they and the British together appointed only three judges to the panel, while the Americans also appointed three. Through his friends Senator Lodge and Justice Holmes, the president pressed the British to favor the American claims, which their representative eventually did. Although the Canadians were incensed at the outcome, Roosevelt's behind-the-scenes moves actually strengthened amity between the United States and Britain.

The single act of his presidency, in domestic and foreign affairs, for which Roosevelt always publicly professed greatest pride also came during 1903. No diplomatic move of any American president would do more to assert a dominant American stake in the Caribbean and Central America; at the same time, practically no action by any president ever did more to tarnish the United States's reputation for morality and straight dealing in the Western Hemisphere. This was Roosevelt's critical role in the armed insurrection of October 1903 that resulted in the secession of Panama from Colombia, and the cession to the United States of a swath of territory running through the middle of the new country. This territory came to be called the Canal Zone. It became the site of the inter-oceanic waterway and would remain under American rule for nearly all of the twentieth century.

Construction of a canal across Central America to link shipping on the Atlantic and Pacific Oceans fulfilled a fifty-year-old American dream. Ever since the United States had expanded to the Pacific, the need had existed to shorten the time and distance required for maritime shipping between the two coasts. The California Gold Rush in 1849 and the Alaskan gold strikes in the 1890s had repeatedly shown how costly, time consuming, and dangerous it was to ship people and goods around South America's Cape Horn, or to transport them by land across the mountainous, jungled, yellow-fever-infested isthmus of Panama. The difficulties of maintaining and reinforcing fleets in the Pacific, even before the Spanish-American War, had demonstrated the strategic boon that an inter-oceanic waterway would provide to the United States Navy. Schemes for the construction of a canal had begun as early as the 1850s, and from 1879 to 1889 a French company, headed by Ferdinand de Lesseps, the builder of the Suez Canal, had tried and failed to dig a canal in Panama. This failure, together with reportedly gentler terrain and a chain of lakes in Nicaragua, prompted many canal advocates to favor a route there instead.

Diplomatic negotiations to secure a route for an American canal across Central America had dragged on for several years before 1903. The Panama route was finally chosen thanks in part to lobbying by investors in de Lesseps's company. American acquisition of the route would allow those investors not only to recoup their losses but also to realize profits of several million dollars. Further complications arose, however, when Colombia, of which Panama was then a part, refused to ratify a treaty ceding the territory and compensating the French investors. The Colombian government was holding out for a bigger payment. An infuriated Roosevelt demanded action. The United States then stationed naval vessels off the principal Panamanian ports, and

Panama's secessionist revolt swiftly followed. Troops from the American vessels helped block Colombian attempts to quell the uprising. Furthermore, the State Department recognized newly independent Panama within hours of the revolt, and already had treaties to acquire the territory for the canal prepared for signing and swift ratification. The representative of the French investors was immediately appointed the minister of newly independent Panama to the United States, and he at once signed the treaty that granted the United States the canal route under the previous terms.

Roosevelt himself retained curiously mixed attitudes toward the Panama affair. The building of the canal, which was not completed until 1914, five years after Roosevelt left office, stood at the head of every list he made of his presidential accomplishments. This gigantic feat of engineering meshed perfectly with his appetite for grandeur and with the enthrallment of Americans and Europeans of that era with triumphs of technology. What better proof of human mastery over nature could be offered than the Panama Canal? It was a magic path between the seas that transported ships for fifty miles over mountain ranges and speeded them toward distant ports. For Roosevelt, the

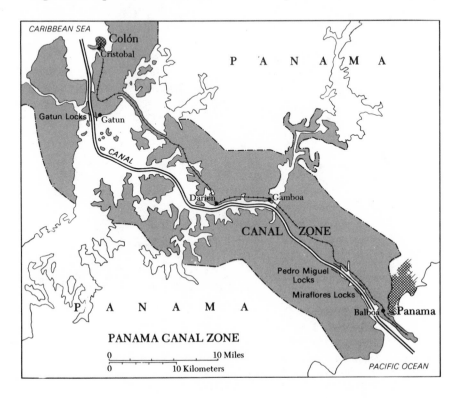

PANAMA CANAL ZONE

emotional high point of his presidency was his trip to Panama at the end of 1906 to inspect work on the canal. On the trip he became the first president to leave the United States while in office, and he revelled at witnessing the massive earth-moving and lock-construction projects. A widely circulated photograph taken of Roosevelt showed him in a white tropical suit at the controls of a huge steam shovel. Nothing depicted him better as an empire builder.

Yet Roosevelt more than once betrayed a trace of guilt over the way the route was acquired. At the first hint of possible American collusion in the Panamanian revolt, the president issued thunderous private denials in letters and monologues to his cabinet, and he leaked his version of the story to sympathetic reporters. After leaving office, he made frequent public declarations of his righteousness, including a lengthy section in his *Autobiography*, published in 1913. "From the beginning to the end," he avowed, "our course was straightforward and in absolute accord with the highest standards of morality." Furthermore, he charged, "it is hypocrisy, alike odious and contemptible, for any man to say both that we ought to have built the canal and that

"The First Spadeful." A cartoon from the New York Herald *suggesting TR's role in securing the Panama Canal.*

Roosevelt posing at the controls of a steam shovel during his visit to the canal, 1906.

we ought not to have acted in the way we did." Those declarations, like earlier statements, had the overwrought quality that Roosevelt's language usually assumed when he was unsure of his moral ground. Elihu Root put his finger on the false note when, after a harangue to the cabinet on the subject of the canal, Roosevelt demanded to know whether he had defended himself adequately. "You certainly have, Mr. President," the secretary of state quipped. "You have shown that you were accused of seduction and you have conclusively proved that you were guilty of rape."

The activist diplomacy of Roosevelt's first term comprised more than bluster and assertiveness. Behind his overbearing public posture often lay more subtle, restrained, cautious dealings with other nations. Whereas Roosevelt bullied smaller, weaker countries, mainly in Latin America, he exercised caution and sensitivity toward nations of equal or greater power, especially in Europe. The mixed character of Roosevelt's diplomacy displayed more than an imperialist's disdain for inferiors and respect for peers. His warnings to Germany over Venezuela, acquisition of the Canal zone, and especially enunciation of the Roosevelt Corollary all sprang from a well-defined strategy of forestalling incursions by European powers in the Western Hemisphere. Roosevelt pursued that goal assiduously for the sake of both his country's security and the world's harmony and order.

With the 1904 presidential campaign on the horizon, Roosevelt became more active still in foreign affairs. At the same time, he became more assertive on the domestic front. "Our place as a nation is and must be with the nations that have left indelibly their impress on the centuries," he declared in May 1903. At home and abroad, Roosevelt urged Americans to tread arduous paths of righteousness and challenge. "I ask that this people rise level to the greatness of its opportunities. I do not ask that it seek the easiest path."

IN HIS OWN RIGHT

More than anything else, Theodore Roosevelt wanted to lead the American people further along the paths that he had preached, and that meant getting elected president in his own right in 1904. As a savvy professional, Roosevelt took nothing for granted. Much of his attention and energy during his first term went toward securing his nomination and election. In this, his caution served him well, as he avoided giving offense to his party's conservatives while at the same time he satisfied the insurgents.

Roosevelt's intraparty maneuverings mirrored his diplomacy on the international scene. While operating quietly and subtly behind the scenes, he supplied plenty of noise and spectacle. This was mainly instinctive on his part, but Roosevelt also aimed at cultivating the press. He was attentive to reporters and editors, with whom he carefully planted leaks and floated trial balloons, and he set up the first facilities for correspondents in the White House. Roosevelt meanwhile manipulated patronage and factional rivalries to gain tight control of his party and shut out possible rivals. A stroke of personal good fortune aided him when his Republican rival, Senator Mark Hanna of Ohio, died suddenly early in 1904. By then, however, not even McKinley's old partner could have stopped the man he had once derided as a "damned cowboy."

Skill and luck conspired together to make 1904 Roosevelt's year of supreme political triumph. By the time the Republican convention met that June he had tightened his control of the party machinery and assured his nomination by acclamation. The 1904 Republican convention and campaign added little new to discussions of public issues. Roosevelt coined a catchy phrase, the "Square Deal," to advertise his program, but he avoided specifics on most issues. Bowing to precedent, he did not appear at the convention, and he followed McKinley's example by staying off the campaign trail. The president also steered clear of provocations to the party's conservative leaders. He allowed them to pick one of their own, Senator Charles W. Fairbanks of Indiana, as his running mate, and he kept the platform noncommittal on controversial issues.

The Democrats obliged Roosevelt even better than his own party did in 1904. William Jennings Bryan cheerfully stepped aside as the standard-bearer, and his followers permitted Northeastern conservatives, who had been blaming the Commoner and his faction for previous Democratic defeats, to take a turn at nominating a candidate and framing party appeals. The Democrats settled on Alton B. Parker, a little-known New York judge and party loyalist. Parker immediately repudiated previous Democratic stands on free silver and other domestic issues, but on the whole, the Democrats vied with the Republicans at ducking controversial questions. There was no mention of the currency or business-regulation issues in the Democratic platform. Only on the well-worn ground of tariff protection did the two parties take opposing positions. The Republicans rehashed the benefits to domestic jobs and wages of high tariffs on imported goods, and the Democrats once more lambasted high prices in their call for lower rates. Parker attempted to shift the focus of debate to Roosevelt himself, especially his "usurpation of authority" and thirst for "personal power." Parker also used his own conservative background and appeals to big business to try to reverse the recent ideological alignment of the two parties.

The effort failed. No noticeable defection from Roosevelt occurred among conservatives. The pro-big business, anti-reformist newspaper,

"FOR PRESIDENT!" An Atlanta Constitution *cartoon depicting the bellicose Roosevelt, 1904.*

the *New York Sun*, rationalized support for him this way: "We prefer the impulsive candidate of the party of conservatism to the conservative candidate of the party which the business interests regard as permanently and dangerously impulsive." At the same time, Parker's attempt to portray the president as an incipient radical endeared Roosevelt still more to Republican insurgents. A few of them, most noticeably Robert La Follette, already distrusted the president as a lukewarm progressive, but most of the growing company of reform Republicans harbored an uncritical devotion for him. Another leading party insurgent, George W. Norris, then a congressman and later a senator from Nebraska, recalled long afterward, "I followed Mr. Roosevelt implicitly in the liberal views that he took, and was impressed always with his sincerity and integrity." Norris even followed Roosevelt, he confessed, "when I had some doubts as to the righteousness of his course." To win the support of the *New York Sun* and of La Follette and Norris was a remarkable political feat.

Although Parker's attacks evidently changed few votes in 1904, they did have important effects in the long term. The aspersions on Roosevelt's love of power stung because they contained more than a grain of truth. Conservatives in the president's own party privately agreed with those charges. The Speaker of the House of Representatives, Joseph G. Cannon of Illinois, once reportedly joked, "Roosevelt has no more use for the Constitution than a tom cat has for a marriage license." Equally discomforting for Roosevelt were disclosures that the president's campaign managers had threatened several trust magnates with government investigations unless they contributed heavily to his campaign fund. With some exaggeration, the Democrats repeatedly charged the Republicans with "blackmailing Wall Street." Roosevelt blasted back by branding their allegations "unqualifiedly and atrociously false"— another example of his inclination toward overstatement when caught with his morals down.

As it was, nothing could hurt Roosevelt in 1904. He won a smashing victory on November 9. He carried thirty-two states for 336 electoral votes and took the popular vote by a margin of more than two-and-a-half million, over 57 percent of the total. Turnout in 1904 fell far below that in 1900: half-a-million fewer people voted in 1904, a decline of eight points in the percentage of eligibles voting. Even so, Roosevelt bettered McKinley's showing four years earlier by more than half-a-million votes, eight percentage points of the total, and five states. Parker carried only his party's Southern strongholds, and even there the president narrowed the margins in eight states.

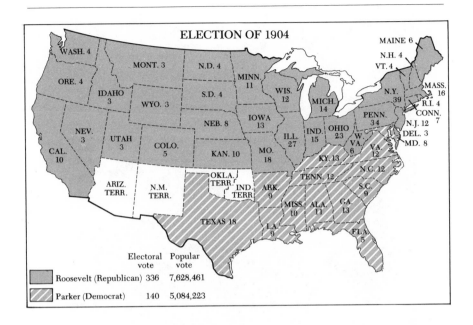

Further signs of trouble for the Democrats came from radical splinter parties. The reconstituted Socialist party garnered over 400,000 votes (3 percent of the total) behind their attractive candidate, Eugene V. Debs. This slender, forty-nine-year-old former railway fireman and union leader was an impressive, impassioned orator who combined infectious compassion for the downtrodden with fierce denunciations of capitalist "exploiters." Debs campaigned from a flag-draped train called the "Red Special," and his vote indicated the small but growing appeal of radical alternatives to an economic system dominated by big business. Even the moribund farmers' protest movement, the People's Party, which had been eclipsed when their platform was taken over by Bryan and the Democrats in 1896, revived to capture over 100,000 votes in the South and West, triple their 1900 showing. The Prohibitionists also gained substantially with over a quarter of a million votes, nearly 2 percent of the total.

The overwhelming endorsement by his fellow citizens moved Roosevelt deeply. On election night he issued a statement in which he observed that although he had not previously been elected he had already served nearly a full term as president. "The wise custom which limits a president to two terms," he announced, "regards the substance and not the form. Under no circumstances will I be a candidate for or accept another nomination." Roosevelt was not speaking impulsively. He genuinely believed that no person should hold such a powerful office

Eugene Debs in 1904.

as the presidency for too long. Yet he also showed an unmistakable need to give the lie to charges that he was power hungry and to square a troubled moral conscience. His promise not to run again was one of the noblest deeds of Theodore Roosevelt's life; it was also the biggest blunder of his public career. From this promise and his steadfast adherence to it over the next four years flowed momentous consequences not only for him but for the development of twentieth-century American politics.

Roosevelt made his pledge at a critical time in his presidency. The vicissitudes of international politics had already launched him on his most significant diplomatic venture. In February 1904, war had broken out in the Far East between Russia and Japan, whose expansionist incursions met head-on in Korea and Manchuria. After sensational Japanese victories, the conflict had degenerated into a stalemate, and the ties of both belligerents to major European powers were straining the international balance of power. For several months, even while managing his nomination and election, Roosevelt conducted delicate, usually informal negotiations with half a dozen world capitals. He was setting the stage for his greatest diplomatic coup—mediation of the Russo-Japanese War—which came in 1905. At the same time he was preparing to enunciate the Roosevelt Corollary to the Monore Doctrine, which he delivered in his annual message to Congress in December 1904, one month after the election.

Roosevelt's pledge was the prelude to equally significant domestic actions. The December 1904 message to Congress opened with observations on "the enlargement of scope of the functions of the National Government required by our development as a nation." Roosevelt also noted that "the relations of capital and labor, and especially organized capital and organized labor, to each other and to the public at large come second in importance only to the intimate questions of family life." He specifically called for further, careful investigation of labor and business conditions and for new, stronger legislation to regulate railroad rates and practices. Privately, Roosevelt hailed his election victory because, "A well-defined opinion was growing up among the people at large that the Republican party had become unduly subservient to the so-called Wall Street men—to the men of mere wealth; and of all possible oligarchies I think an oligarchy of colossal capitalists is the most narrow-minded and the meanest in its ideals. I thoroughly broke up this connection, so far as it existed." Perhaps so, perhaps not; but the president would discover that social discontent was to persist "among the people at large."

3

"Excitement and Irritation"

In March 1906, Theodore Roosevelt complained privately about an "unhealthy condition of excitement and irritation in the popular mind. . . ." He was referring to stirrings that, at several levels of society, among various groups in the nation, and in different parts of the country, were starting to shake the United States. Not all of those stirrings had political origins, and some of them found no resolution in the immediate passage of laws or practices of government. But nearly all of them affected American politics increasingly from 1905 onward.

THE STRUGGLE OVER ACCESS

Much of the excitement and irritation emanated from groups of people who felt excluded from the prosperity and promise of American life. By far the largest such group comprised the nation's women, who made up more than half the population. A rich tradition of feminist criticism of social, economic, and political institutions stretched back more than fifty years. The two aged matriarchs of the nineteenth-century women's movement, Elizabeth Cady Stanton and Susan B. Anthony, remained active until their deaths in 1902 and 1906. Thanks to them, as well as to other pioneering feminists and sympathetic men, American women had moved toward greater measures of legal equality and participation in the work force. School teaching had increasingly become a field for women. The new profession of social work had been begun by Jane Addams, Florence Kelley, the daughter of a Civil War Republican congressman, and Lillian Wald, a New York nurse, who were all outspoken feminists. Clerical and sales jobs were gradually opening to women, and female stenographers and office typists offered a visible though not readily accepted symbol of their advances. Perhaps the most impressive gains had come in higher education. The founding of elite women's colleges and the beginnings of coeducation in a number of public and private universities after the Civil War had changed the face of academic life in America. In 1902, for example, over half the undergraduates at the University of Chicago were women.

Impressive as those advances were, however, two big disappointments continued to worry feminists. One was their evident failure to engage the attention and support of the mass of women. Both the organized women's movement and the colleges drew from economically better-off, native-born whites, usually from the cities and larger towns of the Northeast and Midwest. Their concerns struck little response among poorer women, particularly blacks, newly arrived immigrants, and farm wives and daughters in the South and West. The feminists' other disappointment was the persistent denial to women of the most important political right, the vote, in all but four western states. Repeated efforts to widen women's suffrage had failed at federal and state levels, most recently in unsuccessful referenda in California and Oregon. The question of which goal to emphasize—outreach to the masses or winning the vote—continued to divide the women's movement. With the passing of the older generation, however, concentration on suffrage as the primary, sometimes exclusive goal gained favor, especially in the largest organization, the three-decade-old National Woman Suffrage Association. By 1910, the stage was set for a new drive to win the vote.

The commitment to suffrage did not entirely dispel other feminist concerns. Profession and conscience alike instilled in female social workers a determination to improve the lives of poorer people through education, job training, and family support. Some of these social workers, together with other feminists, joined socialist and labor movements, always emphasizing the women's side of their issues.

One issue above all forged a link between feminists and people who were otherwise indifferent or hostile to their concerns. This was the liquor question. By 1900, agitation against alcohol had come to be identified by the single word "prohibition." Proposals to restrict or, more radically, to ban the manufacture and sale of alcoholic beverages likewise had a long history in the United States before 1900. The battle against "demon rum" exerted a special appeal to evangelical Protestants, who frequently expressed their religious zeal in moral reform

Temperance activist Carrie Nation, ax in hand, depicted in a 1901 cartoon from the Utica Saturday Globe.

drives. A few states and communities had outlawed alcohol for drinking at various times during the nineteenth century. Since 1884, the Prohibition Party had run presidential candidates who were now getting about 2 percent of the popular vote. In the main, however, prohibition resembled the women's movement in having made slender gains.

The turn of the twentieth century brought several hopeful changes to the crusade against alcohol. The feminist connection became clearer and stronger. Not all prohibitionists favored woman suffrage, especially in the South, but nearly all the leading feminists espoused prohibition. In their state campaigns, suffrage advocates appealed to prohibition sentiment among voters; in turn, they encountered major opposition to woman suffrage from the liquor interests. The call for prohibition was amplified too by denunciations of distillers and brewers as yet another arm of predatory big business. During the 1890s, moreover, farmer radicals had supported prohibition, and a number of Southern and Western Democrats continued the agitation. Although William Jennings Bryan was himself a fervent evangelical Protestant and personally eschewed alcohol, he shied away from making prohibition a national issue. Still, Bryan's temperament, if not his political calculations, strongly tempted him and many of his followers in that direction. Some insurgent Republicans in the Midwest and West were meanwhile coming out for prohibition. An alliance was growing between political and economic reform and the abolition of drink.

The rising tide of immigration brought an even bigger change to the prohibition movement, which now became one of the most potent weapons in a cultural conflict that would last for the first third of the twentieth century. The swelling numbers of immigrants, with their growing preponderance of southern and eastern Europeans, were transforming the social context of drinking and, thereby, the thrust of efforts to eradicate it. For these immigrants, like their Irish and German predecessors, social drinking was central to community life. As the tides of first German and later Italian immigration rose, there began to appear "Germantowns" and "Little Italies," where beer gardens and wine shops became community centers and political headquarters, particularly for males.

The immigrants considered prohibition a blow directed at their ways of life, and they were at least partly right in viewing the issue that way. For even the most sincerely humanitarian social workers, concerns about the health, family life, and economic status of immigrants blended with wishes to see newcomers "assimilate" into a presumably superior American culture. Evangelical Protestants mixed moral perfectionism with efforts to stamp out "alien" Catholic influences. For political reformers, the desire to dissolve ties between saloons and corrupt city machines mingled with contempt for immigrants' allegedly "tribal" attitudes toward citizenship. Prohibition had a way of dovetailing the noblest and narrowest motives around an issue that generated more passion than other, often more pressing, matters.

For newly arrived immigrants and other members of ethnic groups, the drive to make them over after a rural or small-town Protestant image was just one more aspect of the travails of adjustment to a different language and culture. Whether they came from cities and towns in Central Europe or peasant villages in southern Italy, Poland, and Russia, these fresh arrivals found the United States a bewildering place. From the time they were admitted to the country, usually through a government quarantine facility—the largest, Ellis Island in New York harbor, had opened in 1892—they had to adjust to what was for them an alien place. Most were poor, and for them the simplest tasks of getting food, clothing, places to live, and jobs loomed as daunting obstacles. Whatever savings or property they had once possessed had gone to pay for their steamship passage, increasingly in the dormitory-

style, steerage class of great passenger liners. Some had skills as car-
penters, bricklayers, tailors, or seamstresses, which helped them find
employment in cities in the construction and garment industries.
Experienced miners from Germany, Poland, and Bohemia flocked to
the mining towns that dotted Pennsylvania, Ohio, Illinois, and Minnesota. But the great majority of immigrants had to settle for unfamiliar, unskilled work in factories, and menial labor in domestic and urban
services. Even the relatively skilled immigrants suffered from the twin
handicaps of unfamiliarity with English and their own numbers, which
depressed their wages.

Yet despite such formidable disadvantages, many immigrants proved
adept at taking advantage of social and political opportunities. Kinship, friendship, and common languages drew immigrants together in
ethnic neighborhoods. Often the proximity of a Catholic church or a
synagogue with a priest or rabbi who spoke their native language served
as the magnet to attract a particular nationality to a particular town or
part of a city. Newspapers in their native languages kept the literate
among them informed about events in their new land, while vaude-
ville, music, and drama performed in neighborhood theaters provided
entertainment and kept them in touch with their cultural heritages.
Stores, restaurants, drinking establishments, and clubs soon lent
neighborhoods the flavor of the "old country," and small enterprises
such as grocery stores, newsstands, and tailor and dressmaking shops
allowed many immigrants their start in business. The newcomers also
responded to institutions of the larger society. The settlement houses
offered training in English, homemaking, child care, and job skills to
adults. The public schools required children to undergo sudden
immersion in the language and culture of their new country. With
youth's greater adaptability to new ways, many of these second-gen-
eration immigrants responded more readily and enthusiastically to
pressures to assimilate. Conflicts developed within most of the immigrant groups about whether or how much to retain their traditional
European ways, although many believed that they could maintain both
older and newer identities.

The strongest political influence on immigrants unquestionably came
from the city machines. Before the advent of the settlement house and
mutual aid societies among ethnic groups, the machines had provided
virtually the only assistance that immigrants received in making the
transition to American life. Even after other agencies began to help in
finding housing, jobs, and education, the machines still furnished a
spirit of uncritical welcome and a sense of belonging. Those good feel-

ings, as much as or more than practical aid, accounted for the willingness of urban ethnic groups to support the machines at the ballot box.

Yet urban immigrant voters were not the blindly loyal sheep that their critics charged. The ethnic blocs that were coalescing in Northeastern and Midwestern cities gradually developed their own power and influence. Although the Irish continued to fill the top spots in most machines until the 1920s and 1930s, representatives of newer groups quickly pushed their way into lower-level positions of leadership. Ambitious young Jewish and Italian politicians often broke with the dominant machines when their own ambitions and their peoples' interests were not sufficiently served.

While the new immigrant groups slowly gathered political strength during the first decade of the twentieth century, they faced not only increasingly aggressive prohibitionists but also a movement representing the most blatant expression of "native" reformers' desire to combat "alien" influences. This was the revived movement to restrict overseas immigration. The immigration restrictionists were not merely purveyors of religious and ethnic prejudice. Some of them unquestionably were bigots pure and simple; others professed to find scientific bases for their social views in applications of Darwinian biological concepts.

"Immigration Restriction Prop Wanted." Uncle Sam straining to keep unwanted immigrants out of the United States.

Madison Grant, a wealthy amateur anthropologist and patron of scientific expeditions, wrote extensively on Nordic superiority and the need to prevent contamination by lesser breeds, thereby offering an intellectual rationale for restrictionist policies. The movement also drew on social and economic arguments for restriction. Some social workers argued that so long as an ever replenishing pool of newcomers diluted efforts to ameliorate conditions, little economic or social improvement, much less assimilation, could be achieved for immigrants already in the United States. Labor union leaders advanced an economic variation of the same argument. They contended that as long as the flood of new immigrants furnished a plethora of hands willing to work for low pay, scant betterment would occur for any workers in wages, hours, or working conditions. Moreover, by offering a ready source of strikebreakers, immigrants hampered unions' drives to organize industrial workers.

The labor leaders' advocacy of immigration restriction had an ironic side, since many were immigrants themselves. The most prominent labor official, the president of the American Federation of Labor, Samuel Gompers, was the London-born son of Russian Jews and had come to New York at the age of thirteen. Gompers supported immigration restriction because he was determined to wean the labor movement away from socialism and convert workers over to his own exclusively economic approach. Once, when questioned about what his long-range goals were for workers, Gompers snapped back, "More, more, more." Like others outside organized labor, Gompers believed that alien radicalism flourished mainly among recently arrived immigrants. Those allegations smacked of smear tactics, but the connection did have a basis in fact. German immigrants had swelled both the leadership and membership of urban, socialist parties since the Civil War. The strongest municipal socialist movement in America had arisen among German-Americans in Milwaukee, where by 1906 the Socialists were already the second strongest party. In 1910, the Milwaukee Socialists elected the party's first mayor of a large city and first member of the House of Representatives.

Fear of radicalism formed one of the broader appeals behind immigration restriction. The leading restrictionist organizations played on the alleged socialist leanings, as well as the strange religions, looks, and customs of southern and eastern European immigrants. They also tried hard to capitalize on the Polish-anarchist background of President McKinley's assassin, Leon Czolgosz. But those efforts bore little fruit in the face of public indifference and organized opposition to

Samuel Gompers in 1902.

restriction. Warnings about immigrants' radicalism fell on deaf ears among business spokesmen, especially the National Association of Manufacturers, who opposed restriction for the same reason that the labor unions supported it—because immigrants furnished low-paid, unorganized workers. Leading Southern whites likewise frowned on restriction. They hoped to attract European immigrants either to work in the region's burgeoning industries, or to become a new class of farmers, in each case diminishing the South's dependence on black labor.

But both of these sources of opposition to restriction were starting to weaken by 1910. Some manufacturers recognized that greater mechanization was making them less dependent upon cheap labor, while Southern whites became increasingly disgruntled at their failure to attract immigrants. At the same time, the restrictionist movement gradually gained strength. Legislation that would require those foreign born seeking entrance to the United States to be able to read and write in their native languages—literacy-test bills—still fell short of passage in Congress, but at each succeeding session the number of votes for these measures rose in both houses.

THE EXCLUSION OF BLACKS

Just as Southern whites were becoming less welcoming toward immigrants from abroad, they were also hardening in their prejudices against blacks in their midst. The movement to disenfranchise black voters—through literacy tests and other devices that did not openly violate the Fourteenth and Fifteenth Amendments—gathered strength after 1900. By the end of the first decade of the new century, nearly all blacks, together with large numbers of poorer whites, had vanished from the electorate throughout the South and in several Border States. There were exceptions, most notably in such cities as Memphis, Houston, and San Antonio, where white-led political machines depended on black votes. Overall, however, the Southern electorate steadily shrank during the first two decades of the twentieth century. In fact some Southern states would be tallying smaller total votes in presidential elections in

"A Triumph for White Supremacy." Disenfranchisement of black voters swept the South after 1900.

the 1940s than they had done in the 1880s, despite population growth and the effective doubling of the electorate by women suffrage.

The first two decades of the twentieth century marked what one historian called the "nadir" for black Americans since the abolition of slavery. Few bright spots relieved the gloomy prospect. Not only were Southern whites bending the law to take away the vote, but they were also erecting legal barriers of social discrimination to build the system known as segregation, or less formally, "Jim Crow." The drive for segregation had started in the early 1880s with laws that required blacks to ride in separate cars on railroads. The movement then broadened, aiming to segregate the races in all manner of facilities—from courtrooms and hotels to restrooms and drinking fountains—and it swept through the South during the next thirty years. Some white southerners justified these actions as humanitarian measures. They argued that disenfranchisement and segregation would make politics and race relations more stable and tolerable by enforcing greater physical separation of the races, imposing the clarity of law on previously loose customs, and eliminating agitation among whites over alleged black political and social threats. These arguments struck black and white critics as examples of hypocrisy: segregation punished the victims of discrimination. Their criticisms made no dent, however, in the overwhelming white will to believe in the benefits of racial discrimination.

Whites outside the South also welcomed segregation. The most important national endorsement came from eight justices of the United States Supreme Court in the 1896 decision, *Plessy v. Ferguson.* Earlier decisions of the Supreme Court had already effectively nullified federal powers to combat racial discrimination under the Fourteenth Amendment. The Court's approval in the *Plessy* case of a Louisiana statute requiring segregated seating on streetcars came, therefore, as no surprise. What was surprising was the sweeping character of the decision. With only one dissent, the justices stated that in itself segregation could not be construed as socially discriminatory, and they laid down the rule that was later termed "separate but equal" to govern all future cases involving segregation. The eight justices stopped short of imposing an affirmative obligation to segregate the races, but their favorable comments on current Southern laws left no doubt that they would smile upon further moves in that direction. Ironically, as has often been observed, the lone dissent came from a white Southerner and one-time slaveowner, Justice John Marshall Harlan of Kentucky. Harlan argued that the Fourteenth Amendment meant what it said about forbidding discrimination on the basis of race. His criticisms failed to slow the segregationist juggernaut, however, as the *Plessy* decision aroused cries of anguish from the black press but little or no comment from Northern whites.

Disenfranchisement and segregation fell spectacularly short of fulfilling the hopes they had aroused in Southern whites. Neither those who predicted racial harmony nor the franker racists who wanted assurance of total white supremacy could take comfort in the events from 1900 to 1915. Depriving blacks of the vote paradoxically made them an even more looming presence in the mind of the white electorate. A succession of colorful but increasingly vicious Negrophobic demagogues set the dominant tone of Southern politics. They began with Benjamin R. ("Pitchfork Ben") Tillman in South Carolina in the 1890s, and they continued through James K. Vardaman, the "White Chief" of Mississippi, Thomas Watson of Georgia, and a host of others between 1900 and the early 1920s. Their appeals mixed virulent racism with advocacy of economic regulation and reform. Tillman and Vardaman were close friends and allies of Bryan in the Democratic party; Watson had been a leading Populist in the 1890s and was their presidential candidate in 1904. Denunciations of Northern big busi-

Tom Watson of Georgia.

ness and cities fitted neatly in these politicians' postures of aggressive Southernism and agrarianism. But they struck their strongest resonance with their followers when they conjured up specters of Negro domination. These demagogues called for repeal of the Fourteenth and Fifteenth Amendments, and they advocated forms of peonage for blacks that would have amounted to virtual re-enslavement. A defeated candidate for governor of Mississippi in 1903 gave eloquent testimony to their influence when he lamented that Vardaman had raised a false issue between them: "Everybody knows that I believe in the divine right of the white man to rule, to do all the voting, and to hold all the offices, both state and federal."

Racism in the South went beyond words as violence between the races escalated after 1900. Although blacks occasionally attacked whites and resorted to self-defense, nearly all the violent acts, particularly organized ones, originated with whites. The most widespread form of documented racial violence was lynching. The victim was usually a black man accused of a crime, particularly murder of a white person or rape of a white woman, or he was a black man suspected of social transgressions, frequently involving interracial sex. After being seized by a mob of whites, he would be tortured and killed, most commonly by hanging, and his body would be mutilated and burned. Nearly every description of Southern lynchings remarked on their joyous, carnival-like atmosphere and the large number of women and children in the crowds. The annual figure for recorded lynchings of blacks in the United States fluctuated between a low of sixty in 1905 to a high of seventy-nine in 1915. Mississippi led the nation in numbers of recorded lynchings, followed closely by Georgia; blacks made up over 90 percent of the victims. By contrast, the largest number of whites lynched in the entire country was forty-six, also in 1915. The great majority of white lynchings occured in the West, often in connection with strikes and labor troubles.

The most widely reported form of Southern violence was the race riot, which was really a rampage of white mobs in black neighborhoods. During the first decade of the twentieth century, three major race riots broke out in the South. The most spectacularly violent one occurred during four days in September 1906 in Atlanta, Georgia, when eleven blacks were killed and sixty were injured, and scores of black homes and businesses were burned down. Respectable Southern whites usually deplored violence, although they often urged sympathetic understanding toward the perpetrators. Some white spokesmen, however, reacted defiantly. Several Atlanta newspapers, especially those close to Tom Watson, excused the rioters in 1906. The following year Pitchfork Ben Tillman defended lynching in a speech on the floor of the United States Senate. Such public remarks served mainly to reassure supporters at home, because lynching and race riots also aroused little concern or criticism from Northern whites. In fact, the fears that prompted racial violence were spreading northward. The first large-scale race riot outside the South occurred in 1908, in Springfield, Illinois, Abraham Lincoln's hometown.

Black Americans responded to these worsening conditions in a variety of ways. The most prominent black spokesman, at least in the eyes of whites, was the principal of the Tuskegee Institute in Alabama, Booker T. Washington. Forty-four years old in 1900 and born a slave, Washington preached doctrines of black pride and self-help. His unbending self-control, eschewal of political protest, and acceptance of a measure of racial separation sometimes made him appear to be an advocate of accommodation to racism. In his most famous and often quoted remark—the statement in 1895 that laid down his so-called "Atlanta Compromise"—Washington had declared, "In matters purely social, we [the two races] may be as separate as fingers, but as the one hand in matters essential to mutual progress." Actually, Washington pur-

Benjamin R. ("Pitchfork Ben") Tillman of South Carolina.

Booker T. Washington.

sued a complex set of strategies for black advancement. He put greatest emphasis both at Tuskegee and in his speeches and writings on basic and vocational education. In the Atlanta Compromise speech he had also avowed, "The opportunity to earn a dollar in a factory just now is worth infinitely more than the opportunity to spend a dollar in an opera-house." Washington was convinced that economic autonomy was essential to any lasting social and political progress for blacks. Thanks in part to his training of teachers, artisans, and farmers and thanks to similar work by others in the South, black illiteracy declined by half—to 30 percent—between 1900 and 1910. Black landownership rose correspondingly by more than ten percent during the decade. At the same time, Washington made himself the conduit for philanthropies from such Northern multimillionaires as Andrew Carnegie and John D. Rockefeller, whose donations were directed at improvement of black health and education.

Behind Washington's façade of dignified acquiescence lay two other facets of the black leader. The more attractive one was what one biographer has called the "secret life" that Washington led as an opponent of segregation and disenfranchisement. Behind the scenes, Washington financed and directed legal challenges against segregation statutes

William Monroe Trotter.

and organized political campaigns against disenfranchisement in the Border States. The other, less attractive facet of his leadership was a bossism that bordered on megalomania. Not only did Washington control access to Northern philanthropists, but he also dispensed the crumbs of political power that remained to blacks within the Republican party. After disenfranchisement, the Republicans faded into phantom organizations in most states of the Democratic South. They survived on federal patronage, of which Washington made himself the arbiter. President Roosevelt confirmed his status with an invitation to dinner at the White House in December 1901. The dinner incited Tillman, Vardaman, and even many usually sober Southern whites to frenzies of denunciation. Roosevelt sneered at the attacks, but he never again entertained Washington or any other black while he was president.

Not all prominent blacks supported Washington's strategies or bowed to his power. During the early 1900s two Northern-born, Harvard-educated black critics challenged him. In 1901 William Monroe Trotter began his Boston newspaper, *The Guardian*, which was dedicated to unceasing agitation for full freedom and equality. Year after year, Trotter denounced all notions of retreat from politics, and he emerged as Washington's most persistent critic. A different attack came in 1903 from a one-time supporter, William Edward Burghardt Du Bois. The thirty-two-year-old Du Bois was already on his way to becoming the greatest black intellectual in American history. Unlike Trotter, Du Bois lauded Washington's accomplishments and shared his emphasis on racial pride and separation, but he rejected the Tuskegeean's exclusive focus on material well-being. Blacks must concentrate instead, Du Bois contended, on higher education for intellectual and political leadership, on devoting resources to training what he called the "talented tenth." Implicit in this emphasis was rejection of Washington's quiescence, which Du Bois soon made explicit by joining forces with Trotter.

Their attacks and Washington's counterattacks led to an internecine conflict among leading blacks and their highly placed white allies. As long as Republicans were in the White House and huge financial benefactions flowed, Washington held the upper hand. Du Bois and others responded in 1906 by forming a militant group called the Niagara Movement. Finding white allies chiefly among the spiritual descendants of Northern abolitionists, they merged into a new organization founded in 1909, the National Association for the Advancement of Colored People. The NAACP pursued a two-pronged strategy. One was a legal-constitutional campaign aimed at resurrecting the power

W. E. B. Du Bois.

of the Fourteenth and Fifteenth Amendments. The other was protest and persistent agitation in an effort to reawaken the moral consciences of Northern whites. In its first decade, the NAACP won a few legal victories, and its journal, *The Crisis,* with Du Bois as editor, became a forum for racially progressive ideas. More substantial results of the NAACP strategy, however, would be a long time in coming.

A common concern haunted both camps of leading blacks. Like the feminists, they worried about whether they were in touch with the majority of their people. Washington and his cohorts claimed to speak to and for the nearly nine million blacks of the South, most of whom were poor, propertyless, and at best, badly educated. Washington himself enjoyed a wide reputation among Southern blacks, but he seems to have been admired less as a spokesman and leader than as a superlative trickster who knew how to get ahead and get money out of rich whites. Trotter and Du Bois were far less known, although their frankly elitist approaches did not immediately require a mass following. By far the best known person among fellow blacks and the most despised Negro among whites was the heavyweight champion prizefighter, Jack Johnson. The tall, muscled, shaven-headed Johnson persistently defeated the world's best white boxers, and was married to a white woman. He set the pattern for a succession of black athletic stars who would become popular heroes by beating whites at their own games. One of Johnson's title bouts had to be fought outside the United States because of white agitation and state laws prohibiting interracial sporting events. Not until 1915, when the thirty-seven-year-old fighter was long past his prime and badly out of condition, did a "white hope" finally wrest the title from Johnson.

For their part, thousands of Southern blacks displayed their discontent with discrimination by engaging in an unmistakable form of protest. If they could not vote with ballots, many voted with their feet. Between 1900 and 1910, over 200,000 black people left the South to settle mainly in cities in the Northeast and Midwest. During the next decade, the rate of migration accelerated as more than 300,000 departed for the North. These were the beginnings of the mass migration that, by the mid-twentieth century, would shift the majority of black Americans outside the South, thereby reducing their proportion of the Southern population and making race relations a truly national affair. Without question, poverty drove many blacks, as it did whites, to leave the South. Economic incentives became particularly important after 1914, when the outbreak of World War I effectively ended European immigration. Northern employers hurried south to recruit blacks for

Jack Johnson, heavyweight champion.

factory work. Before then, however, other motives, especially the yearning to escape discrimination and violence, played the biggest part in precipitating black migration northward. Like fugitive slaves before the Civil War, twentieth-century black Americans were traveling the road to freedom.

At the other end these migrants found urban slums, low-paying jobs, prejudice, and resentment—all of which resembled the conditions encountered by recent European immigrants. Lynching and race riots now spread outside the South because Northern whites scorned and feared these black newcomers. Blacks now faced internal conflicts, like those among the white ethnic groups, between trying to adapt to the dominant culture and maintaining their distinctiveness. Despite the hostility aroused by their color, however, black migrants possessed some advantages. Their Southern ancestry had long since made English their native language and Protestantism their dominant religion. Generations of quiet, stubborn resistance to slavery and racism had fostered Afro-American music and dances, oral traditions, and their own churches, all of which helped preserve their identity and autonomy. Transplanted to northern cities, Afro-American music and literature flowered, especially in New York City's Harlem. The influence of the

"THE MIRAGE." A cartoon in the New Orleans Times-Picayune *questioning the apparent opportunities in the North for Southern black laborers.*

Negro churches combined with the concentration of black people in urban enclaves to lay the future foundations for durable and effective political power.

THE REFORM IMPULSE

The "excitement and irritation" that President Roosevelt had detected in certain social groups in 1906 aroused a sense of foreboding in many observers. Two developments in particular seemed to reflect emerging social tensions. One was the emergence of Eugene Debs as the dynamic, militant leader of the Socialists. On the campaign trail as the Socialist party's presidential candidate again in 1908, Debs once more proved himself the equal of Roosevelt as a personality and of Bryan as an orator, as he continued to demand expropriation of great private fortunes and nationalization of big business.

The other development that fed anxieties about the underclasses was the growth of radical, violent labor unions. These unions sprang up in the early 1890s in the West, chiefly among miners and lumbermen. The isolation of mining towns and lumber camps there, which made them virtual company fiefdoms, had combined with the low pay, long hours, and dangerous working conditions to produce sharp, grating conflicts between workers and owners. With the loose law enforcement and private vigilantism of the region, these conflicts gave rise to a succession of gunfights, lynchings, and bombings.

William D. ("Big Bill") Haywood, an imposing, one-eyed, radical labor leader, had turned one union, the Western Federation of Miners, into an avowedly anticapitalist, rhetorically revolutionary group. Haywood led strife-torn strikes in the copper mines of Coeur d'Alene, Idaho, in 1899. In the early 1900s he shifted his union's activities to Colorado's silver mines, where bloody battles between strikers and company-hired police accompanied strikes in Colorado City and Cripple Creek. In 1906, private detectives kidnapped Haywood and two other union officers from their Denver headquarters and transported them to Boise, Idaho, where they were indicted for the bombing assassination of a former governor. The unionists became known nation-wide after being acquitted in a circus-like trial that featured the famed trial attorney Clarence Darrow for the defense and the state's star orator, newly elected Senator William E. Borah, for the prosecution. The country would soon hear more of Haywood and the union he had founded in 1905, an embracing labor federation that likewise advocated revolution, the Industrial Workers of the World.

It is easy to exaggerate the fear of revolution and radicalism among better-off Americans in the early 1900s. Dread of incipient upheaval and of social threats to private property had been rife in the 1890s, but these fears had subsided by 1900. McKinley's assassination by an anarchist, Debs's verbal pyrotechnics, and Haywood's much-publi-

William D. "Big Bill" Haywood (second from left).

cized words and deeds—although not deeply troubling—did reinforce widespread, vague suspicions that all was not well with the nation's social balance. A few leaders, including Roosevelt, responded to these signs of discontent by pursuing moderate, responsible reform in order to prevent sweeping, destructive change.

Why rumblings of social discontent provoked different responses before and after 1900, especially among middle-class groups, remains one of the most important but also most elusive questions about this era of American history. Economic prosperity was one indisputably important factor in the change. In contrast to the depression-wracked mid-1890s, the first two decades of the twentieth century witnessed a long cycle of economic growth and abundance. Only short-lived recessions in 1907 and 1914 broke the upward spiral. The gross national product rose by half during the first decade of the twentieth century, topping $50 billion for the first time after 1907. Manufacturing continued to power the overall growth of the economy. By 1909 the contribution to GNP from manufacturers alone had risen to more than $8 billion, near double the figure at the beginning of the century. Some older industries, however, registered smaller gains. Flour milling rose by less than one percent during the decade. Book publishing grew by about 30 percent, and whiskey distilling by over 50 percent—despite the efforts of prohibitionists. Industrial output continued to mount, though at varying rates for different industries. Steel production reached 28.3 million tons in 1910, almost triple the amount in 1900. New industries, most notably automobiles, burst on the scene as young giants. The number of motor vehicles registered in the United States rose from 8,000 in 1900 to 458,000 in 1910.

But prosperity bred its own disquiet. The falling value of gold, in conjunction with the near-continuous growth of the economy, stimulated monetary inflation in the American economy for the first time in three decades. Between 1897 and 1913, the estimated cost of living for families climbed 35 percent. Those increases, which averaged a bit over two percent annually, were modest compared with earlier inflationary episodes during and immediately after the Civil War. But to people who had known only falling prices and rising purchasing power, any measure of inflation was profoundly unsettling. Nor did price rises occur gradually. They came in fits and starts, especially in basic home consumption items. Price rises also pinched hard on the fixed incomes of white-collar workers, and on the pay of skilled laborers, who rarely got hourly raises. Although Americans' annual per-capita income rose by about 20 percent during the decade, to over $600 by 1910, industrial workers' wages appear to have risen only slightly more than the inflation rate. Farmers did significantly better as they recovered from the disastrous conditions of the 1890s. Prices for basic agricultural commodities rose by 50 percent between 1900 and 1910, while the farm foreclosure rate dropped. The average value of farms rose from $5,471 in 1900 to $6,444 in 1910. These gains eased farmers' burdens, but memories of the preceding decade and envy of the cities remained fresh.

Another factor that promoted middle-class sympathy toward expressions of social discontent was, perhaps ironically, the conservative political ascendancy. The Republicans' electoral dominance had already been borne out in three successive presidential elections and intervening state and congressional contests. This was reassuring to people who felt a stake in the economy and society, whether great or modest: they did not have to fear dangerous departures. Theodore Roosevelt may have stirred up some nervousness among big businessmen and their Republican allies, but he never aroused the same horror as Bryan did among respectable folk in the Northeast and Midwest.

A relatively new print medium was reaching middle-class readers with a message of social concern. These large-circulation magazines made their first and biggest impact on public life during the early 1900s. The magazines drew attention to the pervasive influence wielded by big business through political corruption, ruthless and immoral commercial practices, and shoddy, unsafe goods for consumption. The magazines did this through the extended exposé reporting which came to be dubbed "muckraking." Investigative journalism was a natural enterprise for popular national magazines, which covered broader areas and longer time periods than the daily newspapers did. Some editors

S. S. McClure.

had run occasional series of articles on social and political problems during the 1890s, but the full-scale outburst of muckraking after 1900 sprang from the feverish brain of the new medium's madcap genius, S.S. McClure.

A classic middle-class success story, McClure had started out on Indiana and Illinois farms as a fatherless immigrant boy from Northern Ireland, worked his way through Knox College in Illinois, and launched publishing ventures while still in his twenties. In 1893, when he was thirty-six, he had started America's first large-circulation magazine, *McClure's Magazine*. He cut the standard price per issue in half and presented a mixture of serialized popular fiction and articles chiefly on science, technology, travel, and recent history. McClure thereby tapped a fresh readership among educated, middle-class people mainly in cities and towns. He attracted readers both through subscriptions, especially with promotional schemes and reduced rates, and through newsstand sales. Other editors soon copied his formula, spreading the "magazine revolution" and establishing the first truly national medium of entertainment and information. McClure himself was never happy without new worlds to conquer. In 1902, after several unsuccessful stabs at empire-building in book and encyclopaedia publishing, he turned to public affairs. "Get out of here, travel, go—somewhere," he reportedly ordered his star writer Lincoln Steffens, who embarked on an odyssey to expose political corruption and promote reform. Once more, where S.S. McClure led, others rushed to follow. Muckraking was underway.

During the next five years, articles on the nefarious influences of business dominated American magazines. *McClure's* set the standard, beginning with Lincoln Steffens's series, "The Shame of the Cities." Reflecting back on his year-and-a-half-long experience, Steffens recalled, "When I set out to describe the corrupt systems of certain typical cities, I meant to show simply how the people were deceived and betrayed. But in the very first study—St. Louis—the startling truth lay bare that corruption was not merely political, it was financial, commercial, social, the ramifications of boodle were so complex, various and far-reaching that one mind could hardly grasp them." The trail led Steffens on to Minneapolis, Chicago, Pittsburgh, Philadelphia, and New York, and everywhere he found the same network of corruption based not upon individual venality alone or even primarily, but mainly upon a system of interlinked business interests and political organizations that required graft simply to maintain themselves and provide some slight satisfaction to their constituents. "Can a city be governed

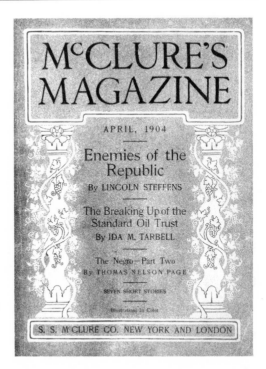

A 1904 issue of McClure's
Magazine.

without any alliance with crime?" Steffens asked after visiting Minneapolis. "It was an open question."

Besides Steffens's "Shame of the Cities" series and his sequel on the
states, several other pieces set the standard for muckraking. One was
Ray Stannard Baker's description of labor conditions, especially in mines
and on railroads, which aroused concern over workers' health and safety.
Baker's accounts of life and labor in Pennsylvania coal towns played a
big part in swaying public opinion against the mineowners during the
1902 strike. The most devastating impact of any *McClure's* article came
with the painstaking two-year series by Ida M. Tarbell, "The History
of the Standard Oil Company." By documenting John D. Rockefeller's
ruthless crushing of competitors and underhanded use of special
advantages, Tarbell made the oil tycoon the nation's most-hated capitalist. These articles in *McClure's,* along with Baker's series on railroads, spawned similar treatments in other magazines, where
muckraking series exposed insurance and patent-medicine frauds, stock-
market jobbery and swindles, and corrupt influences in the United States
Senate. Muckraking became so widespread in magazines that its most
sensational episode occurred largely by accident. Late in 1905, Upton
Sinclair submitted his novel, *The Jungle,* to a New York publisher. Ver-

Upton Sinclair.

ification of his descriptions of the filthy conditions in Chicago stockyards led to a splashy exposé in *The World's Work*, a magazine that
otherwise eschewed muckraking. Sinclair's book, which was in part a
socialist tract, became a best seller, but its author ruefully reflected, "I
aimed at the public's heart, and by accident I hit it in the stomach."

This barrage of investigation and publicity had several effects. Thanks
primarily to Steffens's articles and the lurid series in *Cosmopolitan* by
David Graham Phillips, "The Treason of the Senate," many venal politicians and their machines suffered defeat at the hands of clean government opponents. Articles by Steffens in 1904 made Wisconsin's
insurgent governor, "Battling Bob" La Follette, a national figure and
his progressive Republican faction a model for other reform movements. In many states, new regulatory laws governing banks, railroads,
and insurance companies emerged out of the furor generated by magazine investigations. Prosecutions and convictions galore sprang from
charges leveled in the magazines, and two major political careers got
launched on publicity generated by service as special prosecutors. Charles
Evans Hughes's role in investigating life-insurance frauds in New York
propelled him to the governorship in 1906. Four years later in Califor-

nia, pursuit of transgressions by the railroads furnished the spring-board for Hiram Johnson to win the governorship and lead another important state progressive movement.

Beyond its specific effects on laws, prosecutions, and politicians, muckraking shook public consciousness more broadly, especially among the middle classes. The magazine investigations confirmed the breadth and pervasiveness of nefarious deeds by a few people with unaccountable economic power. Moreover, the style, tone, and content of the exposures were well calculated to persuade the sort of person who read magazines. Not only were the articles larded with facts, figures, names, places, and dates, but they were also written from a professedly neutral perspective. Ostensibly, the writer had no ax to grind, no prescription to offer. Rather, he or she simply reported actual conditions and left it to the reader to make value judgments and decide what, if anything, ought to be done. Where partisan charges by Bryan's Democrats and Socialists might be discounted, these "objective" presentations were hard to dismiss.

But the muckrakers rarely acted as impartial pursuers and presenters of truth. S.S. McClure wanted to arouse readers, in part because he wanted to sell magazines, but more importantly because he yearned

The cover of Sinclair's The Jungle, *1906.*

to exert public influence. Other editors and publishers, especially William Randolph Hearst—who owned *Cosmopolitan* and egged David Graham Phillips on in his work on political corruption—were often crassly commercial, and their efforts bordered on scandal-mongering. Phillips's articles on corruption in the Senate provoked the strongest condemnation leveled at these journalists. Speaking in Washington on April 14, 1906, President Roosevelt compared them to the character in John Bunyan's *Pilgrim's Progress*, "the Man with the Muck-rake, who typifies the man who in this life constantly refuses to see aught that is lofty and fixes his eyes with solemn intentness only on that which is vile and debasing." Although Roosevelt praised exposures of wrong-doing, he decried the person "who never thinks or speaks or writes, save of his feats with the muck-rake." That person was "not a help to society, not a incitement to good, but one of the most potent forces of evil."

Among the muckrakers, Baker alone came close to measuring up to their professed ideal of innocent objectivity. Steffens and Sinclair were committed Socialists anxious to flay the sins of capitalists. The style-setting tone of camera-like realism in Steffens's articles emerged from cuts and revisions that the *McClure*'s editors made in his blatantly slanted first drafts. Tarbell was the daughter of a small independent oil pro-

Ray Stannard Baker.

ducer who had been ruined by Rockefeller, marking her articles with a subliminal strain of family revenge. Phillips had something of the light-hearted sensationalist in him while lesser muckrakers tended to be professionals carrying out assignments. Regardless of the truth of its revelations, muckraking as a journalistic medium contained some false notes.

The heyday of these magazine investigations lasted just five years, from McClure's fist plunge in 1902 until the break-up of his editorial and reportorial team in 1907. Roosevelt's condemnation may have hastened the end of muckraking, but the vogue of large-scale investigative magazine journalism was already waning. Similar work continued afterward, including Baker's series on race relations, "Following the Color Line," but later exposés appeared on a reduced scale and only occasionally. Magazines reverted to a primary emphasis on fiction and non-controversial information, which none of them had abandoned entirely.

The spring of 1906 found Theodore Roosevelt deploring sensationalist journalism as muckraking and social discontent as an "unhealthy condition of excitement and irritation in the popular mind." The president's often overactive imagination led him to fear social revolution unless responsible, farsighted leaders like himself could bring off necessary, constructive reforms, as he had already begun to do. But a better judgment of the state of the nation during the first decade of the twentieth century came around the same time from the newspaper humorist Finley Peter Dunne. Speaking through his fictional bartender, "Mr. Dooley," Dunne declared, "Th' noise ye hear is not the first gun if a rivolution. It's only th' people if th' United States batin' a carpet." Still, Roosevelt's concern about social tensions was legitimate. Mr. Dooley also commented, "But we're wan if th' gr-reatest people in th' wurruld to clean house, an' th' way we like best to clean house is to burn it down." The president had his own way, however, and this most ambitious, energetic, and insightful—albeit conservative—house-cleaner already had his sleeves rolled up.

4

Power and Responsibility
in the Age of Roosevelt

All his life Theodore Roosevelt saw himself as a hero. Starting with his
boyhood struggles against ill health and ending with his last regrets
over missing a final chance to bear arms and lead troops in World War
I, he believed that individuals like himself could overcome adversity,
do great deeds, and inspire others to emulate them. Roosevelt practiced heroism as much in peace as in war, and he gave his most illustrious performance during the middle years of his presidency, from the
end of 1904 through 1906. Those years witnessed his most purposeful
initiatives at home and abroad. In domestic affairs Roosevelt refined
his practice of administrative government, and he mounted legislative
initiatives leading to the passage of two significant sets of laws that
established major economic regulatory functions of the federal government. In foreign affairs Roosevelt played the games of great power
politics with consummate skill. He mediated a war in the Far East,
and he helped to defuse a crisis in Europe. These two years witnessed
the apogee of Roosevelt's political career. Unfortunately for him and
his policies, and even more unfortunately for his party and his successor, the decline from this pinnacle of achievement was swift.

INSURGENCY AND LEGISLATION

The president's basic political task at home remained persuading his
party's stolidly conservative leaders to heed the mounting public dis-

quiet about the growth and power of big business. As his second term began, Roosevelt found his hand strengthened but his task complicated by the increasing influence of the Republican insurgents.

La Follette's group in Wisconsin led the way. The fiery little governor was the archetypal insurgent. Born in 1855 on a small farm in southern Wisconsin and left fatherless when he was less than a year old, La Follette made his way through the University of Wisconsin and trained as a lawyer through a combination of intense work, warm personal charm, and stunning abilities as a speaker and actor. (He briefly contemplated a career on the stage but decided against it after being advised that he was too short to play lead roles in Shakespearean tragedies.) He became an oratorical star in the 1880s, and as a young man in a political hurry, he elbowed aside local Republican machine candidates to get himself elected district attorney and then United States congressman before he turned thirty. La Follette became a reformer only after his defeat for reelection to the House in the Democratic landslide of 1890 and after an alleged attempt by Wisconsin's top Republican boss to bribe him in 1891. Throughout the 1890s, he patiently organized a coalition of disaffected Wisconsin Republicans, particularly Scandinavian-Americans, dairy farmers, and small businessmen burdened with high shipping costs—all of whom felt aggrieved at their treatment by the dominant party factions. At the same time, La

Robert La Follette, Cumberland, Wisconsin, 1897.

Follette made himself the best-known public figure in the state with his tireless speaking and countless appearances at county fairs.

In 1900, after two previously unsuccessful efforts, La Follette captured the Republican nomination for governor and, with the help of his flag-waving oratory, easily won election to his state's highest office. He had stressed three issues in his drive for the governorship—direct primaries for all state and national offices, railroad taxation, and railroad regulation. Of the three, railroad regulation and direct primaries proved to be the most difficult to push through, even though they were the most publicized and most widely popular of the reforms. In 1901, La Follette and his followers quickly revised Wisconsin's tax system to make railroads pay the same rates as farms and other businesses.

Railroad regulation involved complicated technical matters in setting passenger and freight rates for different distances, localities, and products. The charge of rate discrimination had been easy to make for aggrieved shippers, farmers and businessmen alike; it was much more difficult to establish criteria for fair rates. Railroad regulation also required the creation of a new agency that could draw upon expert knowledge independent of the railroad companies. The University of Wisconsin provided much of the needed expertise, although the experts sometimes disappointed progressives by finding the railroads less culpable and arbitrary than their critics had charged. Finally, in 1905 the Wisconsin Railroad Commission was granted powers to investigate railroad practices and to oversee, revise, and overturn rates, subject to court review and injunction. This commission could not set rates, however, as commissions in a few other states could. In all, Wisconsin's experience furnished a model for other states and for the federal government in regulating railroads and other industries.

The direct primary set off a civil war among Wisconsin Republicans. Conservatives, who called themselves "Stalwarts," fought hardest against this reform, which would base the nomination of candidates on the vote of party members, rather than on a convention system. La Follette, in turn, organized his own faction, who dubbed themselves "Progressives." For two years the governor fought for his legislative program, repeatedly spurning offers of compromise, and declaring that "in legislation *no bread* is better than *half a loaf.*" In 1904 La Follette succeeded in sponsoring a thoroughgoing primary law, which was approved that fall in a special popular vote. At the same time, he maneuvered the embittered Stalwarts into bolting and forming a coalition with the Democrats. La Follette once again wrapped himself in the banner of Republican loyalty in a presidential election year, and he and his Progressives romped to victory. In 1905, they broadened their reform program to include more regulatory agencies and such novel devices for popular participation in government as the initiative, which permitted groups of citizens to originate action to pass laws; the referendum, which allowed the electorate to approve or turn down proposed laws and constitutional changes, and the recall, which enabled groups of citizens to attempt to overturn laws and constitutional changes and to remove officials by popular vote.

La Follette's achievements in Wisconsin set precedents for similar leaders and movements throughout the country. A comparable conflict had already broken out among Republicans in Iowa. There, however, Governor Albert Cummins and his insurgents concentrated more on such national issues as the tariff and federal railroad regulation. On the West Coast, reformers in Oregon worked largely outside both parties to enact the initiative, referendum, and recall. In the South, the Mississippi insurgent Democrat James K. Vardaman successfully agitated for enactment of the nation's first primary system. Vardaman went on to blaze fresh trails for Southern reformers. First, he won the governorship of Mississippi in 1903 through flamboyant oratory that combined appeals to white racism with denunciations of big business. Then, as governor, Vardaman abolished convict leasing, regulated corporations, and improved education and social services for whites—but not for blacks. The tempo of reform at the state level accelerated after 1905, as more and more Republican and Democratic insurgents followed the Wisconsin example.

These reformers were also increasingly turning their attention to the national arena, particularly when several of their leaders became senators. La Follette again led the way, elected in 1905 and taking his seat early in 1906. Cummins followed two years later, and Vardaman won a seat in 1911. Meanwhile, other aspiring Republican politicians were also hearkening to cries for reform. In 1905 two of the party's younger oratorical stars began to speak out for governmental powers to curb the trusts. One was Jonathan P. Dolliver, senator from Iowa and protégé of his state's grand old man and conservative leader, Senator William B. Allison. Despite near-filial affection for his senior colleague, Dolliver began echoing the Iowa insurgents' denunciations of the tariff and championing railroad regulation. The other convert was Albert J. Beveridge, senator from Indiana, a flamboyant supporter of imperialist foreign policy, and something of a regional edition of Roosevelt. Beveridge shared the president's fundamental support for economic bigness, which was unusual among Republican insurgents. Yet

Iowa Senators William B. Allison (right) and Jonathan P. Dolliver.

Beveridge also resembled Roosevelt in resenting big businessmen's arrogance and their meddling in politics.

It was the growing power of the trusts that made their regulation so important to Roosevelt, but he was no trust-buster. Prosecutions under the Sherman Antitrust Act proceeded at a steady, though not accelerating, pace during his second term. By the end of his administration, forty-two suits had been brought under the Sherman Act, and the targets included such corporate behemoths as the "Beef Trust"—an arrangement to fix prices among the leading meat packers—and later, the American Tobacco Company, Rockefeller's Standard Oil, and the New Haven Railroad. Curiously, Roosevelt said little about these prosecutions even in private, and most of his public statements hinted at his approval of economic bigness. Nor did he seek additional antitrust legislation. In 1903, after the creation of the Bureau of Corporations under the newly established Commerce Department, Roosevelt had asserted publicly, "Congress has now enacted all that is practicable and all that is desirable to do." In 1908 he privately scoffed at relying upon "the foolish anti-trust law."

The president seemed satisfied to confine what antitrust policy there was to executive action, which suited both his taste for personal responsibility and his preference for administrative oversight. A few economic analysts were beginning to question whether business regulation in general and antitrust action in particular might not be handled best through independent agencies appointed by the president and staffed by experts. Roosevelt was ahead of most such analysts in his thinking, and after 1908 he articulated a full-blown program of administrative trust regulation. During his presidency, however, his avoidance of new antitrust legislation sprang mainly from a desire to maintain control of the issue. He wanted to prevent debate from spilling over into what he regarded as foolish, reactionary attacks on economic bigness itself.

His preference for personal control and administrative leverage likewise colored Roosevelt's approach on two other major concerns—the tariff and railroad regulation. For Republicans, the protective tariff was like the man in the nursery rhyme who was not there and would not go away. Republican conservatives strained to smother discussion of the tariff, a politically dangerous issue that touched on the interests of powerful economic actors. Many Northeastern and Midwestern manufacturers, for instance, felt dependent on the 30 to 50 percent duties that shielded their products from foreign competition. They contributed money and organized support for the Republican party, and their workers contributed votes. But Republican efforts to avoid discussion of the tariff failed, as year in and year out Democrats persisted in denouncing protectionism. That suited the Democratic party's internal needs, because the tariff was virtually the only issue on which Bryanites and Northeastern conservatives could make common cause. Even some Republican insurgents were beginning to link the high tariff with the problems of trusts and inflation.

Roosevelt viewed the tariff question with distaste. For years he had privately confessed to "agnosticism" about it and other economic questions. He had also long recognized that the intricate web of interests bound up in the Republicans' commitment to protectionism made tampering with the tariff perilous. "There is no question that there is political dynamite in it," he had confided in 1902. Ideas about administrative management had also begun to surface in this connection, but tariff-making remained a jealously guarded legislative function whose complexity made it highly resistant to presidential influence and manipulation. As a result Roosevelt shied away from action on the tariff throughout his presidency, leaving the dynamite to explode when he was safely out of political range. But wariness did not prevent him from playing with the tariff as a threat. Republican leaders on Capitol

"TEDLET'S SOLILOQUY: 'Thus the Tariff does make cowards of us all.' " A cartoon in Puck *showing TR as Hamlet in a comment on Roosevelt's indecision regarding the tariff.*

Hill feared the issue even more than he did. Roosevelt therefore frequently hinted to them that he might have to bring it up if they did not cooperate with him on other matters, particularly railroad regulation. The ploy worked. The president got his way on both issues, avoiding the tariff and moving ahead on railroad regulation.

The railroads had always been Roosevelt's favorite legislative target. Discrimination by the railroads in setting shipping rates had long been attacked by Bryanite Democrats. More recently the railroads were the targets of state actions initiated by reform Republicans, and of generalized public concern, especially in the Midwest. Better still from Roosevelt's standpoint, the most frequently proposed statutory remedy to rate abuses lay in vesting rate-making authority in the hitherto severely limited Interstate Commerce Commission. Legislation in this area would not only be clearly focused and widely supported, but it would also enhance administrative power.

The Hepburn Act of 1906, which carried out most of Roosevelt's aims in railroad regulation, stands as one of the three major legislative accomplishments of his presidency. In his December 1904 message to Congress, he made a plea for a law to strengthen the powers of the ICC, and the House soon voted a bill through by an overwhelming margin. This bill, named for its drafter, Republican Representative William P. Hepburn of Iowa, provided for ICC authority to fix maximum rates after hearing complaints from shippers, to inspect railroads' financial records, and to prescribe uniform bookkeeping practices—all of which greatly enhanced regulatory powers. The new rate-making power would be subject to narrowly defined court review, and ICC-fixed rates would take effect within a month, even though the railroads might contest them.

Senate passage of the bill took more time and effort, especially patient, resourceful negotiation and compromise by Roosevelt. Of the Republicans' conservative congressional barons, the wiliest tactician was Senator Nelson W. Aldrich of Rhode Island, who resorted to several stratagems to stymie railroad regulation. One was to assign management of the bill not to Jonathan Dolliver, who was the senior Republican on the Senate Commerce Committee and a strong advocate of the measure, but to "Pitchfork Ben" Tillman of South Carolina, who also favored it but was not on speaking terms with the president. But Roosevelt foiled the maneuver by working with Tillman through intermediaries. Aldrich mounted more serious obstructions through his wonted practice of loading amendments on bills. Roosevelt responded by acceding to one significant amendment that allowed courts potentially broader powers to review and overturn rate decisions by the ICC. With that compromise, opposition to the bill crumbled. The amended bill passed the Senate on May 18, 1906, with just three opposing votes.

The Hepburn Act showed Roosevelt at his best as a legislative leader. He had avoided committing himself too much on details and specifics. He had been willing to work with anybody, no matter how personally obnoxious to him. Above all, he had kept his eye fixed on his main goal, which was to open the door to genuine federal regulation of the railroads. But Roosevelt's willingness to cooperate and compromise exacted a price. Some Democrats and reform Republicans decried the provision for court review and veto as a sellout. La Follette broke with Roosevelt over this "half-a-loaf" approach. The new senator from Wisconsin held out for giving the ICC much more sweeping regulatory prerogatives, including the power to inspect the railroads' finances, set dollar values on their physical assets, and thereby independently establish profit formulas as the basis for rate determination. La Follette's scheme would have stripped much of the control of their businesses from the railroads and vested that control in the ICC. La Follette's conduct confirmed Roosevelt's suspicions that he was a dangerous, impractical fanatic. The president's behavior reinforced the senator's earlier misgivings about him as an opportunist and insincere reformer.

The enactment of the Pure Food and Drug Act and the Meat Inspection Act displayed another dimension of Roosevelt's leadership. The twin problems of impurity and fraudulent representation in medicines and food products had concerned many people for a long time, particularly physicians and pharmacists. Some businessmen had also grown fearful at the threats by several European countries to bar American processed foods, beverages, and other agricultural products, unless the United States government verified the contents of these products. In Congress, the House had twice passed a drug certification bill, and Senator Beveridge of Indiana had sponsored a meat inspection bill in the Senate in 1905. Passage of a bill had nevertheless been stalemated by technical confusions, jealousies between the two houses, conservative resistance to new governmental interference in the economy, and the efforts of lobbyists for patent medicine manufacturers and meat packers.

Roosevelt broke the legislative logjam by arousing public concern, thereby putting pressure on recalcitrant senators and congressmen. Ironically, he was stirring up popular feelings about impurities in food at exactly the same time that he was censuring the muckrakers, who were doing the same. Moreover, Roosevelt received vital aid from the single most spectacular and effective, albeit unplanned, piece of muckraking journalism: Upton Sinclair's *The Jungle.* For two years, Sinclair had been unsuccessfully peddling his novel to New York book publish-

A Chicago meat-packing house early in the century.

ers. Late in 1905 Sinclair sent *The Jungle* to Doubleday, Page & Company, where Walter Hines Page, a senior partner and magazine editor, seized upon the small part of the sentimental, propagandistic story that contained lurid descriptions of filthy conditions in the Chicago stockyards. Page recognized that these sensational disclosures would make news and sell the book. Page's magazine *The World's Work*, which usually avoided muckraking, devoted an entire issue in March 1906 to articles and photographs that substantiated Sinclair's account of abysmal working conditions and a complete absence of quality control in the stockyards. The resulting public furor proved as gratifying to editor and author as it proved galling to meat packers and Chicago sanitation officials.

Roosevelt lost no time in capitalizing on the situation. Page had sent him page proofs of *The Jungle* before publication, and the president had dispatched his own agents to investigate the allegations. When the government investigators produced a damning two-part report on the stockyards, Roosevelt threatened to publish their findings. Congressional opponents of the drug and meat inspection bills continued to stall, whereupon the president published the first, milder part of the report in June 1906. At the same time he warned privately that if passage of a comprehensive bill did not come soon he would release the much harsher second part. The public clamor incited by Roosevelt's revelations blew down the opposition on Capitol Hill, and separately, the Pure Food and Drug Act and the Meat Inspection Act became laws on January 1, 1907. These acts set up a new federal agency, the Food and Drug Administration (FDA), which tested and approved drugs before they went on the market, and empowered the Department of Agriculture to administer a federal program of meat inspection and labeling which helped clean up the stockyards and restore public confidence in food products. The FDA joined the Forest Service and newly empowered ICC to form an institutional trinity that embodied Theodore Roosevelt's commitment to administrative government.

Besides the Hepburn Act and the Pure Food and Drug Act, the president also got Congress in 1908 to enact an employer's liability law for the District of Columbia. Employer's liability was a principle strongly advocated by labor unions, social workers, and many progressives. It established the legal basis for workers to seek compensation for injuries sustained on the job and illnesses contracted as a result of employment. State and federal courts had customarily construed "liberty of contract" to hold workers responsible for such losses as a consequence of their having freely accepted employment. This District of Columbia law was meant to serve as a model for state measures and, some supporters hoped, for a future federal statute.

In one sense, the results of Roosevelt's second-term legislative program were modest. There were only these four statutes, none of them truly far-reaching, and each containing limitations and compromises that disappointed more ardent reformers. In another sense, however, the results were impressive. Considering the resistance that all four acts had encountered, passing them at all had been a feat of leadership. Moreover, the limited scope of this legislative program suited Roosevelt, who did not want to go further at the time, because he feared stirring up radical sentiments among the public. In fact, Roosevelt was frequently striking conservative notes in his public pronouncements. In addition to delivering the muckrake speech, he publicly denounced labor radicalism even while Big Bill Haywood and other Western Federation of Miners leaders were being tried in Idaho.

Theodore Roosevelt had his domestic sights squarely fixed on the center: moderate reform under tight administrative control—that was his chosen path. And this path seemed to be winning the approval of voters. The 1906 state and congressional contests produced the usual mixed results of off-year elections. In the House, the Democrats recovered some, but not all, of the losses that had accompanied their drubbing by Roosevelt in 1904. In the Senate, however, the Republicans fattened their comfortable majority, while reform Republicans continued to gain strength in governorships. Particularly gratifying to Roosevelt was the result in New York, where Charles Evans Hughes turned back a strong Democratic challenge by the sensationalist, sometimes demagogic newspaper and magazine tycoon William Randolph Hearst. Respectability and moderation had triumphed over alleged radicalism in the president's home state. To Roosevelt's sensitive ear for stirrings among the "lower" orders, the only sour notes were the continued modest gains by the Socialists.

But if the president had listened harder, he might have heard other discordant sounds. Women's agitation for the vote and other measures of equality left him cold. "Personally I believe in woman suffrage," Roosevelt told a suffrage leader in 1905, "but I am not an enthusiastic advocate of it because I do not regard it as a very important matter." He had repeatedly declined to endorse woman suffrage publicly, in part because he thought most women were "lukewarm" about having the vote. More important, Roosevelt avowed, "I am more and more convinced that the great field, the indispensable field for the usefulness of woman is as the mother of the family. It is her work in the household, in the home, her work in bearing and rearing the children, which is more important than any man's work, and it is that work which should be normally the woman's special work, just as normally the man's work should be that of breadwinner, the supporter of the home, and if necessary the soldier who will fight for the home."

Neither the fears of immigration restrictionists nor the travails of the immigrants aroused much concern from the president. Roosevelt remained, as he had been for over twenty years, a convinced assimilationist, blithely confident about the ease with which English-speaking culture and American social values would continue to absorb and amalgamate all white newcomers. Non-white immigrants were an entirely different matter, however, as Roosevelt's attitudes would reveal during diplomatic frictions with Japan in 1907. Radical labor agitation likewise aroused in him a stern response. In his 1906 muckrake speech, the president pointedly condemned "a mere crusade of appetite against appetite, . . . a contest between the brutal greed of the 'have-nots' and the brutal greed of the 'haves.' " Privately Roosevelt pronounced Big Bill Haywood and Eugene Debs "as guilty of incitement to or apology for bloodshed or violence. If this does not constitute undesirable citizenship, then there can never be any undesirable citizens." Radical leaders returned Roosevelt's hatred in kind, and workers in the West would turn increasingly against the Republican party in the 1908 and 1910 elections.

No area of discontent elicited less presidential sympathy, however, than relations between blacks and whites in the South. The man who had once stirred the ire of Southern demagogues by inviting Booker T. Washington to dinner at the White House now made an about-face on the racial front. Roosevelt continued to denounce lynching, and he still appointed a few well-qualified blacks to federal offices in the South. Yet throughout his second term, he mainly sought to woo white support below the Potomac. During his 1904 campaign, Roosevelt made quiet overtures toward Southern whites, and his appointments during his second term favored those whites, including several Democrats, at the expense of blacks. The president made his sympathies public in the fall of 1906 when he ordered summary courts-martial for a regiment of black troops accused of rioting in Brownsville, Texas. In two lengthy special messages to Congress about the Brownsville affair, Roosevelt justified his actions by declaring, "A blacker [crime] never stained the annals of our Army." At the same time he told a Southern editor that he recognized "the grave and evil fact that the negroes too often band together to shelter their own criminals, which action had an undoubted

*"DISHONORABLY DIS-
CHARGED." A* Harper's
Weekly *cartoon comments
on the punishment of black
troops convicted of rioting in
Brownsville, Texas, January
1907.*

effect in bringing to precipitate the hideous Atlanta race riots." In these
and other public and private statements, Roosevelt castigated both blacks
and "white sentimentalists" for having caused the August 1906 rampage by whites through the black neighborhoods of Atlanta that left
eleven blacks dead, over sixty injured (there were no whites among the
injured), and millions of dollars in property destroyed. In his own way,
the president was outdoing Southern whites in blaming the victims of
racism. Small wonder that Theodore Roosevelt failed to hear the
anguished cries of distress of these Americans.

THE WORLD STAGE

During the productive first two years of his second term, Roosevelt
gained his most significant diplomatic achievements as well. In fact
Roosevelt played similar roles at home and abroad. With most foreign
powers he exercised the same subtle, crafty, patient negotiating skills
he displayed in working with Congress, and he showed a comparable
willingness to publicize his activity when that suited his purposes.

The war that had broken out in 1904 between Russia and Japan
occasioned his greatest concern and best performance. Russian expan-
sionism on the Asian mainland had long worried Roosevelt. In 1904,
he confided that if he could be sure there would be no wider war, "I

should not in the least mind going to 'extremes' with Russia." The war had broken out after repeated friction between Russia and Japan in Korea and Manchuria, targets of expansion for both the larger powers. The fighting took place mainly on land in Manchuria and at sea in Far Eastern waters. Japan won some early and spectacular naval and military victories, including a surprise attack—launched before war was declared—on a Russian squadron at anchor in Port Arthur, Manchuria. Japan went on to destroy the main Russian fleet, which had steamed all the way from Europe to meet its doom. Most American commentators cheered the plucky little Oriental David for beating the Slavic Goliath. Privately Roosevelt had his own reasons for joining in the applause. "I was thoroughly pleased with the Japanese victory, for Japan is playing our game."

As the Russo-Japanese War dragged on into 1905, however, the president's assessment changed. Japan's emergence as the dominant power in the Far East, accompanied by saber-rattling militarism, made him worry that the war might have replaced one aggressor with another. Japan's newly proven naval prowess posed a potential threat to American interests in the Pacific, especially the Philippines. More immediately worrisome was the protracted, inconclusive course of the war. Though beaten on land and sea, the Russians refused to sue for peace, and the Japanese faced severe economic strains. Further, both belligerents were allied to major European powers, Russia to France, Japan to Britain. Diplomats in Paris and London feared that their nations might be drawn into complications of the war, especially because the conflict

"GOOD OFFICES." A Harper's Weekly *cartoon depicting TR's efforts to bring an end to the Russo-Japanese war.*

threatened their own tightening entente against Germany. Roosevelt, who also regarded Germany as the world's prime troublemaker, supported this Anglo-French entente, and he similarly feared the broader implications of the Far Eastern war.

These concerns led Roosevelt to play peacemaker. Throughout 1904 and the first months of 1905, he worked informally behind the scenes to induce the Russians and Japanese to stop fighting and start negotiating. When the belligerents finally agreed to parley, Roosevelt publicly offered himself as their host, and peace talks opened at Portsmouth, New Hampshire, in August 1905. By initiating negotiations the president gained acclaim throughout the world and enhanced his already stellar popularity at home. But Roosevelt's peacemaking was not simply a disinterested act of benevolence, as most of his admirers assumed. His involvement sprang rather from a deep sense of his own country's stake in the international balance of power and his commitment to an active role in world affairs. During the Portsmouth conference, Roosevelt labored to make the principals moderate their demands and to persuade their respective allies to press them to relent. At one point Roosevelt secretly committed the United States to join Britain in military and economic support of Japan if Russia refused reasonable terms. The belligerents eventually settled, with Japan gaining unlimited control over Korea, as well as naval bases and economic rights in Manchuria, but no financial indemnity from Russia. Peace prevailed, although many Japanese felt cheated out of a larger victory, which they believed should have brought them substantial reparations payments and annexation of Manchuria. Roosevelt's popularity soared still further, and in 1906 he became the first American to win the Nobel Prize for Peace.

By the time he was awarded the Nobel Prize, Roosevelt was playing an even stronger and riskier hand in great-power politics. No sooner had he pushed the Russians and Japanese to the peace table than the Germans threatened to upset the balance of power in Europe. Kaiser Wilhelm II had seized upon French incursions into Morocco as an opportunity to embarrass and weaken France, and by dramatizing the Anglo-French colonial rivalry in Africa, he tried to stir up old suspicions and jealousies of the French among the British. The Germans' larger aim was to weaken the entente between Britain and France against themselves. "The Kaiser's pipe dream this week takes the form of Morocco," sighed the president to Secretary of War William Howard Taft at the outset of the crisis in April 1905. Although "we have no real interest in Morocco," Roosevelt was worried that Germany might pre-

"THE BUSY SHOWMAN."
This Harper's Weekly *car-*
toon accuses Roosevelt of
playing to the public in the
Algeciras dispute.

cipitate a war with France. Accordingly, he officially assured the French
of American backing, while at the same time he urged them to be
conciliatory toward the Germans. Roosevelt also privately communi-
cated through highly placed British and German friends that he would
stand with Britain and France against any effort to push them apart.

The face-saving expedient to defuse the Moroccan crisis was an
international conference held at Algeciras, Spain, in April 1906. Acting on the meager pretext of an American commercial treaty with
Morocco, Roosevelt sent a delegation to the conference, with instruc-
tions to side with Britain and France. At the same time, he repeated
his private assurances of support to London and Paris, and he reiterated his condemnation of adventurism to Berlin. The conference ended
with the French still in possession of their gains in Morocco, but the
Germans took satisfaction in having publicly exposed French incursions in North Africa, making them appear the aggressors. All parties
outwardly appeared mollified, and the Anglo-French entente remained
unshaken. Roosevelt had proven to be a resourceful leader of a great
power in the area of world politics, and he took deserved pride in the
accomplishment.

Roosevelt's diplomatic initiatives were not entirely behind the scenes.
The president continued to avail himself of opportunities to lecture
Americans on their duties to each other and to the rest of the world. In
his December 1906 message to Congress, he dwelled on what "an evil
thing" it would be "for a great and free nation to deprive itself of the
power to protect its own rights and in exceptional cases to stand up for

the rights of others. Nothing would more promote iniquity" than for Americans and other "free and enlightened peoples . . . to render themselves powerless while leaving every despotism and barbarism armed and able to work their wicked will." Roosevelt viewed reform and harmony at home and strength and activism abroad as related parts of the same task. Like the individual, he argued in a speech in May 1907, the nation must spurn "a life of effortless ease, of mere material comfort." The United States "must live up to the ideals of the founders of the nation," both by playing "an ever growing part in the affairs of the world" and by recognizing "our first and primary duty at home . . . to strive measurably to realize certain ideals." It was a noble vision, and the hero in the White House affected to believe that he was leading his people toward its realization.

Sadly, the gap between presidential preaching and national perfor- mance during Roosevelt's second term grew too wide for the president to ignore. He experienced disillusionment first in foreign affairs. Even at the height of his involvement in the Russo-Japanese War and the Moroccan crisis, Roosevelt knew that he had to tread warily around the age-old American stance of noninvolvement in overseas, especially European, power politics. Acknowledging this stance, Senator Henry Cabot Lodge of Massachusetts, who knew intimately and played a large part in Roosevelt's secret diplomacy, defended the president's role in the Moroccan affair. In 1906 Lodge assured his colleagues on Capitol Hill that "in entangling alliances, of course, no man wants to engage his country; we have no concern with the wars of Europe." With Lodge's and Roosevelt's acquiescence, the Senate unanimously attached a res- ervation to the agreements negotiated at Algeciras, stating that consent to them was "without purpose to depart form the traditional American foreign policy." The contrast between the president's activist views and the reluctance of the public and Congress to support him was great.

Even more disturbing to Roosevelt was the situation revealed in 1907 by a new diplomatic controversy in the Far East. Just as he had feared, the Japanese proved troublesome as they pushed for greater power and influence in China. Still, their incursions might not have caused immediate friction with the United States, except for coincidental, inflammatory racial incidents at home on the West Coast. Ever since Chinese laborers had first come to California to work on building rail- roads in the 1860s, white residents had resented their presence and had discriminated against them. Congress responded to the demands of whites in the West by enacting the first immigration restriction law, the Chinese Exclusion Act of 1881, but that measure had not stopped the East Asian influx. Additional Chinese and, increasingly after 1890, Japanese had come to the Pacific Coast through Hawaii. Their numbers had swollen after Hawaii became an American possession in 1898. By 1905, anti-Japanese sentiment had reached a flash point in California, where labor unions and Hearst's newspapers played major parts in fanning fears of the "yellow peril."

Roosevelt used his influence with California's Republican governor to prevent action on a loudly debated bill to exclude all Asians from the state. But he could not restrain the San Francisco school board from requiring segregated facilities for Chinese, Japanese, and Korean pupils. The school board's move, together with a succession of race riots up and down the Pacific Coast in the spring of 1907, sparked anti-American outcries in Japan. Some observers predicted a crisis between the two countries, perhaps even another war in the Far East. Although the dangers were exaggerated, Roosevelt rose to the occasion with his final exercise in deft diplomacy.

At home, Roosevelt's task was to restrain citizens and local governments, and cool tempers. The president showed a surprisingly mild face toward the troublemakers on the West Coast. His unwonted restraint sprang less from the niceties of federal-state relations than from his own social views. "Our line of policy must be adopted," Roosevelt explained soon afterward, "holding ever the view that this is a race question, and that race questions stand by themselves." He had always recognized one overriding fact, he said, namely that "the Japanese

"FRICTION BETWEEN JAPAN AND CALIFORNIA." Roosevelt's comment: *"Be quiet! Youngsters! Have you forgotten my Nobel prize?"*

should, as a race, be excluded from becoming permanent inhabitants of our territory." In short, Roosevelt did not lean harder on the Californians because he approved of what they were doing, even though he often disliked their manner of doing it.

Roosevelt dampened the dispute with Japan through a series of private and public moves. He sent Secretary of War William Howard Taft on a special mission to the Far East, where Taft negotiated an agreement under which the United States recognized Japan's domination of Korea and paramount influence in Manchuria and Northern China. In a coldly realistic way, Roosevelt was appeasing the Japanese. His appeasement meant that the United States was tacitly reneging on its proudly proclaimed Open Door declarations—the public expressions of support in 1899 and 1900 for China's independence and territorial integrity. In return, Roosevelt secured a "gentleman's agreement" from the Japanese, under which they acquiesced in having their citizens barred from immigration to the United States.

Finally, Roosevelt made his grandest gesture on the international stage in December 1907, when he ordered the American battle fleet to make a fifteen-month round-the-world cruise, calling first in Japan. The cruise of what newspapers called America's "Great White Fleet" made a splendid show of force, and it was one of his acts as president for which Roosevelt professed greatest pride.

Roosevelt later disclosed that in sending the fleet around the world,

"Scarecrow of the Pacific." A cartoon in Puck *commenting on Roosevelt's decision to send the "Great White Fleet" around the world.*

"My prime purpose was to impress the American people; and this purpose was fully achieved." Roosevelt deplored the loose talk and thoughtless action of editors and politicians who casually risked war with Japan but remained unconcerned about strengthening the army and navy. When he sent Taft across the Pacific, he secretly warned that the United States must be prepared to give up the Philippines far sooner "than I would think advisable if this country were prepared to look ahead fifty years and build the navy and erect the fortifications which in my mind it should. The Philippines form our heel of Achilles. They are all that make the present situation with Japan dangerous." That admission indicated another, much more painful about-face for Roosevelt. The man who had blown the loudest bugle for expansion in 1900 was now privately sounding retreat. Profound disillusionment about Americans' willingness to play a great role in world affairs fed Roosevelt's pessimism, and he sought to dispel gloom in his characteristic way—by taking action, the more spectacular the better. That was the deepest motive behind the cruise of the Great White Fleet.

Deadlock

The Great White Fleet was a splendid gesture, but it failed to stimulate international awareness among Americans. Roosevelt was deluding himself when he boasted about achieving that purpose. Indeed as domestic difficulties began to mount at the beginning of 1907, self-delusion at home as well as abroad became the hallmark at the White House.

Roosevelt's favorite issue, conservation, occasioned his first serious clash with Congress. Launching the Forest Service in 1905 had only whetted Gifford Pinchot's ambitions. Pinchot made increasingly bold incursions into the jurisdictions of other agencies, particularly the Interior Department. He also aroused impassioned opposition from two otherwise inimical groups—wilderness preservationists and Western developers.

The preservationists, whose most eloquent spokesman was the sometimes eccentric California naturalist and best-selling author John Muir, believed in the primacy of the natural environment for its own sake and, secondarily, for people's aesthetic appreciation. They resented the emphasis of Pinchot and the conservationists on rational, planned exploitation of nature. Muir's quarrel with Pinchot assumed a specific, impassioned focus when the forester championed the drive to create

John Muir.

an additional reservoir for San Francisco by damming Hetch Hetchy, a beautiful, unspoiled valley adjoining Yosemite. The bitter, prolonged battle pitted Pinchot, the Forest Service, and urban Californians against Muir, wilderness preservationists, and later the Interior Department. Roosevelt, for once, avoided taking sides, and the controversy dragged on after he left the White House. Finally, in 1913, the dam forces won, and Hetch Hetchy was flooded. On the other side of the debate, the Westerners wanted to use timber, water, hydroelectric power, and minerals at once to start industries, build towns, and break the soil for farming—all in order to overcome their region's chronic underpopulation and economic backwardness. They resented the aim of Pinchot and the conservationists to sequester resources and restrict their exploitation to limited, gradual uses.

A proposal by Pinchot at the end of 1906 to make the Forest Service financially independent of congressional appropriations gave his enemies on Capitol Hill the opening they wanted. They moved not only to try to clip the chief forester's wings but also to curtail the executive branch's conservation actions. The 1907 appropriation bill for the Department of Agriculture contained provisions that reasserted congressional control of all Forest Service revenues and, most important, that rescinded presidential authority to create forest reserves in all the Western states—except California, where Pinchot's policies were popular.

The battle lines were drawn. Later congressional restrictions further hampered Pinchot's activities, and "Pinchotism" became a favorite campaign slogan for Democrats and Republican conservatives in the West. Even without the combative Pinchot egging him on, Roosevelt would have hit back hard. In February 1907, the president ordered the Forest Service to work around the clock for ten days to map out seventeen million acres of new forest reserves, which he sequestered just hours before his authority ran out. The creation of these "midnight reserves" was nothing less than a massive land grab in defiance of the will of Congress. It was Roosevelt's most high-handed exercise of presidential power. In Roosevelt's scheme of things, the action was heroic, but in its political effects, it was unwise.

Although Roosevelt and Pinchot did nothing else so dramatic during the next two years, the creation of the forest reserves marked the beginning of a bold experiment in executive management of natural resources. Pinchot, who had a streak of mysticism, experienced a vision in February 1907, while he was riding alone on horseback around sunset in Washington's Rock Creek Park. Suddenly, he later recalled, "the idea flashed through my head that there was a unity in this complication" of conservation of forests, land, water, minerals, and energy. "To me it was a good deal like coming out of a dark tunnel." Upon sharing his revelation with Roosevelt, Pinchot got a free hand to shape federal policy in all areas touching upon his now expanded definition of conservation. The chief forester became the Roosevelt administration's czar for domestic policy touching upon his broad concerns.

With the appointment of James R. Garfield as secretary of the interior in March 1907, Pinchot gained both a compliant head of his main rival agency and an eager partner in his grand design for conservation. The two men usually walked to work together. They called once or twice a day at the White House. They also frequently played tennis, hiked, and rode horseback with the president. All the while they entertained more great visions and hatched exciting schemes for government policies. Between them, Pinchot and Garfield sequestered further vast tracts of the public domain from private development and persuaded the president to do likewise. These later withdrawals involved potential water-power sites for cities and agricultural irrigation. Pinchot seized some of them under the pretext of setting up forest ranger stations, while Garfield prodded the Reclamation Service, which was under the Interior Department, to take control of other sites. Roosevelt vetoed congressional bills that sought to halt those withdrawals, and he used his veto messages to preach the conservationist gospel of wise planning and comprehensive public control of water power. He thereby launched a political issue that would persist for the next quarter of a century.

The triumvirate of Roosevelt, Pinchot, and Garfield enjoyed heady times during the administration's last two years. The promotion of these lieutenants heightened the aura of glamor and adventure in public service that already surrounded the White House. But this kind of government carried a heavy political price. Pinchot not only fomented determined opposition on Capitol Hill and denunciations by politicians and newspapers in the West, but he also made enemies within his own branch of government by exercising his license to hunt in other agencies' bailiwicks. The Commissioner of Public Lands, Richard A. Ballinger, quit in 1907 after only a year in office because he was fed up with the chief forester's poaching on Land Office prerogatives, and with what he regarded as the apostasy of his own cabinet secretary, Garfield. Even the outwardly easygoing Secretary of War William Howard Taft bridled at the Forest Service's disregard of legal procedures and its elbowing aside of the Army Corps of Engineers to assert control over the water power sites. A potential political storm was brewing around Pinchot and conservation.

Gifford Pinchot.

That was not the only storm on the horizon. The Congressional attack on the Forest Service at the beginning of 1907 inaugurated two years of deadlock between the president and the legislative branch. Roosevelt remained sensitive to the rising strength of Republican insurgency and to evidence of radicalism in the appeal of the Socialists and such Democrats as William Randolph Hearst and William Jennings Bryan. More than ever he viewed himself as the apostle of moderation between extremes. "In industrial matters our enormous prosperity has brought with it certain grave evils," he declared in April 1907. "It is our duty to try to cut out these evils without at the same time destroying our well-being itself." The president identified the central problem as "how to exercise such responsible control over the business use of vast wealth," and he sponsored further reform measures in 1907 and 1908. Among these were still stricter railroad regulation by the ICC; employers' liability for injuries and illnesses sustained by employees through work done by private firms under government contract; the outlawing of child labor in the District of Columbia, which would again serve as a model for broader state and federal legislation; federal income and inheritance taxes, with graduated rates; and, finally, downward revision of the tariff.

Those proposals hit a stone wall on Capitol Hill. At the ramparts were the Republican conservatives, who viewed such measures as corroborating their long-held suspicion that the president was politically unsound. The congressional barons had a point. Roosevelt was advocating reforms that he had previously rejected as too radical or politically risky. Yet nothing nettled Roosevelt more than allegations that he was a false conservative. He constantly harped on the need for sympathetic attitudes toward business. On antitrust issues, he argued repeatedly that bigness was not just irreversible but beneficial, and that punishing improper conduct was the sole correct aim. Above all, Roosevelt never missed a chance to continue to denounce demagoguery, envy, and class hatred. "Every far-sighted patriot should protest first of all against the growth in this country of that thing which is called 'class consciousness,' " he avowed in April 1908. Americans must cling instead "to those eternal and immutable principles of righteousness which bid us treat each man on his worth as a man without regard to his wealth or poverty."

His protestations fell on deaf ears among conservatives. Party loyalty usually curbed the tongues of Republican opponents, but most of them privately blamed Roosevelt's criticisms of big business for the financial panic that occurred in October 1907. Thanks in part to the president's ready cooperation with J. P. Morgan and other Wall Street leaders, and his mobilization of government funds, both the panic and a mild recession that had preceded it were short-lived, and recovery got under way in the spring of 1908. But those actions did not mollify Republican conservatives on Capitol Hill, who smothered Roosevelt's reform proposals during 1907 and 1908.

Their efforts to frustrate him extended to small as well as large questions. One of Roosevelt's favorite devices to educate public opinion and generate policy ideas was the appointment of presidential commissions to study domestic-policy problems. During his two terms in the White House, nine commissions were named to investigate such matters as water power, conservation, transportation, and rural life. In 1907, congressional critics started blocking appropriations for these commissions' expenses and even the publication of their reports. The president had to seek private funds to support their work and disseminate their findings. By the end of 1908, relations between Roosevelt and his party's congressional leaders had grown so spiteful that when it was announced that he was going to make a safari in Africa when his term expired, Capitol cloakrooms reportedly echoed with the toast, "Health to the lions!"

Roosevelt's relations with the judiciary were even worse. He retained his activist temperament, and he was well acquainted with the new ideas of constitutional interpretation that stressed the latitude that should be allowed executives and legislatures in intervening in social and economic affairs. His temperament and views together made Roosevelt impatient with the federal courts, especially the Supreme Court. These tensions persisted despite his three appointments to the Court—Justice Oliver Wendell Holmes, William H. Moody, and William R. Day— and some moderation in the Court's penchant for striking down regulatory legislation.

Several Court decisions during his first term and early in his second term had reignited Roosevelt's disgust at what he privately called the justices' "reactionary folly." In Roosevelt's eyes, the worst of these decisions came in 1905, in a suit brought by an immigrant German baker in Utica, New York. The baker, Adolph Lochner, contested the constitutionality of a state law limiting the hours of work for bakery employees. The court majority in *Lochner v. New York* struck down the law as an unwarranted intrusion into private enterprise, which violated the Fourteenth Amendment's prohibiton on states' depriving persons of liberty and property without "due process of law." In an acidly written dissent, Justice Holmes asserted, "The framers of the Fourteenth

Amendment did not enact Mr. Herbert Spencer's Social Statics," an allusion to a tract in which Spencer argued that society, like nature, should be governed by survival of the fittest.

In his annual messages to Congress in 1905 and 1907, the president publicly criticized apparent judicial subservience to business interests and raised questions about whether judicial decisions could be made more readily accountable to majority opinion. In his last message to Congress in December 1908, Roosevelt observed that when judges interpret the law "they necessarily enact into law parts of a system of social philosophy." Therefore, he argued, "for the peaceful progress of our people during the twentieth century we shall owe most to those judges who hold to a twentieth-century economic and social philosophy and not to an outgrown philosophy which was itself the product of primitive economic conditions."

Besides indicating Roosevelt's familiarity with more advanced ideas of jurisprudence, which opposed judicial vetoes of federal legislation affecting the economy and society, that parting shot illuminated the depth of estrangement between him and mainstream pro-business Republicans. Though the president's criticisms of the courts attracted comparatively little attention at the time—he couched them in carefully qualified language and buried them in the lengthy state papers that no president since John Adams had delivered in person to Congress—his comments offered another sign of how sour the political situation had turned. Relations might have deteriorated still further if the president and his Republican adversaries had not hidden their differences behind a façade of party unity and superficial good will. Seldom in twentieth-century American party politics have appearance and reality been so far out of kilter. Roosevelt's second term was drawing to a close in stalemate and bitterness, but Republicans of nearly all persuasions were publicly claiming that everything was going splendidly.

This outward harmony rested upon an implicit trade-off between the two sides. Roosevelt was able to pick his party's presidential nominee in 1908, while Republican conservatives dominated all other aspects of the campaign. Choosing his successor in the party presented Roosevelt with a thorny problem. The two men whose abilities Roosevelt admired most, Senator Henry Cabot Lodge of Massachusetts and Secretary of State Elihu Root, refused to be considered. They recognized that their temperaments and conservative views were out of tune with current political conditions. New York's reform Republican governor, Charles Evans Hughes, might have been a logical choice, but personal

"THE COURTSHIP OF BILL TAFT." A Puck *cartoon showing TR interceding on behalf of Taft with "Priscilla," the Republican party, whose response is, "Why don't you speak for yourself, Theodore?"*

relations between him and Roosevelt were not good, and the governor inadvertently rebuffed the president's tentative overtures. By a process of elimination, only one person remained suitable in Roosevelt's eyes: Secretary of War William Howard Taft.

The fifty-year-old Taft brought several sterling assets to his presidential candidacy. He came from a prominent Cincinnati, Ohio, family and was a graduate of Yale. He had enjoyed a distinguished career as a lawyer and as an appointed government official. During the early 1890s, Taft had served as Solicitor General in Washington, where he and Roosevelt became fast friends, and he had afterward returned to Cincinnati as a federal judge. In 1899, President McKinley and then Secretary of War Root had persuaded Taft to become the first civilian governor of the Philippines. By all accounts he did an efficient, fair-minded job of establishing American colonial rule there. Friendship and admiration for Taft's administrative ability had prompted Roosevelt to make him Root's successor at the War Department in 1904. Roosevelt had also employed Taft for delicate diplomatic negotiations and left him in charge of the government during Roosevelt's absences from Washington. Furthermore, unlike Lodge and Root, Taft shared both the president's sensitivity to popular discontent over big business and political machines, and his desire for party unity. Those circumstances made him Roosevelt's inescapable choice as successor.

As a presidential candidate, however, Taft suffered from two glaring drawbacks. First, he had never run for office. He was a likable man, whose height and weight—six feet one and nearly 300 pounds in 1908—lent an appearance of strength and solidity. He was also a good speaker, although nowhere near Bryan's league as an orator or Roosevelt's class as a dynamic public figure. He was not only inexperienced with the rough-and-tumble of elections, but he also had, behind his genial exterior, a sensitive, brooding personality. As a result, Taft never felt at home on the campaign trail or in dealing with hardened professional politicians. His other drawback was obscurity with the general public. He became better-known through favorable publicity about his work in the Philippines and the War Department and a well-orchestrated build-up by sympathetic magazine editors in 1907 and 1908, but Taft's name was no household word. These drawbacks left him totally dependent upon presidential machinations for the nomination. Republican politicians knew that Taft had gotten where he was only because he was Roosevelt's man, which meant they owed Taft next to nothing politically. Those conditions did not augur well for a presidential campaign or a future presidency.

Such weaknesses mattered little at the moment. Roosevelt cranked up his presidential control of the party apparatus to assure Taft's nomination. Insurgent Republicans supported Taft on the grounds that if he was good enough for Roosevelt he was good enough for them. The only resistance came from a few conservatives. They tried to launch a last-minute boom for Governor Hughes, but Taft won the nomination easily on the first ballot at Chicago in June 1908. The Republican convention otherwise belonged to the conservatives. As they had done four years before, they chose a congressional stalwart for vice-president. This time their nominee was one of House Speaker Joseph G. Cannon's henchmen, Congressman James S. Sherman of New York. The conservatives likewise wrote a platform that mixed praise for Roosevelt with pro-business declarations reminiscent of McKinley's 1896 and 1900 campaigns. They also spurned a plea by Roosevelt to include a plank condemning court injunctions against striking labor unions, which Samuel Gompers and the AFL ardently desired. One of the platform's few concessions to reformers was a vague promise to lower the tariff. The temper of the convention was not lost on Roosevelt. The president privately deplored the persistence of "the 'old commercial conservatism' of that Republicanism which dominated the party for many years and culminated in Mark Hanna."

Much of the 1908 campaign harked back to 1896 and 1900. Since the feebleness of conservative Democrats had been proven in Alton Parker's 1904 presidential campaign, the Bryanite wing regained control of the party without much of a fight at the convention in Denver in July. They nominated Bryan on the first ballot by nearly a nine-to-one margin, and they adopted the most advanced reformist platform of any major party. The Democratic platform had planks calling once more for lower tariffs, stronger antitrust laws, and stricter railroad regulation and valuation by the ICC. Reporters noted the similarity between the Democratic platform and the Republican president's recent stands. Many Democrats admitted that they wanted to steal Roosevelt's thunder. Bryan and his cohorts also stole a march on the Republicans by adopting strong pro-union labor planks, including restrictions on court injunctions, comprehensive employer's liability laws, and an eight-hour day for work under government contract. So gratifying were these overtures that Gompers and the AFL abandoned their customary non-partisanship and supported the Democrats. Bryan himself had come out earlier in favor of government ownership of railroads and telegraph lines. During the campaign, however, he backed off from those stands in deference to party unity.

The Commoner's third presidential foray showed that he had lost

Taft on the stump.

none of his eloquence and energy. He made his usual eighteen-hour-a-day whistle-stop train tours, as he hammered away at his slogan, "Shall the People Rule?" Bryan did not content himself with generalities. He again attacked "plutocracy" and the corrupt influence of money in politics, and he leveled specific charges against both conservative Republicans and Roosevelt. Bryan denounced the president's consent to J. P. Morgan's acquisition of the Tennessee Coal and Iron Company during the 1907 panic as a violation of the Sherman Antitrust Act and a sellout to Wall Street. Taft, by contrast, reminded people of McKinley. Here was another amiable Ohioan who exuded an air of calm competence. In fact, Taft originally intended to emulate McKinley's 1896 front-porch campaign. He planned to stay off the stump and instead receive delegations of visitors at his home in Cincinnati, where he would also issue prepared statements to the press.

If Taft was prepared to sit still, however, Roosevelt was not. Rattled by Bryan's large, enthusiastic crowds and personally stung by the Commoner's charges, the president in effect ordered his nominee to hit the campaign trail. In August 1908 he told Taft, "You ought to be on the stump but only speak *once* or *twice* in each state you visit. Do not answer Bryan; *attack* him. Don't let him make the issues." Taft obediently took to the hustings, making two extended trips in September and October. He made a favorable impression, although many observers contrasted his ponderous appearance and speaking style with Roosevelt's dynamic presence. Likewise, although Taft sounded reformist notes and pledged fealty to Roosevelt's domestic policies, the contrast with Bryan made him sound more like a mainline Republican conservative. His performance distressed Roosevelt. "Personally, I wish Taft would hit harder," the president told his sister, "would smash into Bryan in an effective fashion."

Most of the sparks struck by the Republican campaign emanated from Roosevelt's intervention. At one point he upstaged Taft by issuing a public letter in which he blasted back at Bryan's charges. At other times he directed the campaign organization and recruited two of the younger insurgent Republican oratorical stars, Senators Beveridge and Dolliver, to follow the Commoner's campaign. Actually, Bryan's most effective platform competition came from Eugene Debs, who was running for the second time as the Socialist party's presidential nominee. Traveling on his banner-draped train, the "Red Special," the lean, intense Debs became a national figure through the publicity he attracted.

The 1908 returns showed strong similarities to the previous three presidential canvasses. The total popular vote increased by over a mil-

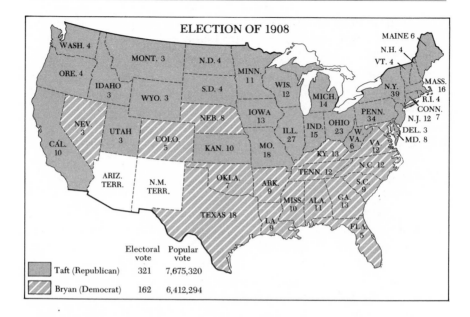

ELECTION OF 1908

	Electoral vote	Popular vote
Taft (Republican)	321	7,675,320
Bryan (Democrat)	162	6,412,294

lion from 1904, but the percentage of eligibles voting remained almost exactly the same. Taft won 29 states with 321 electoral votes. He swept the Northeast and Midwest, and he made a decent showing in the West. His popular margin was more than one-and-a-quarter million votes over Bryan's, a little under 52 percent of the total, or roughly the same as McKinley's margin in 1900. Bryan carried 17 states with 162 electoral votes. His support came from the ever-solid South, along with two Border States and three Western states.

The results brought a measure of disappointment to all the candidates. Glad as he was to win, Taft saw how far short he had fallen from Roosevelt's 1904 showing; he had carried a million-and-a-quarter fewer popular votes and three fewer states. In other races, the Republicans gained no Senate seats, lost three in the House, and suffered further losses at the state level, including the governorship in the president-elect's home state of Ohio. Bryan remained temperamentally buoyant and as ideologically committed as ever. Still, the Commoner felt galled to have lost his last, apparently best chance at the presidency and to have underlined the Democrats' status as a minority party. Most disappointed of all was Debs. The Socialist candidate had bettered his 1904 total by only 18,000 votes and had gotten virtually the same percentage of the total as four years earlier. The failure to garner more votes, despite widespread disquiet about big business, appeared to confirm the Socialists' unpopularity. Their lackluster showing also attested to Bryan's appeal to radical-leaning labor and agrarian voters who might otherwise have warmed to Debs. The Prohibitionists likewise suffered a small loss in their vote and declined to below two percent in their share of the total.

The only major participant in the 1908 election who felt unbridled satisfaction with the outcome was Theodore Roosevelt. Taft's unspectacular victory reaffirmed Roosevelt's standing as the most popular politician in America. Republican losses in the West and reduced margins in the Midwest convinced the president of the wisdom of his flexible, reformist conservatism. No matter how pleased he might feel, however, he faced the sore duty of relinquishing power. During his last year in the White House, Roosevelt often grew depressed. He was laying aside "the burdens of this great nation," he told his military aide, "with a good deal of regret, for I have enjoyed every moment of this so-called arduous and exacting task." Not even his frustrations with Congress made him feel relieved to get out. Nor did the joy of welcoming home the Great White Fleet lighten his gloom for long. Fresh adventures awaited Roosevelt on his African safari and European tour, which would keep him abroad until the middle of 1910. But he was only fifty years old. He was younger when he finished his two terms as president than all but four other men have been when they entered the office. He was in vigorous health and brimming with all his usual energy and ambition. The hero had had his turn at the helm; it was difficult for him to let go.

5

Social Turmoil and Political Ferment in the Taft Years

The first two decades of the twentieth century marked a second golden age of American political leadership. Like the first quarter century after the framing of the Constitution, these twenty years featured more than one presidency that has come to be ranked among the nation's top six or seven. Like the period of the Founders, this era witnessed a depth of thought and discussion about fundamental questions of national life that has been unmatched at almost any other time. Finally, the early twentieth century resembled the previous golden age in witnessing an uncommon breadth of ability and accomplishment among second- and third-rank leaders. Between 1900 and 1920, administrators such as Elihu Root, legislators such as Henry Cabot Lodge, orators such as Albert Beveridge, state governors such as Robert La Follette, and jurists such as Oliver Wendell Holmes epitomized a galaxy of talented people who engaged in political debate and action on a grand scale.

Perhaps the best evidence of the high level of leadership between 1900 and 1920 comes from the comparative failures, who themselves had great gifts and made an indisputable impact on public affairs. Among the losing major-party presidential candidates in the elections of 1904, 1908, 1912, and 1916, only one, Alton Parker, the Democratic candidate in 1904, did not become a historical figure of the first rank. Among the minor-party candidates, Eugene Debs made himself the most influential of American socialists. Of the three men who were elected president between 1900 and 1920, even the one who did not achieve heights of renown in office remained unquestionably a man of substance. This was William Howard Taft.

"Big Bill" Taft entered the White House in difficult circumstances. First, there was the shadow cast by Roosevelt's luminous performance. Any successor would almost certainly have suffered from the comparison. Taft bore an especially heavy burden because he was Roosevelt's choice and owed him so much. Second, American politics had reached a particularly trying moment when Taft became president. The simmering discontents of the previous decade boiled over into full-blown political turmoil. At the same time the insurgencies and reform movements of the time spewed forth a welter of exciting, unsettling ideas and doctrines. It was a far more vexing situation than Roosevelt had faced. Ironically, the ex-president was at the time brooding in his tent in Africa about not having led the country during truly challenging circumstances, during times that he believed might have summoned forth his full measure of greatness. Considering the political stalemate of Roosevelt's last two years in office, it seems doubtful that he could have done a lot better in Taft's place. Yet both men often wished that they could trade places and tackle tasks that seemed better suited to each of them. Soon neither man would be able to forgive the other for his fate.

TIDES OF DISCONTENT

During the Taft years, rising discontent sprang from the same sources that had occasionally roiled more placid conditions under McKinley and Roosevelt. One of these sources was black protest, still in its infancy as an organized movement. The newly formed NAACP had just begun to plot its strategy of legal challenges to segregation and disenfranchisement, which it combined with publicity to arouse Northern white consciences. The first issue of its journal, *The Crisis*, under W. E. B. Du Bois's editorship, did not appear until 1911. Yet such activists as Du Bois and William Monroe Trotter were already exploring avenues for political action. They mounted a challenge to the political bossism of Booker T. Washington, and urged blacks to assert political independence from the Republicans. Trotter, Du Bois, and a handful of black intellectuals publicly supported the Democratic presidential nominees in 1908 and 1912, which was a sign of restiveness among black Americans who had traditionally voted for the party of Lincoln.

Blacks had ample reason to be dissatisfied with the Republicans in

THE CRISIS

A RECORD OF THE DARKER RACES

Volume One	NOVEMBER, 1910	Number One

Edited by W. E. BURGHARDT DU BOIS, with the co-operation of Oswald Garrison Villard,
J. Max Barber, Charles Edward Russell, Kelly Miller, W. S. Braithwaite and M. D. Maclean.

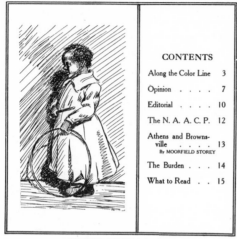

CONTENTS

PUBLISHED MONTHLY BY THE
National Association for the Advancement of Colored People
AT TWENTY VESEY STREET   NEW YORK CITY

The first issue of The Crisis, *published by the NAACP and edited by W. E. B. Du Bois.*

1908. Roosevelt's thinly disguised hostility toward blacks had not less-ened because he had had to rely on black delegates from the South as part of the presidential steamroller at the 1908 convention. During the campaign, he privately scorned old-fashioned "sectional" Republicans who "thought the Negro could be legislated to be as good as the white man, forgetting the natural limitations of the Negro." Taft brought no improvement. As secretary of war he had acquiesced in the punish-ment of the black soldiers involved in the disorders during fall 1906, in Brownsville, Texas. Taft did so despite his own misgivings about the evidence against them and about the fairness of the harsh punishments Roosevelt had ordered without hearing any arguments in defense of the black soldiers. Taft avoided mentioning race on the campaign trail in 1908, but he welcomed overtures from a group of expatriate South-ern whites aimed at making him and his party more attractive below the Potomac. Speaking to a Southern group in New York in December 1908, Taft applauded disenfranchisement laws as intended "to prevent entirely the possiblity of a domination . . . by an ignorant electorate."

The president-elect also declared, "The federal government has nothing to do with social equality."

Republican efforts to abandon blacks came just as they were starting to build a new base of political power in northern cities, where black migrants from the South were forced to settle in separate neighborhoods. Most black newcomers gladly supported urban bosses, after the fashion of European immigrants, but with one main difference. Blacks brought with them a legacy of party loyalty that enlisted them behind Republican rather than Democratic machines. Calls to break those ties, such as Du Bois's in 1908 and 1912, went largely unheeded. Blacks in northern cities felt historic gratitude to the party of Lincoln, and the Democrats either shunned them or appealed to white backlash against them. The 1908 race riot in Springfield, Illinois, had already exposed the racial hatred stirred in the North by black migration. The first recorded lynching of a black outside the South occurred in August 1911, in Coatesville, Pennsylvania, near Philadelphia. This lynching featured the familiar spectacle of the mutilated corpse, festive atmosphere, and plenty of children in attendance. Race relations were becoming truly a national scandal, and neither the Democrats nor the Republicans were inclined to take notice.

Women, by contrast, met speedier success in reaching their main goal, although this did not come easily or completely. At the end of the first decade of the twentieth century, leadership of the nation's feminist organizations was passing to a new group, most of whom focused more exclusively on the suffrage issue. The National Woman Suffrage Association decided in 1906 to petition the president and Congress for an amendment to the Constitution to abolish sex discrimination in voting. Several petitions were presented, but the association fell short in its most ambitious project, a one-million-signature petition; they had to settle for presenting Congress with a petition signed by 404,000 supporters in the spring of 1910. Some younger feminists chafed at those decorous procedures and advocated highly visible, even disruptive action. Elizabeth Cady Stanton's daughter, Harriot Stanton Blatch, who had lived in England, had gotten to know British suffrage leaders and their militant protest tactics. Blatch organized a new group, the Women's Political Union, which staged marches and mass meetings, and sought to reach out to poorer, less-educated women through ties to the labor movement. Such feminist social workers as Jane Addams and Florence Kelley were already pursuing that approach.

The first suffragist victories came at the state level. In November 1910, the suffrage movement finally added another Western state by

Results of Equal Suffrage
in California

Women Do Not Neglect Their Homes. Political activity and service are carried on by women whose children are grown, by women without children or by unmarried women, just as club activities are carried on.

Suffrage Has Proved to be Another Bond of Common Interest between husband and wife. They do not always agree in opinion, but discussion has added to their information and has not broken up any homes.

Women Seldom Seek Political Office. No women ran for the legislature in the first two state elections after their enfranchisement and few have been elected to any but minor positions. Many have been appointed to political positions. Women show a desire to fit themselves for office before seeking it.

Women Do Not Pay a Poll Tax. The Poll Tax is not a voting tax but a school and military tax imposed upon men only, citizens and aliens alike.

Women Are Registered in Their Homes. The regular biennial registration is largely made by house-to-house visits of Deputy County Clerks. There is no trouble or inconvenience about registering.

Women Attend Political Meetings, Often Taking Their Children with them.

Women Conduct Schools of Voting and Teach Men as well as women how to vote correctly.

Polling Places Have Been Made Entirely Desirable. Schools, churches, libraries, club houses and tents are now used extensively. The use of livery stables, barns, barber shops and similar places has been stopped. No man now would question the desirability of having his wife go to the polls.

Women Frequently Serve as Election Judges. They are interested, conscientious and reliable. Several of the county clerks have stated that they prefer to have women as judges.

As a Rule Women Do Not Vote Unless They Understand a Question. Men frequently vote "No" on all propositions they do not understand, but women refrain from voting.

Women Vote More Rapidly and With Fewer Mistakes *than men.* This is generally commented upon by election officials. It is due to the fact that women study the sample ballots and know exactly how they are going to vote.

A Petition to Appeal the Suffrage Amendment Was Stopped as soon as the first few elections demonstrated the sensible way that women would vote.

Those Who Were Anti-Suffragists Register and Vote as faithfully as the Suffragists. Most of them honestly believed that women were not ready for the responsibility of the ballot, but since they have a duty to perform they have accepted their share.

A bulletin published by the National Woman Suffrage Association on the effects of woman suffrage in California.

winning a referendum in Washington. Careful attention to detail and grass-roots mobilization seemed to offer the keys to success. Woman suffrage advocates particularly needed to combat persistent, well-financed opposition by liquor interests. The next year, 1911, brought a bigger reward for these tactics. California became the most populous state to adopt woman suffrage, by a narrow margin, again through a referendum. These wins gave the suffrage movement a long overdue shot in the arm. Referendum campaigns were mounted in six states in 1912, and the suffragists prevailed in three: Arizona, Kansas, and Oregon. Their losses were disheartening, however, because they occurred in the large states of Ohio, Michigan, and, despite active assistance from Senator La Follette and his Progressives, Wisconsin. In Michigan and Wisconsin, brewers once more played a big role in defeating the suffrage measures. Those failures convinced many suffragists of the futility of a piecemeal approach. State campaigns continued with mixed results after 1912, but nation-wide suffrage through a constitutional amendment was now the overriding goal of women's organizations. Some leading feminists, most notably Jane Addams, had already entered national politics to achieve that goal.

Advocates of prohibition were making a similar switch to the national arena, and they too would ultimately seek an amendment to the Constitution. Ties between the woman suffrage and temperance movements remained strong, especially in the eyes of their foes. Because the brewers, distillers, and saloon-keepers helped finance and organize opposition to suffrage referenda, they usually suffered when women won the vote. Stricter municipal and county-option laws were enacted soon after suffrage victories, thereby "drying up" larger and larger areas in those Western states. But the overlap between the movements was far from complete. Despite those Western coalitions, the flamboyance of such anti-liquor zealots as Carrie Nation, and the strength of the Women's Christian Temperance Union (WCTU), the prohibition movement was not predominantly feminine enterprise. Nothing showed the disparity between suffrage and prohibition more clearly than the mushrooming popularity of prohibition in the South, where the suffragists made little headway. By 1910, county-option statutes were drying up the South even faster than the West. In 1907, Oklahoma entered the union as the nation's second "dry" state, along with Maine, where alcoholic beverages had been illegal since the 1850s.

State-wide prohibition now became the thrust of the temperance movement. The WCTU and the Anti-Saloon League mounted simultaneous campaigns to lobby legisatures and to drum up popular votes. By 1914 they had banished alcohol from eight more states through legislative action, all in the South and West. When liquor interests stymied them in five other state legislatures, the prohibitionists won by carrying referenda. Two years later, in 1915, the prohibitionists added nine more, for a total of twenty-three dry states. Yet like the suffragists, the drys suffered disappointing setbacks. They were unable to get prohibition on the ballot in most Northeastern and Midwestern states, and they failed in hard-fought referendum contests in California in 1914 and 1916. In 1912 the Prohibition party's presidential showing fell by nearly 50,000 votes from its 1908 tally, again declining to below two percent of the total. Two years later, however, a California district elected the first Prohibitionist to Congress, with Democratic support. William Jennings Bryan still declined to inject his personal anti-liquor views into national politics, but in 1910 he broke with fellow Nebraska Democrats to support county option. In 1913, when he was appointed secretary of state, Bryan set a personal example of temperance when he banished alcohol from official entertainment. Critics jeered when he served grape juice instead. Also in 1913, his friend and political cohort, Secretary of the Navy Josephus Daniels, made the fleet dry by forbidding drinking on shipboard.

Having secured only a mixed record in the states, the prohibitionists—like the suffragists—shifted their attention to the federal level. Experience with local and county option had long since demonstrated the difficulty of enforcing prohibition in areas adjoining "wet" enclaves. Moreover, distillers were openly advertising mail-order whiskey in dry states. Responding to demands by the temperance organizations, Senator William S. Kenyon of Iowa, an insurgent Republican, and Representative Edwin Y. Webb of North Carolina, a Bryanite Democrat, sponsored legislation to forbid the shipment of liquor into dry states. In January 1913, better than two-thirds majorities in both houses of Congress approved the Webb-Kenyon Act. Its supporters had to override a veto by President Taft, who opposed prohibition and doubted the law's constitutionality. The Supreme Court upheld the Webb-Kenyon Act in 1917, but doubts such as Taft's led prohibitionists to envision a constitutional amendment as the surest form of dry legislation. The whopping congressional majorities behind the Webb-Kenyon Act made that goal appear attainable. Later in 1913, the Anti-Saloon League publicly announced a drive for nationwide prohibition through amendment to the Constitution. The WCTU soon joined the drive.

The campaign to make the United States a dry nation drew together disparate constituencies. The geographical pairing of Iowa's Senator Kenyon with North Carolina's Representative Webb epitomized the movement's strength in the South, West, and to a lesser extent, Midwest. Their political backgrounds demonstrated prohibition's appeal to the reform wings of the two parties. Prohibition drew upon both positive and negative sentiments among its supporters. Its anti-urban perspective reflected suspicions both of immigrants, with their alien ways and support for corrupt political machines, and of big businessmen. Its vision of moral uplift contained roughly equal measures of evangelistic Protestant conformism and humanitarian impulses to improve health, safety, and family life. Later, critics would emphasize the repressive,

intolerant motives behind prohibition, to the exclusion of its sympathetic concerns. The same people who jeered at Bryan's grape juice
would fix the image of the entire movement.

Reform and prohibition did not entirely overlap in the first decades
of the twentieth century. Some leading reformers, most notably Senator La Follette, stood strongly against the prohibition movement, though
his stand was often dismissed as a bow to his notoriously "wet"
Wisconsin constituents. By contrast, in 1915, Bryan finally would add
nationwide prohibition to his repertoire of political, social, and
religious causes. Because he symbolized so perfectly the rural and small-
town Protestant culture of the South and West, the Commoner sharpened the polarization over prohibition between "native" groups on one
side and urbanites on the other. By 1915 the crusade against alcohol
had become the focal point of a titanic political, social, and cultural
conflict that would reverberate for another decade and a half.

The sides and the issues in that cultural conflict were already forming by 1910. Although prohibition offered the strongest rallying point
for defenders of rural and small-town Protestant culture, other issues
also offered vehicles for their discontent. Woman suffrage gathered
support for a curious mixture of modernist and traditional motives.
Many feminists expressed contempt for old-fashioned ways and attitudes. The emancipated behavior of "new women," which included
smoking cigarettes and frank talk about sex, shocked traditionalists.
Yet, as the prohibitionist-suffragist connection demonstrated, much of
the support for woman suffrage drew upon notions that women would
uphold moral values and protect families against "alien" and modernist threats. This was evident in the South, where some suffragists argued
that white female votes would further buttress white supremacy. Still,
the suffragists fared poorly in the South not only because stodgier views
of woman's "place" prevailed there but also because many whites feared
that any reform in voting would weaken black disenfranchisement.

Immigration restriction presented an equally strange yoking of disparate interests. European migration to the United States continued to
accelerate, topping one million a year for the first time in 1905, and
reaching a peak of almost 1.2 million a year in 1907. The numbers
declined thereafter until 1913 and 1914, when they again exceeded a
million. These waves of European immigrants fed a backlash that
resembled the resentment among Northern whites toward newly arrived
blacks. By 1910, despite their interest in cheap labor, Southerners were
converting to the cause of immigration restriction. They joined fellow
Protestants of other sections in revulsion against the rise of "alien"

"G.W.: HOW THEY HAVE CHANGED!" A cartoon expresses revulsion at the new immigration, 1909.

religious and cultural influences. As did prohibition, the cause of immigration restriction was overlapping more and more with political and economic reform. Not all reformers were restrictionists, however. All three presidents between 1901 and 1920 opposed measures to restrict immigration, and Senator La Follette argued eloquently for maintaining an open door to newcomers. But Bryanite Democrats and insurgent Republicans supplied leadership and majorities in Congress for measures aimed at stemming the influx from abroad. Such support in part reflected the influence of labor unions and social workers, who favored restriction as necessary to improving the lot of industrial workers and immigrants already here. More generally, reformers supported restriction simply because it was opposed by businessmen who wanted to maintain a supply of cheap labor.

Despite the reformist, pro-labor impulses behind the restrictionist bills in Congress, these measures most strongly embodied ethnic and religious biases. The long-proposed literacy test transparently discriminated in favor of Nordics and against southern and eastern Europeans, most of whom came to the United States unable to read and write in their native languages. Persistent agitation by restrictionist organizations and the AFL finally won passage of a literacy-test bill by both houses of Congress in February 1913. President Taft promptly vetoed the bill. Supporters mustered the necessary two-thirds in the Senate to override his veto; they failed in the House, but by only five votes.

Woman suffrage, prohibition, and immigration restriction all reflected in some degree an underlying clash of cultures in America. This conflict pitted country against city, hinterland against metropolis, Protestant against Catholic, native against immigrant, and, more vaguely but pervasively, old against new. The sharpest single issue in this cultural conflict was just beginning to creep back into public life in 1910. That was internecine strife among Christians, chiefly among Protestants, over whether modern scientific theories could be reconciled with the traditional teachings of the Bible on creation and the nature of the universe. These controversies had been brewing since the publication of Charles Darwin's account of evolution in 1859. To many they seemed teapot tempests among theologians and scriptural hairsplitters, but the basic issue was whether or not to accept materialistic, scientific explanations of physical reality and biological life, including human life. This issue had brought on wrenching divisions within American denominations, but after 1890 the Darwinist controversy seemed to subside. More liberal, sophisticted clergymen, who were called modernists, had apparently effected an accommodation between science and religion. The modernists were willing to read Biblical accounts of the creation, Garden of Eden, and miracles as metaphors, and sometimes to admit error in parts of the Scripture. Most important, they believed that modern scientific findings and theories could be comfortably subsumed within a tolerant, critical Christian faith.

The calm on the religious front was deceptive. Evangelical clergymen and laymen, especially in the South, Midwest, and West, did not accept any such reconciliation. They were preparing not only to counterattack within their denominations but also to spread the conflict to a broader public. In 1909 a group of anti-Darwinist ministers founded the World's Christian Fundamentals Association, which began to publish a series of tracts entitled, *The Fundamentals: A Testimony to the Truth.* The advent of fundamentalism not only roiled the Protestant denominations in fresh fights over Biblical literalism, but it also presented a potent counterforce to fascination with human feats of science and technology. A new generation of popular evangelists, epitomized by the colorful ex-baseball player Billy Sunday, tapped a huge audience of people who ached to hear messages of certainty from the "old-time religion." The most prominent evangelical layman, William

Billy Sunday.

Jennings Bryan, mixed political messages with religious disquisitions. For several years the Commoner had been voicing misgivings about scientific theories that depicted human beings as animals and glorified brutal struggle. Bryan did not yet propose taking political action to combat such views, but other fundamentalists did. A few were beginning to advocate a ban on the teaching of evolution in public schools. This was the educational equivalent to prohibition.

THE ALLURES OF MODERNITY

These attacks by radicals and religious fundamentalists had made few dents in Americans' faith in industry and technology. The nation's economy continued to generate wonders of production, employment, and innovation. The pace of growth accelerated steadily during the first two decades of the twentieth century. The gross national product, which was estimated at $35.3 billion in 1910, nearly tripled in the next decade, to $91.5 billion in 1920.

But economic growth was not uniform: it had already begun to slow in older, maturing industries. The rise in steel production declined from

more than double between 1900 and 1910 to about 60 percent during
the following ten years. Between 1900 and 1910, railroads added another
47,000 miles of track, but only an additional 7,000 miles by 1920. Growth
in employment likewise sagged. Job expansion lagged from a nearly
30 percent rise between 1900 and 1910 to less than 10 percent in the
succeeding decade. Several factors contributed to this uneven economic growth. Much of the fall-off in job creation reflected disruptions
caused by the outbreak of World War I in 1914, which shut off large-
scale immigration from Europe. At the same time greater mechanization and plant reorganizations were starting to reduce the need for
industrial workers and reduce pressures on employers to pay higher
wages. For the time being, however, they tended to boost workers' wages
and productivity, and to aid the growth of new industries.

One of the biggest and most dynamic new industries was in automobiles. From just 8,000 in 1900, the number of motor vehicles registered in the United States had exploded to 458,000 by 1910. By 1920,
notwithstanding cutbacks in civilian production during World War I,
the number of automobiles would total 8 million. In 1909, William
Howard Taft became the last president to ride to his inauguration in a
horse-drawn carriage; in 1913, he and his successor rode in an automobile. Newspapers and magazines routinely carried advertisements
for automobile goggles, driving hats, and auto coats. Those products
soon fell by the wayside with the production of enclosed sedans with
glass windows. A road construction boom smoothed out cobblestones

The assembly line at the Ford Motor Company.

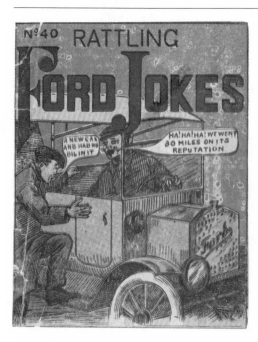

Rattling Ford Jokes. *A book of jokes featuring Ford's Model T: "What's the difference between a 1910 model Ford and a 1916?" "Six years."*

and paved streets in cities and towns, causing farmers and small-town merchants themselves to clamor for paved highways. In 1913 a North Dakota newspaper carried an advertisement: "For sale: Velie 30 auto—drove it from Illinois; on account of roads I cannot drive it back." "Good-road" movements joined other reform drives. The demand for public funds for streets and roads was so great that proposals were being advanced for unprecedented forms of federal aid to states and municipalities. Perhaps the most important advance in automobiles came in 1910, with the introduction of the electric "self-starter." Now that laborious hand cranking was no longer required to start the engine, driving ceased to be the exclusive sphere of strong men and wealthy women such as Alice Roosevelt, who had servants to start their cars for them.

A mammoth new industry was emerging. Employment in automobile factories rose from less than 10,000 in 1900 to 37,000 in 1910 and would grow to over 200,000 in 1920. Detroit, Michigan, became the center of the auto industry, in part for its easy access to raw materials via railroads and the Great Lakes, but even more through the presence of inventive manufacturers. The city's name increasingly became a synonym for cars. More than any other industry, automaking embodied the latest in production techniques. One man above all led the way in implementing innovations to supply affordable cars to clamoring customers—Henry Ford. Forty-seven years old in 1910, Ford was already a folk hero. Born on a farm in Michigan, he had loved machinery from childhood. "My toys were all tools," Ford later remembered. "They still are." He had gone to work as a machinist in Detroit at age 17 and had started tinkering with engines in the 1880s, eventually building his first car in 1896. In 1903 he founded the Ford Motor Company and began to experiment with faster, more highly mechanized methods of production, particularly the assembly line. In 1908 Ford introduced the world's first mass-produced automobile, the Model T. During the next two decades Ford would sell more than 15 million of these automobiles, and in the process make a slang term of unknown origin—"flivver"—a synonym for low-priced cars in general and the Model T in particular. Competitors soon challenged Ford's preeminence in the auto industry, but no one from Detroit ever matched his hold on the popular imagination.

The impact of technology extended to the airplane and radio, which were still in their infancy but becoming increasingly noticeable. After Orville and Wilbur Wright made the first successful flight near the Atlantic beach at Kitty Hawk, North Carolina, in December 1903, other aviation pioneers quickly joined them at home and abroad. Flying demonstrations became a regular feature at fairgrounds and expositions, and fresh distance records were continually being set. In 1911, after his return from abroad, Theodore Roosevelt became the first president to fly in an airplane. The following year, Harriet Quimby became the first American and first woman to make a flight across the

The Wright Brothers' flight at Kitty Hawk, North Carolina, 1903.

Harriet Quimby.

English Channel. Even though aviation still remained something of a sideshow (commercial flight would not be viable until the 1920s), it was having an impact on popular consciousness. One indication was that the age-old scoff—"he can no more do that than he can fly"—was no longer heard.

Radio was meanwhile finding practical uses. Developed during the 1890s by the Italian engineer Guglielmo Marconi, wireless telegraphy had carried its first transatlantic message in 1901 and quickly came into widespread use by ships at sea. Ironically, the wireless won its greatest public notice in April 1912 with the sinking of the luxury liner *Titanic,* when nearby ships failed to respond to the stricken liner's distress signals. At the time, this new medium could not yet transmit voices over long distances; that advance in radio would not come until 1920. Well before that the telephone was carrying voices over longer distances. The number of telephones increased nearly six times during the first decade of the twentieth century, and by 1910, the United States had over a million of them.

The greater ease of travel and communication afforded by cars, telephones, and the wireless epitomized the growing impact of industrial development not just on material goods and jobs, but in all spheres of life. School enrollments continued to mushroom. The number of high school graduates per year tripled between 1900 and 1920, to over 300,000—nearly 17 percent of the nation's seventeen-year-olds. Colleges and universities declined slightly in number during the first decade of the century as educational organizations tightened standards for accreditation. The college student population grew, however, by more than half, to 355,000 in 1910—over 5 percent of the country's eighteen- to twenty-year-olds. By all these measures, the United States continued to lead the world and was widening its margin of preeminence.

Such genuine progress inspired both boastful and thoughtful celebrants. Newspapers and magazines continued to devote much of their space to accounts of inventions, massive construction projects, and faster, more comfortable travel. Of all American magazines, *The World's Work* trumpeted triumphs of technology, production, and social improvement loudest, with factual accounts and photographs displacing fiction and line drawings. Nearly every popular magazine shared that upbeat, optimistic tone, which in some entirely supplanted muckraking and in even the most ardent investigative journals brought about curious mixtures of exposés and cheers.

Leading clergymen in the major Protestant denominations likewise blended denunciation of political and economic corruption with applause for material and social progress. Since the 1870s liberal Protestants, many of the same people who were attracted to theological modernism, had subscribed to the ideas that came to be called the "Social Gospel." They believed that Christ's teachings of love for fellow men and women, concern for the poor, and distrust of material wealth required Christians to promote social, economic, and political reform. The two best-known clerical exponents of the Social Gospel after 1900 were Washington Gladden, a dynamic Congregational preacher from Columbus, Ohio, who served in local government and supported Roosevelt's programs, and Walter Rauschenbusch, a Baptist professor at Rochester Theological Seminary, who wrote the most sophisticated books expounding the need to make life better and more humane. Social Gospel clergymen exerted great influence through their sermons, their articles in both religious and secular magazines, and their widely read books. The most notable of these were Josiah Strong's *Our Country* (1885), William T. Stead's *If Christ Came to Chicago* (1893), and Charles M. Sheldon's phenomenal best-seller *In His Steps* (1896), of which the latter two pondered what might happen if Jesus visited America at the beginning of the twentieth century. Despite the Social Gospelers' influence, however, their absorption in the works of this world sometimes skirted close to denial of the basic Christian precepts of original sin and otherworldly salvation. Even such sophisticated clerical exponents of the Social Gospel as Gladden and Rauschenbusch concentrated so much on the establishment of the Kingdom of God on earth that their fundamentalist critics accused them of heresy.

The 1912 disaster to the "unsinkable" *Titanic,* which went down with only 705 people surviving out of over 2,200 passengers and crew, spread some doubt about the promise of technology, but those doubts were soon forgotten. Instead, it took the outbreak of World War I in 1914 and the swiftly unfolding horrors of modern technological warfare on the Western Front to begin to shake the general belief in progress and human betterment. Even then, disillusionment spread much faster and further in Europe than in America.

Among those who did raise doubts about the prevailing optimism were a collection of acidulous critics who would become well known in the 1920s as representatives of a "lost generation," but who were already emerging on the literary scene by 1910. That year, Harvard College graduated perhaps its most illustrious class. Two of the brightest stars, the poets Thomas Stearns Eliot and Alan Seeger, immediately expatriated themselves to Europe in search of a richer culture. Eliot, who went to London and worked in a bank, soon wrote some of his best-known poems, such as "The Lovesong of J. Alfred Prufrock" (1917) and "The Waste Land" (1922), but his fame awaited the onset

John Reed.

Max Eastman.

of fashionable disillusionment after World War I. Seeger blazed two trails that later writers followed. First, he settled in Paris, living among artists and intellectuals on the Left Bank; then, when World War I broke out, he joined the French Foreign Legion. Seeger went to fight less out of patriotic devotion to France than in search of "experience" on the battlefield. His most famous poem, "I Have a Rendezvous with Death" (1915), anticipated both the mood of the post-war "lost generation" and his own death on the Western Front in 1916.

Another of their college classmates, a boisterous young Westerner and ex-Harvard cheerleader named John Reed, became a devotee of a radicalism that combined cultural rebellion with economic and political dissent. Reed and kindred spirits were gathering in Greenwich Village, the run-down New York City neighborhood where the wealthy divorcée Mabel Dodge had set up a salon that brought youthful artistic and literary experimentalists together with such labor radicals as "Big Bill" Haywood of the IWW. In 1911 Max Eastman, another youthful habitué of "the Village," launched *The Masses,* a magazine which broadcast dissents from established social and cultural values, celebrations of modern art, poetry, and drama, and applause for revolutionary stirrings at home and abroad. Besides Eastman, contributors to the

Masses included Reed, who reported on IWW strikes and the revolution in Mexico; the playwright Eugene O'Neill, who wrote theater criticism; the gifted political cartoonist Art Young; and the Ashcan School painter John Sloan.

In painting and sculpture, the main innovative influence was coming from Europe, and the sensation of the time was the Armory Show in New York at the beginning of 1913, which featured works by such rising masters as Pablo Picasso and Marcel Duchamp, and received not only wild applause from Greenwich Village but even a mildly favorable notice from Theodore Roosevelt. The Armory Show had an unanticipated effect on the development of American painting. Before 1913, Europe's revolutionary schools of art—Impressionism and Post-Impressionism—had exerted an impact on expatriate American painters such as James Abbott McNeill Whistler and Mary Cassatt, who lived and worked abroad. The more established painters influenced by these movements—such as the portraitist John Singer Sargent, and Childe Hassam, best remembered for his "flag paintings"—studied in Europe and pursued transatlantic artistic careers. But the Armory Show brought these vibrant European influences home, and their effect on the major American artistic movements—the Ashcan school and other types of realism—was chilling. It made the realists' work and the concerns of some with social expression seem staid, overly earnest, and dated. After 1913, modern art in America took a decidedly different turn, toward cubism and other forms of abstraction. "I'm afraid it may be more of a calamity than a blessing," noted one painter at the time, "though it's a damn good show."

Elsewhere in the United States, literary dissenters were questioning both the distribution of power and the adequacy of traditional values. Some of the most vivid new poetic voices came from outside the metropolis. Among these were the vagabond Illinois poet Vachel Lindsay, who incorporated folk ballad rhythms and the beat of black music into such works as "General William Booth Enters into Heaven" (1913) and "The Congo" (1914); the Chicago lawyer, Edgar Lee Masters, whose sad, mocking verses, collected in his *Spoon River Anthology* (1915), captured the loneliness of life in the rural Midwest; and the New Hampshire ex-teacher Robert Frost, whose volume of bleak, deceptively simple lyrics, *A Boy's Will*, was published first in England in 1912. Also in Chicago, two struggling novelists were writing works that flew in the face of nearly everything traditional in American culture. One was Theodore Dreiser, whose 1912 novel *The Financier* was the first volume in a trilogy that drew damning portraits of fabled tycoons

Sherwood Anderson.

and the whole economic system. The other notable Chicago fiction-writer was Sherwood Anderson, whose first novel, *Windy McPherson's Son*, published in 1916, unmasked hypocrisy and repression in small-town life. At the time, Anderson was also publishing a gripping series of stories that would be collected in 1919 as *Winesburg, Ohio* and would offer possibly the most damning portrait of middle-class life and values in all American literature.

Dreiser and Anderson would not attract a large readership for several years after 1910, but even among best-selling authors there emerged a new stress on realistic portrayals of the brutal, seamy side of life, especially in factories and cities, mixed with a tinge of political radicalism. The popularity of Upton Sinclair's *The Jungle* might be considered exceptional, but Jack London's consistent success could not. One of the most popular novelists in America between 1900 and his death in 1916, London was a self-educated former laborer and prospector who first achieved fame for his adventure stories of the Klondike gold rush. He retained his broad following even when his novels turned more political. *The Iron Heel* (1906) and *Martin Eden* (1909) frankly portrayed economic exploitation and political oppression, and called for socialist remedies to be achieved through violent revolution.

H. L. Mencken.

Among literary critics, two men stepped forward to attack the poverty of imagination they saw in their nation's culture, and to advocate greater openness to cosmopolitan influences. One was another young Harvard man who had fled to Europe upon graduation in 1907, Van Wyck Brooks. After his return home in 1912, Brooks wrote a series of essays that condemned even the greatest of American writers for lack of maturity, paucity of ideas, and unwillingness to experiment. These essays would be published in 1915 as the provocatively titled book, *America's Coming-of-Age.* The other critic was the Baltimore newspaperman H. L. Mencken, who needed neither college nor foreign travel to prompt his attacks on the inadequacies in American art, music, education, religion, ideas, and taste. By the time he became co-editor of the New York magazine *Smart Set* in 1914, Mencken was perhaps the wittiest and nastiest debunker of progress, optimism, and conventional morality on the literary scene. He was also the fiercest foe of restrictions of all kinds, whether on drink, immigrants, or thought. As early as 1909, Mencken dismissed the prohibitionists' ideal of life as "too austere, too drab, too nearly bloodless. They forget that there is such a thing as an art of life." The next year he lampooned "that maudlin theory of liberty which, in the United States, makes the vote of a negro loafer as potent as that of . . . Thomas Edison."

Champions on both sides of the clash of cultures were waiting in the wings by 1910, but the time had not yet come for them to take center stage. Prohibition, woman suffrage, and immigration restriction as yet occupied secondary places in public debate; they ranked behind and still served as adjuncts to political and economic reform. Nothing better illustrated the priorities of public attention than the roles played by two intellectuals who burst onto the journalistic scene just before and just after 1910. One was a formerly obscure, forty-year-old architectural critic, Herbert Croly. In 1909 Croly published his book of political criticism, *The Promise of American Life*, which supplied a formidable philosophical rationale for Theodore Roosevelt's approach to government. Like Roosevelt, Croly endorsed the growth of big business as a vehicle of economic efficiency and enlightenment, and he likewise sought to vest political leadership in a broad-visioned elite imbued with, in Croly's phrase, "a New Nationalism." Croly's book did not attract a large readership, but it reached the people who counted. Roosevelt read *The Promise of American Life* on safari in Africa, lavishly praised it on his return, appropriated the "New Nationalism" as his own slogan, and drew Croly into his inner circle.

The other new intellectual in journalism was yet another star of the Harvard class of 1910, Walter Lippmann. Despite his promise as a philosopher, Lippmann forsook academic life to plunge into politics. First, he honed his journalistic skills by serving as Lincoln Steffens's assistant, and then he got a taste of politics and government by becoming secretary to the Socialist mayor of Schenectady, New York. His few months in local politics bored Lippmann and tempered his socialist idealism. He assuaged his disenchantment by borrowing from fresh European psychological concepts, particularly the theories of Sigmund Freud, to reinterpret political life in his first book, *A Preface to Politics*, published in 1913. "Men desire first, then they reason," Lippmann wrote.

Lippmann also frequented Mable Dodge's salon in Greenwich Village, and joined Croly as an advisor to Roosevelt. In 1914 he published his second, more ambitious book, *Drift and Mastery*, in which he attempted to reconcile his earlier stress on political irrationality with his reformist involvement. "Rightly understood science," he argued, furnished the means by which people could "treat life not as something given but as something to be shaped." Correctly educated leaders could,

Walter Lippmann (left), with the young Franklin Delano Roosevelt (center).

in his view, "use the political state for interesting and important purposes." For Lippmann, the direction of correct leadership at that time lay along Roosevelt's and Croly's lines of transcendent nationalistic ideals.

That same year Croly and Lippmann joined forces as editors of *The New Republic*, which, during its first years of publication, became the most exciting, sophisticated American magazine. The editors, who also included the reform-minded economist Walter Weyl, produced weekly political commentaries of piercing insight and deep reflectiveness. They drew contributions on public affairs from a host of excellent writers at home and abroad, including the English novelist and science-fiction writer H. G. Wells, the British Socialist theorists Beatrice and Sidney Webb, the rising American historian Charles A. Beard, and the controversial lawyer and economic reformer from Boston, Louis D. Brandeis. They covered literature and culture through reviews and essays, many of which were written by a junior staff member and youthful radical, Randolph Bourne, and they carried creative pieces by younger writers such as the poet Robert Frost. In all, the *New Republic* editors concocted a heady brew of political, social, and cultural commentary. Not all their projects turned out happily, especially their relationship with their erstwhile mentor, Theodore Roosevelt. The ex-president broke bitterly with the *New Republic* just a few months after its founding, when the editors declined to endorse some of his more bellicose stands on foreign policy. Their synthesis of modernist, cosmopolitan perspectives and basically hopeful engagement in public affairs sometimes grew strained, even at the outset. Yet *The New Republic*'s assumptions that there could be a reconciliation of criticism and progress, of cultural ferment and political reform, demonstrated the prevailing optimism among Americans that the problems besetting the United States in 1910 and the years immediately following could be solved.

COLLISIONS IN POLITICS

Americans would need more than optimism to solve their nation's major social and economic problems, which were growing worse. The specter of turbulence among workers had grown since Roosevelt's remark in 1906 about "excitement and irritation." Union organization and labor violence had both increased. Membership in AFL unions nearly tripled between 1900 and 1910, from 548,000 to over 1.5 million. The · unions' political involvement likewise increased, despite Samuel Gompers's dislike of partisan commitment. He and other AFL leaders pressed politicians of both parties for legislative relief from Supreme Court decisions that had made unions subject to the Sherman Antitrust Act. They also sought legal protection for their efforts to organize workers and to limit working hours. President Taft and Republican conservatives either ignored or rebuffed their entreaties. Some Democrats also gave unions a cold shoulder, but Bryan and his followers had already endorsed their program in the 1908 election. A number of Republican insurgents, especially La Follette and his supporters in Wisconsin, likewise proved friendly to the unions. After his return home in the middle of 1910, Roosevelt himself started warming up to the more conservative unions.

The more radical unions formed the most visible segment of the labor movement, however. After "Big Bill" Haywood's acquittal in Idaho in 1907, the IWW expanded under his leadership. The "Wobblies" continued to make their greatest inroads in the West, where they organized miners, lumberjacks, and other workers. Still, their strikes were marked by violence, whether or not they instigated it. In 1911 a boycott by printers against the *Los Angeles Times* reached a violent climax when a bomb was set off at the newspaper's plant, killing twenty-one workers. Although the union leaders accused of the bombing were not associated with the IWW, the Wobblies nevertheless bore the brunt of public revulsion because of their call for a general strike after the bombing. As in the trial of Haywood and the mine union leaders in 1907, Clarence Darrow defended the union, but this time his clients were convicted when it was revealed that they had planted the bombs. The IWW was meanwhile moving eastward to mount organizing drives among textile workers. Haywood's fundraising efforts for well-publicized strikes at Lawrence, Massachusetts, in 1912 and at Paterson, New Jersey, in 1913 brought him in contact with Mabel Dodge and the Greenwich Village intellectuals.

Business interests became the target of a public outcry in March 1911 when a fire gutted the Triangle Shirtwaist Company on New York's Lower East Side, killing nearly 150 young women workers. The Triangle fire dramatized the lack of safety provisions and generally poor working conditions in the garment industry. It also gave a big boost to the passage of state laws regulating safety conditions, heat and ventilation, and lighting in the workplace, particularly for women workers.

The responsibility for such incidents was so clear, and distrust of big business so widespread, that labor radicalism had significant appeal to middle-class groups. At no time in American history was there greater tolerance and openness toward socialism than in 1910 and several years afterward. That year, the Socialist party elected its first big-city mayor in Milwaukee. During the next four years, more cities would choose socialist mayors, including Butte, Montana; Berkeley, California; and Schenectady, New York, where Lippmann worked briefly. Socialist positions drew support as well outside the cities. The largest-circula-

Casualties of the fire at the Triangle Shirtwaist Company, 1911.

tion Socialist newspaper, *The Appeal to Reason,* was published in Girard, Kansas. In 1912, when Debs ran for the third time as the party's presidential candidate, he rolled up his biggest shares of the vote, 16.1 and 17 percent respectively, in Nevada and Oklahoma.

Reformers in both major parties likewise took decidedly radical turns after Roosevelt left the White House in 1909. Among Democrats, the Bryanites now stood less in the vanguard on political and economic issues; they found themselves closer to the center of the party as more and more Northeastern Democrats joined them in denouncing trusts and machines. The clearest indication of the Democrats' ideological realignment occurred in 1910, when a bright star emerged as the newly elected governor of New Jersey. He was Woodrow Wilson, former president of Princeton University and an erstwhile conservative spokesman, but now an unmistakably "progressive" figure. On Capitol Hill, the new leader of the Democratic minority in the House, Congressman Champ Clark of Missouri, quietly drew his cohorts together into a near solid bloc of votes for reform measures. By 1910 it was clear that, despite Bryan's third defeat, his party hewed more faithfully than ever to his ideological course.

The growth of reformist sentiment among Republicans was even more striking, and had profound political consequences. The division between insurgents and conservatives in the party grew so wide after 1908 that it threatened to destroy William Howard Taft's presidency. To an extent, Taft was a victim of circumstances. He tried to uphold Roosevelt's reform conservatism, but he did not possess his predecessor's political capital or skills, and he tried to do this at a time when the Republican center would not hold. The insurgent contingent on Capitol Hill was not only larger after 1908 but much better organized than earlier. At the same time, the old-guard leaders remained as obdurate as ever. Even with such allowances, however, it must be said that Taft was the author of much of his failure as president. He never overcame his natural distaste for bargaining and intrigue, and he never developed an appreciation of the public dimensions of politics.

Taft's shortcomings became painfully apparent even before his inauguration. Early in 1909 he got off on the wrong foot with the insurgent Republicans in the House. Led by Congressman George W. Norris of Nebraska, the insurgents had been trying for several years to curb Speaker Joseph G. Cannon's autocratic rule. The president-elect at first apparently encouraged their revolt, but then, on Roosevelt's advice, he decided to cooperate with the House Speaker and Senate leaders, who were threatening to scuttle his legislative program if he encour-

Speaker Joseph G. Cannon.

aged the insurgents. The choice was perhaps unavoidable, but failure to bargain with both sides was unwise. The grizzled "Uncle Joe" Cannon relied on his own cunning and patronage, together with some conservative Democrats' votes, to stifle the challenge to his ascendancy in March 1909. He repaid his political debt to Taft by allowing the House to pass a bill requested by the new president to make moderate downward revisions in the tariff.

The Speaker's victory was short-lived. Cannon launched costly reprisals against Democrats and insurgent Republicans who wanted to lower the tariff still further, and who denounced the administration-sponsored measure as a sham. Those reprisals weakened Cannon's support in the House and helped pave the way for his dethronement. In March 1910, Congressman Norris outfoxed the speaker in a parliamentary coup. House members at last got a chance to vote on a proposal to democratize the rules by stripping the Speaker of his chairmanship of the Rules Committee, and of his authority to appoint committee chairmen. After three days of stormy, round-the-clock debate and maneuver, the reforms passed. Of the 191 votes in favor, 46 came from Republican insurgents; 145 came from Democrats, nearly nine-tenths of whom Champ Clark delivered.

By the time of Speaker Cannon's downfall, President Taft had long since exposed his inability to overcome the divisions in his party. Taft tried earnestly to follow in Roosevelt's footsteps, and in many ways he succeeded. He maintained a high caliber of personnel among his appointees. Roosevelt and Gifford Pinchot grumbled privately about a plethora of corporate lawyers, but the new Cabinet retained one secretary at the same post and shifted another to a different department. As Secretary of State, Taft appointed Philander C. Knox, who had served earlier as Roosevelt's attorney general, and as secretary of the interior, he named Richard A. Ballinger, who had served briefly under the previous administration as commissioner of public lands. Later, he picked another Roosevelt protegé, Henry L. Stimson, to be secretary of war. Accidents of death and retirement allowed Taft to choose five Supreme Court justices, some of whom turned out to be conservative or undistinguished, and none as great a jurist as Roosevelt's appointee, Oliver Wendell Holmes. But one did approach that stature in a series of opinions that espoused more progressive constitutional views: the governor of New York, Charles Evans Hughes, who was appointed in 1910.

Taft practiced administrative government as assiduously as Roosevelt had done, and he often improved on the performance. Henry Stimson, who would eventually hold seats in the cabinets of three presidents, later judged Taft to have been the most orderly, efficient chief executive he had served. In policy, too, the new president preserved continuity. Antitrust prosecutions increased. Taft and his feisty attorney general, George W. Wickersham, believed much more unreservedly than Roosevelt had in enforcing the Sherman Act. "I think the law is a good law that ought to be enforced," the president had declared, "and I propose to enforce it."

Ninety antitrust prosecutions were brought during Taft's four years in office, compared with fifty-seven during Roosevelt's nearly eight years. Taft's prosecutions resulted in the two biggest and most publicized dissolutions of corporations yet in American history. In 1911, the Supreme Court ruled in favor of the government in separate cases against Rockefeller's Standard Oil Company and the American Tobacco Company—the "tobacco trust" formed by the Duke family. The companies were convicted of having conspired to stifle competition and restrict access to the marketplace, and the Court ordered them broken up into a number of smaller, independent units.

The government's victories carried a price, however, because the Court majority again interpreted the Sherman Antitrust Act in ways that allowed great latitude to big business. In the *Standard Oil* decision, Chief Justice Edward Douglass White laid down a "rule of reason" to govern enforcement of the antitrust law. The Sherman Act, White held for the Court, did not prohibit all restraints of trade but only "unreasonable" ones. It would be up to the courts to decide in future cases

John D. Rockefeller (center) and his lawyers entering court during the antitrust investigations of the Standard Oil Company.

just what was or was not "reasonable," but the Court maintained that there was no intent to prohibit any arrangements, "whether resulting from combination or otherwise, which did not unduly restrain interstate and foreign commerce." These opinions angered not only Democrats and insurgent Republicans but also the president, who initially viewed the decisions as unwarranted judicial intervention to amend the law. Even members of the Court felt the same way. In one of his last dissents, Justice John Marshall Harlan pounded his fist on the bench and accused the Court majority in the *Standard Oil* case of putting "words into the antitrust act that Congress did not put there."

The biggest suit against a corporation under the Taft administration ultimately failed, but not before it caused considerable political fallout. In June 1910, the president had ordered the attorney general to cooperate with a House committee investigating the United States Steel Corporation, and he encouraged a Commerce Department investigation which revealed that over 20,000 steel workers—one-quarter of the total—put in twelve-hour shifts, seven days a week, while over 40,000 of them earned less than eighteen cents an hour. In October 1911 Taft approved plans by the Justice Department to bring an antitrust suit against U.S. Steel. One of the charges against the corporation involved its acquisition of the Tennessee Coal and Iron Company in 1907 which, unknown to Taft, Roosevelt had personally approved after J. P. Morgan had appealed to him to help stem the spreading financial panic. The suit against U.S. Steel would play an important part in the estrangement between the ex-president and his successor. The case dragged on until 1920, when the Supreme Court finally ruled in favor of U.S. Steel. In the meantime, the Court's decisions in 1911 and the steel suit fed agitation for a new, stronger antitrust law.

Taft went beyond antitrust prosecutions in carrying on Roosevelt's policies of strengthening the government's role in economic regulation. He also enlarged the executive role in tariff making through a measure granting the president authority to lower duties under reciprocity agreements with other countries. He won legislation that established the Federal Children's Bureau, which oversaw child labor laws and other child welfare concerns, started a savings system under the Post Office as an alternative to private banks, strengthened the Interstate Commerce Commission by empowering it to originate as well as reduce railroad, telephone, and telegraph rates, and taxed dangerous, unhealthy phosphorous matches out of existence. Under other political circumstances, those accomplishments might have earned Taft accolades for governmental competence and reformist intentions.

But for all his administrative talents, Taft seemed entangled always in political debacles. Immediately after the inauguration, Taft called Congress into session to honor the vague pledge in the 1908 Republican platform to lower the tariff. Despite Cannon's cooperation, the affair went wrong from the outset. The House bill contained an income-tax provision, which the president supported only lukewarmly because he doubted its constitutionality. Taft's doubts about the tax provision disappointed supporters of the measure in Congress and impelled them to sponsor a constitutional amendment that granted government the power to levy income taxes. Thanks to long agitation by Bryanite Democrats and a growing number of Republican insurgents, the income tax was an idea whose time had come. In the midst of the tariff debate, the income-tax amendment won two-thirds votes in the Senate and House in July 1909. Ratified by the states in February 1913, the income tax became the Sixteenth Amendment—it was the first of four amendments that would be added to the Constitution during the second decade of the twentieth century.

When the tariff bill reached the Senate, a familiar scenario unfolded. The last time a president had tried to lower the tariff, in 1894, protectionist senators, aided by lobbyists, had gutted a comparably mild revision through amendments. One senator who had learned well from that previous encounter was Nelson Aldrich of Rhode Island. He had subsequently refined his obstructionist tactics in the duel with Roosevelt over railroad regulation. Now in 1909 the Senate once again nullified nearly all of the House's downward revisions through amendments, although executive authority to revise rates under reciprocity agreements was retained.

But the Rhode Island senator won a pyrrhic victory. Insurgent Republican senators, now increased in numbers, banded together to fight Aldrich and the Old Guard. Led by La Follette, the dissident Republicans divided the tariff bill into separate areas, for which each mastered the details. With their expertise on the tariff issue and the oratorical talents of La Follette, Beveridge, and Dolliver, they unmasked the bogus revisions contained in the Senate bill and denounced the influence of lobbyists. Worst of all from Taft's standpoint, the senatorial insurgents ensured that Republican disharmony received wide public exposure, and they handed the Democrats a potent campaign issue for the next year's congressional elections.

The tariff imbroglio on Capitol Hill presented the president with the same quandary he had faced in the challenge to Speaker Cannon.

A 1909 cartoon showing Taft pleading with Senator Aldrich while TR glares and the Big Stick gathers dust.

Should he side with the insurgents, or should he go along with the congressional leaders, who now promised him "great influence" over the House-Senate conference committee that would hammer out a compromise bill? Once again, the president chose the path of the regulars, and the final bill largely resembled the Senate's protectionist version: it lowered rates on only a few products, left most rates unchanged, and actually raised rates on many imports. This was not a case of a gullible Taft being snookered by a wily Aldrich or a perfidious Cannon, however; Taft believed that the new executive power to revise rates compensated for the bill's conservatism on duties. Furthermore, like Roosevelt, Taft harbored a strong distaste for the insurgents, particularly La Follette, and for what struck him as their self-righteous grandstanding. Unlike Roosevelt, however, Taft made no effort to mollify the insurgents, and he exacted no price for his support from the conservatives beyond the new executive powers granted by the bill. Taft then defended his actions publicly in ways that made matters worse. On a speaking tour in September 1909 he praised the congressional leaders, ignored the insurgents, and touted the new tariff as "the best bill the Republican party ever passed."

Taft's fight with Congress was repeated the next year in a struggle over regulation of railroads, telegraphs, and telephones. Taft's original bill not only expanded the ICC's powers over railroad rates, but would also have extended its authority to oversee their issuance of stocks and bonds. True to his preference for judicial decisions, the president also proposed creation of a new Commerce Court to hear appeals from ICC decisions. The Democratic-insurgent–Republican coalition in the House amended the bill to include La Follette's scheme for physical valuation of railroad assets and regulation of interstate telephone and telegraph companies, and to weaken seriously the Commerce Court. Senator Aldrich once more rose in opposition. He displayed his wiles by bargaining with the Democrats, who wanted admission of Arizona and New Mexico as states, to defeat the insurgents' House bill, and to strip away the president's proposal for railroad securities regulation. In the end, the Mann-Elkins Act of 1910 gave Taft a larger half loaf than he had gotten with the tariff, and it marked an important step forward in railroad regulation by granting the ICC powers to initiate and overturn rates on its own. The act also established the first federal regulation of telephones and telegraphs. As with the tariff, however, Taft received no credit, only blame from his party's insurgents, and he reciprocated by becoming more convinced than ever that La Follette and other reform Republicans were dangerous, deceitful men. The tariff and railroad regulation fights had created an irreparable split within the Republican party, which the Democrats exploited in the 1910 elections when they seized upon the mild tariff revision and linked it in the public mind to the rising cost of living.

In foreign policy Taft departed from the path forged by Roosevelt. Despite his experience in the Philippines and as Roosevelt's advisor and envoy, Taft did not engage in anything like Roosevelt's activist, great-power diplomacy. He did continue a supervisory role for the United States in the Western Hemisphere, which included maintaining American protectorates in the Caribbean. The foreign policy of Taft and Secretary of State Knox could not be called Big Stick diplomacy and was more aptly, though derisively, christened Dollar Diplomacy. The policy had two sides, neither of which was really new. One was the use of diplomacy to promote private trade and investments abroad; the other was the use of private banks as a source of loans to foreign governments, particularly to China and countries in Latin America whose support the administration coveted. Roosevelt had quietly pursued both kinds of dollar diplomacy, but Taft and Knox boasted publicly about what they were doing. They thereby drew more criticism, especially from Democrats and insurgent Republicans who accused them of catering to big business.

But Taft's foreign policy was actually more idealistic and pacific than Roosevelt's. In the Far East the Taft administration reversed Roosevelt's appeasement of Japan. Dollar diplomacy in the Orient involved proposals for loans to China that were intended to offset Japanese financial domination. Those projects sprang from the fertile mind of the young director of the State Department's Far Eastern Bureau, Willard Straight, who wanted to help Chinese nationalists then in revolt against the moribund Ch'ing dynasty. The Taft administration's most important move in the Western Hemisphere was painstaking noninterference in Mexico, where a revolution began in 1911 with the overthrow of the long-time dictator Porfirio Díaz. Taft's determination not to intervene in Mexico required him to resist pressures from American business interests, which had prospered under Díaz and feared the radicalism of some revolutionary elements. As it was, America's refusal to allow dissident Mexican conservatives to buy arms in the United States permitted the fragile new government of Francisco Madero, a sincere but ineffectual democrat, to survive for nearly two years, thereby helping to ensure the eventual success of the revolution.

Taft's proudest accomplishment in foreign affairs came in 1911, when he concluded an arbitration treaty with Britain that ruled out armed conflict in nearly all disputes between the two powers. As a lawyer, Taft believed strongly that domestic and foreign disputes should be settled by an impartial judgment of the competing claims. Unlike his predecessor, Taft gave more than lip service to the movements for international arbitration that had flourished since the late 1890s and had led to treaties among individual nations and to the multilateral pacts negotiated at the Hague Conferences of 1899 and 1907. Also in contrast to Roosevelt and despite his own service as secretary of war, Taft had no love of fighting and military life. The 1911 arbitration treaty with Britain expressed Taft's own beliefs, and caused Roosevelt's first public break with his successor. The ex-president denounced the scheme as a piece of "offensive hypocrisy." He also abetted Henry Cabot Lodge's successful effort to attach severe reservations to the Senate's consent to the treaty. The president, in turn, withdrew the treaty rather than ratify it in what he regarded as an emasculated condition.

What dramatized the Taft-Roosevelt split to a broader public was the colorful dispute that erupted soon after the tariff fight: the so-called "Ballinger-Pinchot Affair." None of Roosevelt's cronies had mourned his departure more keenly than Gifford Pinchot, and Taft's assurances of continued influence failed to satisfy the chief forester. His fears were well founded. Pinchot enjoyed nowhere near the same intimacy with the new president, and Taft replaced the compliant Garfield at the Interior Department with Pinchot's old bureaucratic foe, Richard Ballinger. Ever alert to the uses of publicity, Pinchot started making speeches during the summer of 1909 in which he insinuated that Ballinger was undermining Roosevelt's conservation policies. Pinchot's strong identification with those policies and with Roosevelt ensured receptive audiences among conservationist organizations and magazine editors.

The situation became explosive when Pinchot learned that Ballinger was being investigated for allegedly corrupt dealings while he had served as Roosevelt's land commissioner. The chief forester and his lieutenants gleefully leaked information about the investigation to *Collier's Magazine*. Taft reviewed the case, decided that Ballinger was innocent, and ordered a halt to all allegations against him. In January 1910, after Pinchot only mildly reprimanded his assistant for further leaks and then publicly repeated charges against Ballinger, Taft fired him. The president acted with more political courage than shrewdness. Since Ballinger's reputation had been damaged, whether deservedly or not, Taft's smartest move would have been to let both men go. But Taft believed Ballinger had done no wrong, and he did what he thought was right, regardless of the consequences. "I would not have removed Pinchot if I could have helped it," Taft privately moaned.

Consequences followed swiftly and spectacularly. After the chief forester's dismissal, the Ballinger-Pinchot Affair turned into a battle to sway both public opinion and Roosevelt's opinion. Ballinger, and through him Taft, lost in both arenas. A congressional investigation began three weeks after the firing. *Collier's*, which feared possible libel suits for publishing the charges against Ballinger, retained the Boston attorney and economic reformer Louis D. Brandeis as counsel. Brandeis saw to it that Pinchot's side was presented in the best possible light and that the administration's case was made to look suspect, even fraudulent. Although the investigation ultimately cleared Ballinger, the slowly unfolding story, the clash of personalities, and the uncovering of an apparently juicy scandal concerning a clumsily post-dated document supplied irresistible copy to newspapers and magazines during the first half of 1910. The contest for Roosevelt's support was just as heated. Taft, Lodge, and Root wrote letters to the former president in Africa defending the administration. Pinchot, once he had testified, went abroad to tell his own story. He met Roosevelt in Italy in April 1910, and they talked for several hours, in what Pinchot called, "one of the best and most satisfactory talks with T. R. I ever had." That same evening Roosevelt confided to Lodge, "I don't think that under the Taft-

"*Sec. Ballinger: 'Well, I think I am going to have a white Christmas.'*" *A cartoon accusing Taft Republicans of a whitewash in the investigation of Ballinger.*

Cannon-Aldrich regime there has been a real appreciation of the needs of the country, and I am certain that there has been no real appreciation of the way the country felt."

During the spring and summer of 1910, people all over the world were watching for signs and portents. Halley's Comet was making another appearance on its seventy-six-year circuit, accompanied by predictions from the frivolous to the cataclysmic. In the United States the writer Mark Twain, who had often foretold his own death—"I came in with it, and I'll go out with it"—died in April, just as the comet became visible. Others tried to read political omens as the rift in the Republican party widened. During the summer of 1910, Taft publicly backed conservatives in party primary battles with insurgents. This first attempt by a twentieth-century president at a party purge failed miserably. Several conservatives lost, incumbent reformers won renomination, and in two states even bolder insurgent movements forged ahead. In Wisconsin, La Follette's forces regained complete power after a brief lapse. In California the Republican faction headed by Hiram Johnson seized control of the state party and swept all the offices. But no event attracted more attention or excited greater hopes and fears than Theodore Roosevelt's return in June 1910. The ex-president was greeted in New York by fireboats spouting plumes of water and by a tickertape parade. Nearly everybody seemed to be wondering what this political phenomenon was going to do next.

6

The Emergence of Wilson

Even without the coincidental appearance of Halley's Comet, Theodore Roosevelt would have evoked comparisons with a spectacular force of nature after he came back to the United States in 1910. During the next two years he reshaped the course of a major reform movement; he split an established political party; he founded a new party; he raised searching questions about the nature and direction of government and society; and he fostered the emergence of his own greatest rival. Roosevelt's performance sparked a keen response at the time. The sharpest comment came from the man who sought to best him in the 1912 presidential election. Just one month before the November vote, Woodrow Wilson observed of Roosevelt, "We have a very erratic comet sweeping across our horizon." Wilson knew what he was talking about. So much would have turned out differently without Roosevelt's extraordinary performance, including the rapid rise of Wilson's own rival star.

The Return of the Hero

When Roosevelt returned home in June 1910, the Republicans were on the verge of civil war and he himself was in a quandary about what to do about it. He knew that he should support his handpicked successor and maintain at least a façade of party unity, but he was also consumed with concern about the nation and about his own role in history.

Privately, Roosevelt had given up on Taft at the first hint of trouble. "The qualities shown by a thoroughly able and trustworthy lieutenant are totally different," he had told his friend Senator Henry Cabot Lodge ". . . from those needed by the leader, the commander." Further, he believed that "much of what has been called leadership in the Republican party consisted of leadership which has no following," whereas, for all their faults, the insurgents stood closer to "real Republicanism . . . the creed of the Republican party of Lincoln."

Roosevelt tried to carry water on both shoulders in the congressional elections of 1910. He kept up appearances of cordiality with Taft, and he made no direct criticism of his successor's policies. But while the president aided the campaigns of conservative Republicans, Roosevelt took to the hustings during August and September in support of the insurgents. He used his campaign speeches to restate his basic approach to politics and to take stands that were plainly at variance with the policies of the Taft administration. In his most extended address, Roosevelt borrowed Herbert Croly's phrase to call for a "New Nationalism." He called for a creed that put "the national need before sectional or personal advantage," that regarded "executive power as the steward of public welfare," and that required judges to "be interested primarily in human welfare rather than property." His demand for stricter railroad regulation, stiff federal income and inheritance taxes, and abolition of child labor pleased insurgents and irked conservatives. But nothing sowed greater disquiet on the part of Taft and congressional leaders than Roosevelt's criticisms of the courts. Distorted newspaper accounts of a speech at Denver made it appear that Roosevelt sought legislative powers to overturn Supreme Court decisions. In fact, he was merely reiterating the views of constitutional interpretation that he had presented in several earlier presidential messages: that courts should allow executives and legislatures great latitude in dealing with economic and social problems.

But Roosevelt's political position in 1910, which appeared erratic to some observers, was characteristically complex. His support for insurgent Republicans was constantly colored by a steadfast conservatism. Roosevelt bared his political soul soon after the elections. "I am a radical," Roosevelt confessed in December 1910, "who most earnestly desires the radical programme to be carried out by conservatives. I wish to see industrial and social reforms of a far-reaching nature accomplished in this country, . . . but I want to see that movement take place under sober and responsible men, not under demagogues." In the 1910 elections, Roosevelt campaigned not only for insurgents but also for

Roosevelt calling for a "New Nationalism," August 1910.

such conservatives as Massachusetts's Senator Lodge and the Ohio Republicans' gubernatorial nominee, Warren G. Harding. He refused to speak on behalf of La Follette's senatorial reelection bid, and he devoted his most strenuous efforts to the two Republican candidates whom he regarded as "sound" reformers. Those were Senator Albert J. Beveridge, who was running for reelection in Indiana, and Henry L. Stimson, who was the party's choice to succeed Charles Evans Hughes as governor of New York.

To both Taft and Roosevelt the results of the 1910 elections spelled disaster. With some notable exceptions, Republicans lost all across the country. Their majorities on Capitol Hill withered away. The loss of fifty-seven seats in the House cost them control of a chamber of Congress for the first time in sixteen years. Congressman Champ Clark of Missouri became House Speaker, and the Democrats' diligent tariff expert, Congressman Oscar W. Underwood of Alabama, assumed the post of House majority leader. The loss of ten Senate seats did not cost the Republicans control of that body, but their reduced margin transferred the balance of power to an informal coalition of insurgents and Democrats. Gubernatorial losses were equally heavy. Democrats took away the governorships of New York, New Jersey, Connecticut, and Indiana, while they retained the governor's chair in Ohio. To the chagrin of Taft and his allies, nearly all the Democratic gains came at the expense of conservative Republicans.

The results were equally disheartening to Roosevelt. Henry Stimson's defeat for his old office in his home state was a particularly hard blow. So was Beveridge's narrow defeat in Indiana—one of the few losses suffered by a prominent insurgent. The bright spots on the gloomy Republican horizon were insurgents' victories, but those failed to warm Roosevelt's heart. In Wisconsin, La Follette handily won reelection to the Senate, while his followers recaptured control of the state government and proceeded to enact a new agenda of regulatory measures. In California, Hiram Johnson's movement seized power and passed sweeping primary and referendum laws. Also on the West Coast, a less dramatic Republican revolt triumphed in Washington. Those victories troubled Roosevelt almost as much as his friends' defeats. During the campaign he grumbled about "Western radicals," and after the election he fretted that many insurgents "tended to make progress sideways instead of forward."

Whether the president and ex-president liked them or not, the insurgents represented a rising force among Republicans, and now they gave themselves a potent new name. They had long called themselves "progressives" in Wisconsin, California, and other states, but now in January 1911, a group of senators and congressmen led by La Follette formed a national organization, which they christened the Progressive Republican League. The group, still a part of the Republican party, adopted a platform that demanded new federal regulatory laws for transportation and trusts, denounced corrupt business and machine influence, and opposed President Taft for renomination by the party in 1912. The question of whom to support against Taft was a difficult one. Even though Senator La Follette mistrusted Roosevelt and others resented his coolness toward them, the Progressive Republican League turned first to the ex-president. He rebuffed their overture, but he did not completely close the door. Except for opposition to Taft, Roosevelt confided that he "already *in principle* supported all the things the Progressive Republican League stands for." Publicly restating his advocacy of reform measures, Roosevelt now included measures that he had previously avoided: popular election of senators, the initiative, and the referendum. Meanwhile, the Progressive Republican League turned to one of its own, Robert La Follette, who eagerly answered the call and started to campaign against Taft during the spring of 1911. The party's civil war had escalated into open combat.

Bad as their internecine conflict was, however, the worst aspect of the Republicans' predicament lay in the Democrats' newfound strength, vitality, and appeal. Lost governorships and House seats in 1910 were the least of the Republican worries. For some years the Democrats had been stronger than they seemed to be. Since reaching their low point in 1904, they had been electing more governors in Midwestern states and steadily narrowing the Republican margin in the House. The Democrats had not elected more senators largely for procedural reasons. Since Senators were elected by state legislatures, the overrepresentation of rural and small town areas in the Northeast and Midwest disproportionately favored Republicans. But thanks in part to continuous Democratic and insurgent Republican agitation, by 1911 more than half the states had passed laws requiring a popular vote to elect senators. In May 1912, the Democratic–progressive-Republican coalition in Congress mustered the necessary two-thirds to pass a constitutional amendment. Ratified by the requisite states in May 1913, the Seventeenth Amendment required all senators to be elected by the people, beginning in 1914.

Republicans tried to explain away some of their losses in 1910 as expected mid-term attrition and bad luck. "The voters are like a man who's going to roll over in bed," Elihu Root had warned, "whether he needs to or not." But the turnover in House seats and governorships was the largest since the mid-1890s, and with Champ Clark now Speaker of the House, the Democrats acquired a fresh national figure. Moreover, because Clark delegated policy leadership to the House majority leader, Oscar Underwood, the party gained a second major new spokesman. Furthermore, nearly all the most salient issues in the 1910 elections—tariff reform, regulation of business, attacks on the influence of wealth—were questions which, thanks mainly to Bryan's long labors, Democrats could address with enthusiasm and a modicum of unity.

The worst news for the Republicans and best news for the Democrats came from the states. Local factors played a large role as usual in gubernatorial contests, but Democratic breakthroughs in populous Northeastern and Midwestern states showed how widespread the voters' desires for change were, and how willing voters were to look for leadership in unaccustomed places. The Democrats' biggest liability since 1896 had been their reputation for radicalism and riskiness in the minds of the electoral majority in the nation's heartland, while the Republicans' biggest asset had been their reputation for soundness and conservatism in the minds of that majority. But political agitation and journalistic exposés about the trusts and moneyed corruption had made identification with big business by Republican conservatives and their Democratic counterparts much less attractive than earlier. Likewise, Taft's performance and the open warfare between insurgents and regulars had sullied the Republican image of competence. Most important of all, the Democratic governors together presented a bright new face that seemed to displace the received image of their party.

New Star Rising

The Democrats' most striking new governor in 1910 was a long-jawed, bespectacled former professor of government and college president, who was the son, grandson, nephew, and son-in-law of Presbyterian ministers. This was the governor of New Jersey, Woodrow Wilson. He was fifty-three years old in 1910, and he won the governorship in his first race for any public office. With his neat dress and polished speaking style, Wilson inescapably reminded people of his background in classrooms, libraries, and churches. His emergence as the Democrats' brightest star after 1910 seemed odd at the time and later. Wilson was just one of a crop of new Democratic governors, and New Jersey was not the most politically significant state in which the party won the statehouse in 1910. But Wilson soon outdistanced his fellow governors, including Judson Harmon of Ohio and John A. Dix of New York, in public attention and stature. This occurred in part because he did a demonstrably better job in office, yet the roots of Wilson's almost instantaneous political blossoming lay elsewhere.

While Wilson was beginning to show his mettle first as a campaigner in 1910 and then as a governor in 1911, he faced the same question over and over from reporters. Though usually more politely phrased, the question went: how is it that an ivory tower academic can do so well in the rough-and-tumble "real world" of politics? Wilson, who belied his austere appearance with a ready wit, developed a stock answer: "After dealing with university men," he asserted in one version on the campaign trail, "the men I am striving with appear as amateurs. I fail to find the same subtle political games that I found in the university." Playful as it was, Wilson's reply made two essential points about his political emergence. First, his academic background was not just a coincidental prelude, but provided preparation for his political career. Second, his appearance as a learned man, with his evocation of books, pulpits, and lecture platforms, was not a liability. Like Roosevelt's upper-class background and manner, Wilson's academic image made him distinctive and noticeable. It was one of the secrets of his success in politics.

Journalists compared Wilson to Roosevelt from the start, despite the obvious differences between the two men. Wilson had been born in the medium-sized town of Staunton, Virginia, and raised in the larger towns of Augusta, Georgia, and Columbia, South Carolina. His family had never possessed more than modest financial means, and Wilson had never enjoyed a private income like Roosevelt's. Moreover, Wilson was neither an outdoorsman nor a war hero; he had not served a long apprenticeship in politics, and he was a lifelong Democrat. Yet the comparisons were apt in that Wilson shared with Roosevelt an identity as an intellectual, a reliance on the new public dimensions of politics, and, up to a point, similar views about the active role government should play in addressing social and economic problems.

Wilson's standing as an intellectual was indisputable. His father and favorite uncle had been not only Presbyterian ministers but also seminary professors. Growing up among them had exposed the young "Tommy" Wilson, as he was called as a boy, to some of the most liberal, sophisticated religious influences in late nineteenth-century America. But the young Wilson had never been inclined toward the pulpit; instead, he had yearned to enter politics and to become a "statesman" after the manner of Daniel Webster, or the British Prime Minister William Ewart Gladstone. After his graduation from Princeton in 1879, Wilson had studied law at the University of Virginia. For a brief time he practiced the law, but abandoned this when he decided it did not offer good opportunities for a political career.

Wilson was also strongly attracted to writing and to the study of politics. He did graduate work at Johns Hopkins University and received his Ph.D. in 1886. (He would be the only holder of that degree to become president.) The year before he received his doctorate, Wilson had published his first and best book, *Congressional Government.* He went on to hold professorships at Bryn Mawr College, Wesleyan University in Connecticut, and after 1890, Princeton. Wilson became renowned as both a classroom and a public lecturer, and as a writer on historical and political subjects for higher-toned popular magazines. During the 1890s he established himself as a leading academic political scientist, and as 1900 passed he was planning to write a great comprehensive work to be entitled, "Philosophy of Politics."

In 1902, however, Wilson's career took another unexpected turn when he was chosen president of Princeton. He soon made himself the most

*Woodrow Wilson at Prince-
ton University.*

famous college president in America. Wilson transformed Princeton,
which had only begun calling itself a university in 1896, into a front-
rank educational institution. He constructed buildings, established
laboratories, and attracted star faculty members from leading universities at home and abroad. But Wilson achieved his greatest renown as
an educational reformer. In 1905 he introduced the "precept" system,
under which he recruited fifty young academics to teach undergradu-
ate students in small groups, thereby maintaining the intimacy of a
college within a modern, research-oriented university. In 1907 he
attempted to abolish Princeton's exclusive, fraternity-style social clubs
by creating a college system with resident faculty, partly after the model
of Oxford and Cambridge. Opposition by alumni and trustees foiled
Wilson's effort, but the wider publicity he received for fighting the
snobbish clubs made him a national figure. Finally, in 1909 and 1910,
he became embroiled in a struggle over where to locate Princeton's
embryonic graduate school. Wilson favored mixing graduate students
with undergraduates in an effort to raise the intellectual tone of the
university. When his foes prevailed, he was ready to leave Princeton.
Ironically, it was the sponsorship of New Jersey's conservative Democratic bosses for the 1910 gubernatorial nomination that provided his
springboard into politics.

Throughout his academic career, Wilson had retained a practical
bent. He had originally forsaken law for teaching in hopes of becoming

what he called "an outside force in politics," by which he meant a commentator and advisor. As a teacher and writer, Wilson had fixed his gaze on how politics and government really worked, and how government could be made more efficient and more popularly accountable. Through study and observation he had developed broadly activist ideas about how much law and government could do to meet the needs of society. But it was only after he became president of Princeton and thereby acquired greater visibility that Wilson began to play the role that he had originally envisioned as an "outside force" in contemporary affairs. The publicity he attracted as a bold reformer of Princeton's intellectual and social life, and as a battler against social privilege and conservatism, heightened his attractiveness as a potential candidate for office.

New Jersey's conservative Democratic leaders were attracted to this activist college president because, before he became a reformer, Wilson was known as a political conservative. Wilson was quite capable of opportunism in his politics, and his early conservatism sprang more from circumstances than from convictions. After Alton Parker's defeat by Roosevelt in 1904, Northeastern conservative Democrats needed a fresh spokesman for their anti-Bryanite position. The newspaper publicity and speaking opportunities that Wilson had gained through his Princeton presidency brought him to their attention. He seized upon the opportunity they offered and began publicly criticizing both Bryan and Roosevelt from a states-rights, limited-government standpoint. This conservative message proved advantageous to Wilson as an entree into active politics, and as a signal to the New Jersey bosses who eventually handed him the gubernatorial nomination. Intellectually, however, the right-wing Democrats' strict preference for limited government, which they justified with genuflections to a Jeffersonian heritage, suited Wilson badly. "Ever since I had independent judgments of my own I have been a [Hamiltonian] Federalist," he had stated early in his academic career. By 1906, moreover, conservatism was plainly waning in popularity, and Wilson had no taste for a political voyage aboard a sinking ship.

As soon as Wilson hit the campaign trail in 1910, his unmistakably reformist profile emerged. He immediately distanced himself from his conservative patrons and espoused measures advocated by New Jersey progressives in both parties. Like much of the rest of the country, New Jersey was ripe for a move away from the Republicans, and, thanks also in part to his increasingly attractive campaign style, Wilson won election by the second largest majority ever given to a New Jersey gubernatorial candidate of any party. Once in office he put through a stunning program of reform legislation which included party primaries, strict campaign spending limitations, statutory protection for workers against unsafe working conditions, and business regulation. Wilson's success as governor came through an ingenious combination of party leadership—which had been a major theme in his academic studies—and popular politics. His frequent public appearances, sensitivity to the press, and appeals to the people allowed him to use his talents as a speaker. No wonder he reminded people of Roosevelt. Not only was Wilson advocating many of the same reform measures, with the same spirit of strong, energetic governmental action, but he also conveyed a similar aura of intellectual excellence and social glamor. Even without Roosevelt's upper-class background, Wilson had gained social status as president of a leading university, and he, too, was a personification of moral and religious respectability.

The social and intellectual similarities with Roosevelt made Wilson an almost instant front-runner for the 1912 Democratic nomination. Even before his gubernatorial successes, newspapers and magazines were mentioning him as a presidential candidate. A drive to get him the nomination started in January 1911, and was centered among expatriate Southerners like himself. Walter Hines Page, the editor of *The World's Work*, drummed up national publicity for his candidacy, but the most effective organizer and real leader of the Wilson band-

Wilson as governor of New Jersey.

wagon was a Georgia-born New York businessman, William Gibbs McAdoo.

His bandwagon did not take the party by storm, however. Wilson's earlier attacks on Bryan and lack of strong ties to the Democratic party created problems. Moreover Wilson faced stiff competition from Speaker Champ Clark, who became a presidential contender by virtue of his office and his connections with party organizations, as well as his long friendship and support for the Commoner and his programs. Majority Leader Underwood likewise entered the race for the nomination, drawing nearly all his support from fellow Southerners, who saw a chance to put forward a candidate who was really one of their own, rather than an expatriate like Wilson. Throughout 1911, however, as the New Jersey governor enacted his reforms and made well-publicized speaking tours in the Midwest and West, he seemed the most likely man to get the nomination.

Wilson's prospects depended, fittingly enough, on the Republicans' conflict and particularly on Roosevelt's part in it. The fight between conservatives and the Progressive Republican League soon turned into a standoff in which the ex-president hovered menacingly at ringside. On Capitol Hill, the pitch of debate and intra-party discord heightened. Senator Aldrich's deal with the Democrats in 1910—to trade conservative Republican support for a bill to grant statehood to Arizona and New Mexico, in return for Democratic support for the Mann-Elkins railroad regulation bill—had come unstuck. In 1911 the Arizonans adopted a "radical" constitution that included provisions for the recall of judges. Taft vetoed the enabling legislation, to howls of protests by Democrats and insurgent Republicans. Only after a temporary retreat by the Arizonans were the two states admitted to the union in 1912, bringing the total number to forty-eight and rounding out the continental United States.

Taft gradually made matters worse for himself by drawing Roosevelt into the fray. The government's antitrust suit against U.S. Steel included charges concerning Roosevelt's cooperation with J. P. Morgan during the 1907 panic, particularly his assent to Morgan's acquisition of the Tennessee Coal and Iron Company. Roosevelt regarded those charges as a slur on his honor. Issues in conservation and foreign affairs also brought the two men into opposition. Early in 1911 Taft appointed a respected conservationist to replace Ballinger as secretary of the interior, but that move did not allow Roosevelt to forgive Taft for having fired Pinchot, nor did it diminish his admiration for the former chief forester. Taft's arbitration treaty with Britain prompted Roosevelt's first public criticisms of his successor. Ironically, opposition to the treaty threw him together, not with the insurgents, but with his conservative friends, Lodge and Elihu Root, who were otherwise urging him to maintain peace with the administration.

Taft's troubles did not automatically spell victory for the progressive Republicans in the fight for the party's 1912 nomination. La Follette's indefatigable campaigning during 1911 drew almost as much criticism as applause. The Wisconsin senator suffered from some of the same liabilities as Bryan. He struck many sophisticated city dwellers as a small-town provincial. H. L. Mencken, for example, later sneered at "the Progressive martyr" and "poor Bob and his sanguinary battles for the lowly." La Follette's fiery oratory raised, to many, specters of unsoundness and radicalism. Perhaps because their hearts really belonged to Roosevelt, even some of La Follette's progressive supporters did not regard him as a truly national leader.

By the fall of 1911, few observers believed that La Follette could wrest the Republican nomination from President Taft. Pressures grew on Roosevelt to reconsider and enter the race, but the ex-president persisted in his refusals. At the same time, he continued to take strong public stands alongside the progressives on most issues, including the touchy question of recall of judicial decisions. Among the Democrats Wilson continued to be the probable nominee. His potential appeal to reform Republicans remained an important asset so long as the Republican breach did not yawn too wide, enabling any Democrat to win regardless of extra-party appeal. Wilson had the best chance to win against a relatively undivided Republican ticket, and Democratic party leaders were cheerfully willing to sacrifice this relative newcomer should he lose. When 1911 ended, however, Taft appeared increasingly likely to fall before any Democratic nominee, and all calculations and prospects changed. With the Democratic nomination really worth having, the party professionals wanted it for one of their own.

HATS IN THE RING

Roosevelt precipitated the change when he decided in January 1912 to run for the Republican nomination. He first persuaded several governors to join in issuing a public request that he seek the presidency. After long consultations with both insurgents and conservatives, he announced in February, "My hat is in the ring." A bit of luck simplified his course when La Follette collapsed while making a speech in

Philadelphia. The senator's illness furnished most members of the Progressive Republican League with the excuse they wanted to desert ·him for Roosevelt. La Follette soon recovered and refused to drop out of the race, bitterly spurning all suggestions of cooperation with his erstwhile supporters in any progressive alliance. He later broke with two of his top lieutenants in Wisconsin because they tried to persuade him to make peace with Roosevelt.

The ex-president decided to enter the 1912 race for a complicated set of reasons, which curiously enough did not include either a real hope of winning the nomination and election, or personal and ideological sympathy with the insurgents. Roosevelt grasped the practical wisdom of standing aside and letting Taft lose. At worst, such forbearance would make him the odds-on favorite to reunite the Republicans and re-enter the White House in 1916. That eventuality might happen even sooner, counseled his conservative friend Elihu Root, if Roosevelt only sat tight; there was a good chance that Taft would not run again, and then the party would rally to Roosevelt. But shrewd counsel such as Root's was wasted on Roosevelt in 1912, because he was no longer thinking of practicalities. Knowing as he did the potency of the presidential steamroller at Republican conventions, Roosevelt was never optimistic about taking the nomination away from Taft; he predicted that the conservatives would use any means, fair or foul, to beat him. If they did, Roosevelt told Root, he was ready to bolt the party.

Despite his frequent references to himself as a "radical," Roosevelt clearly had his differences with the insurgents. "I am keenly aware that there are not a few men who claim to be leaders in the progressive movement," he admitted privately, "who bear unpleasant resemblances to the lamented Robespierre and his fellow progressives of 1791 and '92." It was in fact Roosevelt's conservatism that convinced him to lead the revolt against Taft. "I wish to draw into one dominant stream all the intelligent and patriotic elements," he confided, "in order to prepare against the social upheaval which will otherwise overwhelm us." Several advisors, including his oldest son, tried to convince Roosevelt to stay out of the race. They argued that a Republican defeat in 1912 would not be a bad thing, especially since Wilson was the probable Democratic nominee. Roosevelt emphatically rejected their suggestions. He dismissed Wilson as "pretty thin material for a President," and he argued that there was "no ground for permanent hope in the Democratic Party." The Democrats were divided between "bourbon reactionaries" and "foolish radicals," and they were all wedded to "States' rights as against National duties." In Roosevelt's view, La Follette and other Republican progressives shared the Bryanite Democrats' failing of "servility toward the majority whether it goes right or wrong." This conservative reasoning left him no choice but to save the progressives from themselves, and thereby rescue the nation from class division and incipient revolution.

Roosevelt was obviously inflating the significance of social divisions in order to justify his chosen role. No themes occurred more often in his public and private utterances after 1910 than comparisons between current controversies and those of the Civil War era and, more specifically, between himself and Abraham Lincoln. Theodore Roosevelt had left the White House oppressed by the belief that he had not presided in momentous enough times to call forth heroic leadership. Just before his return home from abroad, he had observed that "if there is not the great occasion, you don't get the great statesman; if Lincoln had lived in times of peace, no one would have known his name now." By 1912 Roosevelt aspired to play a Lincolnian role in two ways. One was to be the exemplar of inspired moderation between the extremes of selfish, unenlightened conservatism and dangerous, irresponsible radicalism. The other was to stand as the large-visioned statesman who perceived transcendent ideals and rallied the people to rise above pettiness, narrowness, and selfishness. This heroic tendency had always lurked in Roosevelt's political personality. Earlier he had tempered it with practicality and caution, but now he was determined to unleash his yearning for greatness.

Calculation did not disappear completely from Roosevelt's thinking in 1912. If, as he believed likely, the conservatives cheated him out of the party nomination, then he would lead a separate movement that would re-enact the Republicans' original course in the 1850s and 1860s. He might possibly lead this new party to victory in 1912, but winning was not essential. If the Democrats nominated a party hack or a Southerner without much appeal to party progressives, then his movement would attract both Bryanites and Republican insurgents into "one strong progressive party" that would resemble the Republicans after their first race in 1856, which positioned them for their victory four years later. Though a Democrat might beat both Taft and Roosevelt, the new party would be "able to take control if the Democrats failed as they ought to do." The prospect was thrilling. It offered Roosevelt the chance to play a truly fulfilling role in history. In retrospect, the iffiness and wishful thinking seem glaringly obvious, but they were not so apparent at the time. Rather, it was remarkable how close other actors in the events of 1912 came to granting Roosevelt's wish.

Taft's withdrawal from the race had remained a possibility until his predecessor openly challenged him. The personal break with Roosevelt pained Taft deeply, but he believed that self-respect required him to defend himself. The president revealed his attitude in another memorably unfortunate remark during the spring of 1912: "Even a rat in a corner will fight." Taft was responding to more than the personal challenge in his decision to run: even before Roosevelt's return, the president had brooded about his friend's "Napoleonic" bent, and Roosevelt's criticism of the courts had offended Taft's regard for law and judicial procedures. He shared Roosevelt's fears of radicalism among the Republican insurgents, but rather than try to moderate or co-opt them, Taft was convinced that he must oppose them. Roosevelt correctly divined that Taft was determined to use his control of the party machinery to beat back all challengers. The president was no more sanguine about the election than his critics, but he also believed that he was playing for the highest political stakes. In June 1912, on the eve of the convention in Chicago, Taft told a friend, "I can stand defeat in November if we retain the regular Republican party as a nucleus for future conservative action."

Most of the established party leaders, including Roosevelt's old friends Lodge and Root, shared Taft's convictions. They had no illusions about the imminence of defeat in the election. It might seem strange that such hard-bitten professional politicians would stick with a likely loser rather than flock to their party's only potential winner, and some Republicans did support Roosevelt despite disagreement or indifference toward his stands on the issues. But most party leaders stayed loyal to Taft, in part because Roosevelt's reformist stands had made him unpalatable to them. Other Taft loyalists shared Roosevelt's faith in the Democrats' unsoundness, particularly on economic questions, and predicted that the currency and tariff policies of a Democratic administration would frighten business, cause a depression, and swiftly sweep their party, under conservative control, back into office. At one point during the 1912 convention an irate insurgent reportedly shouted at one of the bosses, Senator Boies Penrose of Pennsylvania, "Don't you realize you're wrecking the Republican Party?" Penrose, who stood six feet four and weighed over 300 pounds, thundered back, "Yes, but we'll own the wreckage."

It was wreckage that the Republicans unquestionably wrought at their June 1912 convention. "Mr. Dooley" correctly forecast their gathering in Chicago as "a combynation iv' th' Chicago fire, Saint Bartholomew's massacre, th' battle iv' th' Boyne, th' life of Jesse James, an' th' night of th' big wind." The party leaders displayed blatant highhand-edness in awarding nearly every contested seat to Taft. Those seats were not really needed for Taft's nomination, but the action provided a dramatic pretext for nearly all the Roosevelt delegates to walk out. Meeting in a rump session at a nearby auditorium, they heard their leader admonish them to oppose this "crime which represents treason to the people," perpetrated by a "corrupt alliance between crooked business and crooked politics." Reveling in the martial ardor of his own language, Roosevelt urged them to join him in fighting on "with unflinching hearts and undimmed eyes; we stand at Armageddon and we battle for the Lord." At that meeting and again when Roosevelt's supporters gathered in August 1912 to found the new Progressive Party, they sang "Onward Christian Soldiers" and the "Battle Hymn of the Republic." Soon afterward, when a reporter asked him how he felt about running, Roosevelt shot back, "I feel as fit as a bull moose!" Now, the ex-president had found not only his crusade and his new party, but his most fitting symbol.

The pivotal point in Roosevelt's calculations actually rested with the Democrats. If they obliged him by nominating a conservative candi-date, his scenario to win in 1912 or at least establish his party as the only progressive party might well come to pass. But if they chose their nearest counterpart to him, the man who competed so well in appeal-ing to progressives—Woodrow Wilson—his hopes would almost cer-tainly go awry. As events transpired, the Democrats nearly did do Roosevelt's bidding. At the beginning of 1912, Taft's weakness and

"The Challenge." The Progressive bull moose chasing the Democratic donkey and the Republican elephant into the hills.

Roosevelt's challenge had the predictable effect of tightening the race for the Democratic nomination. Despite Speaker Champ Clark's uninspiring speeches and his support from some unsavory city machines, he defeated Wilson in several primaries and also gathered large numbers of delegates through organization channels. Underwood hurt Wilson in their native South, where both conservatives and agrarian radicals distrusted Wilson because of his long residence in the Northeast.

The New Jersey governor's resemblance to Roosevelt had hurt him among Democrats almost as much as it had helped him outside the party. Opposition by such Southern agrarian radicals as James K. Vardaman and Tom Watson sprang from both regional patriotism and their dislike of Wilson's association with Northeastern intellectual and social elites. Their suspicions of him were analogous to some of the Republican insurgents' mistrust of Roosevelt. Some of these agrarians, such as Tom Watson, who would later back Roosevelt, were being more Bryanite than the Commoner, who by the spring of 1912 had found Wilson quite acceptable. Wilson had been cultivating Bryan since early in 1911 in an effort to live down his conservative past. At the same time, Wilson had proclaimed himself for the first time a "Jeffersonian"—not as a devotee of states' rights but as a champion of "the men who are on the make, and not of the men who are already made." Wilson also repeatedly called himself a "radical" in 1911 and 1912. In contrast to Roosevelt, however, he avowed "that the so-called radicalism of our time is nothing else than an effort to release the energies of our people. This great people is not bent upon any form of destruction. This great people is in love with the realization of what is pure, just, and of good repute, and it is bound by the clogs and impediments of our political machinery."

By the time the Democratic convention met in Baltimore at the end of June 1912, Wilson's star had faded. Clark secured a majority vote on the tenth ballot and seemed sure to win the two-thirds needed to head the ticket. One of Roosevelt's sons was reported as saying, "Pop is praying for the nomination of Champ Clark." Those prayers were disappointed, ironically, by the Democrats' antiquated two-thirds rule for nomination, which was anathema to nearly every reformer, including Wilson. Wilson was able to stem the tide at the convention through his ironclad stop-Clark agreement with Underwood's forces, and through the steadfastness and shrewdness of his managers, particularly McAdoo. Southern loyalties finally swayed Underwood's backers, who preferred one of their own, even an expatriate, to Clark. Wilson's forces engaged in extensive behind-the-scenes maneuvers to woo boss-led Midwestern delegates away from Clark. William Jennings Bryan finally made the difference for Wilson. When Clark refused to repudiate support from Tammany Hall, the Commoner ended his neutrality during the convention and endorsed Wilson. The former college president finally received the nomination on July 2, 1912, on the forty-sixth ballot.

1912: THE GREAT CAMPAIGN

The election of 1912 featured three presidents, past, present, and future, as candidates, and in Theodore Roosevelt and Woodrow Wilson, it pitted the most vivid political presence since Andrew Jackson against the most accomplished political mind since Thomas Jefferson. It was a grand moment in American politics.

Wilson and Roosevelt were the main contenders, as everyone recognized at the time, and during the campaign they aired their alternative visions of economic regulation and reform, the purposes of governmental action, political leadership, and the nature of the good society. Taft stayed in the race to bear the standard of Republican conservatism, and to make sure that Roosevelt lost. He broke the traditional ban on an incumbent president campaigning to give a few low-key speeches in which he reminded voters that he was still running and that his regular Republicans stood firm behind tariff protection and sound business conditions. Eugene Debs once more brought his magnetic eloquence to the presidential contest, running for the third time as the Socialists' candidate. Although Debs drew larger crowds than ever, few observers regarded his campaign as more than an attractive side-show. Almost no one expected him to do any better than he had done in his two previous races, especially because the action in the main ring was so spectacular. The last three-cornered presidential election with a split major party had occurred in 1860, and the fate of the Union had rested on the result. Roosevelt's frequent invocations of Lincoln and the Civil War never convinced many people that this election was equally momentous, but there was no question about its excitement.

By coincidence, Roosevelt and Wilson opened their campaigns on the same day, August 7, 1912. The former president stood before 15,000 cheering delegates and spectators at the Progressive convention in Chicago. He was the first presidential candidate of any party to accept his nomination in person. In his acceptance speech, "Confession of Faith," Roosevelt declared, "The old parties are husks, with no real

soul within either." Their new party was "a movement of truth, sincerity, and wisdom, a movement which proposes to put at the service of
all our people the collective power of the people." He demanded national
primaries to choose presidential candidates, measures to make courts
answerable to the people, stronger regulation of manufacturing and
transportation, laws to establish maximum hours and mimimum wages
for workers, abolition of child labor, government-run insurance and
pension programs, and nation-wide woman suffrage. Despite his bold
language and proposals, Roosevelt still sounded some familiar conservative notes. He denounced "class government" and claimed that
the Progressives offered "a corrective to Socialism and an antidote to
anarchy." He also rejected previous antitrust approaches as "Toryism
and reaction" in contrast to his determination "to penalize conduct and
not size."

As the delegates' hymn-singing enthusiasm indicated, the Progressives aroused plenty of zeal and hope. Jane Addams delivered one of
the nominating speeches, in which she lauded the party's endorsement
of woman suffrage and promotion of social justice. Writers and intellectuals—"literarys" as La Follette derisively labeled them—flocked to
the cause. Herbert Croly, Walter Lippmann, and the widely respected
Kansas newspaper editor William Allen White served as campaign
advisors to Roosevelt. Youth predominated at the convention and in
local Progressive parties. Roosevelt's younger backers in 1912 included
such diverse figures of future fame as Alfred M. Landon, Henry A.
Wallace, Felix Frankfurter, and Dean Acheson. But the Progressives
lacked the experience and organizational skill necessary to launch a
successful political party. Among leading Republican insurgents, only
Albert Beveridge, Hiram Johnson and his Californians, and a few others became Progressives. Such congressional veterans of the fight against
Taft and the conservatives as Albert Cummins, George Norris, William E. Borah, and most of their brethren remained Republicans,
although some personally endorsed Roosevelt. La Follette refused to
back anyone openly, but he made it clear privately to his followers and
in public statements on issues that he preferred Wilson.

Roosevelt, whose own crusading fervor had cooled somewhat, blamed
the lukewarm response of veteran reformers on their timidity and ego-
tism. He was right in that personal bitterness loomed large with La
Follette and his supporters, while for others, Republican ties stretching
back to Civil War childhoods proved too hard to sever. But broader
considerations also underlay the hesitance of Republican reformers to
support Roosevelt. Some of them had begun to share La Follette's doubts

about Roosevelt's reform convictions. Nothing raised such misgivings more than the trust issue. Roosevelt's insistence upon defending economic bigness and scoring reactionary antitrust views, together with the prominence in Progressive circles of such tycoons as the newspaper publisher Frank Munsey and the former Morgan partner George W. Perkins, underscored the differences between the new party's candidate and most reform-minded Republicans, even many of those who did follow him into the Progressive party.

Wilson's campaign opened more sedately at the summer residence of New Jersey governors at Sea Girt. The Democrats observed the tradition of officially notifying their nominee by a party delegation, but the stilted practice did not prevent Wilson from issuing his own call for a new, independent politics. "We stand in the presence of an awakened nation," he declared in his acceptance speech, "impatient of partisan make-believe." Most of the nation's problems sprang from "very small, and often deliberately exclusive groups of men who undertook to speak for the whole country . . .—a poor substitute for genuine common counsel. No group of directors, economic or political, can speak for a people." Wilson advocated many of the same reform measures as

Wilson on the campaign trail, 1912.

Roosevelt—except for woman suffrage, which he regarded as a question for the states—and he concluded his speech on a mixed note of partisanship and progressivism. "We have set ourselves a great program, and it will be a great party that carries it out. It must be a party without entangling alliances with any special interest whatever. It must have the spirit and the point of view of the new age."

Wilson's main advantage over his rivals lay in having behind him a long-established, well-organized, united party. At worst he could win the election merely by retaining the Democrats' traditional following, while Roosevelt and Taft split the Republican vote. But Wilson wanted to make a much better showing, and in order to do that he had to win over Roosevelt's constituency of reform-minded Republicans. In turn Roosevelt's chances depended on holding their loyalty and attracting reform-minded Democrats. In short, the two leading candidates faced the same task: they had to keep their own constituencies intact while wooing each other's supporters. Roosevelt's and Wilson's pursuit of that common strategy in 1912 brought out the worst and the best in them. In vying for reform voters, each misrepresented the other as he strove to brand his opponent a false "progressive." But in defending himself against the other's charges, each man had to develop his own position in depth and with some complexity.

On August 28, Wilson met with the Boston attorney and economic reformer Louis Brandeis. The encounter between the Presbyterian governor and the Jewish lawyer witnessed a remarkable meeting of minds. Like Wilson, Brandeis was a fifty-six-year-old expatriate Southerner who had gone to the Northeast for his education and stayed there to pursue his career. A graduate of Harvard Law School, where he had compiled a brilliant record, Brandeis had made himself rich as a corporate lawyer. But he had also taken on unpopular clients, advanced bold new legal ideas, and championed labor unions—all of which had earned him the sobriquet of "people's attorney" and the enmity of economic and judicial conservatives. Because he had long been a critic of the inefficiencies and injustices of big business, Brandeis could supply the specific economic focus that Wilson's reform bent required.

The new advisor's impact on the campaign quickly became evident as he convinced Wilson to make the first attack and concentrate his fire on Roosevelt's most vulnerable point: his stand on the trusts. In his first appearance on the hustings, Wilson praised the Progressives for wanting to aid labor and protect the disadvantaged, but he blasted them and their leader for seeking "a consummation of the partnership between government and monopoly." That would mean control of government by monopoly, instead of the revival of competition, which the Democrats sought. "In other words, ours is a program of liberty, and theirs is a program of regulation." Those remarks conveyed the essence of Wilson's argument about the trusts in the 1912 campaign. After the election the slogan "the New Freedom" would be applied to his program, but its basic themes were present from the beginning.

Roosevelt struck back fast and hard, dismissing antitrust talk by Wilson as "a make-believe assault on monopoly," in contrast to the Progressives' "definite and concrete" program to correct real abuses and achieve real results. Roosevelt likewise struck at Wilson's most vulnerable points: his academic background, lack of political experience, and erstwhile conservative views. Roosevelt sneered at Wilson's earlier views on limiting the powers of government as a "bit of outworn academic doctrine which was kept in the schoolroom and the professorial study for a generation after it had been abandoned by all who had experience of actual life." The Progressives intended "to use government as the most efficient instrument for the uplift of our people as a whole, . . . to protect all those who, under Mr. Wilson's *laissez-faire* system, are trodden down in the ferocious, scrambling rush of an unregulated and purely individualistic industrialism." It is worth noting that the downtrodden whom Roosevelt wanted to protect were not black Americans, women, or other particular groups victimized by social discrimination, but only the economically disadvantaged in general. That desire to extend government protection conveyed the essence of Roosevelt's arguments in 1912, which he had subsumed under the slogan "the New Nationalism."

Wilson showed that he was the suppler thinker of the two as he turned most of Roosevelt's charges to his own advantage. The trust question gave him some trouble, because he seemed to sympathize with his opponent's approval of bigness. Wilson distinguished between a "trust," which was "an arrangement to get rid of competition," and a "big business," which "has survived competition by conquering in the field of intelligence and economy," and he avowed, "I am for big business, I am against the trusts." Roosevelt had been making a similar distinction between "bad trusts," which conspired to stifle competition, and "good trusts," which rose to pre-eminence by being the best competitors. Bothered by the similarity, Wilson asked Brandeis to help him clarify his stand. After a second conference between the two men at the end of September, Wilson condemned businesses that reached "the point of bigness . . . where you pass the point of efficiency and get to the point of clumsiness and unwieldiness." During the rest of the cam-

"Wilson's Suggestion for a Cartoon." Wilson argued that TR's program of monopoly regulation played into the hands of the big trusts.

paign, Wilson said little about the appropriate size of businesses and concentrated on the need to restore competition in the economy.

Wilson found Roosevelt's aspersions on his views about government easier to refute. Although he reaffirmed his Jeffersonian allegiance, Wilson stated that "there is one principle of Jefferson's which no longer can obtain in the practical politics of America." That was the idea "that the best government is that which does as little governing as possible, which exercises as little power as possible." The time for such views had passed. "I am not afraid of the utmost exercise of the powers of the government," declared Wilson, ". . . provided they are exercised with patriotism and intelligence and really in the interest of the people who are living under them. But when it is proposed to set up guardians over those people and to take care of them by a process of tutelage and supervision, in which they play no part, I utter my absolute objection." Therein lay the difference between Roosevelt and himself, Wilson insisted. They disagreed, not about the power and activity of government, but about its purposes and accountability.

Wilson turned back Roosevelt's slurs on his academic background even more easily. From the earliest days of the campaign he gloried in being "a schoolteacher." Wilson believed that to be a leader was to be an educator, which entailed a two-way process of communicating with people to arrive at the right policies and programs. He contrasted his notion of leadership with Roosevelt's and the Progressives' claims that

modern political, economic, and social problems were so complex that
only a small body of trained experts could master the job of governing.
If the people did not "understand the job, then we are not a free people," Wilson declared again and again during September and October
1912. He scorned "big-brother government," asserting, "I do not want
a government that will take care of me. I want a government that will
make other men take their hands off so I can take care of myself." As
a leader, Wilson avowed, "I do not wish to be your master. I wish to be
your spokesman."

Roosevelt likewise found the trust question hard to handle. He tried
to shift the discussion to such matters as workers' protection, minimum
wages, limitation of hours, abolition of child labor, and assurance of
quality products for consumers. "The truth is," Roosevelt asserted, "in
this discussion we are losing sight of the main thing—men and women.
We're for men. Free competition and monopoly—they're all the same
unless you improve the condition of the workers." Roosevelt contended
that government's most important role in the economy was not to set
conditions in the marketplace but to safeguard workers and consumers
against the unchecked, unaccountable powers of big business. Eventually, however, he felt compelled to modify his antitrust stand. Two
weeks before the election he issued a statement calling for both a new,
more comprehensive antitrust law and a regulatory commission to
oversee business practices. In that statement Roosevelt unwittingly
echoed the program that Wilson had just outlined.

Roosevelt also ignored his opponent's denials and continued to flay
Wilson for adherence "to the old flint-lock, muzzle-loaded doctrine of
States' Rights." Wilson reciprocated the misrepresentation by continuing to imply that Roosevelt was a pawn of the trusts and by calling his
followers "the third party" or "the irregular Republicans," but almost
never the Progressives. Wilson likewise insinuated that Roosevelt was
an insincere reformer by frequently praising "that indomitable little
figure Bob La Follette" and by pointing out that "such genuine progressives" did not support the ex-president and his "third party." Between
his own attacks and his opponent's counterattacks, Roosevelt found
himself by the middle of the campaign in a predicament that required
a dramatic incident to get him on the right track.

The incident occurred on October 14, 1912, when a deranged bartender shot Roosevelt on his way to a speech in Milwaukee. Though
gravely wounded in the chest, the candidate insisted on keeping the
engagement. "I can tell you with absolute truthfulness," Roosevelt
affirmed, "that I am very much uninterested in whether I am shot or

not. It is just as when I was a colonel of my regiment." Not only was the colonel "occupied with the absorbing desire to do his duty," but he also claimed that the assassination attempt "emphasizes to a peculiar degree the need for this Progressive movement." The Progressives were striving "to prevent the coming of the day when we shall see in this country two recognized creeds fighting one another, when we shall see the creed of the 'Havenots' arraigned [sic] against the creed of the 'Haves.' When that day comes then such incidents as this tonight will be commonplace in our history." His party wanted to restore the values "which are the foundations of good citizenship in this great Republic of ours." Roosevelt praised the Progressives for upholding "that common weal. I have fought for the good of our common society."

This was Roosevelt's finest hour. By likening himself to a commander leading dedicated troops he conveyed his central vision of transcendent nationalism. But circumstances muted his drama: Roosevelt did not die from his wound like a soldier fallen in battle. After a two-week convalescence he recovered sufficiently to make a final major speech. On October 30, 1912, Roosevelt ended his campaign with another ringing statement of his beliefs. The Progressives, he avowed, were determined never to "permit the brutal selfishness of arrogance and the brutal selfishness of envy, each to run unchecked its evil course." Rather they would show justice and compassion and build "character, the sum of many qualities, but above all the qualities of honesty, of courage, and of common sense" among all citizens. Roosevelt closed with an invocation of the Civil War, "the common heritage of honor which belongs to all our people, wherever they dwell." Now as then Americans sought "to wrest justice from the hands of injustice, to hearten and strengthen men and women for the hard battle of life. We stand shoulder to shoulder in a spirit of real brotherhood."

That noble vision evoked an equally noble countervision. On a triumphant swing through the Midwest and West during the first half of October, Wilson dwelt on his major theme of social and economic renewal through equal opportunity for those starting out. The trust issue came down to one question, he asserted, "Are you going to have fresh brains injected into the business of this country, and the best man win, or are you going to make the present combinations permanent?" On this tour Wilson wrapped himself in Bryan's mantle and coined his slogan by admonishing Democrats "to organize the forces of liberty in our time in order to make conquest of a new freedom for America." Wilson also reached out beyond his party both by likening himself to La Follette and the Republican insurgents, and by invoking the aegis of Lincoln as "the Great Emancipator." He urged Americans "to repudiate this [economic] slavery just as emphatically as we have repudiated the other."

Wilson halted his campaign until his opponent recovered from his gunshot wound. When the campaign resumed, Wilson sketched once more his vision of regeneration through social and economic mobility. The future of the nation depended, he declared, "upon the invention of unknown men, upon the origination of unknown men, upon the ambition of unknown men." Citing a metaphor that he had often used before, Wilson observed in another speech, "For energy in a nation is like sap in a tree; it rises from the bottom up; it does not come from the top down." Wilson invoked Lincoln a final time as the luminous example that there was "no class in America so high that men haven't climbed into it from the bottom, if there is any bottom." Therein lay America's pride, "and if out of the average men we can't get our great men, then we have destroyed the very springs of renewal in this America which we built in order to show that every man born of every class had the right and privilege to make the best of himself."

Between them, Roosevelt and Wilson had conducted the greatest debate ever witnessed in an American presidential campaign. Curiously, however, some of the best observers at the time and later doubted the quality and value of the debate, and wondered especially whether any real differences separated the two candidates. As William Allen White wrote a decade later, "Between the New Nationalism and the New Freedom was the fantastic imaginary gulf that has always existed between tweedle-dum and tweedle-dee." White did appear to have a point. Roosevelt's and Wilson's mutual pulling and hauling over antitrust policy was just one example of the similarities in their specific stands. They also advocated similar reform measures for workers, farmers, consumers, and businesses, and their party platforms differed mainly in the Democrats' greater stress on agriculture and the Progressives' on labor and the tariff.

Their differences on the tariff did not go much beyond their respective platforms, however. Partly to compete with Taft, Roosevelt affirmed his belief in protection, but he argued that such protection must be instituted on a "scientific" basis by an expert regulatory commission. In an unusual move for a Democrat, Wilson endorsed protection in principle at the same time that he lambasted it in Republican practice as special privilege. In view of the damage that the "political dynamite" of the tariff issue had done to Taft and the Republicans, it was curious that the question aroused so little concern in 1912. The lack of debate

*"Big Ball, Little Club, 1912."
Taft had little chance in the
1912 election.*

reflected the growing public consensus in favor of lowering the tariff, and boded well for future efforts at tariff reform. From these positions there followed little debate on the tariff between Roosevelt and Wilson.

The issue of woman suffrage also seemed to disappear during the campaign. Although Roosevelt supported and Wilson opposed a constitutional amendment, neither man took a strong stand on the issue. "I am rather in favor of the suffrage, but very tepidly," admitted Roosevelt. Wilson, who had taught at Bryn Mawr and who had two suffragist daughters, called his own judgment "an uncertain balance," and he continued to favor leaving the matter to the states. Still of limited public concern, foreign policy did not enter into the campaign at all.

The plight of black Americans also evoked little interest or disagreement from Roosevelt and Wilson. Bolting the Republicans offered the ex-president a clean slate in seeking white Southern support. The Progressives fielded "lily white" parties in Southern and Border states. Roosevelt avoided mentioning race during the campaign, but he evidently made his distance from blacks clear enough to reap some modest electoral rewards. His acceptable position on race, combined with doubts about Wilson, earned him Tom Watson's endorsement, and Roosevelt finished second in eight Southern states. Wilson held no strong racial views, which was unusual for a Southern-born white of that era.

During the campaign he did not discourage the black support organized by Du Bois, but he did refuse to make public statements about racial matters, and he declined to appear before black audiences. In all, despite their discontent and growing activism, black Americans as well as woman suffragists remained nearly invisible to the major presidential candidates in 1912.

There were fundamental disagreements between Roosevelt and Wilson on the economics underlying the trust issue, the nature of democratic leadership, and conceptions of human nature. Although they overlapped on antitrust policy, the two men diverged sharply in their analysis of the American economy. Roosevelt believed that there were, in his terms, more "good trusts" than "bad trusts" and that the current distribution of power among businesses was likely to last. For him, therefore, the solution to present problems was to offset the private power of big business with greater governmental power. This was an essentially conservative economic assessment, which contemplated management of a basically unchanging situation. Wilson believed that there were, in his terms, more "trusts" than "big businesses." He was convinced that, without unfair interference, the current distribution of economic power would not last because fresh competitors would succeed in wresting dominance from the trusts. For him, therefore, the solution was to use governmental power to keep open the arena of competition. This was an essentially liberal economic assessment, which contemplated promotion of a fundamentally dynamic situation. The two men may have advocated virtually the same policies, but the aims behind those policies were not at all alike.

Roosevelt and Wilson left no doubt about the contrast in their ideas of democratic leadership. Mounting once again to his "bully pulpit," Roosevelt believed that a leader must evangelize his followers to rise above base and selfish motives. In the root sense, he saw the task as one of inspiration—to breathe into people higher, better values than they would otherwise possess. As ever the "schoolteacher," Wilson believed that a leader must instruct his followers about the proper realization of their best interests. To Wilson the task was one of education—to draw out of people an enlightened, refined appreciation of their own needs and wants. The difference between them was also a difference between liberalism and conservatism in basic political terms. As an aristocrat, Roosevelt held the classic conservative belief that better people should hold political sway over their less able fellows. As a democrat, Wilson held the classic liberal belief that nearly all people could take better care of themselves than anyone else could, no matter how gifted or well intentioned.

The heart of Roosevelt's and Wilson's differences lay in their conceptions of human nature. Roosevelt did not believe that people, if left to themselves and left free to pursue their own interests, would act to promote the public good. This was the source of his evangelism: people had to be made better than they naturally were. Untypically for a conservative, Roosevelt believed that heroic leadership and political evangelism could make ordinary folk rise above their individualistic, selfish ways. He held a pessimistic view of human nature, but an optimistic view of the means to transcend it. Wilson believed that people, if left to themselves and left free to pursue their own interests, would usually act to promote the public good. This was the source of his belief in education: it was necessary to elicit, inform, and shape the innate goodness of people. Wilson held an optimistic view of human nature and an easygoing realism about how average people could be expected to behave.

In the end, despite mutual misrepresentations, the two men were right to accentuate their differences. On the fundamental question of political philosophy, from which everything else flowed—the nature of human beings and the public good—they held opposing views. That Wilson and Roosevelt articulated those views so well made them the twentieth-century counterparts to Jefferson and Hamilton, whose political visions for America had clashed over a century before. Unlike those great statesmen, Wilson and Roosevelt did not differ over the size, structure, or power of government. They both believed in big, strong government, although they wanted it to serve different purposes. In some ways they reversed their predecessors' estimates of commerce, industry, and progress. Roosevelt, the Hamiltonian, rejected materialism; Wilson, the Jeffersonian, celebrated enterprise and mobility. The twists they gave to their respective ideological legacies demonstrated how much had changed during the century and a quarter since Jefferson's and Hamilton's debates. Roosevelt's and Wilson's agreement in practice on so many important policies illuminated the degree to which political options had been narrowed by the rise of large-scale industry and private economic power. With socialism an unlikely option in the United States, the political implications of America's social and economic development all pointed to an expanded regulatory state.

The narrowness of the options for public policy offered one explanation for the only mystery surrounding the 1912 election. Why, after such drama and eloquence, did this contest fail to produce a political upheaval? Why did Roosevelt and Wilson, in contrast to Jefferson and Hamilton before them, fall short of creating lasting electoral alignments?

The results of the 1912 election were an anticlimax. Wilson won easily, as nearly everyone expected. He got almost 6.3 million popular votes, and carried forty states with 435 electoral votes. Roosevelt came in second with 4.1 million popular votes and six states with 88 electoral votes. Taft finished fairly close behind. He had just under 3.5 million votes, but won only two states with eight electoral votes. The total vote rose less than the population had grown since 1908. Just 58.8 percent of eligible voters participated, down from 65.4 percent in 1908. Wilson's appeal did not extend beyond his party; in fact, he fell 115,000 votes below Bryan's 1908 showing. Wilson won popular majorities only in the South and in Arizona.

Roosevelt and Taft did no better. Their combined total was almost 70,000 votes less that Taft's 1908 showing. Second place offered scant consolation to Roosevelt. He ran far ahead of all other Progressive candidates, and his party did well only in California and Washington. Taft took some solace in the Republican party's showing. Although the

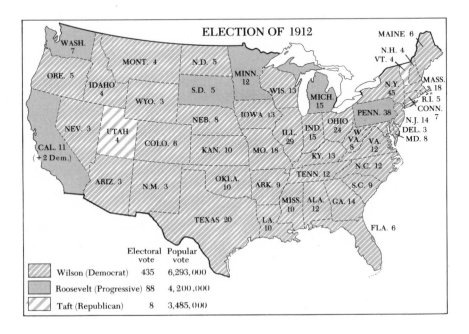

ELECTION OF 1912

	Electoral vote	Popular vote
Wilson (Democrat)	435	6,293,000
Roosevelt (Progressive)	88	4,200,000
Taft (Republican)	8	3,485,000

Democrats won control of the Senate, the Republicans retained 44 seats, as against one for the Progressives. Despite a top-heavy Democratic majority, the Republicans also still held 127 House seats, compared with 15 for the Progressives. Taft also consoled himself with the conviction that in a short time "the incapacity of the Democratic party and their leader will make itself known to the country in a way unmistakable."

The one real surprise of the election was the Socialists' showing. Debs more than doubled his vote from four years before. He gained over 900,000 popular votes, 6 percent of the total. This was the largest share of the vote ever won by a Socialist candidate for president before or since. Socialists attributed the increased appeal to more than Debs's considerable talents and appealing presence as a campaigner. They believed that neither Roosevelt nor Wilson had really addressed many people's longings for stronger measures to combat big business. There was something to that view. Debs's strong showing in the West and Wilson's decline from Bryan's performance in twelve of the seventeen states that the Commoner had carried in 1908 suggest that the Democrats and Progressives had failed to satisfy radical yearnings in 1912.

In explaining the decline in turnout in 1912 and the failure to break the established alignment of the two major parties, some observers contended that the absence of a close contest, with Wilson's victory almost universally predicted, dampened incentives to get out the vote. Republican conservatives viewed the persistence of the electoral alignment that had existed since 1896 as vindication of their assessment that progressivism was a passing fad, and they looked forward to a reassertion of their own enduring appeal to Northeasterners and Midwesterners on economic grounds. Some supporters of Roosevelt and Wilson believed that their candidates' sophisticated political arguments had gone over most people's heads in 1912. Perhaps the best explanation for why Roosevelt and Wilson failed to budge many voters out of their customary political grooves involved the similarity in their stands on immediate issues. It was hard for many to see what difference their grand visions would really make.

Despite the magnificent debate it sparked, the election of 1912 left many open questions. The political agendas of women and blacks were ignored; cultural issues such as prohibition or the teaching of evolution had gone unmentioned; and though immigration restriction was an exception, Roosevelt, Taft, and Wilson all opposed it. Foreign affairs aroused no comment from any of the candidates, despite Roosevelt's longstanding concern with America's international duties. It remained to be seen whether progressive issues really cut much ice with the electorate. The election of 1912 was the beginning, not the end, of the confrontation between Roosevelt and Wilson, and the views they represented. The debate would continue down through the new century.

7

The New Freedom

The most significant practical difference between Woodrow Wilson's New Freedom and Theodore Roosevelt's New Nationalism lay in the opportunity Wilson had after 1913 to turn his words and thoughts into deeds. The New Nationalism would always remain a label applied to a set of ideas advanced between 1910 and 1912. It described a road not taken in American politics, especially for American conservatism. The New Freedom would describe the accomplishments of a presidential administration, the main course of American liberalism, and, more generally, the spirit of the years immediately before America entered World War I.

No career in the history of the United States better justified the study of politics as preparation for the practice of politics than Woodrow Wilson's. Journalists and professional politicians continued to scratch their heads in wonder at this professor-turned-president. Too many of them tended to write off his accomplishments as the results of luck, or of talents unconnected with or unspoiled by his academic career. Those assessments misread the secret of Wilson's success. He succeeded so well as a scholar in politics precisely because he had been a scholar of politics. Woodrow Wilson was putting into practice the reflections, analyses, and theories he had developed during his years as a professor and college president.

One recurring question had absorbed Wilson's attention as an academic political scientist. How, he had repeatedly asked, does power really work in politics and government, particularly under the American system? Furthermore, how can power be made to work more hon-

"Mr. Wilson Taking Charge of the School." A cartoonist's view of the professor-turned-president.

estly, more efficiently, and in a way that would be accountable to the public? Wilson's answers to those questions had revolved around two points. First, government should be opened to greater public debate, and second, political parties should be used as the means to overcome dispersion of responsibility between the executive and legislative branches of government. Starting as a college student in the 1870s, Wilson had argued for refashioning American government after parliamentary models such as Britain's. He had modified that argument in later years, but it still formed the core of his approach to office. In January 1913, two months before his inauguration as president, Wilson stated his conviction that the American people expected their president "to be the leader of his party as well as the chief executive officer of the government. . . . He must be the prime minister, as much concerned with the guidance of legislation, as with the just and orderly execution of law."

Prime ministership, party leadership, and the importance of passing legislation: these ideas formed the core of Wilson's conception of the presidency, and he put them to work even before he entered the White House. Breaking with tradition, he dodged the swarm of office seekers and took a three-week trip to Bermuda right after the election. Having separated himself from the hurly-burly to think and plan, he weighed appointments to his administration on the bases of party service, sectional support, and competence in formulating and executing policy. The result was a mixed bag. Partly out of deference to his party lead-

"The Sphinx." Wilson dodged the office seekers greeting him at the start of his administration.

ership and partly because he was the only prominent Democrat with much of a record in foreign affairs, William Jennings Bryan became secretary of state. A veteran congressional Democrat, Albert S. Burleson, of Texas, took over the Post Office. Wilson's campaign manager, William Gibbs McAdoo, brought some financial experience to the Treasury Department, but few others in the new cabinet had made great marks as either politicians or policymakers. Overall, Wilson's appointments had a distinctly Southern and a strongly partisan flavor. They seemed a far cry from both Roosevelt's glamorous activists and Taft's lawyerly managers. Despite his reformist views, Wilson never intended to use any instrument except his party to achieve his ends, and his appointment of Bryan, Burleson, and McAdoo to the cabinet showed this.

Wilson gave his highest priority to formulating legislation, a great change from his Republican predecessors' stress on administrative government. This emphasis reflected not only the new president's approach to government but also his party's need to establish its credibility in government after years spent in opposition. Because he believed that the success of his presidency depended upon enactment of great statutes, Wilson broke with tradition to become the first president to lay out a legislative program in advance. "We have itemized with some degree of particularity the things that ought to be altered," he declared in his inaugural address on March 4, 1913, and he spelled out much of the major legislation that he would propose and Congress would enact over the next three-and-a-half years. Though soberly eloquent rather than frenetically exciting, Wilson's inaugural address echoed Roosevelt's themes of high and stirring purpose. "This is not a day of triumph; it is a day of dedication," Wilson avowed. "Men's hearts wait upon us; men's lives hang in the balance; men's hopes call upon us to say what we will do."

Wilson was also the first president to hold regularly scheduled press conferences. Initially he met reporters twice weekly, but soon he cut back to once a week. Reporters in attendance could not quote him directly, but they could ask any questions they wished. Wilson engaged in witty, informal give-and-take, although he manipulated the correspondents with his answers as much as he enlightened them. Nor did he enjoy the encounters as much as he affected to do. After two years, Wilson used the delicacy of diplomatic dealings surrounding World War I as an excuse to cancel the meetings, and he rarely held any

A woman suffrage march held in Washington the day before Wilson's inauguration in 1913.

Joseph P. Tumulty.

thereafter. Like his pre-inaugural retreat to Bermuda, this episode demonstrated the solitary side of Wilson's character. Fortunately for the new president, his able secretary, Joseph P. Tumulty, attended to the details and personal dimension of press and congressional relations. An amiable Irish-American who had served Wilson in the same capacity as governor, "Joe" Tumulty made up for his chief's reclusive ways.

Another departure from tradition came when Wilson called Congress into special session in April 1913 and, breaking with the custom begun by Jefferson, became the first chief executive in 112 years to appear in person before either house. Wilson wanted to show that the president was "not a mere department of the Government hailing Congress from some isolated island of jealous power . . . but a human being trying to cooperate with other human beings in a common service." It was the right touch, and it marked the beginning of a long series of personal appearances before Congress. During the next six years, Wilson addressed joint sessions annually on the state of the union, and frequently on important legislation and national emergencies. The president also used special sessions of the Senate as his favorite platform for policy pronouncements. By the end of his tenure in the White House, Wilson had appeared before Congress more often than any president before or since. On the whole Wilson gave public speeches much more frequently than any of his predecessors, including Roosevelt.

THE FIRST WILSON PROGRAM

Wilson's original legislative program consisted of major acts in three areas: tariff revision, with income taxes attached; banking reform, which established a new reserve system; and antitrust regulation, which tightened and enlarged the existing laws and created a new regulatory agency. Tariff reform was the subject of Wilson's initial address to Congress. In tackling this issue at the outset, he was taking his easiest but also his riskiest shot. Tariff revision seemed an easy task because Democrats of nearly all persuasions favored a lower tariff, and because the House majority leader, Oscar Underwood of Alabama, had already steered a revision bill through that chamber in 1912. In 1913, Underwood quickly repeated his earlier feat and attached a graduated income-tax measure to the new revision bill. The House passed these new bills by two-to-one margins just a month after Wilson's speech. The risk for Wilson lay in the Senate, the graveyard for previous efforts at tariff reform. History appeared ready to repeat itself once more as protectionist lobbyists and their senatorial allies stood poised to attach crippling amendments to the House bill.

It was the perfect occasion for Wilson to stage a public appeal. In a statement to the press on May 26, 1913, the president denounced "so insidious a lobby" for pouring out vast sums of money and for exerting stealthy influence "to overcome the interests of the public for their own private profit." The ploy worked. Senator La Follette seized upon the statement to mount an investigation into tariff lobbying and the potential benefits of the proposed amendments for his colleagues' holdings. With the public pressure on, senatorial revisionists succeeded in lowering rates still further, and the final act, known as the Underwood-Simmons Tariff, passed the Senate by a comfortable margin in September 1913. The final version lowered rates by an average of 24 to 26 percent. The accompanying income tax went further than Wilson had originally wanted. It affected mainly wealthy Americans, starting at one percent for annual earnings of $20,000, and rising by steps to six percent for earnings above $50,000. The victory tasted particularly sweet to Wilson because he had succeeded where his predecessors had failed

"A NEAR-FUTURIST PAINTING BY PRESIDENT WILSON, ON THE SUBJECT OF THE TARIFF." A clever play on Duchamp's Nude Descending a Staircase, *depicting Wilson as a "near-futurist" artist.*

or feared to tread. Better still, it began to rid the Democrats of their reputation for ignorance and unsoundness or, as they had once been labeled, "the organized incompetence of the country."

Wilson and his party asserted their newfound competence most strikingly in the second major legislative area, banking reform. Repeated waves of bank failures, particularly during the financial panic of 1907, together with the scarcity of credit and banking facilities in the South and West, had convinced nearly everyone concerned that a new reserve system was needed. The difficulty was that different interests wanted different arrangements in any new system. Wilson grasped the thorniness of banking reform when he confided to a friend, "There are almost as many judgments as there are men. To form a single plan and a single intention about it seems at times a task so various and so elusive that it is hard to keep one's heart from failing." Instead of losing heart Wilson met the situation with one of his deftest exercises of presidential leadership.

Earlier, as university president and governor, Wilson had generally practiced a collegial style of leadership. He had tried to avoid an overly dominant role and had allowed others to present initiatives and develop programs. Wilson continued the practice in the White House, especially on the issue of banking reform. Soon after the election, while still president-elect, Wilson had conferred with Congressman Carter Glass of Virginia, chairman of the House Banking Committee, and had given Glass the go-ahead to draft a bill in consultation with experts. In the process, two principal, crosscutting matters of contention became clear. One was whether the reserve system should be centralized or decentralized; the other was whether the system should operate as a government agency or as a private institution under some degree of government supervision. Four combinations were possible, and each had its ardent proponents. Glass and his committee, backed by Southern and Western bankers and businessmen, framed legislation for a decentralized private institution with minimal government oversight. Republican conservatives, backed by Wall Street and other established financiers, advocated a centralized private institution, like a European central bank. Some reformers favored a centralized government agency, while Bryanite Democrats and some Republican insurgents wanted a decentralized governmental system. Wilson's task was to reach a compromise among these plans, and then to make it work.

The president avoided commitments and let the situation reach a stalemate among the contending factions before he sought advice once more from the economic reformer Louis Brandeis, who argued strongly for government control. Wilson thereupon instructed Glass to revise the committee's bill, and on June 22, 1913, the president made his second appearance before Congress. Wilson demanded a reserve system comprising "the best and most accessible instruments of commerce and industry," which must remain free from the grip of monopoly. That meant that control of the new system "must be public, not private, must be vested in the Government itself, so that the banks may be the instruments, not the masters, of business and of individual enterprise and initiative." If Wilson's message sounded mixed, it was because he in effect embraced three of the four possible plans. The revised bill combined decentralization in the form of regional reserve banks, with centralized control by a supervisory board in Washington. There would also be a blend of private and public authority. The reserve banks would hold the deposits of private member banks and allow these banks to name some of the directors of the regional bodies, but the president would appoint most regional bank directors and all central board members. Only the advocates of a private central bank seemed left out, but in practice the New York reserve bank, which was dominated by Wall Street, came to overshadow the rest of the system within a few years.

The compromise Wilson had engineered still had to be sold to Congress. Conflict persisted in the House, and the president called upon Secretary of State Bryan several times to bring around his recalcitrant followers, who still yearned to cut private bankers out of the system altogether. Once the House passed the bill in September an equally protracted wrangle ensued in the Senate, where conservatives attempted to weaken government control of the proposed banking system. At the same time some reformers, most prominently La Follette, denounced the bill as a sell-out to "the interests." Wilson finally won through patience, firmness, and old-fashioned horse-trading.

At last, on December 19, 1913, the Senate passed the Federal Reserve Act, Wilson's biggest single legislative monument. It created the Federal Reserve System, with a publicly appointed board of governors who were empowered to oversee and veto the interest rates charged by the regional reserve banks. This central control was intended to introduce order and stability into the American banking system, thereby preventing panics or at least containing the damage caused by economic downturns. The regional banks actually administered the funds in the system and lent them to individual banks. This regional autonomy was intended to make credit more readily available in all regions of the country, especially the South and West, and to liberate smaller banks from control by Wall Street and other metropolitan financial institutions. The Federal Reserve System became the Wilson administration's most important and, though it was substantially changed in the 1930s, most lasting contribution to America's government and economy.

The third legislative area, the antitrust issue, presented similar problems of technical complexity and competing interests. Wilson held off

"Whipt." A comment in the St. Louis Star on passage of the Federal Reserve Act, 1913.

"The Squealers." An approving view of Wilson's antitrust initiatives, from the Harrisburg Patriot, *1914.*

consideration of antitrust matters until the end of 1913 in order to keep the agenda clear for banking reform. He also wanted once more to let the main points of contention fully emerge before he made any commitments. In January 1914 the president made his fifth appearance in less than a year before a joint session of Congress. In urging new antitrust legislation, Wilson echoed his 1912 campaign theme of bringing "new men, new energies, a new spirit of initiative into the management of our great business enterprises." He called specifically for a two-pronged attack on the trusts: a more detailed antitrust statute, and a new regulatory agency that would extend to antitrust problems the kind of supervision already exercised over transportation by the ICC.

The new antitrust law proved suprisingly easy to draft and, despite lengthy debates, to pass. The only really controversial sections of the law, which came to be called the Clayton Antitrust Act, involved its application to labor unions. In 1894 the Supreme Court had declared unions subject to the Sherman Act's ban on restraint of trade, and thereby subject to federal court injunctions which severely hampered their ability to strike. Ever since, Gompers and the AFL had been lobbying for exemption of labor organizations from antitrust laws. Wilson personally sympathized with the unions, but he believed that their demands raised legal difficulties. As a result, he agreed to press Congress only for a partial exemption from the antitrust laws. The new law declared that unions should not be "construed to be illegal combinations in restraint of trade," and it also forbade federal courts from issuing injunctions against striking unions "unless necessary to prevent irreparable injury to property." Those gestures earned Wilson almost pathetic gratitude from Gompers and effusive praise from the AFL for having made the Clayton Act "Labor's Magna Charta." The exemption marked a further milestone in the entente that Bryan had initiated between unions and the Democrats.

The Clayton Act, which received final congressional approval in October 1914, differed from its predecessor, the Sherman Act, in being a lengthy, detailed, tightly drafted statute that specified prohibited business practices, such as combinations to allocate and control markets, and prescribed penalties and remedies for infringements. It became another of the Wilson administration's lasting contributions to government and the economy. Though occasionally amended and variously interpreted, the Clayton Act remains in operation after three quarters of a century as the nation's basic antitrust law.

The new regulatory agency, which was called the Federal Trade Commission (FTC), proved harder to create. The proposed new agency would be empowered to hear complaints about unfair business practices under the antitrust laws, initiate its own investigations of suspect dealings, and issue cease-and-desist orders without having to go through lengthy litigation in the courts. Wilson had to overcome opposition from Bryanite Democrats and some Republican insurgents, who turned back on him his own campaign rhetoric against Roosevelt's support of regulation. They denounced the proposed agency as a covert servant of the trusts. There was poetic justice in the charge, but Wilson had really swung around to the regulatory approach for reasons that shared none of Roosevelt's fundamental approval of bigness. Instead he once again followed the advice of Brandeis, who argued that an expert regulatory commission could do a better job than the courts in curbing the trusts, because it could stay abreast of constantly changing technological and business conditions. What he wanted, Wilson told one Democratic senator, "is elasticity without real indefiniteness, so that we may adjust our regulation to actual conditions, local as well as national." Wilson did agree with his great rival, however, in viewing the antitrust issue as politically vital. Their party could not, he warned another Democratic senator, "afford to show the least hesitation or lack of courage on this point which is going to be the point of attack during the 1914 campaign, as Mr. Roosevelt so kindly reminded us."

Through the summer and fall of 1914 as Wilson pushed the bill to establish the FTC, he sustained attacks not only from die-hard anti-trusters but also from Roosevelt and some Progressives, who alleged that he did not sincerely embrace regulation. Their charges had some merit. In August 1914 Wilson allowed conservative senators to weaken the FTC's powers by permitting businesses to appeal its decrees in the courts under broad powers of judicial review. Later Wilson appointed commissioners who did not pursue vigorous antitrust policies. But his acquiescence in weakening the new agency did not spring from lack of commitment to the regulatory approach. Rather, he was suffering from twin distractions—the outbreak of World War I and his wife's death—both of which also occurred in August 1914. As it was, even though the FTC disappointed some of its more ardent advocates, it became yet another lasting feature of American government.

In all, Wilson staged a stunning performance during his first year-and-a-half in office. He had passed more legislation through Congress in a shorter time than any previous president. It was a triumph for Wilson's notion of party leadership, though circumstances also helped him along in 1913 and 1914. Partly because his party had regained power after sixteen years in opposition, all the Democratic leaders in Congress, including House Speaker Champ Clark and Majority Leader Underwood, were anxious to cooperate in making his administration a success. Moreover the Republican-Progressive split in 1912 had swept a horde of unusually cooperative freshman Democrats into the House. Finally, Wilson had Bryan at his side. The Commoner's undisputed standing as party spokesman on major issues and his loyal factional following offered repeated assistance at critical junctures. A severe test of Wilson's party leadership would come when and if he no longer enjoyed either such a big majority in the House or Bryan's patronage.

Wilson's exclusive, openly acknowledged partisanship carried a price, however, and the president's political triumphs soon began to include some sour notes. Ideologically sympathetic Republicans and Progressives were able to save face only by adopting Roosevelt's earlier criticism of Wilson as a sham reformer. They lambasted Wilson for not going further to push such measures as woman suffrage, abolition of child labor, aid to agriculture, and stronger pro-union actions. At first blush the charges seemed to ring true. Wilson turned down demands from some Democrats as well as opposition leaders to endorse additional reform measures. The only exception was an act pushed by La Follette to regulate safety and working conditions among merchant seamen. Moved by the testimony from union leaders about the low pay, dangerous work, and near absolute subservience of sailors in the merchant marine, the Wisconsin senator persuaded the president to support the reform measure, which passed Congress as the La Follette Seamen's Act in February 1915. But Wilson refused to back further reform legislation for tactical, not ideological reasons. He personally favored most of those measures, but believed that he had gotten everything he could out of Congress. Also, rather like Roosevelt during his first term, Wilson wanted to see which way the political winds were blowing in the mid-term congressional elections.

Wilson's type of leadership, successful though it was in passing needed legislation, carried another price that troubled the president. Wilson was painfully aware that he did not share Roosevelt's instinct for self-dramatization, nor his hold on the popular imagination. In March 1914 Wilson publicly bemoaned false impressions of him as "a cold and removed person who has a thinking machine inside," saying instead that he felt "like a fire from a far from extinct volcano." And a few months later, he publicly confessed regret "that I did not myself have a first name that yielded to the process" of a nickname. If only people could have called him "Woody" or "Tommy," the way they had called his predecessor "Teddy." Yet something deep within Wilson made him guard his personal and family privacy. He never could indulge in the expansive promotion of personality and kin that seemed second nature to Roosevelt. Solitariness lay at the heart of Woodrow Wilson's political personality. At many junctures, the ability to detach himself from the hurly-burly of politics and to reflect amid the welter of conflicting advice and pressures proved one of his greatest strengths. At other times, Wilson's excessive reliance on his own judgment and difficulty in dealing with subordinates and opponents would become a severe liability.

NEW FREEDOM FOR WHOM?

Wilson's inability to call forth and sustain popular enthusiasm for his positions left him vulnerable to the turmoil that continued to bubble over from domestic social sources. The cultural conflict between Protestants and Catholics, "natives" and ethnics over such matters as prohibition, woman suffrage, and immigration restriction sharpened further during his first term. After Taft had vetoed the literacy-test bill passed in 1912, restrictionists redoubled their efforts in the next Congress. A more comprehensive measure to regulate immigration, which again included the literacy test, won in the House in February 1914, by the two-thirds margin of 253 to 126. In January 1915 the Senate passed this bill by an even larger margin, 50 to 7. Wilson vetoed this legislation, and the House once more narrowly failed to override the veto. By then, however, the issue had been altered by the outbreak of World War I. The carnage in Europe and the specter of hordes of refugees added a new dimension and fresh passion to the issue. Restrictionist organizations and the AFL redoubled their efforts, and in 1916 huge majorities in both houses repassed a bill requiring all adult immigrants to pass literacy tests in their native languages. In February 1917 they overrode Wilson's veto. It was the first step toward ending large-scale immigration from Europe.

Prohibitionists and woman suffragists were meanwhile pursuing their goals at the state level and through constitutional amendments, which could not help stirring the political pot. The 1914 elections brought the first Prohibitionist to Congress and witnessed extensive fallout from "wet" versus "dry" fights within the established parties. For example, that year the Democrats lost gubernatorial and senatorial contests in Ohio in part because their attempts to evade the issue of statewide prohibition had angered both supporters and opponents. The Republicans suffered the same fate in Ohio two years later, again partly on the same grounds. More generally, in the Northeast and Midwest, agitation over immigration restriction and prohibition heightened tensions between small-town and rural "native" Protestants on one side and mostly Catholic urban ethnics on the other. These issues still did not occupy the center of the political stage, but they were moving inexorably into more prominence, along with the drive for woman suffrage, which was so often linked to prohibition by both supporters and opponents.

The broader, feminist assault on women's roles in both the workplace and the family was making itself felt in some conspicuous ways. The biggest expansion of women's participation in the work force occurred between 1900 and 1910, when their share of the total rose from 23.5 to 28.1 percent. The numbers of working women kept growing after 1910, although the percentage of women employed remained virtually unchanged over the next twenty years. What changed most during these years were the kinds of jobs they held and the social prestige attached to their work. The feminization of schoolteaching advanced from the primary grades into secondary schools. More and more women became salesclerks in stores and secretaries in offices. Women college graduates already dominated the field of social work, and they were

Julia Lathrop.

moving into civil-service positions. In 1910, when President Taft appointed Julia Lathrop director of the newly established Federal Children's Bureau, she became the first woman to head a federal agency. Not everyone, male or female, welcomed these new entrants into white-collar and other types of employment. Magazines regularly featured articles that cried alarm about threats to the home and decried, in the words of a woman novelist in 1910, the young woman "with surprisingly bad manners" who insisted upon earning "her own living . . . won't go to church" and flaunted her "views upon marriage and the birth-rate, . . . while her mother blushed with embarrassment."

It was unclear whether the feminists really made much headway in this war of words and ideas about woman's proper "place," but there were unmistakable changes in women's appearance and behavior. Charles Dana Gibson's drawings of the "Gibson Girl" and her real-life embodiments, most notably Alice Roosevelt, had already furnished women at the turn of the century with a new ideal of physical vigor and personal independence. Advertisements in women's magazines increasingly pictured women driving cars, and their appeals to the "outdoor girl" were a sharp contrast to earlier pale, indolent images of submissive femininity. After 1910 freer conduct advanced still further.

The daring dancer Isadora Duncan promoted unfettered approaches to art and life, discarding classical ballet's restraints by dancing in bare feet and abbreviated tunics modeled after classical Greek costumes. She scorned marriage, bore children out of wedlock, and embraced radical politics. Other dancers, such as Ruth St. Denis, wore Oriental costumes, drew inspiration from Asian art forms, and founded the modern dance movement. Their innovations found a ready platform in the women's colleges. Their loose, flowing costumes and celebration of the female body accelerated the movement of women's fashions away from binding corsets and elaborate overdressing. The most conspicuous signs of change in appearance were rising skirt lengths, which reached mid-calf by 1915. Likewise, short, bobbed hair, which made its first appearance in 1912, became the rage within two years.

The most widespread influences toward newer feminine fashions and behavior emanated from motion pictures. "Movie" stars, both male and female, became popular idols, often as much for their off-screen lives as for their acting, although gossip about actors' and actresses' wild ways was not yet as widespread as it would later become. The exquisite, heart-shaped faces, full lips, and trim figures of Lillian Gish and Mary Pickford made American women more beauty conscious. Ordinary young and not-so-young women did more than dream of being

After 1910 it became more acceptable for women to smoke in public.

Margaret Sanger (left), an early advocate of birth control.

like their idols; they spent millions of dollars to buy dresses like theirs and to use cosmetics like theirs. Earlier, lipstick and face powders were worn largely by stage actresses, who were barely respectable at best, and prostitutes. After 1910 the social stigma surrounding make-up vanished, and cosmetics became a big business.

Before this period it was considered "the gesture of the brothel" for a woman to smoke, but after 1910, smoking became fashionable with both sexes. Some society women, such as the daughter of Senator Henry Cabot Lodge, smoked in public. Such behavior encountered fierce resistance from the heads of women's colleges and other guardians of female respectability. Behind their concerns about smoking, dress, and the influence of movie stars or other "scandalous" women lay the scarcely veiled matter of female sexuality. Older taboos and reticence about sex were plainly under attack. Books, magazines, stories, plays, and—ever-so-gingerly—movies depicted a franker recognition of sex. The titles of magazine articles in 1913 and 1914 proclaimed that "Sex O'Clock in America" had struck, and celebrated "The Repeal of Reticence." A 1916 popular song entitled "A Dangerous Girl" contained such lyrics

as "You dare me, you scare me, and still I like you more each day . . .
you've got a dangerous way."

To some, the most disturbing element of all in these changes was
that a few women were also advocating birth control, mainly through
the use of condoms. Cities and states passed anti-contraceptive laws,
which made not only the sale of condoms but also the dissemination
of information about methods of birth control illegal. Those laws did
not deter Margaret Sanger, a thirty-year-old New York nurse, from
starting the work in 1914 that later led to the founding of the American
Birth Control League. Two years later Sanger underwent the first of
many arrests for passing out birth-control information. "Regardless of
the outcome," she declared, "I shall continue my work, supported by
thousands of men and women throughout the country." Sanger was as
good as her word, and in 1916 she opened the first public clinic to
advise on birth control and distribute contraceptive devices. American
women were clearly seeking and finding varieties of "new freedom"
during the second decade of the twentieth century.

Black Americans, by contrast, found little new freedom, and they
seemed to be losing old opportunities. W. E. B. Du Bois, William Monroe
Trotter, and fellow activists quickly regretted their support of Wilson
in 1912. The new Democratic administration, with its strong white
Southern component, took away government jobs hitherto held by blacks
and gave them to whites. Wilson's two terms witnessed a decline in the
percentage of federal government positions that went to blacks, although
the number of blacks so employed increased modestly, thanks to the
overall growth of government, especially during World War I. Nor would
that situation improve when the Republicans regained power in the
1920s. Blacks' share of federal employment would not rise for another
thirty years.

In 1913 and 1914 Southern demagogues, particulary Senator Vardaman of Mississippi, lambasted Wilson for appointing two blacks to
the positions of minister to Haiti and register of deeds for the District
of Columbia. The president appeased those Southern critics when he
permitted several Cabinet members to announce plans to introduce
segregated facilities and employment into their departments. These
officials intended to set up separate dining facilities and restrooms for
black and white employees and to have them work, for the most part,
in separate rooms. They were particularly concerned about stamping
out all cases of blacks supervising whites.

Black leaders and sympathetic Northern whites fought hard and, to
an extent, successfully against these moves. The NAACP met the attempt

to segregate parts of the federal government with a campaign of protest in the Northern press that denounced these moves as unfair and discriminatory. Some politicians, most notably Senator La Follette, championed the black government workers' cause and excoriated the administration for its regressive conduct. The outcries sufficed to get the segregation plans shelved, but Trotter and a delegation of black leaders bearded Wilson himself at a White House meeting in November 1914. "Have you a 'new freedom' for white Americans," Trotter asked the president, "and a new slavery for 'your Afro-American fellow citizens?' God forbid!" Infuriated, Wilson retorted, "You have spoiled the whole cause for which you came," and dismissed the visitors. He soon repented his response, privately confessing, "When the negro delegate threatened me, I was damn fool enough to lose my temper and to point to the door." Yet, despite rescinding the segregation orders, Wilson made no public apologies to blacks, nor did he evidently entertain any regrets about the substance, if not the implementation, of the policy.

Seven months later the NAACP won another battle when the Supreme Court unanimously struck down Oklahoma's grandfather clause in *Guinn v. the United States.* These clauses, which Southern and Border states had passed along with their disenfranchisement measures in the 1890s and early 1900s, were blatantly discriminatory loopholes in supposedly impartial literacy tests. Illiterates whose grandfathers had voted before 1866 were exempted from taking literacy tests. Since only whites could have voted in these states before 1866, the clauses plainly violated the Fifteenth Amendment's ban on racial tests for voting. The Wilson administration's solicitor general, John W. Davis, argued the federal government's case against the Oklahoma law on the narrow ground of its violation of the Fifteenth Amendment. The NAACP, in an *amicus curiae* brief, raised the broader ground of the law's violation of the "equal protection" clause of the Fourteenth Amendment. The Court's decision held to the government's ground, and it would not be until the 1930s that the Supreme Court would apply the Fourteenth Amendment to cases of social discrimination. For black Americans, this legal victory was at once pyrrhic and portentous. Oklahoma immediately passed another law that re-registered previously eligible whites but effectively barred blacks from voting. Still, the *Guinn* case pointed down the long road of constitutional challenge that would bring the downfall of segregation nearly four decades later.

The retreat from government segregation and the Supreme Court decision in the *Guinn* case offered just about the only glimmers of hope for black Americans in 1915. That year the former muckraker Ray Stannard Baker published a magazine article entitled, "Gathering Clouds along the Color Line," and its images of gloom and storm aptly described race relations at the middle of the decade. With Booker T. Washington's death in November 1915, blacks lost their most influential leader among whites and, his critics notwithstanding, the one who commanded the broadest following among his own people. Washington was at least able to die peacefully in bed. Seventy-nine other black Americans met violent deaths at the hands of lynch mobs during 1915, which marked the peak for lynchings, black and white, during the twentieth century. Worse still, organized anti-Negro sentiment received a boost when a band of white Georgians burned crosses at Stone Mountain on a summer night in 1915. They were founding the twentieth-century reincarnation of the Ku Klux Klan. These latter-day Klansmen had drawn their inspiration from D. W. Griffith's immensely popular 1915 film, *The Birth of a Nation*, which portrayed the Klan of Reconstruction times as an heroic, romantic organization. The new Ku Klux Klan offered an ironic tribute to the cultural impact of the movies.

Hostile as these sheeted crusaders were toward blacks, this Klan would devote more attention to combating "alien" menaces among whites, principally from Jews, Catholics, immigrants, and modernists. The most publicized lynching in the South during 1915 had as its victim not a

A Ku Klux Klan rally, 1915.

black man but a Jew. This was the infamous case of Leo Frank, a factory owner in Atlanta, Georgia, who in 1914 had been convicted for the rape and murder of one of his employees, a 14-year-old white girl named Mary Phagan. Frank's trial had taken place with mobs screaming outside the Atlanta courtroom and with cries for his blood in the press, especially from the veteran racist demagogue and ex-Populist Tom Watson. When the governor of Georgia commuted Frank's death sentence in June 1915, Watson howled, "Our grand old Empire State has been raped!" He demanded for Frank "the same thing that we give to negro rapists." Two months later a disciplined band of armed men abducted Frank from the state penitentiary and hanged him. The rope and the victim's clothing became prized souvenirs. More than 15,000 people flocked to view the corpse.

Forty-five other whites met their deaths at the hands of lynch mobs in 1915. Nearly all of these lynchings occurred in connection with labor troubles in the West. IWW organizers accused of committing violence were the victims in most of these lynchings. Strikers and their families also made up the bulk of the casualties in such incidents as the massacre at Ludlow, Colorado, in April 1914. Thirteen people, all children and wives of IWW strikers, were killed in a raid on a tent colony by private police. Federal troops had to be called in to restore order. But the Wobblies and their supporters were not always innocent victims; they carried out their share of the dynamiting and shooting. Their most celebrated martyr, Joe Hill, was executed by a Utah firing squad in 1915, after being tried for murder, under conditions inflamed by hostile publicity. Still, Hill had most likely committed the killings for which he was convicted, as well as others.

Radicalism flourished in the midst of the violence and attempts at repression in the West. In 1914 a new agrarian protest organization, the Non-Partisan League (NPL), which eschewed both major parties, sprang up among embittered wheat farmers on the Great Plains. The NPL demanded new forms of government intervention on behalf of agriculture in the form of direct aid to farmers, and higher taxes and stricter regulation of big business. The largest geographical region of the country, the West, was clearly seething with social and political conflict as Wilson's New Freedom moved forward and World War I erupted in Europe.

A broader source of public disquiet lay in the state of the economy in 1914. A business downturn had begun late in 1913, evidently spurred by credit restrictions and fears of war in Europe. The faltering economy soon plunged the United States into the worst depression since

Funeral for Joe Hill, Chicago, Illinois, November 1915.

the 1890s. With the new Federal Reserve system not yet in place, little could be done to counteract contractions of credit or shore up faltering banks. Business failures mounted rapidly, and industrial production fell. Job losses hit cities and heavy industries such as coal and steel particularly hard. Massachusetts unions found that nearly a fifth of their members were unemployed at the end of 1914. Other surveys found comparable levels of unemployment in most major industries in the Northeast and Midwest.

The war in Europe came at first as an additional curse, but it eventually brought salvation to the American economy. The war's sudden outbreak in August 1914 fomented financial panic and disrupted international trade. The rapid mobilization of armies as war enveloped first Austria-Hungary and Russia, then Germany and France, and finally Great Britain and Turkey, along with smaller nations, threw the world's economies into a tailspin. With its vast naval power, Britain's entry into the war swept the ships of enemy nations from the seas, hurting their trading partners among the neutral nations. Conditions worsened in the United States during the fall of 1914, especially in export-oriented sectors such as cotton growing. By the spring of 1915, however, the situation had turned around dramatically. War orders from across the Atlantic not only arrested America's slide into depression, but also began to fuel an economic boom that would last for the rest of the decade.

REFORMERS AT A CROSSROADS

Social tensions, cultural conflicts, political unrest, and economic hardship formed the background to the congressional elections in 1914, which offered the first tests of public reaction to Wilson and the Democrats. Although local conditions affected the results as always, the political direction was unmistakable. The tide that had swept reformers upward for nearly a decade had crested and was ebbing fast. Nearly everywhere Republican conservatives proved the biggest winners as they bounced back from their nadir of 1912. Primary results had forecast their resurgence. In Kansas, Senator Joseph Bristow, a veteran insurgent, lost his bid for renomination. In Wisconsin, factional strife between La Follette and rival Republican Progressives allowed the Stalwarts to prevail. Third-party Progressives fared even worse in November 1914. Albert Beveridge, Gifford Pinchot, James Garfield, and a host of leading Progressives went down to defeat at the hands of Republican conservatives. Only in California, where Hiram Johnson's organization had pre-empted the Republicans, did the Progressives hold their own. Even there a Democrat, albeit a progressive one, won the race for a Senate seat.

The president's party fared only slightly better. In the Northeast and Midwest, Democrats relinquished many of the House seats and governorships they had captured in 1910 and 1912. Their losses included Wilson's former gubernatorial chair in New Jersey. Overall, the Democrats lost sixty-one congressmen, reverting to the narrower margin they had held in the House after the 1910 elections. One ray of light did relieve the Democrats' gloom. It came from the West, where they added the senator from California, two governors, and held nearly all their House seats. Comparisons of the Western results in 1914 with those in 1912 made it evident that the Democrats had grabbed a big slice of the votes that had previously gone to Roosevelt and the Progressives. Clear sectional contrasts highlighted the 1914 results. The South remained as stolidly Democratic as ever, while the Northeast and Midwest appeared on the way back to their traditionally conservative Republican allegiances. But the West appeared to be up for grabs. At least that was how Wilson read the returns. He took "solid satisfaction," he told a friend, from the Democrats' showing in the West, "the real heart of America. . . . We have had a change of venue. A different part of America now decides, not the part of America which has usually arrogated to itself a selfish leadership and patronage of the rest."

Others interpreted the results of the 1914 elections differently. Republican conservatives took gleeful satisfaction in their victories. "We have squeezed Roosevelt out," Taft exulted to a friend, "and we can attend to the Democrats in two years." Conservatives also felt relieved and gratified at how well they did in the newly adopted state primaries and popular elections of senators. In Pennsylvania, Boies Penrose, who handily beat both Gifford Pinchot and A. Mitchell Palmer, a respected Democratic congressman who later entered Wilson's cabinet, took special delight in his re-election. He had been wrong to oppose primaries and the Seventeenth Amendment, Penrose chortled: "I thought they were going to be bad, but they were wonderful. In Pennsylvania a grateful people has just sent me back to the Senate when no Republican legislature would have dared to re-elect me." Another Republican conservative who had won a senatorial contest in 1914 was Ohio's Warren G. Harding, who soon emerged as a comer in the party. The 1914 elections appeared to have vindicated the Republican conservatives' earlier strategy. "Owning the wreckage" of the Republican party seemed well worth the price they had paid in 1912.

Theodore Roosevelt read the results of the 1914 elections in the same way as his conservative foes. "The fundamental trouble was that the country was sick and tired of reform," he told the journalist William Allen White. Thanks to the ongoing depression, people were feeling "the pinch of poverty; they were suffering from hard times. They wanted prosperity and compared with this they did not give a rap for social justice or industrial justice or clean politics or decency in public life." Roosevelt was disappointed with the Progressive defeats, but beyond that he was growing increasingly disenchanted himself with the Progressive party. In part this stemmed from his own shift in concern from domestic reform to foreign affairs. More important, his 1912 defeat had revived Roosevelt's long-standing preference for practical politics over popular agitation and crusading programs. Well before the outbreak of war and the 1914 elections, Roosevelt was again grumbling about the irresponsible radicalism of many Progressives, whom he publicly dubbed the "lunatic fringe." By the beginning of 1915, the Progressive captain was anxious to abandon ship.

Wilson bid openly to offer Progressives an alternative vessel. He regarded Democratic gains in the West as pivotal, and he wanted to extend them to the rest of the country. When newspapermen pressed the president for public comments on the 1914 elections, he answered, "My comment will, I hope, be the action of the next two years." Wilson delivered with major action on the reform front. The new Congress, which did not convene until December 1915, found itself presented with a legislative agenda that rivaled Wilson's initial program. This second installment of the New Freedom included no single measures to match the trio of monumental accomplishments of 1913 and 1914, but it did contain a greater number of specific legislative acts that added up to equally significant governmental departures.

The New Freedom program that Wilson pushed through Congress between January and September 1916 included seven pieces of important reform legislation. One extended the executive role in tariff making by establishing a Tariff Commission. The commission had only advisory powers, but its establishment represented a further incursion of administrative-style expertise into congressional tariff making. Another new agency established in 1916 was the Shipping Board, which exercised regulatory authority over passenger and freight rates for the merchant marine. Both shippers and the carriers themselves had sought government regulation in order to try to revive a dying industry. The Rural Credits Act of 1916 established the first outright federal loan program to any group of citizens. It answered the generation-old demand of Bryanite Democrats for credit that would give farmers financial leeway to pay storage fees and market their crops when they chose, and to buy fertilizers and farm implements without having to pay high interest rates to the banks. Another law enacted in 1916 crowned the long drive by social workers, reformers, and unions to ban child labor on any manufactured product sold in interstate commerce. This act was later struck down by the Supreme Court. Yet another statute required workmen's compensation for injuries and illnesses incurred on all work done under government contract. Reformers hailed this measure as a further step toward a comprehensive statute that would require workmen's compensation for all businesses engaged in interstate commerce.

The two most politically potent pieces of legislation passed in 1916 concerned taxation and labor relations. Led in the Senate by La Follette and in the House by Claude Kitchin of North Carolina, Underwood's successor as the Democrats' majority leader and chairman of the Ways and Means Committee, a determined group of insurgent Republicans and Bryanite Democrats doubled the tax rates on incomes over $5,000 to two percent, imposed a new ten percent surcharge on incomes over $40,000, and enacted inheritance taxes ranging from one percent on $50,000 estates to five percent on estates over $450,000. Much of the initiative for the taxes came from critics of increased military spending, who wanted to make the wealthy and big businesses pay for the build-up, and who also levied stiff duties on the munitions industry. Advocates of the new taxes openly boasted about "making the rich pay," while Southerners and Westerners conceded that the revenue measure would make the Northeast and Midwest bear heavier tax burdens. President Wilson approved the tax bill, but he played little part in its passage.

The new labor law, by contrast, came almost entirely on his initiative. At the end of August 1916 Wilson appeared before Congress to urge enactment of a statute requiring an eight-hour day for interstate railroad workers. Railroad workers typically put in a ten-hour day without overtime, and their unions were threatening a nation-wide strike in the face of management's adamant refusal to grant their demands. Wilson lobbied hard to get Congress to enact the first federal legislation regulating the number of hours that private employees worked. On August 31, 1916, the House passed the bill easily by a vote of 239 to 56, but Republican senators opposed the bill as a sell-out to special interests. Finally, the Senate approved the measure, which was known as the Adamson Act, by a vote of 43 to 28, and the president signed it into law that same night. Wilson had averted a paralyzing strike and fulfilled a goal of organized labor that dated back to the 1880s.

Louis Brandeis.

Wilson's hardest lobbying campaign on Capitol Hill in 1916 was not an effort to pass legislation, but to get the Senate to confirm an appointment. On January 28 he nominated the Boston attorney and his economic advisor Louis Brandeis to a vacancy on the Supreme Court. Wilson had previously favored Brandeis for appointments as attorney-general, and to an earlier Supreme Court vacancy; the president had allowed himself to be talked out of both. Wilson's 1916 nomination of Brandeis engendered opposition that was both organized and prestigious. Leaders of the bar, including law-school deans, the president of Harvard, and ex-president Taft all urged the Senate to reject the nomination. Their opposition probably reflected some covert, even perhaps unconscious anti-Semitism, since Brandeis was the first Jew to be proposed for the Supreme Court. The openly stated reasons for opposition revolved around his highly visible, often controversial stands against big business and in favor of promoting competition. Skillful behind-the-scenes lobbying by the president and the nominee himself finally secured Brandeis's confirmation on June 1, 1916, by a vote of 47 to 22.

Wilson's success in passing this second set of New Freedom measures was an even more impressive legislative achievement than the first, for Wilson now faced bigger distractions and a more tangled politics. Troubles in Mexico had occupied much of his attention in 1913 and 1914, but foreign affairs had become far more pressing by 1916 because of both the world war and renewed Mexican difficulties. The Democrats' shrunken margin in the House did not offer as great an obstacle to passing legislation as some had feared. Good party discipline, heightened by the upcoming presidential and congressional elections, helped keep Democratic congressmen in line. But a truly formidable obstacle to party discipline and legislative accomplishment lay in the defection of William Jennings Bryan, who in June 1915 had resigned as secretary of state in protest over Wilson's policies toward the European beligerents. The Commoner opposed Wilson on issues related to the war and on the military and naval programs that the president was also pushing through Congress. Wilson not only had to get domestic and defense legislation enacted in 1916, he also had to break Bryan's generation-old sway over Democrats. It was Wilson's finest hour as a party leader.

As before, Wilson's strong reliance on his party incurred political costs, including the alienation of Republican insurgents who found themselves caught between the rising conservatism of their own party and Wilson's pre-emption of most of the reforms they advocated. A few of them, most conspicuously George Norris of Nebraska, who had been elected to the Senate in 1912, and the redoubtable Robert La Follette, supported reform measures as strongly as ever. But they were the exceptions as most of the insurgents lined up alongside their conservative party brethren in opposition. Some justified their actions with tortuous arguments in which they continued to dismiss Wilson as a false prophet of reform. There emerged in 1916 a sharper division between the two major parties in Congress, and nothing showed the alignment more clearly than the Senate vote in June on Brandeis's nomination to the Supreme Court. Just one Democrat broke ranks to vote against Brandeis. Just two other Republicans joined La Follette, Norris, and Miles Poindexter, the Senate's lone Progressive, to furnish the only non-Democratic votes for him.

As Poindexter's vote indicated, the Progressives found their choices harder still. By 1916 Roosevelt had decided to scuttle the party, if necessary, in order to join a united front against Wilson. Some observers, particularly Republican conservatives, suspected that the ex-president was conspiring to gain their party's nomination for himself. But grounds for the suspicion were weak, and Republican leaders honored his desire to bury the hatchet by not demanding abject terms of surrender. When their convention met in Chicago in June 1916, the presidential nomination fell almost by default to Charles Evans Hughes, a former governor of New York, moderate reformer, and proven campaigner. Hughes's greatest asset in 1916 was that as a justice of the Supreme Court since 1910 he had taken no part in the strife of 1912 and had taken no stands on any recent issues. This made it easy for erstwhile Progressives to return to the party. The Republican platform was likewise designed to be broadly palatable. It avoided mention of controversial domestic issues and flayed Wilson for all manner of failings.

Roosevelt welcomed the chance to return to the Republican party. He repeatedly refused to accept the nomination that was offered him by the Progressives, who met in Chicago at the same time as the Republicans. He declined to attend the Progressive convention, and sent a public telegram in which he suggested the conservative Henry Cabot Lodge as his choice for the Progressive party's nomination. As slavishly as most Progressives worshiped Roosevelt, they could not help feeling betrayed. Some delegates muttered "apostate" and "running out" as his final telegram of refusal was read to them. The convention broke up without nominating anyone and with most party members uncertain about where to turn. Few Progressives shared either Roosevelt's detestation for Wilson, or his all-consuming concern with foreign affairs. Most of them remained committed to domestic reform, and some, such as the *New Republic* editors Herbert Croly and Walter Lippmann, had publicly begun to reconsider their earlier rejections of Wilson and the Democrats.

Wilson did everything he could to make it easy for Progressives to choose to follow him. He drafted the platform that the Democrats adopted almost verbatim at their convention in June 1916. It contained long recitations of the administration's legislative achievements, pledges of further reform, and statements about governmental responsibility for social and economic welfare. Later Wilson personally endorsed the women's suffrage amendment, partly in an effort to gain votes from women in the states where they had won the vote, and partly out of newfound conviction. Wilson frequently referred to his party as the "Progressive Democrats," and he made sure that campaign literature stressed how his administration had enacted virtually every plank in the 1912 Progressive platform. Wilson's more or less open courtship of Roosevelt's followers later led some historians to argue that in 1916, under the spur of the political necessity to attract Progressive voters, he had converted from the New Freedom to the New Nationalism. It was true that he wanted to win, and he certainly did calculate how to woo voters, but Wilson underwent no ideological conversion in 1916. He readily admitted that he was making tactical changes, and none of Wilson's moves in 1916 betokened acceptance of Roosevelt's fundamental beliefs in collective bigness or devotion to national ideals that transcended self-interest. In fact, Wilson sensed the differences between Roosevelt and his Progressive followers, and he was betting that what they really wanted was not the New Nationalism but a full-blown, updated edition of the New Freedom.

Much of the outcome of the 1916 election would turn on the correctness of Wilson's assessment and his skill in appealing to erstwhile opponents. If nothing else, he had shifted the terms of debate to what he believed were highly favorable grounds for himself. With Roosevelt's unwitting assistance, Wilson had identified his party and administration with the main reform issues of the last decade. At the same time, his opponents had come together, if not on conservative grounds, at least on grounds that de-emphasized domestic reform. That was just the way the Republican leaders, although not Roosevelt, wanted the election to be fought. After their comeback in 1914, they were more convinced than ever that recent reform issues were ephemeral and that economically based voter alignments in the Northeast and Midwest would complete the conservative restoration to power. In short, both sides were setting the stage for a possible re-enactment in 1916 of the kind of confrontation that had occurred twenty years before between Bryan and McKinley. Much had changed, however, since 1896, and the shadow cast by the terrible war that had been raging in Europe for two years had already fallen over the presidential contest and much of American life.

8

Armageddon Abroad

The Great War, as it was originally called, ended one hundred years of general peace in Europe. Its sudden outbreak, rapid spread, and unprecedented scope jarred the imagination. When a Serbian nationalist assassinated the heir to the Austro-Hungarian throne, Archduke Franz Ferdinand, at Sarajevo on June 28, 1914, it proved the pretext for the delicately balanced alliance system of the great powers to crumble into world-wide war. Austria-Hungary's moves against Serbia following the archduke's murder tripped a chain of connections that, by the beginning of August 1914, brought that empire, joined by Germany, into armed conflict against Russia and France. Germany's march across neutral Belgium toward France caused Great Britain to join France, Russia, and Serbia—the Allies—against Germany and Austria-Hungary—the Central Powers—which were soon joined by Bulgaria and Turkey. The war spread around the world as Japan, allied with Britain, seized Germany's Far Eastern possessions. The British Commonwealth countries of Canada, Australia, New Zealand, and South Africa likewise intervened, dispatching troops to Europe and the Middle East and conquering German colonies in Africa and the South Pacific. In 1915, Italy entered the war on the Allied side, as did Rumania in 1916.

The circumstances of its outbreak and rapid spread left most people groping for terms to comprehend the conflict. Natural catastrophe offered a ready frame of comparison. "This dreadful conflict of the nations came to most of us like lightning out of a clear sky," wrote one congressman. The novelist Henry James called it "this plunge into an abyss of blood and darkness." Theodore Roosevelt declared that the war was "on a giant scale like the disaster to the *Titanic.*" Most often, however, Americans invoked supernatural terms. In a country where Bible-reading Protestantism was the largest cultural influence, one word was inescapable. That was "Armageddon"—not the Old Testament battle that Roosevelt had invoked in 1912, but the vision from the book of Revelation of the kingdom-shattering miracle that would precede the Day of Judgment. "Now Armageddon has a real meaning," asserted *The World's Work.* ". . . If this be not Armageddon we shall never suffer the final death grip of nations."

DISTANT THUNDER

In their initial shock over World War I (as it would later be called), Americans resembled the Europeans who found themselves swept so swiftly from bright summer's peace into dreadful carnage. Yet attitudes on the two sides of the Atlantic differed in a critical respect. For Europeans the war quickly smashed the prevailing optimism and the faith in inevitable progress that had been sown by the scientific and industrial advances of the preceding century. For Americans the war was, in the phrase they coined later, "over there." It was a horrible calamity that was happening to somebody else, far away. This feeling of remoteness from the war resulted from more than geographical distance. To many Americans the conflict seemed to confirm age-old beliefs in a moral, political, and cultural dichotomy between a despotic, warlike Old World and a democratic, peaceful New World. When the Panama Canal opened in August 1914, the same month as the outbreak of World War I, the normally sober *New York Times* crowed editorially, "The European ideal bears its full fruit of ruin and savagery just at the moment when the American ideal lays before the world a great work of peace, goodwill and fair play."

Such gloating was not typical. Some Americans felt genuine sympathy for the people caught in the war, particularly women and children, and worked to aid the afflicted. Charitable organizations raised money and dispatched food, clothing, and medical supplies for civilian casualties, refugees, and orphans on both sides. The most impressive American effort to aid victims of the war was the massive enterprise that fed and clothed the entire population of German-occupied Belgium. The Committee for Relief of Belgium, which became renowned as the CRB, required delicate diplomacy to allay suspicions by the Allies

An American condemnation of the outbreak of war in Europe.

that the supplies might aid the Germans. The CRB also mounted prodigious feats of management to gather, transport, and distribute supplies to five million people. The wizard who performed these seeming
miracles was an American volunteer who was living in London in 1914.
He was an Iowa-born, California-educated engineer who had spent
most of his adult life in mining and business ventures around the world.
His name was Herbert Hoover, and he would ultimately outstrip any
other American in the fame and subsequent career that were opened
up to him by World War I.

During the first nine months after the war's outbreak in August 1914,
the prevailing public mood in America remained one of detachment,
sympathy, and interest, but no pressing concern. Few observers believed
that the United States would ever be drawn into the war. Secretary of
State Bryan, who had been promoting the peaceful settlement of disputes through treaties that committed adversaries to "cooling off"
periods, was determined to maintain good relations with all belligerents in order that the United States might be in a position to bring
them together for negotiations. President Wilson was less optimistic
about early prospects for peacemaking, but he shared Bryan's wish to
keep the United States in a properly detached, balanced, and friendly
posture toward the belligerents. In August 1914, Wilson issued a public statement in which he urged Americans to "be neutral in fact as
well as in name . . . impartial in thought as well as in action." He wanted
the United States to be a nation "which keeps herself fit and free to do

what is necessary and disinterested and truly serviceable for the peace of the world."

Some leaders, most notably Theodore Roosevelt, did think that the war's ramifications vitally affected the nation, and he tried to arouse popular awareness. President Wilson privately shared some of Roosevelt's views, but he confined his public statements to affirmations of impartiality. What little discussion there was in the press of America's relations with the warring nations continued to revolve around mediation possibilities. During these months Americans regarded the war, in the somewhat bitter words of the British ambassador, "as an immensely entertaining spectacle," or, as one jounalist later wrote, like a baseball game with themselves as fans in the bleachers.

Shortly after the 1912 election, Woodrow Wilson had casually remarked to a friend, "It would be an irony of fate if my administration had to deal chiefly with foreign affairs." Despite his long study of politics, Wilson had devoted little attention before he became president to foreign affairs. The single exception had come at the turn of the century, when Wilson had briefly become an ardent imperialist, strongly resembling Roosevelt, and had become an admirer and friendly acquaintance of Roosevelt. In the ten years preceding his election as president, however, Wilson had thought, written, and spoken little about foreign affairs.

Secretary of State Bryan, by contrast, had spoken and written extensively on both American foreign policy and international politics. He had maintained his anti-imperialist stance and had led the Democratic party's opposition to most of the diplomatic initiatives of Republican administrations, including Roosevelt's incursion in Panama, his protectorates in the Caribbean, and Taft's dollar diplomacy. More broadly, Bryan's evangelical Christian faith fed an idealism in international relations that bordered on pacifism. His most frequently delivered lecture after 1907 was "The Prince of Peace," which argued that all but a few wars in history—such as the American Revolution and the Civil War—had been wrong, and that leaders must heed the duty to promote peaceful means of settling disputes among nations. During the first year after becoming secretary of state in 1913, Bryan had devoted his greatest energies to negotiating his compulsory delay pacts, popularly called "cooling off treaties," with thirty other countries.

Despite their differences, Wilson and Bryan worked well together. In the Far East, the pair flaunted their idealism when they hastened to recognize the new republican government that overthrew the mori-

Bryan as secretary of state.

bund Ch'ing dynasty in China. By mid-April 1913, after only a month in office, the president was ready to extend diplomatic recognition to the newly installed regime in Peking in order to help it become "a peaceful and progressive republic," and Bryan agreed. On May 2 the United States became the first major power to recognize the Chinese Republic. It was the beginning of a Far Eastern diplomatic course that abandoned previous efforts by Roosevelt to appease Japan and reasserted the support for Chinese independence and territorial integrity embodied in John Hay's "open door" policy of 1899 and 1900. Wilson and Bryan also swiftly repudiated Taft's dollar diplomacy in China by withdrawing government support for a huge private loan by American banks. The administration clashed with Japan over further discrimination against Japanese immigrants on the West Coast, where Wilson and Bryan unsuccessfully tried to modify local segregation laws, and over the administration's support of China. The first year of the Wilson administration featured a trying, often fumbling shake-down cruise in foreign affairs.

The worst diplomatic fumbling occurred in Latin America, where the president and the secretary of state actually extended the previous Republican administrations' interventionist policies in the Caribbean and Central America. Bryan negotiated treaties with Nicaragua maintaining the American control over its financial affairs that had begun under the Taft administration, and he and Wilson sent the navy and the marines to establish protectorates in Haiti and the Dominican Republic. Contrary to later interpretations of their "missionary diplomacy"—which suggested that Wilson and Bryan became interventionists because of their professed idealism—their willingness to bully weaker nations in the Western Hemisphere stemmed more from an unwillingness to leave their neighbors alone.

But nowhere was American diplomacy more tortured than immediately south of the border. The most pressing diplomatic concern for the United States in 1914 was not the European war but Mexico, where political and social turmoil had followed the revolution that had overthrown the long-entrenched dictator Porfirio Díaz in 1911. President Taft's hands-off policy had prevented United States involvement, even though persistent violence threatened American lives and property in the region. In February 1913, Francisco Madero, Díaz's successor as president, was deposed and killed in a military coup led by General Victoriano Huerta, who proclaimed himself the new president. Taft, who was to leave office in less than a month, had declined to recognize Huerta and passed the problem on to his successor.

A brief investigation in the spring of 1913 sufficed to suggest not only Huerta's part in the murder of Madero but also the complicity, albeit unwittingly, of the American ambassador, Taft's appointee. The Wilson administration thereupon continued non-recognition and decided to cut off military aid to Huerta, instead aiding his opponents. Wilson's policy toward Mexico stood in contrast to his speedy recognition and encouragement of the new government in China, and it was the prelude to the most extensive effort yet mounted by any president to bring down a regime in the Western Hemisphere. Wilson believed his policy would foster democracy in Mexico and thwart pressure from American business interests, particularly Rockefeller's oil companies—which were pro-Huerta—to shore up an authoritarian regime. But Huerta proved a slippery, tenacious adversary, inasmuch as he refused to give way under American pressure and proved adept at arousing Mexican nationalism. "The apparent situation changes like quicksilver," Wilson complained privately in September 1913, his patience wearing thin.

That impatience, together with a growing yen for Roosevelt-style action, led Wilson to try to weaken Huerta through military intervention at Veracruz in April 1914. A complicated, petty quarrel erupted over whether Mexican troops in Tampico and Veracruz should salute the Stars and Stripes when American naval vessels, which were on

A comment on Wilson's policies in Mexico, provoked by the Veracruz incident, April 1914.

patrol to stop arms shipments, steamed into the harbors of those port cities. Wilson used the incident as an excuse to order the marines to land in Veracruz. His aim was both to embarrass Huerta and to rally his foes in support of American liberators, but the affair turned into a fiasco. Fighting broke out as soon as the American forces landed, although it was not clear who fired the first shots. Nineteen American servicemen were killed, and 71 were wounded; 126 Mexicans were killed and 195 wounded. Huerta posed legitimately as a Mexican patriot. His opponents likewise denounced the move, while Wilson's domestic critics such as Roosevelt and Lodge castigated the president as spineless and inept.

The best that can be said about the Veracruz incident and Wilson's subsequent policies toward Mexico is that they taught the president valuable lessons. The reaction of Huerta's opponents made him appreciate the strength of other peoples' nationalism and the limits of American power. Equally important, the Mexican revolution gave Wilson a glimpse of great underlying social forces—primarily the aspirations of colonial peoples to rule themselves—that had begun to overturn the international order. "There are in my judgment no conceivable circumstances," he avowed in August 1914, "which would make it right for us to direct by force or threat of internal processes of what is a profound revolution, a revolution as profound as that which occurred in France [in 1789]."

The Veracruz incident bolstered Huerta only temporarily. He fell late in 1914, and the revolutionary forces themselves dissolved into internecine warfare. By the end of 1915 the one-time bandit and dissident leader Pancho Villa was trying to provoke American intervention. He expected foreign aggression to strengthen his hand as it had earlier strengthened Huerta's. In January 1916 Villa and his men shot sixteen Americans who were travelling on a train in northern Mexico. On March 9, he raided the border town of Columbus, New Mexico, and killed another ten citizens. Reluctantly bowing to outraged calls for action, Wilson sent a punitive expedition commanded by Brigadier General John J. Pershing to pursue Villa across the border into Mexico. Pershing's troops never caught Villa, who made several more raids on American territory, but they did have some tense confrontations with the armies of Villa's opponents.

Mexico became an issue in the 1916 elections, as Roosevelt and many Republicans flayed Wilson for refusing to mount a full-scale intervention. American forces withdrew in early 1917, but social turmoil continued in Mexico into the early 1920s, and pressures for American intervention would arise again from time to time. But Wilson steadfastly refused to commit U.S. forces, and eventually he would have to fire Bryan's successor as secretary of state, Robert Lansing, for apparently conspiring to intervene in Mexico. The president had learned the hard way that he must let the Mexicans manage their own affairs. With that much experience at hand, Wilson now faced a much more dangerous test across the Atlantic.

WAR IN EUROPE

When World War I broke out in August 1914, Wilson privately believed that the United States could not fail to be touched by the results of that conflict. "It is perfectly obvious that this war will vitally change the relationships of nations," Wilson confided to his brother-in-law. Henceforth, he believed, all nations must have equal rights, there must be some form of disarmament, and "an association of the nations" must be set up to punish peacebreakers. In November 1914 he also told a journalist, off the record, that a "deadlock in Europe" without any "exemplary triumph or punishment" would be the best outcome. Wilson's public calls for impartiality expressed not indifference to the war, but his deep concern about the emotions that it might stir in America among the ethnic groups drawn from the belligerent nations. In December 1914, in response to efforts by Roosevelt and Senator Lodge to raise military preparedness as an issue, Wilson asserted that big defense increases "would mean that we had lost our self-possession, that we had been thrown off our balance by a war with which we have nothing to do, whose causes cannot touch us, whose very existence affords us opportunities for friendship and disinterested service which should make us ashamed of any thought of hostility or fearful preparation for trouble."

Others drew different conclusions about the war's likely effects on the United States. Roosevelt's reactions blended emotional, strategic, and domestic considerations. After initial hesitation at taking sides, the ex-president privately condemned Germany for having violated Belgian neutrality by brutally overrunning that country. He also soon came to regret that, as neutrals, Americans enjoyed "no opportunity for the display of heroic qualities." Obligations to the Progressives, who still put domestic reform uppermost, curbed his tongue in public about the war and military preparedness until after the November 1914 elections. Meanwhile, however, Roosevelt wrote a series of magazine articles in which he laid out a grand design for foreign policy. Roosevelt drew a relatively narrow perimeter of America's vital interests, and for the first time he publicly disclosed his belief that the United States should withdraw from the Philippines. He also suggested that parts of the Western Hemisphere might not require American supervision. Most important, he called for "a great world agreement among all the civilized military powers to *back righteousness by force.* Such an agreement would establish an efficient world league for the peace of righteousness." Roosevelt thereby became the first major public advocate of a league of nations with the United States as an active member.

The issue of America's military preparedness divided political leaders and popular sentiment. The United States possessed the smallest land force of any large nation in the world in 1914, with only 100,000 officers and men in the regular army, and no reserve forces except the often poorly maintained National Guard units in each state. During Roosevelt's presidency Secretary of War Elihu Root had introduced a modern general-staff system—modeled on Germany's—and other reforms, but many officers and civilians believed that the army required further modernization, adequate ready reserves, and the ability to raise large-scale forces rapidly through conscription. The navy stood in better shape, with a battleship fleet exceeded only by Britain's and Germany's. But the navy lacked a modern command structure, and many officers and some civilians, most notably Roosevelt and Senator Lodge, were convinced that the United States needed a much larger and still more modern naval force, second only or equal to Britain's.

When Roosevelt and Lodge attempted to arouse concern about military preparedness in the fall of 1914, only a few upper-crust Northeastern Republicans joined them. Progressives either failed to follow their leader or even opposed him, as did most of the insurgent Republicans. Conservative Republicans generally avoided the issue, although Taft joined Wilson in scoffing at the cries of alarm. With a handful of isolated exceptions, Democrats rallied enthusiastically behind their administration's opposition to major defense increases. Along with the belief that the war in Europe did not affect the United States, antipreparedness sentiment sprang from long-standing hostility to the military among Democrats, insurgent Republicans, and Progressives. They agreed that boosts in military spending diffused reform efforts at home, imposed tax burdens on ordinary citizens, and fattened the earnings of munitions manufacturers and the Wall Street tycoons who financed them. More generally, many Americans shared age-old suspicions of large, standing armies and conscription as tools of European despotism, and as menaces to democracy. The ease with which Wilson handled the preparedness issue at the end of 1914 confirmed the lack of alarm about the war in the United States.

"CLOSE UP THESE FACTORIES! . . . BE NEUTRAL!" A pro-preparedness cartoon showing the German Kaiser urging the closing of American arms manufacturers.

Roosevelt came closer to mirroring popular opinion, however, in his expressions of sympathy for Belgium and the Allies and by his condemnation of Germany. The ex-president began making his views public just months after the outbreak of war. In November 1914 a poll of 400 newspaper editors by the magazine *Literary Digest* found that slightly over half said they were impartial. Among the remainder, pro-Allied sentiment ran five to one. The poll of editors showed considerable regional variation. Impartiality ran lowest and favor for the Allies ran highest among editors from the Northeast and the South. In the Midwest and West, impartiality stood much higher, at about 75 percent; pro-Allied and pro-German sympathy was about equally divided among the rest of the Midwestern and Western editors. Support for the Allies did not, however, run deep. Few who expressed sympathies for the Allies shared Roosevelt's covert yearning to fight alongside Britain and France. Instead, as the *Literary Digest* noted, their sympathy was "that of a detached observer." In April 1915 the British ambassador ruefully agreed. "It is, I think, useless and misleading to depend upon these people for practical sympathy."

Many influences shaped the positions Americans took toward the war. Ethnic ties accounted for some pro-Allied sentiment, though relatively few Americans were of recent British or French extraction. Hostility toward Germany's partner in the Central Powers, Austria-Hungary, did sway some people from subject nationalities of that empire, such as Czechs, Slovaks, and Croats, but those sentiments existed among relatively few enthusiasts in restricted urban enclaves. Ethnic-based sympathy for the Central Powers and hostility to the Allies were less widespread but much more potent. Confined as they were almost exclusively to German-American and Irish-American communities, these attitudes made up in commitment what they lacked in numbers.

Early in the war both sides used propaganda in an effort to influence opinion and policy in the United States. The Germans, however, ran a better-financed and more sophisticated propaganda machine in the United States between 1914 and 1917 than the Allies did. The German embassy in particular cultivated sympathetic politicians, writers, and editors, and their side received ample coverage in the press. They also worked through German-American and Irish-American organizations to lobby in Congress and to try to influence elections. A national federation, the German-American Alliance, already linked local clubs and fraternal societies. It had been organized several years earlier as a front for brewing interests to combat prohibition. As soon as the war began, the German embassy took over the alliance and used it as a propaganda outlet and lobbying tool. The British and French mounted smaller, less visible operations. Given the preponderance of sympathies in the United States, they found their work easier than their foes did. In all, the influence of propaganda on public opinion and foreign policy at the time has been considerably exaggerated.

The German invasion of neutral Belgium was the decisive influence on the positions of many Americans. Accounts of the invasion were magnified by lurid descriptions and trumped-up atrocity stories, but the simple fact of the Germans' unprovoked aggression and tyrannical occupation of "brave little Belgium" could not be denied. The invasion put the German cause at a moral disadvantage in American eyes, and no outpouring of counter-propaganda ever enabled the Germans to recover much benefit of the doubt. One ironic effect of Germany's violation of Belgium was to reinforce notions of America's moral superiority to Europe, which in turn inclined even those with pro-Allied sentiments, except in scattered cases such as Roosevelt's, to feel even further removed from the war.

The grinding horrors of the stalemate that developed along the Western Front in Belgium and France added to Americans' revulsion from the war. Newspaper and magazine accounts, illustrated with battlefield photography, brought home to Americans the miserable squalor of the war. Millions of soldiers were mired in the trenches, confined by barbed wire and exploding shells, only to be gunned down by the thousands when they were ordered "over the top" to attack enemy positions. Even more repelling were the war's technological horrors, such as aerial bombing and particularly poison gas, which was first used early in 1915. Small wonder even ardently pro-Allied Americans did not yearn to fight.

But America could not remove itself completely from the war. With their vast naval superiority, the British from the outset choked off virtually all of the Central Powers' overseas trade, including a fairly sizable direct trade between Germany and the United States. The Allied blockade raised complex, touchy issues with the United States, and potential disputes arose in the fall of 1914. Only the unwillingness of Wilson and Bryan to provoke what appeared to be a fruitless quarrel temporarily prevented full-scale diplomatic confrontation between the United States and Britain over the strangling of overseas trade with the Central Powers.

For the Allies, a happy side effect of their blockade was that only they could buy supplies and munitions from the United States. The German embassy responded in the fall of 1914 by prompting German-

American organizations to lobby Congress for an arms embargo. Since an embargo on the sale of arms to both sides would be a blow to the Allies and a boon to Germany, Wilson and Bryan denounced the measure for its one-sidedness. Still, the idea had a seductive appeal to many. In January 1915 another *Literary Digest* poll of editors found 40 percent in favor of an embargo, with strong support everywhere except the Northeast. The following month an arms embargo amendment to a shipping bill won thirty-six votes in the Senate, despite active opposition by Bryan, Lodge, Roosevelt, Taft, and Wilson. At the same time there began to appear a few cracks in the public's detachment from the war. Britain's tightening blockade hurt certain export commodities, particularly cotton and copper, and diplomatic disputes were arising over Allied interdiction of goods bound for neutral countries bordering Germany such as the Netherlands. The growing anger among Southern cotton growers and traders posed special political problems for a Democratic administration.

Germany's military response to Britain's naval superiority was to proclaim submarine warfare in February 1915. Since the kaiser refused to permit the German surface navy to challenge the British, the new undersea craft seemed to hold the only promise of counteracting the Allied naval advantage. But German submarines in 1915 were frail, slow-moving craft with short cruising ranges and a small capacity for carrying torpedoes. So despite high hopes that the submarines would sink enough British merchant shipping to cut the Allied overseas lifeline of food, supplies, and munitions, their only real value as a weapon lay in surprise attacks that violated existing rules of warfare and alarmed neutral shippers. Worse, the Germans had only twenty-one submarines at the beginning of 1915, far too few to make a dent in the daily flow of hundreds of ships into Allied ports. The Germans were gambling on a magic weapon of unproven, severely limited capacity, and in doing so they risked bringing the biggest, richest neutral nation into the war against them.

The submarine decree aroused little reaction in the United States because no one was sure what these new undersea weapons could do or whether the proclamation might be a bluff. President Wilson and Secretary Bryan initially answered by warning that Germany would be held to "strict accountability" for all losses that Americans might incur, but they did not spell out what they meant. During February and March 1915 a few American ships were attacked by submarines, and an American citizen who was travelling as a passenger on a British freighter was killed. These incidents did raise some comments from the press and demands for a diplomatic response.

Two poles of argument soon formed within the Wilson administration about how to respond. Bryan sought means to ensure against any danger of American involvement in the war. His number-two man in the State Department, Robert Lansing, an international lawyer and conservative Democrat, took the contrary position that all rights under international law and usage must be strictly maintained. The danger to American interests lay not in attacks on U.S. ships, since relatively few of them sailed the North Atlantic, and the Germans usually left them alone after those first incidents. The real danger was the vulnerability of American citizens who travelled as passengers and crew on Allied merchant vessels, which carried allegedly defensive armaments. The practical choice facing the Wilson administration was whether to warn Americans against such voyages, as Bryan suggested, or to demand that Germany safeguard them, as Lansing argued. Wilson tried to have it both ways. He made no haste to face the issue but persisted in counseling calm. In a speech in April the president asserted that "the supreme test" of a nation was "self-possession, the power to resist excitement, to think calmly."

THE SHOCK OF RECOGNITION

The shock of World War I hit home for nearly all Americans within the space of a few hours during a single afternoon. On the morning of May 7, 1915, a German submarine sank the British passenger liner *Lusitania* within sight of the coast of Ireland. The 1,198 people who were killed included 128 Americans. That afternoon the news reached the United States with such impact that ten years later a writer found that everyone he interviewed still vividly remembered where they had been, and what they had thought and felt, when they first heard the news. The sinking of the *Lusitania* furnished twentieth-century Americans with their first great conscious-searing event. It was not just a huge catastrophe, like the loss of the *Titanic* three years earlier; it was a sudden, stunning revelation to Americans that their own lives had changed forever. The world war was no longer only "over there."

Expressions of outrage flared. Theodore Roosevelt dramatically denounced the attack as "Piracy, pure and simple." Yet, almost no one called for war. In a poll of newspaper editors throughout the country,

Americans were outraged when a German torpedo sank the Lusitania *on May 7, 1915.*

only six out of more than 1,000 respondents said that the United States should fight Germany. The lack of belligerency astonished many who remembered the war fever that had followed the sinking of the *Maine* just seventeen years before. The reason for the difference was not hard to find: There were few illusions in 1915 about a "splendid little war." Rather, as one politician subsequently observed, "Our people had read in the newspapers [since 1914] of the horrors of the European war. They had visualized their sons at the battlefront." To add to the familiar horrors of trench warfare, the first publicized use of poison gas had occurred a week before the sinking of the *Lusitania*.

The classic conundrum of peace and honor underlay the tortuous diplomacy that the Wilson administration conducted with Germany and, collaterally, with the Allies over the next two years. Speaking in Philadelphia three days after the sinking of the *Lusitania*, Wilson declared, "There is such a thing as a man being too proud to fight. There is such a thing as a nation being so right that it does not need to convince others by force that it is right." The "too proud to fight" speech instantly drew passionate reactions for and against; quickly grasping its unfortunate implications to a public outraged by the *Lusitania* incident, Wilson retracted his phrase the next day. His position, however, remained unchanged. Wilson stubbornly clung to the conviction that he could convince Germany to apologize for the sinking of the *Lusitania* and restrict submarine warfare without really risking American intervention in the war. He believed that he could have both peace and honor.

Bryan meanwhile continued to plump for warning citizens off Allied merchant vessels, and he urged Wilson to send a peace signal to Germany. Lansing likewise stuck to his advocacy of a stiff stand on international law, demanding that Germany repudiate the sinking of the *Lusitania* and guarantee the safety of all Americans on Allied ships. Lansing's position got strong support from the secretary of war, Lindley M. Garrison, and from Colonel Edward M. House, a presidential confidant and advisor on foreign affairs who was visiting European capitals to sound out possibilities for mediation. House was a wealthy Texan who lived on a private income in New York and whose rank was strictly honorific. During the 1912 campaign he and Wilson had formed a close friendship which was based upon the colonel's constant availability, ingratiating manner, and acquaintance with Democratic politicians. After Wilson's inauguration House had carved out foreign affairs as his field of activity, and the president had indulged his friend's hobby

Colonel Edward M. House.

by allowing him to go to Europe to explore possibilities for a larger American role in great power politics.

Wilson continued his search for a middle way. "I wish in all my heart I saw a way to carry out a double wish of our people," he told Bryan, "to maintain a firm front in respect of what we demand of Germany and yet do nothing that might by any possibility involve us in the war." Wilson sent a toughly worded protest to Germany over the *Lusitania* affair, demanding an apology and promises to restrict future submarine operations, but he made no threats of specific action. Wilson also contemplated but rejected for the time being Bryan's proposal of offering private assurances to Germany that the United States expected a peaceful outcome to the dispute. The president's middle way did not satisfy the secretary of state, who thought he was wrongly risking war. After agonized soul-searching, Bryan resigned in protest on June 8, 1915.

The Commoner announced that he intended to take the issue of war and peace into the political arena, where a few politicians, most notably Senator La Follette and others with German-American constituencies, were already calling for a peaceful resolution of the controversy. Some Democratic congressional leaders likewise warned the administration that they would not support a belligerent response to the *Lusitania* sinking. A neat symmetry placed Bryan and Roosevelt at opposite political poles following the *Lusitania* sinking. Roosevelt demanded that Americans must not "earn as a nation measureless scorn and contempt, if we follow the lead of those who exalt peace above righteousness." Instead Americans must "do the duty imposed upon us in connection with the World War." Roosevelt stopped short of advocating intervention, but he privately ached to join the Allies. A few Northeastern Republicans, including Senator Lodge and Elihu Root, joined him in demanding a hard line toward Germany.

Roosevelt and his cohorts also revived their earlier agitation on the issue of military preparedness. The *Lusitania* crisis lent the issue a new immediacy, and in response Wilson reversed his previous opposition to expansion of the armed forces. To strengthen the thrust of American diplomacy, the president came out for a big naval expansion program, including construction of ten battleships, ten cruisers, fifty destroyers, and one hundred submarines. Wilson's ambitious aim was naval parity with Britain in five years, or a "navy second to none." For the army he proposed a more modest program that would increase the regular army to 250,000 and create a new national reserve force—called the Continental Army—to replace the National Guard. Wilson did not, however, endorse conscription. Roosevelt and other preparedness enthusiasts predictably denounced the proposals as too little too late, even though Wilson called for larger increases in the navy than they had advocated. Bryan meanwhile renewed his own long-standing opposition to a big army and navy. By the summer of 1915, the lines were drawn for full-scale political battle over military preparedness.

Beyond the immediate concerns of war there were issues of long-term peace. By 1915, movements to reform international relations through arbitration, adjudication, and disarmament stretched back nearly two decades. World War I had obviously dealt a blow to earlier hopes for a new world system, but some advocates of international reform viewed the conflict as an opportunity. A group of American diplomats and lawyers began meeting early in 1915 to discuss establishment of an international body empowered to maintain peace by force if necessary. Ex-president Taft became head of this group, which was formally organized in June 1915 as the League to Enforce Peace. It was the first organization in the United States dedicated to promotion of a league of nations. Following Roosevelt, Taft became the second major public figure to endorse American participation in such a league. "We have got to depart from the traditional policy of this country of isolation from power politics outside the Western Hemisphere," Taft declared at the inaugural convention of the League to Enforce Peace. He justified this departure on two grounds: first, the war in Europe had demonstrated that America "must assume certain obligations in the interest of the world and in the interest of mankind"; second, the current crisis with Germany threatened that "we are likely to be drawn in ourselves."

Within days of the league's convention, Bryan delivered the first dissent. He condemned the program as a false promotion of peace. It would require a repudiation of traditional American policies against permanent alliances, and the abandonment of the Monroe Doctrine, in order to make "ourselves partners with other nations in the waging of war." Far better, maintained Bryan, to "remain true to the ideals of the fathers." Surprisingly, another stinging rejection came soon afterward from Roosevelt. In August 1915, less than a year after his endorsement of a league of nations, he attacked the program of the League to Enforce Peace as "childish make-believe" that distracted from military preparedness and real participation in international politics. Instead, admonished Roosevelt, America must be "willing by deeds to make good on the promises that we have already made."

Taft, Bryan, and Roosevelt together had staked out the basic positions in a major conflict over the proper basis of American foreign policy. Their respective positions corresponded to internationalism, isolationism, and traditional nationalism. The first round in that debate, which would rage for the next quarter of a century, occupied the year following the sinking of the *Lusitania.* The threat of involvement in World War I did what the war's outbreak and the earlier debate over American imperialism had failed to do—it made foreign policy a major, lasting issue in American politics. Concern about international affairs would wax and wane after 1915, but, despite recurrent efforts to banish such concern, there would never again be a real relapse into inattentiveness toward the rest of the world.

During the rest of 1915 and the first three months of 1916, President Wilson clung to his diplomatic middle course of trying to combine peace with honor. But with Bryan now gone, Wilson's conduct of foreign policy changed. As his new secretary of state, Wilson chose Robert Lansing, despite his doubts about Lansing's strength of character and intellectual ability. The president also began to rely more on his confidant, Colonel House, who now assumed a major role in dealing with the European belligerents. And Wilson, in perhaps another expression of his solitary nature, began to conduct America's foreign policy increasingly on his own.

The submarine controversy with Germany remained Wilson's overriding concern. Neither the first *Lusitania* protests nor the further exchanges of notes in the summer of 1915 drew any satisfactory reply from the Germans. Then in August a submarine sank the British liner *Arabic* and injured two American passengers. Wilson unofficially threatened to break relations with Germany unless such submarine attacks ceased. The threat prompted Germany, which also included hard-line and moderate factions in its government, to pledge to spare passenger ships. That pledge, however, was ambiguous and limited. It did not cover cargo vessels, and it came unstuck when more surprise attacks on liners took place in the fall. In January 1916 Secretary Lansing proposed a *modus vivendi* under which the Germans would restrict submarine attacks and the Allies would disarm their merchant ships. This proposal would have complicated American relations with both sets of belligerents, and House's urgent relay of outraged British objections to disarming their vessels convinced Wilson to drop the *modus vivendi* at the end of February 1916. Soon afterward, on March 24, 1916, a German submarine attacked the English Channel steamer *Sussex,* injuring several Americans. Wilson thereupon formally threatened to sever diplomatic relations unless the Germans pledged to abandon submarine attacks without warning on all merchant vessels.

"The Octopus." A New York Sun *cartoon depicting German U-boats in the Atlantic.*

The *Sussex* crisis precipitated a showdown in Berlin in April 1916 between advocates of submarine warfare and skeptics who questioned its effectiveness. When Wilson made the threat of war implicit behind a diplomatic break, he was, without knowing it, finally calling the Germans' bluff. They decided to meet his demand for a pledge to cease attacks without warning, although they hedged the guarantee by reserving the right to resume such attacks in the future. The Germans backed down in the face of Wilson's threat not because they feared the United States as a military foe; rather, the German army confidently expected victory that summer on the Western Front and did not want to be distracted by what they considered small-scale naval maneuvers and minor overseas complications. Wilson's diplomatic victory was welcome, but it rested on shaky underpinnings.

Relations with Germany were just one aspect of Wilson's diplomacy at the beginning of 1916. Another initiative aimed at the settlement of the war through mediation. Before and after his resignation Bryan had demanded a public appeal to the belligerents to sound out peace prospects. Wilson preferred quiet, though not strictly official, diplomacy. In December 1915 he sent Colonel House on a mission to Europe to spring a plan for a mediated settlement of the war. Unfortunately, the colonel was not straightforward with anyone, including himself. House spun secret fantasies about managing events on the world stage, and he covertly harbored pro-Allied, interventionist views similar to Roosevelt's. In Paris and London he deceitfully presented Wilson's plan to offer mediation to Germany as a pretext for the United States to enter the war. Writing and cabling back to Wilson, however, he exaggerated British and French interest in the proposal, and he depicted their alleged interest as evidence of a genuine desire to make peace. House's behavior sprang from a complex, murky set of motives. In part he deceived himself about the importance of his activities, and in part, he tried so hard to ingratiate himself with both Wilson and the Allied leaders that he told them only what he thought they wanted to hear.

On February 12, 1916, the British foreign secretary, Sir Edward Grey, initialed a document drawn up by the colonel. This House-Grey memorandum proposed joint Anglo-American mediation, which would be followed in the event of a German refusal by entry of the United States into the war on the Allied side. House had eagerly relayed British objections to Lansing's *modus vivendi* of January 1916 because he wanted nothing to interfere with his own project. At all events, the

Secretary of State Robert Lansing.

colonel's scheme for mediation or intervention soon went awry. When Wilson saw the memorandum, he added the word "probably" to the clause about the likelihood of American intervention. The British meanwhile secretly brushed the offer aside as a distraction from their military plans on the Western Front in the summer of 1916. Just like their foes, the British confidently expected to win on the ground and wanted no troublesome complications from pesky Americans offering mediation. The British never mentioned the House-Grey memorandum in any of their diplomatic communications with the United States. This potentially dangerous piece of deception died quietly of inattention, and House's influence with Wilson soon declined.

Everything seemed to happen at once during the first three months of 1916. As if the submarine crisis with Germany, the expedition against Pancho Villa in Mexico, and secret mediation overtures did not sufficiently challenge Wilson, he also had to wrest control of the Democratic party from Bryan. The issues of military preparedness and submarine diplomacy dovetailed to create a climactic confrontation between the two men. When the administration's preparedness program was presented to Congress in December 1915, the Commoner's followers, who controlled the House Military and Naval Affairs Committees, promptly bottled it up.

Wilson responded with a classic carrot-and-stick approach. The stick was to revive his earlier practice as governor of New Jersey of appealing over the heads of legislators directly to the people. The war had, ironically, given Wilson the opportunity that he had previously lacked to make himself a popular leader. Now, for the first time, he had an issue with which he could arouse public sentiment. In January and February 1916 the president made a whirlwind two-week speaking tour in an effort to educate the public on the need for a stronger army and navy. Over and over Wilson hammered away at the argument that Americans were involved in a dangerous world, whether they wanted to be or not. As he asserted in one speech, "We live in a world which we did not make, . . . which we cannot think into a different condition from that which actually exists." In another speech he warned, "The world is on fire and there is tinder everywhere."

Wilson's carrot was compromise. Most of the Democratic opposition to Wilson's preparedness program focused on his proposal for a national reserve force, the Continental Army. As soon as Wilson returned from his speaking tour he announced that he no longer supported the proposal. That decision prompted Secretary of War Lindley Garrison, an outspoken hard-liner on defense and diplomatic issues, to make good on repeated threats to resign. Wilson shrewdly used the occasion to mollify congressional critics further by choosing as his new secretary of war Newton D. Baker, the well-known reform Democratic mayor of Cleveland, Ohio, and former opponent of increased preparedness. Now there remained only a hard core of intra-party opposition to the defense program. The army and navy bills subsequently passed in both houses with little further controversy. Wilson had won the first round in the struggle with Bryan.

The second, deciding round transpired soon afterward over the submarine issue. At the end of February 1916 panic broke out on Capitol Hill when rumors of war accompanied the collapse of Lansing's *modus vivendi*. A Bryanite Democrat in each house, Senator Thomas P. Gore of Oklahoma and Congressman Jeff McLemore of Texas, had already introduced resolutions embodying the Commoner's proposal to warn citizens off belligerent merchant vessels. In a flurry of excitement, demands arose for passage of those resolutions. Rather than let things cool down, Wilson chose to bring the matter to a head. After conferring with congressional leaders and reassuring them that he did not want war, the president sent Postmaster General Burleson and Secretary of the Treasury McAdoo to the Capitol armed with a handwritten letter from him to show to Democrats. The letter asked them "to relieve the present embarrassment of the Administration in dealing with the foreign relations of the country" by means of "an early vote" to defeat the resolutions. "No other course would meet the necessities of the case." Bryan likewise hurried to Washington to lobby for the Gore and McLemore resolutions.

Wilson won decisively. The senators fell into a confused wrangle over the Gore resolution before they rejected it on a 68 to 14 vote to table on March 2, 1916. All but two Democrats deserted the measure: even Gore himself voted to table the resolution. However twelve Republicans, mostly Midwestern and Western insurgents, including La Follette, George Norris, and Albert Cummins, stuck by it. Four days later the House provided a clearer test of political sentiment when it tabled the McLemore resolution on a vote of 276 to 142. Three-quarters of the Democrats voted to table. Many said they favored the measure in principle, but, as one of them observed, "the issue presented in this context is whether we shall stand by the President in this crisis or not." By contrast, just over half the House Republicans voted against tabling; they were joined by five of the six Progressives and the lone Socialist. Republicans divided on the McLemore resolution partly along ideological but most clearly along sectional lines. Nearly two-thirds of the Republicans who voted against tabling were from the Midwest. They included both insurgents, such as La Follette's Wisconsin followers, and conservatives; many from both factions represented strong German-American constituencies.

Wilson's victory marked the beginning of a major reversal in American foreign policy. Before 1916, as commentators had often noted, Democrats had generally followed Bryan's lead in opposing a more assertive, interventionist role in world affairs. Now, by pointing them toward such a role, Wilson was carving out a new stance for them in foreign policy. This was, in one way, an even more impressive feat of party leadership than his domestic legislation. In domestic affairs, Wilson had built upon a political base prepared by others, particularly Bryan. There he was refining and extending the positions on industrial concerns that Democrats had been taking since 1896. In foreign affairs, however, he was pushing his party in a direction that ran counter to nearly all its inclinations during those twenty years. Two votes to table congressional resolutions did not signal a permanent policy reversal. Yet the votes of congressional Democrats on the Gore and McLemore resolutions came on the heels of the party's conversion on military preparedness and in the context of an inescapable choice between past and present leaders. The outcome pointed toward a major shift of political alignments surrounding foreign policy.

Congressional Republicans' votes disclosed the start of a comparable shift in the opposite direction. The party's support of the Spanish-American War and acquisition of the Philippines, together with the influence of such advocates of activism as Roosevelt, Lodge, and Elihu Root, had earned Republicans a reputation for favoring a larger role for the United States in world affairs. Taft's more pacific foreign policies and the dissent of some insurgents from dollar diplomacy had not dimmed that reputation. Since the outbreak of World War I and especially since the sinking of the *Lusitania*, the loudest Republican voices had joined Roosevelt's in denouncing Wilson for not taking tougher stands toward Germany and for not pushing for still larger increases in the army and navy. Two days after the House vote on the McLemore Resolution Roosevelt issued a statement to the press in which he warned that in 1916 no party should "nominate me unless the country has in its mood something of the heroic." The majority of Republican congressmen, together with all but one of the Progressives, had already answered him by supporting the cautious, pacific McLemore resolution. Their votes proved equally embarrassing to Lodge, Root, and other pro-Allied Republicans, who were exposed as being out of step with much of the party's rank-and-file, particularly outside the Northeast. Those votes of congressional Republicans in March 1916 were also only a straw in the wind, but they pointed toward a repudiation of their party's previous advocacy of an America active on the world stage.

The debate over managing international relations in the long term also advanced during the latter half of 1915 and first months of 1916. Taft and Bryan maintained their respective positions for and against a league of nations. A few congressional politicians took up the issue during the debates over preparedness and submarine warfare. Bryan's isolationism received seconds from a handful of his followers in the House, but the most prominent converts to his stand were two Republican senators. One of them, John D. Works of California, an insurgent, declared in March 1916 that the proposal by the League to Enforce Peace "to compel a nation to keep the peace by force of arms . . . is entirely inconsistent with what I think a peace organization should be." The other, Porter J. McCumber of North Dakota, a moderate conservative, decried attempts to make America abandon "our ancient policy of aggrandizement in the arts of peace, a policy which our splendid isolation makes possible." Taft's internationalism drew support from a scattering of Democratic and Republican congressmen, one of whom asserted, "America, world-renowned for the justness of its conceptions, has outgrown any fear of foreign entanglements."

Roosevelt similarly stuck to his nationalistic guns. With equal fervor he condemned the Wilson administration, Bryan and his followers, Republican and Progressive opponents of tough diplomacy, and the League to Enforce Peace. His line of attack on Taft's proposals elicited little agreement, even from his closest cohorts. In June 1915, Senator Lodge had endorsed the idea of an international peace-keeping organization, which he had dubbed a "united nations." Although Lodge did not join the League to Enforce Peace, he spoke in favor of the organization's approach at its annual convention on May 17, 1916.

That convention also featured a public endorsement of the league's ideas by President Wilson. Although Wilson declined to commit himself on specifics, he did affirm that the "great nations" must agree "as to what they hold to be fundamental, and as to some feasible method of acting in concert when any nation or group of nations seeks to disturb those fundamental things." He called for all peoples to be able to choose their governments, equal rights for all nations, freedom from aggression, a negotiated peace in Europe, free use of the seas, and an international tribunal for settlement of disputes and maintenance of fundamental rights. Most important, he promised "that the United States is willing to become a partner in any feasible association of nations formed in order to realize these objects and make them secure against violation."

It was a measure of Wilson's confidence that he would disclose his internationalist convictions and propose such sweeping future commitments. He had much to feel confident about by the end of May 1916. The second installment of his New Freedom program was moving through Congress, and he was about to win the hard-fought battle for Louis Brandeis's confirmation to the Supreme Court. The preparedness program was likewise making its way on Capitol Hill, and the *Sussex* crisis the previous April had occasioned no revival of the Gore and McLemore resolutions or even much expression of congressional concern. The face-off with Germany over the submarine attacks had turned out well, and the threat of involvement in war appeared to be receding. Best of all from Wilson's standpoint, he had proven himself master of the institution that mattered most to him: his party. Not only had he wrested leadership decisively away from Bryan, but his recent successes at home and abroad had compelled the Commoner to stop dropping ominous hints about not supporting Wilson's renomination.

Personal happiness added to the president's confidence in 1916. The death of his wife Ellen in August 1914 had come close to shattering his emotional stability. Colonel House had gained his greatest influence during the next year and a half through his soothing presence.

Wilson with his second wife, Edith Bolling Galt Wilson.

Then, in March 1915, Wilson had met a forty-three-year-old widow, Edith Bolling Galt. Almost at once the fifty-seven-year-old president fell madly in love, with all the emotional and physical ardor of an adolescent. Wilson instinctively adopted the old axiom that power is the most potent aphrodisiac. He shared secrets of state and major policy decisions with Mrs. Galt from early in their courtship, at the time of the sinking of the *Lusitania* and Bryan's resignation. The attractiveness of man and office quickly melted the widow's reserve, and she became Wilson's closest advisor for the rest of his life. Well before their marriage in December 1915 Edith Wilson had displaced the Texas colonel, whom she disliked from the first, and everyone else as the president's chief source of emotional and political support. Altogether the skies looked clear and the winds felt fair as Wilson faced his re-election campaign in the middle of 1916.

9

"He Kept Us Out of War"

After the middle of 1916 American politics and foreign policy went through a kaleidoscope of changes in a few months. The presidential campaign lived up to advance billing as a hard-fought contest, although the closeness of its outcome confounded nearly everyone's predictions. The abatement of the submarine crisis had produced what Colonel House privately called "a lull in foreign affairs," yet this happy turn of events did not banish American troubles with the European belligerents or concern with the war. Nor did the reprieve from the danger of involvement last. In January 1917 the Germans decided to reopen and widen the submarine campaign, which brought a final crisis for the United States. The first three months of 1917 witnessed a set of dramatic turns, mounting tensions, bruising arguments, and painful choices, all of which culminated in American entry into World War I.

Close Call at the Ballot Box

The first surprise in the 1916 presidential race was that neither candidate chose the main themes of his campaign; instead, each man found the major issues thrust upon him and his party. Woodrow Wilson's well-laid plans for a balanced, orderly presentation of his administration's accomplishments, with the heaviest emphasis on domestic reform, went awry at the June 1916 Democratic convention in St. Louis. In the keynote speech ex-Governor Martin Glynn of New York unintentionally electrified the delegates with an offhand reference to the president's success at avoiding war. When the audience started chanting "What did we do? What did we do?" Glynn bellowed back, "We didn't go to war!" Subsequent speakers seized upon the peace theme, and the delegates began shouting "Bryan! Bryan!" Invited by acclamation to give an unscheduled speech, the Commoner literally wept with joy at his party's "love feast." He waved aside past differences with Wilson to praise his reform legislation and to "join with the American people in thanking God that we have a President who does not want this nation plunged into war." Thus was born the battle cry of Wilson's re-election drive. Democratic propagandists translated it into the slogan, "He kept us out of war!"

Charles Evans Hughes and the Republicans took longer to find their banners to rally behind. Candidate and party both initially put a premium on papering over the divisions left from 1912. But their 1916 platform stand for tariff protection and miscellaneous attacks on the opposition did not lay promising groundwork for a presidential campaign. Hughes's early performance came as a disappointment to those who remembered a dynamism that had once earned the bearded New York governor the nickname, "animated featherduster." Some observers speculated that six years of political seclusion on the Supreme Court had blunted Hughes's edge as a candidate. Others suspected that the

Charles Evans Hughes.

Republicans' priority on avoiding intraparty strife was making the candidate pull his punches. At all events the former justice's reserved manner and mild speeches soon earned him the new nicknames of "iceberg," "bearded lady," and, in private from Roosevelt, "whiskered Wilson." As the summer of 1916 ended, the Republicans' tepid campaign needed a shot in the arm.

Two pieces of Wilson's second New Freedom program gave them their lift. As the income-tax bill neared passage in July and August, Republicans on Capitol Hill repeatedly denounced the measure as a Southern and Western raid on the wealth of the Northeast and the Midwest. Party propagandists seized upon those arguments to highlight sectional divisions more vividly than in any election since Bryan's campaigns in 1896 and 1900. The 1916 tax measures welded Wall Street and most leading manufacturers and financiers into a near solid phalanx behind Hughes. "I believe the whole business and intelligent part of the community to be thoroughly roused against Wilson," observed Taft with satisfaction. Even more dramatically divisive was the Adamson Act, the eight-hour law for interstate railroad workers, which became the hottest single issue of the 1916 campaign.

Hughes denounced the Adamson Act as Wilson's "surrender" to the railroad unions. The Republican candidate declared, "Transcending every other issue is the issue that has presented itself—whether the Government shall yield to force." Hughes pressed the issue constantly, and he was joined by conservative Republicans, insurgents, and leading former Progressives, including Roosevelt. They condemned the Adamson Act as "class legislation," accusing the Democrats of granting peculiar, unfair advantages to a special interest—labor. On several occasions Roosevelt lambasted the Adamson Act as "craven surrender" and a flagrant abandonment of governmental "disinterestedness." Further, charged Roosevelt, such dispensing of benefits to interest groups unmasked the president's "frank cynicism of belief in, and appeal to, what is basest in the human heart." Among insurgents only La Follette and a few others held back from the attack.

Just as the tax and labor issues tended to unite Republicans on conservative grounds, they pushed Democrats in the opposite direction. The party fell in gladly with Wilson's appeals to Progressives. Democratic publicity trumpeted the administration's enactment of the 1912 Progressive platform, and it dwelled on public endorsements of Wilson by prominent progressives, including a majority of the party's 1912 platform committee and *New Republic* editors Herbert Croly and Walter Lippmann. In 1916 the Democrats for once bested the Republicans at mounting a smoothly run, tightly organized campaign. They excelled particularly at targeting appeals to specific blocs of voters, such as ethnic groups, farmers, and Westerners. But they aimed their appeal to one sector above all: organized labor. In return for the exemption of unions from the antitrust laws through the Clayton Act, and now the passage of the Adamson Act, the AFL and its constituent unions backed Wilson strongly and actively. Even the IWW treated him with benevolent neutrality. The president, in turn, frankly advocated government assistance to disadvantaged groups, especially labor and farmers. During the campaign Wilson frequently cited labor for special attention, and urged aid to get them "upon the same footing as the other industrial workers of the country," by which he meant white-collar employees and businessmen.

On domestic issues the lines were more sharply drawn between the two parties in 1916 than in any election since 1900. But both parties tried to get mileage out of diplomatic as well as domestic issues. Peace appeared to be the Democrats' trump card. They brandished the "He kept us out of war" slogan, and they unleashed Bryan for another of his familiar whistle-stop campaign swings. "Honor,"—standing up to foreign aggression—likewise seemed the Republicans' strong suit. They harped on their preparedness record, and they welcomed Roosevelt back for another of his familiar barn-storming forays on the hustings.

The Wilson bandwagon in 1916.

He obliged by assailing the president and his diplomacy with mounting fury as the contest unfolded. The ex-president's indictment of Wilson's inaction during the foreign crisis culminated on the eve of the election in a macabre word-play on Shadow Lawn, the name of the New Jersey seaside estate where Wilson was spending the campaign. "There should be shadows enough at Shadow Lawn," intoned Roosevelt in reference to the casualties of submarine warfare, "the shadows of men, women, and children who have risen from the ooze of the ocean bottom . . . the shadows of lofty words that were followed by no action; the shadows of the tortured dead."

But the foreign-policy debate in the 1916 campaign was more opportunistic than principled. Wilson privately professed dismay at the "He kept us out of war" theme, complaining, "I can't keep this country out of war. Some damned little German lieutenant can plunge this nation into war through a calculated outrage." On the campaign trail, however, he showed no shyness about accepting Democratic claims on his behalf. "There is only one choice as against peace," Wilson asserted on September 1916, "and that is war." He added that in view of their current attacks on his policies, "the certain prospect of the success of the Republican party is that we shall be drawn, in one form or another, into the embroilments of the European war." When German-American organizations and some anti-British Irish groups openly opposed Wilson for his earlier stand against German submarine warfare, the president made the most of a golden opportunity to wrap himself in the flag. Wilson scorned support from "disloyal Americans" and appealed for "one hundred percent Americanism." Hughes, by contrast, declined to repudiate endorsement by some of the same groups.

The Republican candidate also criticized Wilson for not having been tougher with the Allies, a charge which now appeared politically promising. The British had aroused American opposition by keeping a blacklist of American firms suspected of ties to the Germans, and interdicting mail to Europe. Moreover, the British were at the time trying to smother the independence movement in Ireland, which had been sparked by the Easter Rising in Dublin in April 1916. Their brutal conduct in Ireland, which included several hundred summary executions, had tarnished Britain's moral position in American eyes and had eroded much pro-Allied sentiment in the United States. Wilson himself soured on Britain in the wake of its diplomatic intransigence and callous brutality in Ireland. He privately voiced scorn for the Allies in the fall of 1916, to the dismay of his covertly pro-Allied advisors Colonel House and Secretary of State Lansing.

Not even Roosevelt's rhetoric was straightforward in the 1916 campaign. Many of his slams at Wilson's "high sounding words" and "shabby deeds" referred to Mexico rather than Europe. Republicans attacked Wilson's diplomacy with Mexico more than any other aspect of his administration's foreign policy. The Democrats themselves invoked "He kept us out of war" more often with reference to Mexico than to Europe. On his campaign swings Bryan used Mexico as his chief example of maintaining the peace. Wilson frequently expressed gratitude for Bryan's aid, especially because the Commoner was concentrating his efforts in critical Western states. For his part, Bryan was not just making an altruistic gesture or yielding to an irresistible urge to be on the stump. In December 1916, shortly after the election, he made a bid to reassert his party leadership by demanding that Democrats commit themselves to his program of further reform, woman suffrage, and prohibition. He also demanded pursuit of an isolationist foreign policy based on a constitutional amendment "to submit every declaration of war to a referendum of the people, except in the case of *actual invasion of the country.*"

On the issue of international cooperation for peace the party positions were unclear as well. At their convention, the Democrats revealed their ambivalence when they adopted a platform plank that pledged membership in a league of nations but applauded keynote speaker Glynn's praise for "the American policy of neutrality and isolation." Wilson again endorsed the league-of-nations idea in the fall of 1916. He may have had some thoughts about using the campaign to educate the public on the issue, but he dwelled on it less as the election neared. Hughes's stand mirrored Wilson's. At the outset of the campaign he endorsed an "international organization" backed by "the preventive power of a common purpose," and he declared that "there is no national isolation in the world of the Twentieth Century." Later, however, Hughes rarely mentioned the league idea. Roosevelt avoided criticizing it during the campaign, but his erstwhile imperialist and Progressive comrade Albert Beveridge denounced Wilson for daring to contemplate any form of alliance. What America needed, insisted Beveridge, was a "broader, deeper, stronger nationalism."

In 1916, as earlier in 1900, attempts to turn a presidential election into a foreign-policy referendum flopped. By November, few attentive observers found much to distinguish between the candidates on these grounds. Reactions to the European war and Mexico must have swayed some voters, but it was difficult to detect any large influence of foreign policy in the outcome. Perhaps the best explanation for this was that the campaign and election took place during a "lull in foreign affairs."

At the time American involvement in the world war did not seem imminent.

As election day approached, both candidates genuinely expected to win. Wilson no longer enjoyed the free ride conferred by a split opposition, but he did benefit from unusual advantages for a Democratic nominee. Besides incumbency, he had a well-oiled organization which made no mistakes and employed the latest publicity techniques, including public endorsements by movie actors and sports stars such as baseball's Ty Cobb. Wilson's legislative and diplomatic achievements earned him unusually broad endorsement in the press, although the majority of newspapers remained faithfully Republican. For his part, Hughes hit his campaign stride after a rocky start. Reverberations from the 1912 split between Republicans and Progressives plagued his campaign. They seemed particularly harmful in California, where conservatives embarrassed Hughes by keeping him away from the Progressive governor, Hiram Johnson, even though the two men's paths crossed during Hughes's visit there. It was a costly affront, but by October order had been established in the Republican campaign and an able manager had been found in a veteran Indiana operative, Will Hays. Between Hays's skillful deployment of money and manpower and Hughes's hammering away at tax and labor issues, they narrowed the race as election day approached.

The returns produced the closest contest in three decades. The two candidates finished virtually even in popular and electoral tallies, and neither won a popular majority. Wilson garnered slightly over 49 percent of the votes cast, and nearly 600,000 more than Hughes, who won 46 percent. Total votes cast and participation by those eligible to vote were up from 1912, but the percentage of eligibles who voted stood just a little over 60 percent, far below the turnouts of 1896 and 1900, and under 1904 and 1908 as well. Hughes bettered the Roosevelt-Taft 1912 total by a million votes, while Wilson gained nearly three million over his previous total. Minor party votes declined. The Prohibitionists fell off slightly, and because Eugene Debs had retired from politics, the Socialist vote declined by more than a third.

The electoral college was much more closely divided: 277 for Wilson, 254 Hughes. In California, with 13 electoral votes, the outcome was in doubt for several days before barely tilting toward Wilson. Hughes's inadvertent snub of Hiram Johnson may have tipped the scales there. If California had gone the other way the Republicans would have won with a one-vote electoral majority. Congressional margins were comparably thin. The Democrats' majority shrank in the Senate,

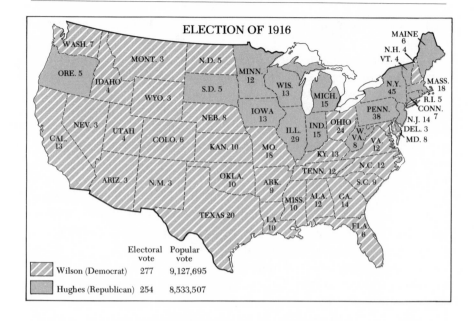

while in the House they retained only a six-seat plurality over the Republicans. The remainder of the seats were scattered among splinter-party congressmen.

A familiar pattern of sectionalism re-emerged in the 1916 results. The two parties retained almost exactly the same sectional constituencies they had held for the last twenty years. The Democrats' great crescent of the South and West went almost solidly for Wilson. He swept the South and lost only three Western states not bordering on the Mississippi. Wilson actually improved upon Bryan's earlier achievements in the West, where the president owed much of his success to the support of Roosevelt's 1912 voters. The Republicans' heartland, the Northeast and Midwest, went almost but not quite solidly for Hughes. He lost only two states east of the Mississippi and north of the Potomac and Ohio Rivers. There, majorities of former Progressives returned to the Republican fold, and economic conservatism once more predominated. The Republicans came as close as they did to victory in 1916 because of their traditional hold on electoral majorities in these sections. The crucial exception was Ohio, which Wilson carried largely through his appeal to labor. Without Ohio, Wilson's western sweep would have been unavailing, and Hughes would have won.

On the whole, the labor issue allowed the Democrats to broaden their base in the Northeast and Midwest. Although Republican denunciations of the Adamson Act and new taxes persuaded significant numbers of middle-class voters, the Democrats managed to draw the support of industrial workers, organized and unorganized. Wilson exceeded previous Democratic percentages in every Northeastern and Midwestern state, and most of the increase came from urban, industrial areas. These inroads in the heartland pointed toward possibilities for a future national Democratic majority.

More immediately, the 1916 results confirmed the retreat from reform that had become evident two years earlier. Although Wilson's appropriation of progressive issues to himself and the Democrats clearly played a big part in his slender victory, his first-term successes as a party leader had undermined the broader reform coalition. Most insurgent Republicans and Progressive leaders drifted into opposition to the New Freedom mainly out of desperation about where to turn politically. Deeper ideological concerns caused Roosevelt and a few others to reject Wilson's programs. But either way, the broad areas of agreement among parties, factions, sections, and classes that had supplied a reform consensus before 1912 no longer existed. The conservatives had barely lost, and their odds on making further gains appeared excellent.

A PEACE OFFENSIVE

Wilson felt the weight of foreign affairs with redoubled strength almost at once after the 1916 election. German moderates had privately warned Wilson in the fall of 1916 about pressures to resume submarine warfare unless he could end the war through mediation. The president responded by plunging ahead with a peace offensive on several fronts. He overrode objections by House and Lansing, who feared that mediation would only hurt the Allies, and started to draft a formal diplomatic note that asked the belligerents to state possible peace terms. At the same time, Wilson, who had grown disillusioned with the Allies, saw the chance to use economic pressure to speed a settlement.

War orders in the United States had piled up a huge indebtedness for the British, who acted as banker, purchasing agent, and shipper for the Allies. Their growing dependence had begun to be evident late in 1915 when the J. P. Morgan firm, which represented the Allies in the United States, had had great difficulty floating a half-billion-dollar loan for Britain and France. The volume of their purchases soon exhausted that loan. The British government ignored the worsening situation until the fall of 1916, when a young Treasury official who oversaw Anglo-American exchange finally exposed how desperate their circumstances were becoming. The British official, John Maynard Keynes, warned that a crisis was looming sometime early in 1917, when the Allies would exhaust their collateral in America. By that time, Keynes implicitly suggested, they would need such massive and rapid infusions of credit and supplies that they would, in effect, need the United States at their side as a co-belligerent. These warnings contributed to the mood of sober reappraisal that accompanied the parliamentary coup in December 1916 that made David Lloyd George prime minister at the head of a coalition government.

Wilson decided to use their financial vulnerability to pressure the Allies for peace. In November 1916, right after the election, Wilson maneuvered the Federal Reserve Board into issuing a statement that deplored excessive lending by American banks to foreign borrowers. The board's statement, which Wilson personally revised, sent an unmistakable message to the Allies, who were the borrowers in question. The statement also caused a flurry of alarm on Wall Street and among some Allied sympathizers. A much bigger flurry arose when Wilson dispatched his peace note on December 18, 1916, and made it public two days later. The note not only urged the warring nations to state their war aims, but it also asserted "that the objects which the statesmen of the belligerents on both sides have in mind are virtually the same." The note claimed that both sides wanted security against aggression not only for themselves but also for weak and small nations. Moreover, the note implored all nations "to consider the formation of a league of nations to insure peace and justice throughout the world," and it pledged that the United States would be "vitally and directly interested" in full participation in such a league.

Wilson's peace note set off frantic debates at home and abroad. Discussions commenced in London, Paris, and Berlin over how to reconcile the president's request with Allied and German war plans. Early in January 1917, the British sent a gentle, noncommittal reply; the Germans, by contrast, told the Americans to mind their own business. At home, Roosevelt, Lodge, and a few others speedily denounced as pro-German the request for terms and the recognition of all the combatants' war aims. Within the administration, House and Lansing took the same view, and they tried to counteract Wilson's apparently anti-Allied thrust. The colonel told one British contact that by acknowledging the war aims of the Central Powers the note was aimed at "restraining the German submarine policy." The president, House said, wanted to buy time because he feared that "England would not be able to hold out long enough for American assistance to become effective."

"ASKING A FAVOR." "THE KAISER: 'I say, Wilson, my friend, I shall be extremely obliged if—You will kindly do your best to get me peace on reasonable terms.' " Many considered Wilson's actions a response to the threat of resumed submarine warfare.

House also assured the British, another contact reported, "that the attitude of the Administration toward Britain has not changed from that which he explained [in presenting the House-Grey Memorandum] in February."

While House misrepresented the president behind the scenes, Lansing publicly bent the truth in order to scuttle the peace note. He told reporters the day after the note's publication, "We are drawing nearer the verge of war ourselves. . . . The sending of this note will indicate the possibility of our being forced into the war." Aghast when he read a transcript of Lansing's remarks, Wilson ordered him to issue a further statement declaring "that your utterance of this morning had been radically misinterpreted" and especially "that it was not at all in your mind to intimate any change in the policy of neutrality which this country has so far so consistently pursued in the face of accumulating difficulties." The secretary meekly complied. Unlike Bryan, who had resigned as secretary of state to protest the president's policies, Lansing, a weak man, stayed on. Wilson failed to fire Lansing for this episode because he was playing more and more of a lone hand in foreign affairs, and showing an astonishing tolerance for unreliable, even disloyal lieutenants.

Wilson's note became the target of attack not only for its alleged pro-German bias but also for its commitment to a league of nations. Bryan registered only private dissent from the league proposal, but one Republican senator expressed public opposition along isolationist lines. William E. Borah of Idaho, a veteran insurgent, now emerged as a leading isolationist spokesman. Early in January 1917, Borah told his Senate colleagues that Wilson was adopting the program of the League to Enforce Peace, which would thrust America into "the storm center of European politics." The president's course, Borah argued, would take America down "that course which, in my humble judgment, is not to promote peace but to promote war." Borah received private congratulations from Bryan and Roosevelt, who also told him his criticisms "did not go nearly far enough." The ex-president renewed his public attacks on the League to Enforce Peace as a "wicked" organization that "interferes with the all-essential movement for spiritual and material preparedness."

Roosevelt and Borah had vastly different reasons for opposing the league idea, but their joining hands further disclosed the political realignment that the March 1916 votes on the Gore and McLemore Resolutions had begun to reveal. This realignment was the Republicans' shift toward an isolationist policy. Another sign of the shift came when Henry Cabot Lodge joined Borah in criticizing Wilson's proposal for a league of nations. Speaking in the Senate on the same day as Borah, Lodge warned that Wilson was thrusting the United States "into the field of European politics" where Americans had "no national or legal concern." Lodge hesitated to reject the league idea, but he observed "that it is departure form the hitherto unbroken policy of this country" of avoiding alliances for the sake of entering into "the political system of another hemisphere." A Senate resolution supporting the peace note but not the commitment to join a league of nations drew votes from 38 Democrats and 11 Republicans; 16 Republicans and one Democrat opposed the resolution. Foreign policy divisions were becoming more sharply partisan.

Wilson intensified the domestic debate by escalating his peace offensive. Neither Britain's evasive reply to his note nor Germany's harsh rejoinder deterred him from presenting his own terms for ending the war. On January 22, 1917, the president made a surprise appearance before the Senate and delivered one of his greatest speeches. In it he called for a new international order. "There must be, not a balance of power," he asserted, "but a community of power." The one way to achieve that was through "a peace without victory. . . . Only a peace among equals can last, only a peace the very basis of which is equality and a common participation in a common benefit." Such a peace required the guarantee for all nations of fundamental rights, equal sovereignty, freedom from aggression, freedom of the seas, and eventual disarmament. Wilson argued that a lasting peace also required establishment of a league of nations. In a ploy to disarm isolationists Wilson argued that "all nations [would] henceforth avoid entangling alliances" because there could be "no entangling alliances in a concert of power." Withal, he avowed, "These are American principles, American policies. We could stand for no others."

Wilson had delivered a noble utterance. He had laid out a grand design for world politics and a new course for his country's foreign policy. Praise for the speech was vociferous and widespread. Senator La Follette, who rushed up after the speech to shake the president's hand, stated afterward, "We have just passed through a very important hour in the life of the world." Democratic and some Republican insurgent senators echoed La Follette. Outside the Senate, Bryan lauded Wilson's "brave and timely appeal to the war-mad rulers of Europe," but the Commoner reiterated his disagreement over "the wisdom of joining a league to enforce peace." Taft expressed public approval, but he grumbled privately that Wilson had endorsed the league idea "in such a way as to embarrass me, because I don't agree with much of what he says in respect to the kind of peace that ought to be achieved." Although he was not an interventionist, Taft hoped that the Allies would win, and he believed that they would if the United States did not pursue misguided ideas about mediation.

There was also loud criticism of the speech, though it was more narrowly based. Borah renewed his isolationist criticism by declaring, "What this passion-torn world needs and will need are not more leagues and alliances, but a great, untrammeled, courageous neutral power, representing not bias, not hate, not conflict, but order and justice." Another veteran insurgent Republican senator, Albert Cummins of Iowa, took a similar stand, asserting that a league with "the power to use armies and navies to enforce its decrees" would only "provoke war instead of suppressing it." Roosevelt predictably damned the whole enterprise. "Peace without victory is the natural ideal of the man who is too proud to fight," he sneered. Roosevelt's erstwhile imperialist and Progressive cohort Albert Beveridge again attacked the abridgment of sovereignty under a league, and he was joined by another ex-Progressive, Senator Miles Poindexter of Washington, who rejected "the proposition that we shall surrender our independence." The most searching criticism came from Lodge, who now recanted his earlier attraction to the league idea. Lodge professed "no superstition in regard to Washington's policy" against alliances, but he believed that there was "in this tortuous and distracted world nothing but peril in abandoning our long and well-established policies." For Lodge, those traditional policies of avoiding permanent alliances were "as clear as the unclouded sun at noonday, and are not collections of double-meaning words." By 1917 the league idea had clearly emerged as a major political issue.

CRISIS RENEWED

The European belligerent governments reacted with surprising calm to Wilson's call for a "peace without victory." It would prove indeed the calm before the storm because on January 9, 1917, the German government had decided to resume and widen submarine warfare, starting on February 1. The Germans realized that their action could hardly fail to bring the United States into the war against them, but they reasoned that they now had sufficient numbers of submarines to make deep inroads against Allied shipping. Their plan was to cut their foes' transatlantic lifeline of munitions, food, and supplies, and thereby win the war long before the Americans could mobilize enough forces to make any impact. This calculated military risk almost succeeded. Allied losses to submarine attacks in the spring and summer of 1917 came close to knocking Britain out of the war. Only the last-minute decision by the British to adopt the convoy system, under which naval vessels escorted merchant ships in packs, provided an effective defense against undersea attacks and thus foiled the submarine campaign.

Yet the German plan contained a fatal flaw. By 1917 British credit in the United States was about to collapse, which would have cut the Allies' overseas supply lines without submarine attack. When added to the Allies' other setbacks in 1917—the collapse of Russia, weakness in Italy, mutiny in the French armies—that blow might well have cost them the war. Incredibly, the Germans either knew nothing of Britain's financial plight or underestimated its importance. The decision to renew submarine warfare was an expression of German contempt for a "shop-keeper's war"—one waged through economic attrition. Germany's leaders wanted to win a crushing victory through strictly military means. But by recklessly provoking the United States, they were trading probable victory for near certain defeat.

Ten days after the decision to unleash their submarines, the German foreign secretary, Arthur Zimmermann, secretly cabled their embassy in Mexico City. Zimmermann warned of the approaching resumption of submarine warfare, and he instructed his envoys to seek an alliance with Mexico in the likely event of war between Germany and the United States. This cable—soon to be famous as the Zimmermann Telegram—offered the Mexicans recovery of lost territory in Texas, New Mexico, and Arizona should they enter the war against the United States. Through their cable-tapping and code-breaking operations, the British knew the contents of the Zimmermann Telegram within hours of its transmission on January 19. Because they took elaborate precautions to conceal their interception, the telegram was not released to the Americans for several weeks. With the resumption of submarine warfare imminent, and American participation in the war therefore likely, the British could afford to be unruffled by Wilson's proposal three days later for peace without victory. The British seemed to know that all they had to do was wait.

On January 31, 1917, the German ambassador informed the State Department that submarine warfare would commence against all shipping the next day. The news sent shock waves through the United States. Heated debate about an appropriate response swirled around the president, who still struggled to avoid having to choose between war and submission. Wilson broke diplomatic relations with Germany. It was, he explained to a joint session of Congress on February 3, the only "alternative consistent with the dignity and honor of the United States." But it was not, he insisted, a step toward war. "Only actual overt acts," by Germany could bring hostilities. Germany was quick to supply these. The submarine campaign opened with full force, sinking American as well as Allied ships and killing scores of citizens.

Wilson's response was to call for an armed neutrality, and with some reluctance he sent to Congress a measure to arm merchant vessels. Speaking to another joint session on February 26, the president asserted that the armed ships bill was intended solely to defend "those rights of humanity without which there is no civilization." On March 1 the House passed the bill by 403 to 14, and an amendment to prohibit American vessels from carrying munitions failed with 293 against. The 125 congressmen who favored the amendment showed that there still was strong sentiment against American entry into the war.

On February 28, the Zimmermann Telegram was published. The British had turned the telegram over to the Americans four days before. After taking steps to verify its authenticity, Wilson decided to release the telegram in order to bolster public support for armed neutrality.

"ON THE AMERICAN PLAN." A disgruntled Uncle Sam asks the waiter, Wilson: "Here, Waiter, I can't wait forever. Where's my airplane soup?" "Cook begins on that next month, sir." "Next month! And my grilled rifles?" "Rifles too old to cook, sir." "Then bring on the canned ships." "No ships in the house, sir; nor in sight, sir." The preparedness issue persisted through the early war years.

The telegram had a stunning effect, especially after Zimmermann publicly acknowledged having sent it. Many Americans had previously regarded the submarine controversy as a remote affair which involved only a few wealthy transatlantic travelers and scruffy merchant seamen. Now the threat of Mexican involvement, no matter how farfetched it seemed, brought the war closer to home. Some previously uncommitted politicians and editors now called for war, but most persisted in seeking some honorable alternative. Anti-interventionists dug in their heels. Senator La Follette was already opposed to the armed ships bill, and what he regarded as a war scare over the Zimmermann Telegram only stiffened his resistance.

A group of eleven senators, led by La Follette and composed almost equally of Republican insurgents and Bryanite Democrats, prevented the House-approved armed ships bill from coming to a vote in their chamber. Through parliamentary maneuvers and lengthy speeches, the opponents consumed the time that remained before the expiration of the Congress at noon on March 4, 1917. Tempers flared, and physical violence threatened to break out on the Senate floor. One senator was ready to use a file as a dagger, while La Follette had brought in a revolver, which his son quietly removed from his desk. Supporters of the bill took revenge by consuming the session's final hours, depriving La Follette of his coveted chance to close the debate with a carefully prepared statement. Wilson blasted the filibuster with a stinging rebuke: "A little group of willful men, representing no opinion but their own, have rendered the Great Government of the United States helpless and contemptible." But when advised by the attorney general that the president already had the authority to do so, Wilson ordered the ships armed. His words and deeds were now reminiscent of Roosevelt's, and he was following his predecessor's footsteps by resorting to executive action to circumvent Congress.

While most Americans remained as torn as ever between war and peace, Allied losses at sea climbed, and in Russia a relatively bloodless revolution at the beginning of March toppled the czar. The Russian revolution expunged a blot of autocracy from the Allied cause, but it also raised doubts about the viability of their already shaky Eastern

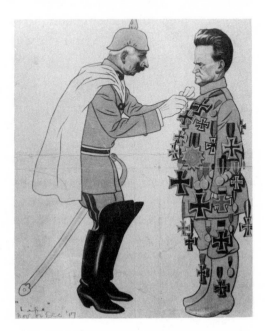

A Life *cartoon depicting Sen. La Follette as a traitor for his opposition to the armed ships bill.*

Front. The president meanwhile gave few indications of his thinking. On March 9, Wilson called Congress into special session for April 16, and on March 21, he moved the date up to April 2. He also authorized limited naval action against German submarines, and he permitted an American admiral to travel incognito to London to consult with the British. At no time, however, did Wilson indicate to anyone that he regarded these actions as steps toward war.

Wilson went through an agony of the soul as he wrestled with what to do. Cabinet meetings witnessed sharp exchanges as Secretary of State Lansing, Postmaster General Burleson, and Secretary of Treasury McAdoo tried to push the president toward intervention. "You are appealing to the spirit of the code duello," Wilson once snapped at Lansing, when he suggested that German violence against the United States required a response in kind. Another time Wilson avowed that he would "submit to anything and any imputations of weakness or cowardice" in order to stay out of the war. Wilson shared the fears of many anti-interventionists about undoing reform achievements. If the United States went to war, he told one cabinet member, "you and I will live to see the day when the big interests will be in the saddle." Further, as he privately confessed to a newspaper editor, he shrank from awakening "the spirit of ruthless brutality" that would infect "the very fibre of our national life." Above all, Wilson ached at the prospect of abandoning "peace without victory." American intervention would remove "a preponderance of neutrality" from world politics. No longer would there be "bystanders with power sufficient to influence the peace terms. There won't be any peace standards to work with. There will only be war standards."

When the new Congress convened on April 2, 1917, the first woman in either House took her seat: Representative Jeannette Rankin of Montana, a Republican. Democratic control of the House was now tenuous and required horse-trading with a remaining handful of Progressives. But the most anxious attention focused on the White House. Everybody awaited the president's address to a joint session that night, and nobody knew what he was going to say. When Wilson spoke, his first words gave no hint of his intentions, as he recounted recent diplomatic events. Only gradually did the drift of his remarks become clear: armed neutrality was an insufficient response to German attacks. "There is one choice we cannot make," Wilson declared, "we are incapable of making: we will not choose the path of submission." A storm of applause arose from the senators and representatives, many of whom waved small flags. Conspicuously silent was Senator La Follette, who

Jeannette Rankin, the first woman elected to Congress and a dedicated pacifist.

sat with his arms folded and his mouth grimly set.

Wilson acknowledged his "profound sense of the solemn and even tragical character of the step I am taking." The words "solemn," "tragic," and "grave," cropped up again and again in ways that lent a somber beauty to the speech. He made no exalted claims for America, which he described as "but a single champion" of right. In urging defense of the nation's ideals, he proclaimed that "the world must be made safe for democracy." He admonished his countrymen to "fight without rancor" and to uphold "with proud punctilio the principles of right and fair play we profess to be fighting for." Wilson's war address reverberated with the sense of tragic necessity. It was the most philosophical call to arms that any American president ever sounded. Wilson's deepest thoughts came at the end. "It is a fearful thing to lead this great peaceful people into war, the most terrible and disastrous of all wars, civilization itself seeming to be in the balance. But the right is more precious than the peace." America would fight for her greatest values, for democracy, freedom, "for the principles that gave her birth and happiness and peace which she has treasured. God helping her, she can do no other."

Wilson's last words were instantly recognizable as a paraphrase of Martin Luther's declaration, "God helping me, I can do no other." The president was casting his nation in the role of Luther's Christian in a sinful world. People and nations, no matter how righteous, could not avoid sin. In seeking to do God's will they must, in Luther's words, "sin boldly." Wilson was asking his countrymen, in seeking a better, freer, more peaceful world, to "sin boldly" by entering World War I.

Thus in April 1917 the man who until then had "kept us out of war" proposed to take the United States into World War I. Why? Why, in the face of his vivid apprehensions about the horrors of war at home and abroad did Wilson nevertheless make the decision to intervene? It was not a case, as Roosevelt and some others believed, of his being forced in against his will by public outrage. Every insightful observer, no matter what his or her own wishes were, agreed that Wilson could have carried congressional majorities with him for whatever policy he chose. Nor was it a case, as some writers later argued, of his embracing an idealistic crusade to purify the world. Wilson entertained sadder, more sober thoughts.

For all his emotional agony, the president chose war largely through calculations of cost and benefit. Armed neutrality, it rapidly became clear, entailed many of the costs of war, including lives and property lost, and inflamed public passions. But it brought none of the benefits of war, which included psychological release and, most important, the chance to shape the peace settlement. Wilson had come to see the European conflict as a war "deprived of glory." It was combat reduced to "mechanical slaughter," technological horror, and immobility in the trenches which brought "the sacrifice of millions of men." The world desperately required a new basis of order such as he had outlined in his peace without victory address. In the end, Wilson could see no alternative but to seek that order through entering this war.

Following the president's war message it was not Senator La Follette but Senator Lodge who rushed up to shake his hand. "Mr. President," Lodge exulted, "you have expressed in the loftiest possible manner the sentiments of the American people." This time La Follette stood aside, his arms still folded, his mouth still firmly set. Although Lodge and Roosevelt continued in private to pour verbal vitriol on Wilson for having waited so long, in public they and other interventionists called for an all-out crusade—arm-in-arm with the glorious Allies—to smite the evil Huns. Seven senators, including La Follette, Norris, Gore, and Vardaman, opposed the war resolution. La Follette got his chance to deliver a long, impassioned speech in which he heaped scorn on any notion that joining the Allies meant fighting for democracy. The bitterest denunciation came, however, from the normally low-key George Norris of Nebraska. "The object in having war and in preparing for war is to make money," he declared. "Human suffering and the sacrifice of human life are necessary, but Wall Street considers only dollars and cents. . . . We are going into war upon command of gold."

Senator Norris's declaration expressed a deep-seated progressive attitude toward foreign affairs. Not only the anti-interventionists but also Wilson himself suspected big business of fomenting wars in order to profit from arms sales; progressives also accused political conservatives of seeking entanglements abroad in order to distract popular attention and stifle reform at home. Since in 1917 the Allies had been borrowing vast sums of money from American financiers, and using the Morgan firm as their agent, there seemed to be some credence to charges of nefarious economic influences behind American intervention. Years later, when the imminent peril of Allied financial collapse became widely known, disillusioned liberals and revisionist historians would allege that Wilson had plunged the United States into the war not just because he had always been partial to the Allies himself, but more specifically because he wanted to save Wall Street's financial stake in the Allied effort. Such charges were false, inasmuch as the president retained little partiality toward the Allies by 1917, and thought the worst of big business, especially since its spokesmen had so recently fought against his re-election. The notion that the United States entered World War I primarily for economic reasons persuaded few in 1917, but in later years it would furnish a potent underpinning to American isolationism.

The great majority of senators and representatives favored the war resolution, many simply affirming that it was the proper response to German attacks. Some seemed to think that American participation in the war would be limited to naval engagements and sending supplies. Few anticipated full-fledged combat on the Western Front. The Senate passed the war resolution on April 4, 1917, followed two days later by the House, where fifty representatives opposed the action. Compared with other declarations of war before and since, this was substantial opposition. Only the War of 1812 received more negative votes in either chamber of Congress.

The House vote, on April 6, 1917, completed the constitutional process of declaring war. It was Good Friday, and the United States had entered World War I.

10

"Over There"

The war had always seemed elusive to Americans, who for a while did not know what to call it. Early on, the English-speaking belligerents had dubbed the conflict the "Great War," but that name never caught on in the United States. The one that eventually did, ironically, came from the enemy. For years before 1914, the Germans had talked and written about a "world war" as the necessary means to fulfill their "world politics" and attain their coveted status of "world power." The first American to call the European strife a world war had been Theodore Roosevelt in 1914. The ex-president had grasped the global implications of the conflict, and he had prophetically foreseen its effects on the United States. American intervention transformed the conflict from a European war with far-flung ramifications into a genuine world war.

A CALL TO ARMS

Before the term "world war" caught on, another phrase filled the breach—"over there." Taken from the composer George M. Cohan's popular song of the same title (1917), those two words captured the way Americans felt about the war. "The Yanks are coming," the song pledged, "and we won't come back 'til it's over, over there." It was a brave boast, but it left a lot of questions unanswered: Which Yanks and how many were going? where? to do what? Those questions plagued politicians, journalists, and most Americans in April 1917. Few Americans knew clearly why they were at war. President Wilson may have made the initial choice to go to war for honor and to secure larger ideals, but his job of educating the public had just begun. Mobilization required more than massing troops and matériel; it also required instilling morale and a sense of public purpose.

Opposition to American intervention in the war did not disappear. Many opponents remained critical and unreconciled, and it was unclear how far some of them would go down the path of obstruction. Particularly vociferous in their continued opposition were the Socialists. Eugene Debs ended his political retirement to lend his oratorical gifts to denunciations of the war. A few party leaders supported intervention, but the bulk of Socialists stood firm against belligerency. Debs and other Socialists denounced the conflict as a squabble over profits for big businesses and munitions makers, in which capitalists and aristocrats were sacrificing the workers of the world on the altar of their greed. Although many Socialists were German-Americans, such as former Representative Victor Berger of Wisconsin, most of them condemned both sides as equally reactionary and imperialistic. In the fall of 1917 Socialist candidates for municipal offices made much stronger showings than usual, almost entirely on their anti-war stands. In New York, Morris Hillquit increased the party's mayoral vote fivefold, to

"ARMY MEDICAL EXAMINER: 'At last a perfect soldier!'" An attack on America's entry into the war, appearing in The Masses.

nearly a third of the total. In the West, some IWW leaders called for strikes and sabotage against war-related work in mines and lumber camps.

A radical farmers' uprising in Oklahoma, the Green Corn Rebellion, tried to impede the induction of recruits into the armed forces. In August 1917, over 500 tenant farmers in southeastern Oklahoma banded together in an attempt to stage a march on Washington to protest the draft. A special posse surrounded the marchers after they had walked only a few miles, arrested them without violence, and hustled them off to jail. Of the 450 men arrested, 150 were convicted for incitement to rebellion and about half of them served terms in prison. The rate of conviction was not higher because the local people were afraid and unwilling to testify against their neighbors. These same counties in eastern Oklahoma had been a center of agrarian radical strength in the 1890s and had recorded some of the highest voter percentages in the entire country for Eugene Debs's candidacy on the Socialist ticket in 1912.

So much dissent and soft support would have created difficulties in waging war under any conditions, but one circumstance made the problem acute. For over a century no major nation had been able to mount a large-scale mobilization without resorting to conscription to fill the ranks of its armed forces. The United States had instituted a draft during the Civil War with mixed results. The practice of paying for substitutes, usually newly arrived immigrants, had allowed wealthy young men such as Theodore Roosevelt's father and J.P. Morgan to avoid military service. Resistance to the draft had provoked occasional violence, particularly three days of rioting in New York City in 1863. Memories of the Civil War draft and dislike of conscription, especially among immigrants, had combined to make the draft a political hot potato in the preparedness debates of 1915 and 1916. Roosevelt had been the only major figure to endorse the idea. Nevertheless, military experts agreed that a draft was essential, not only to raise armies but

"THE DRAFT—IT'S ALL IN THE WAY YOU SEE IT" was the comment in the St. Paul Pioneer Press, *1917.*

also to funnel workers toward exempted civilian jobs that were vital to war production.

Wilson endorsed a draft bill in Congress two weeks after the United States entered the war. As earlier in the preparedness fight, he met resistance from his own party, and he had to rely on support from Republicans such as Senator Lodge. Bryanite Democrats and the usually loyal speaker of the House, Champ Clark, broke ranks. Clark opposed the draft with a speech that included the crack, "In the estimation of Missouri there is precious little difference between a conscript and a convict." Despite such resistance the draft act passed with surprising ease in both houses, largely because of frenetic lobbying efforts by such preparedness organizations as the National Security League and the Navy League, and Wilson's customarily skillful legislative maneuvering.

The president signed the draft act into law on May 18, 1917, but legislative enactment was just the first hurdle. The War Department had laid careful plans to administer the draft as quietly and smoothly as possible. The army's Judge Advocate General, Enoch H. Crowder, and his principal assistant, a raspy-voiced, horse-faced cavalry officer, Captain Hugh S. Johnson, actually ran the effort. The administering agency, formally entitled the Selective Service Administration, was separated from the military and was staffed almost exclusively by civilians, particularly by unpaid volunteers at the local level. Johnson invested his thought and energies mainly in a public relations campaign to dispel impressions that a distant, impersonal government was snatching young men out of peacetime pursuits and sending them away to fight, perhaps to die.

Johnson's management of the draft, which eventually helped earn him a brigadier general's star, encompassed a variety of subterfuges to soften its impact. The system vested the selection of conscripts with the volunteer personnel who made up several hundred local boards. The letter that ordered draftees to report opened with phrases that would bring bitter smiles to the next three generations of young male Americans: "Greetings from the President of the United States: You have been selected by a committee of your neighbors for service in your country's armed forces." Such sugar coating may have helped the pill go down, but the fact remained that millions of men were being forced to abandon their chosen paths, to submit to absolute discipline, and to risk life and limb at the command of central authority. The psychological effects on those who went through the experience were varied and largely imponderable, but, if nothing else, the draft delivered a massive lesson that contradicted some of the most hallowed American social values. It taught young men and their families that individuals were not always masters of their fate, and that they could not always shape their destiny through self-reliance.

The draft functioned smoothly. On June 5, 1917, ten million American men between the ages of twenty-one and thirty-five registered for the draft at 4,000 polling places; by the war's end, over twenty-four million—44 percent of American males—had registered. Inductions began in July when the blindfolded secretary of war, Newton D. Baker, pulled capsules containing registration numbers from a clear glass bowl. After physical examinations and deferments, nearly six-and-a-half million men were found eligible for service, and slightly over 2.7 million draftees subsequently entered the army during the course of the war. Enlistments also ran high, comprising another 1.5 million in the army and 520,000 in the navy and marines. Social and economic inequities plagued the draft less in World War I than during the Civil War, but the local board system proved susceptible to pressures from local interests to defer or pass over favored people and groups of farmers and workers.

Not everyone complied with the draft. The rate of evasion ran at around 11 percent, or about 340,000 men in the course of the war. The

Secretary of War Newton Baker drawing the first draft number, 1917.

Justice Department mounted occasional raids, particularly in cities, to round up draft dodgers, and officials estimated that they caught about half of the evaders. Almost 65,000 registrants declared themselves objectors to military service, mostly on ground of religious beliefs. Draft boards honored the claims of nearly 57,000 of them. Just under 21,000 objectors were drafted to serve in non-combat roles. Many then changed their minds about bearing arms, including the later combat hero Alvin York, a deeply religious Tennessee mountaineer. York had searched the Bible and his conscience before deciding that it was moral for him to take up arms against fellow human beings. On one day in October 1918, Corporal York, who had acquired his proficiency with firearms as a backwoods hunter, singlehandedly killed 14 and captured 132 Germans. Other objectors served as stretcher-bearers or support troops. The 4,000 who refused to participate at all suffered imprisonment and often harsh treatment at the hands of military authorities.

The smoothness of the draft betokened America's efficiency in training, arming, and transporting forces to fight on the Western Front. American mobilization was the great success story of World War I. Its speed and extent surprised friend and foe alike. Within a little over a year, the United States expanded its armed forces twenty-fold to nearly five million men and women. By the time the fighting ended in November 1918, more than two million American troops were in Europe, along with vast quantities of equipment that included 45,000 horses, nearly 40,000 cars and trucks, and 2,000 airplanes.

This phenomenal mobilization required the coordination of military, industrial, logistical, and financial efforts, and it demanded new forms of organization under central planning and direction. Curiously for a politician who had once scoffed at "experts" and long lauded the capacities of ordinary people, Wilson turned most of the war effort over to professionals and highly trained technicians. Of all American wars, World War I belonged most to career officers, who enjoyed minimal interference from civilian authorities and political critics in formulating strategy, dispatching forces, and managing troops in the field.

"Politics is adjourned" was the phrase Wilson coined in May 1918 to describe his war policies. The claim was self-serving and often inaccurate, but partisanship and the promotion of future electoral stars played much less of a role in World War I than in any previous American war. Ever since the Revolution, generalships and combat heroism had offered well-worn, often deliberately chosen paths to political preferment. Roosevelt's charge up San Juan Hill in 1898 was just the most recent example. World War I proved an exception. Only two military veterans

America's mobilization for World War I was massive. This Cleveland, Ohio, factory assembled tanks for the war effort.

of the war would eventually become president, and then long afterward and for reasons largely unrelated to their war-time service: Harry S Truman and Dwight D. Eisenhower. By contrast, the war service of two civilians helped boost careers that led to the White House: Herbert Hoover and Franklin D. Roosevelt.

The secretary of war, Newton D. Baker, had occupied his office only a year when the United States entered the war. Despite his lack of military background, and his previous coolness to the draft and increased preparedness, Baker established cordial relations with his senior officers, particularly General Peyton C. March, the Chief of Staff, and General John J. Pershing, who was named commander of the American Expeditionary Force (AEF) in Europe. Baker proved a capable executive and staunch defender of his department against political attacks.

Civil-military relations were different at the Navy Department, where the North Carolina newspaper editor and friend of Bryan's, Josephus Daniels, remained as secretary. Cordially hated by old-fashioned admirals and big industrial contractors, Daniels had long since become a prime target for attacks by Roosevelt, Lodge, and other advocates of preparedness. Worse, his deputy, assistant secretary Franklin Roosevelt, had aided and abetted his opponents. A distant cousin of the ex-president and husband of his niece, the younger Roosevelt had frequently lampooned his chief's Southern accent and small-town manners at upper-crust social gatherings, and he had leaked damaging information to Republican critics on Capitol Hill. Only Daniels's sweet temper, patience, and political sagacity kept him from firing Roosevelt, who gradually came to appreciate and admire the secretary as a shrewd administrator and genuine friend of the navy. As chief of naval operations, Daniels appointed Admiral William S. Benson, with whom he worked well. Once the United States was in the war, he named Admiral William S. Sims fleet commander in European waters.

The navy made one of the United States' three biggest contributions to winning the war. Naval combat in World War I focused primarily on the submarine. When the United States entered the war, the German submarine campaign seemed to be fulfilling its aim of speedy victory. In April 1917 the Germans sank 900,000 tons of Allied shipping, at which rate, experts on both sides calculated, Britain could hold out for no longer than four months. When Admiral Sims reached London, the British Admiralty apprised him of the true extent of the submarine peril, which they had kept hidden even from their own people and Parliament. The one glimmer of hope lay in the proposal by a

General John J. Pershing.

group of junior British officers to adopt the convoy system. Sims sided with the convoy advocates against senior British and American admirals, who sneered at playing nursemaid to merchantmen. Sims's influence tipped the scales toward prompt adoption of the convoy system, which soon cut sinkings to bearable levels. That decision, together with the growing use of American destroyers as escorts, played a major part in the eventual Allied victory.

The second great American contribution to the Allied victory was financial. Just as the convoy system stopped German submarines from cutting Allied lifelines of overseas supplies, huge American loans forestalled the crumbling of foreign exchange that would have accomplished the same result. In April 1917, the British sent a mission headed by the new foreign secretary, Arthur James Balfour, to Washington with the main task of disclosing their desperate need for money. As it turned out, the Balfour mission failed to avert an exchange crisis in June. Only a flurry of desperate negotiations and a second special mission prevented the collapse of Allied credit, as the American treasury made a series of emergency loans totalling over $500 million. After that, money flowed smoothly to British and French purchasing agents, even though Secretary of the Treasury McAdoo and others continued to suspect that wily Europeans might be trying to swindle gullible Americans. These events sowed seeds of mistrust over war debts that would rankle international relations during the next two decades.

The third major American contribution to winning the war was military. Convoys and credit for the purchase of supplies enabled the Allies to stave off defeat during the dark days of 1917. That year witnessed a string of military reverses for the Allies. These included mutinies in the French army, the Italian defeat at Caporetto (brilliantly described by Ernest Hemingway in *A Farewell to Arms*), which caused a partial collapse of their front, and the relentless crumbling of the new provisional government in Russia, which culminated in November with the Bolshevik Revolution. The Russians, it was estimated, had suffered over nine million casualties in the war since 1914. Their economy was in a shambles, with industries stripped of manpower and starvation rampant because of the lack of laborers to plant and harvest crops. The Bolshevik leader, Vladimir I. Lenin, was determined to get Russia out of the war, and his victory in the revolution virtually guaranteed a separate peace between Russia and Germany. That separate peace came in March 1918 in the Treaty of Brest-Litovsk, allowing the Germans to concentrate nearly all their military might against the Western Front.

The failure of the Germans' offensive—which encompassed the most massive ground combat up to that time in history—sealed their defeat. The German generals stubbornly refused to learn the lessons of the preceding four years of war: artillery and machine guns gave entrenched defenders an overwhelming advantage against even gigantic offensives. In staking their all on yet another offensive, the German generals squandered the manpower that could have allowed them to hold out against the fresh American forces that began to reach France in strength in June 1918. As earlier in their submarine campaign, the German leaders gambled everything to win a sweeping military victory. This time they ensured their defeat in a way that would poison their nation's politics and help to foment another world war in twenty years.

Few American troops fought in the effort to stop the giant German offensive in the spring of 1918. General Pershing resisted the pleas of Allied commanders to integrate small American units at once into the established battle lines. As an American nationalist and an ambitious general, Pershing insisted that the AEF must fight as a separate army under his sole command. He did relent in some particularly desperate cases, such as the heroic stand by army artillery units at Cantigny in May and the brave fight by marines at Belleau Wood in June. But the thin lines of battle-weary French and British veterans withstood the final German onslaught with scant assistance from their newly arriving friends. The European Allies justifiably resented American claims of having saved them from annihilation in the darkest hour of the war. Yet in a broader sense American forces were essential to victory. The British and French knew that if they could just last a little longer the Yanks would be coming. That psychological lift, no matter how imponderable, played an indispensable part in enabling them to hold out this one last time. Moreover, after blunting the German offensive it took the swift infusion of American forces to achieve victory.

American troops saw their first substantial action on May 28, 1918, at Cantigny, a village near Rheims, France, when several regiments of artillery and infantry joined French units in blunting one of the last salients of the German offensive. A week later, in division-sized engagements along the same section of the Western Front, the United States marines participated in the recapture of Belleau Wood. The marines' advance was like a descent into hell, as shells burst constantly, clouds of gas and smoke swirled and settled, and piles of dead and wounded men mounted. At one point, Sergeant Dan Daly, twice decorated with the Congressional Medal of Honor, urged his platoon forward by shouting, "Come on you sons of bitches, do you want to live forever?" Out of 8,000 marines in action, over 5,000 were killed or

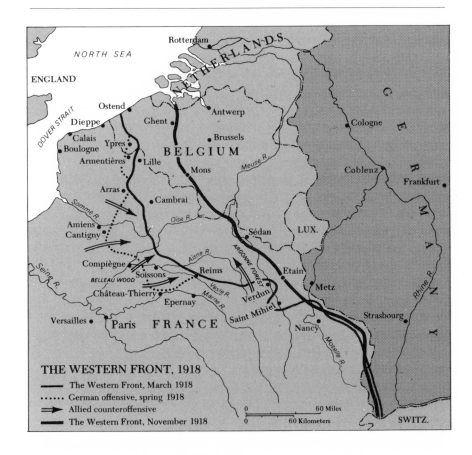

THE WESTERN FRONT, 1918

——— The Western Front, March 1918
•••••• German offensive, spring 1918
⟹ Allied counteroffensive
━━━ The Western Front, November 1918

0   60 Miles
0   60 Kilometers

wounded in taking Belleau Wood. In July 1918, 75,000 men from the
United States Army joined the French in their slogging, month-long
Aisne-Marne offensive. German leaders later confessed that when they
encountered the fresh American troops they knew that they had lost
the war.

In August 1918, the Allied counteroffensive opened in earnest with
the first independent American operation in the Aisne-Marne sector
of the front, which involved 550,000 troops in bloody fighting to retake
the city of Chateau-Thierry. By September, over a million American
soldiers had reached France, and General Pershing insisted upon running his own sector of the front. After some hesitation, the Allied supreme
commander, French Marshal Ferdinand Foch, granted the Americans
their wish by assigning them an area south of Verdun along the Meuse
River. On September 12, Pershing commenced operations against
German positions at St. Mihiel, which his divisions captured after four

days of fierce combat and monumental transport foul-ups. It was the largest single American engagement in the war. Pershing commanded over a million troops in that offensive, which involved slow slogging through the mud in almost constant rain, and claimed over 100,000 casualties in the first two weeks. Logistical failures continued to plague Pershing as the traffic jam became synonymous with the AEF. For two weeks in October, Pershing halted nearly all field operations while he relieved commanders, shifted units, and whipped his forces into better shape. Foch then ordered Pershing to shift the bulk of his forces north of Verdun, where they pushed the Germans back along a twenty-four-mile battle line that stretched through the Argonne Forest.

By November 1, 1918, over two million American troops had reached France. Pershing now had forty-two divisions under his command, twenty-six of which were on the battle line. Allied war plans called for a crossing of the Rhine early in 1919, with American forces to play the major role in an invasion of Germany. Instead the German government, weakened by military setbacks and a political crisis at home, sued for peace and signed the Armistice that ended the war on November 11, 1918. The Yanks deserved much of the credit for ending the first world war so soon.

Soldiers of the U.S. 16th Infantry, First Division, celebrating a victory over the Germans in France.

Just a little over a year and a half had elapsed from intervention to Armistice, and in that brief span United States forces lost over 52,000 soldiers killed in action, and sustained nearly 200,000 more wounded. Though Americans saw much less large-scale military action than the British, French, Russians, or Germans, participation in the war had a sizable impact on those Americans who fought in Europe, and on those who stayed at home. The nearly five million men and women who either volunteered for or were drafted into the armed forces underwent a massive common experience. Even troops who had remained stateside had been uprooted from local communities and moved around the country for training and duty. Although local units and state divisions stayed together, as for example New York's renowned, largely Irish-American Sixty-ninth Regiment, some outfits deliberately drew men from all over the United States. One of these was the Forty-second Division—called the Rainbow Division because, by including National Guard units from many states, it symbolically drew together the colors of the flag—which was commanded by the army's youngest general, the dashing Douglas MacArthur. Other divisions comprised similar mixtures, not by design but by chance, depending on the draftees who happened to be sent to them.

Wounded American troops' shelter in the ruins of a church, Argonne, 1918.

Military training in World War I introduced many young men to modern technology and hygiene for the first time. The army and navy required daily bathing and shaving. They issued the newly developed safety razor to all male personnel, thereby, as one writer observed, changing the shaving habits of a generation. As part of the overall emphasis on scientific expertise, the services conducted both intelligence and psychological testing to learn more about the new inductees, and experimented with indoctrination programs about the purposes of the war and proper conduct. Soldiers and sailors received frequent lectures and warnings about the dangers of drink and venereal disease, and the navy mounted campaigns to clean up red-light districts near bases and shipyards. One such effort in 1917 closed down Storyville, in New Orleans, where many black jazz musicians had gotten their start playing in the bawdy houses.

The army's and navy's emphasis on moral uplift had positive as well as repressive aspects. Both services brought in clergymen, psychologists, social workers, recreation specialists, entertainers, and journalists to make military life more wholesome and enjoyable—perhaps a hopeless task. Army camps in particular featured a variety of organized athletic, musical, and theatrical activities. Professional actors and singers, such as Al Jolson and Douglas Fairbanks, performed on military posts, and major league baseball teams played exhibition games there. Every post had its own newspaper, which provided information and humor within the limits of military discipline. Although a few fugitive army newspapers had sprung up during the Civil War, these World War I journals represented the first officially sponsored efforts. Military journalism made a further leap forward in 1918 with the establishment of a daily newspaper for the AEF, *Stars and Stripes,* which was distributed to all soldiers. The army was still the army, but now it included some of the ties and values, if not the comforts, of home.

The war had its greatest effect of course on the two million servicemen who crossed the Atlantic, particularly the several hundred thousand who saw combat. The newly arrived Americans encountered the squalor and misery in the trenches that their European counterparts had been enduring for nearly four years. The trenches were dirty, constantly crumbling from the reverberations of artillery shells, infested with rats and lice, and usually filled with at least several inches of standing water. The most frequent complaint from soldiers in all armies was that they could never get dry. Shoes and clothing rotted in the constant damp. Skin infections were rampant. Colds, pneumonia, and influenza flourished among the chilled, confined, exhausted troops.

A convalescent soldier reading the lastest issue of Stars and Stripes, *France, 1918.*

Thanks in part to the recent beginnings of psychiatry as a branch of medicine, the mental and emotional damage of combat began to be diagnosed and treated in rudimentary ways. The special strains of confinement and persistent artillery pounding in the trenches had already given rise to the term shell shock. Over 7,000 American soldiers were officially diagnosed as suffering from shell shock, and an indeterminate number of others carried unacknowledged psychological scars from their experiences.

But combat was not an unrelieved horror. Because most American troops saw action in the summer and fall counteroffensives of 1918, they experienced the exhilaration of a war of movement. World War I produced its share of colorful tales of fighting and inspiring stories of heroism, such as Corporal, later, Sergeant York. Equally celebrated heroes had already emerged from the ranks of aviators. The minuscule but highly publicized air war had long provided both the movement missing on the ground and the opportunity for knight-like individual combat. Before 1917, enough Americans had joined the French air arm to form the nucleus of the Army Air Corps in France. Captain Eddie Rickenbacker, a former automobile racer who went to France as General Pershing's chauffeur and learned to fly there, downed twenty-six German aircraft and later became a pioneer in civilian aviation.

Many American soldiers and sailors were not sorry to make the break from home. The thrill of first-time foreign travel compensated at least in part for the rigors, confinement, and boredom of military service.

Sergeant Alvin York, war hero.

Paris exerted its special allure for these young Americans and gave rise to a popular witticism, "How are you going to keep 'em down on the farm, once they've seen Paree?" These youthful newcomers usually found a warm welcome in France. After all, they were not only military saviors but they also had money to spend. The Americans' pay—$25 a month for privates, with an $8 a month bonus for foreign duty—was much higher than that of British and French soldiers, and it gave a new twist to the soldiers' nickname, "doughboys," which had originated in the Civil War. Despite the incessant propaganda and the watchful eyes of chaplains and social workers, many doughboys reveled in the tastes of French wines and brandies, and enjoyed the company of French women. These experiences may have affected only a small minority of American soldiers, but a considerable number of young men had literally and figuratively tasted a different way of life.

Two particular groups of Americans—one tiny but inordinately influential, the other large and mainly ignored or despised—had bittersweet experiences overseas. The first was the knot of young writers and intellectuals whom Gertrude Stein later dubbed the "lost generation." Their most renowned members included the future novelists Ernest Hemingway and John Dos Passos, the poet e. e. cummings, and

Ernest Hemingway.

the critic Malcolm Cowley. These youthful literary men, most of whom were graduates of leading colleges, enlisted not as combatants but as ambulance drivers, and not out of patriotic fervor but in search of experience. Their writings and reputations later fixed the image of World War I as a rite of passage for idealistic American youth. These young men, so the stories emphasized, found disillusionment amid the horrors of the trenches, and they returned home fed up with their country's narrowness and hypocrisy. The best of their novels were Dos Passos's *Three Soldiers* (1919) and Hemingway's *A Farewell to Arms* (1929), in which the hero expresses the disillusionment of his generation: "That was what you did. You died. You did not know what it was about. You never had time to learn. They threw you in and told you the rules and the first time they caught you off base they killed you." Bent on the hedonistic flaunting of social taboos and restrictions, particularly prohibition, this lost generation spent the postwar years eschewing political commitment, laughing at idealism, and drinking compulsively. Many besides Hemingway and fellow novelist F. Scott Fitzgerald expatriated themselves to Europe in search of a "freer" atmosphere. The stories wove a charming legend, which within a decade formed the prevailing view of the American experience in World War I.

The other group with bittersweet experiences overseas were the 367,000 black Americans who served in uniform during World War I. Black enlistments ran high, evidently out of mingled desires to demonstrate patriotism and escape discrimination. Draft calls also ran higher for blacks than for whites. The navy accepted only 5,000 blacks as sailors, all in separate, menial assignments; none served in the marines. The army segregated blacks as a matter of course; even the Rainbow Division was all-white. Blacks were relegated to separate areas in training camps, allotted inferior facilities and equipment, and provided with few of the new social services available to whites. Interracial tensions soon surfaced, particularly in cities and towns near bases. In August 1917 a riot involving black soldiers in Houston, Texas, left nineteen people dead, including four white policemen. The army's punishment was swift, harsh, and arbitrary. Thirteen black soldiers were hanged at

Members of the U.S. 369th infantry regiment, which was awarded the Croix de Guerre for bravery at the battle of Meuse-Argonne.

once and six more soon afterward, while over fifty were sentenced to life imprisonment. The War Department made no provision for commissioning or training black officers until protests by the NAACP led to the establishment of one officer candidate program in June 1917. By war's end 1,200 black officers had been commissioned.

Black soldiers who went to France had mixed experiences there. The AEF originally intended to employ them solely in labor squads, but further pressures by the NAACP caused two black divisions to be formed, one of which briefly saw front-line duty. The black troops' combat record appeared contradictory. One regiment fought well, but more attention focused on the other units that reportedly had to be forced to fight. These black divisions suffered from several problems. Their highest ranking officers were whites who resented the assignments and looked for trouble. Inadequate training plagued lower-ranking black officers, who often had little idea about how to lead troops. In all, their perceived inadequacies furnished a self-fulfilling prophecy to the army's white, often Southern upper echelons, who pulled the black troops off the front lines as soon as possible. Exaggerated tales of incompetence and cowardice under fire in World War I would plague black soldiers for the next three decades.

Despite discrimination and unfair treatment, however, black sol-

Home from the war, these troops are welcomed at a club in Newark, New Jersey, 1918.

diers enjoyed many of the same horizon-expanding experiences as their white counterparts in France. They also reaped a special benefit. For the first time they encountered a society with little or no reflexive color prejudice against them. The breadth and depth of the impressions left by these tastes of freedom must remain imponderable, but clearly many black Americans could never again regard segregation and inferiority as unalterable states of affairs. Whites back home certainly feared that blacks' experiences in France were having such effects and returning black veterans stirred special dread. President Wilson privately grumbled that equal treatment overseas had "gone to their heads." Southern white spokesmen fixed on the emotionally loaded issue of interracial sex. In the upsurge of lynching in 1919, ten black victims were soldiers, several of whom were hanged and mutilated in their uniforms. Allegedly "uppity" black veterans with notions about "social equality" became favorite targets for vigilante action by the rising Ku Klux Klan. In the short run at least, World War I probably worsened race relations in the United States.

The War at Home

Military mobilization on a vast scale required an equally impressive civilian mobilization, which was mainly economic and psychological. In the United States, as in Europe, mobilization during World War I witnessed the first real attempts at governmental planning and management of the economy. America's economic mobilization differed, however, from that of Britain, France, and Germany in that it relied less on compulsion and more on persuasion. The differences reflected ideological preferences in part, although conservatives seemed willing to shelve their opposition to governmental interference, at least temporarily, in support of the war. Some of them discovered a positive enthusiasm for state power as a means of suppressing political and social radicalism. Progressives of various persuasions likewise welcomed opportunities to experiment with new forms of governmental economic and social intervention in civilian as well as military life. The main opposition to the expansion of wartime state power sprang from some progressives and radicals who had opposed intervention and who now recoiled from governmental coercion to stifle dissent.

There was less coercion in America's mobilization than in Europe's in part too because the Wilson administration lacked the governmental instruments to force Americans to mobilize. The United States had almost no centralized bureaucratic agencies, with corps of trained personnel and efficient channels of communication and information gathering, to run its war effort. For example, neither the Selective Service System nor the Justice Department could draw upon any sort of national police to enforce the draft and other wartime laws. The first step in that direction occurred in 1917 with the founding of the Bureau of Investigation, which would be renamed in 1923 the Federal Bureau of Investigation. Enlistment of local and state police forces only partially filled the breach. Instead, the administration had to seek a high degree of voluntary compliance, which required popular support. This approach nicely fit Wilson's ideas about democratic leadership through the education of the public.

The man who did most to shift America's economy from peacetime production to support of the war effort was Bernard M. Baruch, the chairman of the War Industries Board (WIB). Southern-born like most members of the Wilson inner circle, this tall, handsome, self-proclaimed speculator on Wall Street took over the newly constituted WIB in March 1918, after nearly a year of fumbling by the military services and civilian agencies over production and procurement. The WIB was charged with coordinating the work of various committees that had

Bernard M. Baruch.

been set up during 1917 to oversee production and distribution in various industries, so that military procurement requirements could be met. The proliferation of these committees, over 150 by the end of 1917, their lack of real authority, and the suspicions of the War Department all severely hampered "industrial mobilization," especially when it came to shipping and delivering matériel to the army. Wilson appointed Baruch, who was also a large Democratic campaign contributor and outspoken admirer of the president, to clean up the mess. Wilson charged Baruch with general oversight of production and delivery for the military, but he wanted the WIB to retain "its present advisory agencies" and he gave Baruch no new powers as chairman.

Despite limited means to force compliance, the new WIB brought a semblance of order to war production. Through personal charm, seemingly encyclopedic command of information, and carefully cultivated relations with the press, Baruch created the appearance and, thereby, something of the reality of being a czar who could award contracts, set prices, demand compliance, fix standards, and punish offenders. One major struggle involved getting the automobile industry to convert its plants to war production. During the summer of 1918, when the car manufacturers balked at Baruch's demands, the WIB head announced, "You won't get your steel; that is all." The automakers soon came around and shifted most of their plants to making trucks and tanks for the army. Actually "Dr. Facts," as he was nicknamed by reporters, operated much more through bluff and wheedling, but his artfully contrived reputation smoothed and speeded war production and delivery.

To harness the nation's resources for the war effort, the Wilson administration enlisted both academic and business experts into civilian service. The businessmen, most of whom continued to be paid by their private firms, received $1 per annum from the government, thereby giving rise to the term "dollar-a-year-man." With coal and oil for the army and navy a critical need, Wilson appointed his friend, Harry A. Garfield, son of President James Garfield and president of Williams College, as fuel administrator. To manage the production and distribution of food to American forces and the Allies, Wilson appointed Herbert Hoover, whose work in Belgium had ended when America entered the war, as food administrator. Both the Fuel and Food Administrations achieved mixed results in allotting their resources. Difficulties in getting coal-mine owners and meat packers to agree on prices and deliveries forced rationing of home heating supplies in January 1918 and the institution of "meatless Mondays." Through constant sloganeering, the Food Administration got large numbers of

Herbert Hoover as general food commissioner, marshalling American agriculture for the war effort.

Americans to forego various foodstuffs on meatless and wheatless days, and to grow their own vegetables in war gardens. The Wilsons set an example by having sheep graze on the White House lawn. Baruch, Garfield, and especially Hoover believed that better results could be achieved through businessmen's voluntary compliance, and the "dollar-a-year-men" soon discovered business advantages to be gained through a friendly attitude toward government.

Not everything functioned well through persuasion and partnership. Though some sectors of war production did fine, especially automobiles, clothing, and small arms, other sectors did badly, particularly artillery, tanks, and aircraft. Because of bad planning and conflicts between the government and private industry, the United States supplied almost nothing in the way of big guns, tanks, and planes to the Allies. In other areas, compulsion replaced voluntarism. Transportation was so critical and the railroads proved so inept and recalcitrant that Wilson ordered a government takeover on January 1, 1918. The railroad managers had either failed or refused to cooperate with government requests to move men and matériel. Troop movements had been delayed, and shipments of munitions and food had arrived at seaports late, often missing the sailings of cargo ships. To run the railroads, the president appointed the hard-driving William Gibbs McAdoo, who was chafing at the difficulties of dealing with bankers in financing the war as secretary of the treasury. Even the WIB began to rely more on compulsion. Because the army command thought the agency was not meeting their requirements fast enough, they detailed Hugh Johnson to be their man on the scene. The energetic officer soon became one of Baruch's right-hand men, even as he exerted more military-style discipline over contractors. Another agency that helped enforce economic discipline was the Price-Fixing Committee, headed by the academic economist Robert S. Brookings. The committee's efforts reduced inflation during 1918, but its policies also sowed discontent among some farmers and manufacturers, who resented alleged favoritism toward Southern producers.

War finance in 1917 and 1918 would have tried the patience of a more placid person than McAdoo. The cost of fighting in World War I finally amounted to over $24 billion for the United States, not counting $11 billion in loans to the Allies. The war brought the nation its first real taste of truly large-scale government spending. Federal expenditures had totaled $1 billion for the fiscal year that ended June 30, 1916. They doubled the following fiscal year, and then they skyrocketed to $14 billion for fiscal year 1918 and $19 billion for fiscal 1919. The national debt, which had amounted to $1 billion in 1915, grew to $20 billion by 1920. Wilson had promised in his war address that ordinary Americans would not have to make financial sacrifices. He and McAdoo originally planned to pay at least half the cost of the war through taxation, especially on excess profits, business earnings, higher incomes, and large inheritances. Others were even more determined to make the wealthy and big business bear the brunt of war finance. Senator La Follette and Congressman Claude Kitchin fought doggedly to shape tax bills that included stiff corporate imposts and steeply graduated income and inheritance rates. Although La Follette and Kitchin fell short of complete success, the Revenue Acts of 1917 and 1918 levied the first substantial taxes on earnings of businesses and individuals in American history. They also shifted the main source of government finance away from tariffs and excise taxes.

La Follette's and Kitchin's agitation embarrassed Wilson and McAdoo. Their own political and economic sympathies with the tax program notwithstanding, they could not embrace the "soak the rich" approach, inasmuch as they depended on wealthy people and the financial community to buy bonds. Moreover, ballooning expenditures quickly ruled out their plan to rely on taxation as the primary means of financing the war. Eventually, just under $9 billion, slightly more than a third of direct American expenditures, came from taxes. The remainder had to be raised from borrowing, and for the Wilson administration this posed a difficult choice between borrowing in large amounts from wealthy investors and financiers, through high-denomination Treasury issues, or borrowing in small amounts from average citizens, through mass, low-denomination bond drives. Large-unit borrowing, primarily on Wall Street, had the advantages of raising money quickly and of enlisting the financial community behind the war. But it was expensive. Since market forces determined interest rates, such massive, repeated borrowing could not fail to worsen the already severe inflationary pressures that hit the American economy hard in 1919. Moreover, this kind of borrowing to a degree mortgaged war finance to Wall Street. It required the administration to modify its tax policies in an effort to appease businessmen. Large Treasury issues, 48 during and immediately after the war, became the government's chief source of short-term financing for the war effort.

Long-term financing was a different story. Most of it, a total of $21.4 billion, came though a series of five popular, small-denomination bond drives. The first four were called Liberty Loans and the last, launched in April 1919, was renamed the Victory Loan. The Liberty Loans, McAdoo's triumph, offered a cheaper, less inflationary means to pay for the war. The Treasury fixed successive interest rates at 3-1/2, 4, 4-1/2 percent, with thirty-year maturities and partial redemption after fifteen years. Those terms, together with the work of Brookings's Price-Fixing Committee, formed the basis for the administration's relatively successful control of inflation during 1917 and 1918. From the administration's standpoint, however, the Liberty Loans had some drawbacks. To make the bonds attractive to purchasers, their earnings were made exempt from federal taxation. That exemption induced businesses and wealthy individuals to buy them in large numbers, and cost the government in lost tax revenues. Moreover, the Federal Reserve Board ruled that banks which bought these bonds could count them as assets against which to issue notes. That ruling increased the money supply and partially foiled the administration's anti-inflationary efforts.

Whatever their economic shortcomings, the Liberty Loans conferred an inestimable psychological advantage. They offered an opportunity to sell the war, in several ways, to the American people. Besides getting ordinary citizens to open their pocketbooks, the Liberty Loan

A Liberty Loan poster.

drives furnished superb vehicles to build morale on the home front. McAdoo and others employed the latest advertising and public-relations techniques to sell the bonds. Posters and newspaper and magazine advertisements promoted the drives with visually arresting images that were sometimes luridly violent and sometimes bordered on sexual suggestiveness. Businesses and private clubs staged competitions to boost contributions. Patriotic societies and vigilante groups occasionally coerced reluctant subscribers and physically punished scoffers and skeptics.

Above all, Liberty Loan drives served as occasions for staging huge rallies. Every major city witnessed several mass gatherings, and millions of people turned out at rallies in New York. With official prodding, businesses gave employees time off to attend. Famous sports and entertainment figures added to the draw. Movie stars such as the swashbuckling, romantic hero Douglas Fairbanks and the beautiful starlet Mary Pickford, the comedian Charlie Chaplin, singers as different as operatic virtuoso Enrico Caruso and ex-vaudevillian Al Jolson, sports idols such as baseball greats Ty Cobb and Babe Ruth all spoke and performed at rallies. Their appearances were recorded for still broader audiences by newspaper photos and newsreels. These stars'

Douglas Fairbanks at a Liberty Loan rally.

roles in the Liberty Loan further attested to the growing influence of movies and big-time professional sports in American culture. The four Liberty Loans and one Victory Loan elicited over 60 million subscriptions, representing a broad segment of the American population. The drives' razzle-dazzle sales pitches and enforced patriotic conformity helped set the tone of American popular sentiment toward the conflict "over there." The Liberty Loan unquestionably played a big part in selling the war at home.

Selling the war was the specific task of a new agency that was established in April 1917, the Committee on Public Information (CPI). Headed by a respected reformer and magazine writer, George Creel, the agency emerged from a combination of Wilson's desire to guide and arouse public opinion, and journalists' fears of heavy-handed news management by the government. Creel was a Californian who had written favorably about Wilson and done publicity work for his re-election in 1916. He spearheaded a drive by his professional colleagues to be allowed to administer information policy themselves, and he was the inescapable choice to head the agency. A man of drive and sophistication, Creel acquitted himself well in many respects. The CPI, or Creel Committee as it was also known, recruited journalists, psychologists, artists, movie directors, writers, and scholars to publicize America's war effort at home and abroad. The CPI's foreign propaganda shaped the European Allies' knowledge of their new co-belligerents by supplying copy to newspapers and publishing books and leaflets in their own languages. The staple of this literature was President Wilson's own words, and the CPI was mainly responsible when his phrase "safe for democracy" took on a life of its own as a sometimes misleading justification of intervention. It also distributed the hundreds of thousands of photographs of the American president that turned him into an international cult figure. The CPI likewise smuggled and air-dropped into Germany and Austria-Hungary more than a million copies of the president's liberal war-aims statements, translated into German, Czech, Hungarian, Polish, and other languages.

The Creel Committee concentrated its major efforts, however, within the United States. As one observer noted, the CPI saturated the country with "information," often attractively packaged and ingeniously presented. Some posters urged young men to volunteer, as in James Montgomery Flagg's finger-pointing self-portrait as Uncle Sam—"I Want You"—and others admonished people to buy liberty bonds or simply to support the war. Fact books about both the Allies and the

James Montgomery Flagg's
Uncle Sam.

enemy poured off the presses, often in foreign languages for the benefit of recent immigrants. Annotated versions of Wilson's speeches were a staple of the CPI's publications at home, too. Films and phonograph records also lauded American intervention in the war.

The Creel Committee's most widely used and probably most effective device was the enlistment of speakers. A system of local committees, resembling the Draft Boards, organized about 75,000 clergymen, lawyers, teachers, and other citizens to deliver short, set speeches, with texts supplied from Washington. Officially titled "Four-Minute Men," the volunteers received a new speech every ten days on such topics as "Why we are fighting" and "Maintaining morals and morale." One model speech, calling the Germans "Prussians," charged that they pursued a "deliberate policy of terrorism" that led to "almost unbelievable besotten bestiality," and asked "Now, then, do you want to take the slightest chance of meeting Prussianism here in America?" Another speech thundered ". . . in the great struggle our country *is* right, supremely right, overwhelmingly right, sacredly right." Creel's claim that his Four-Minute Men gave over 7.5 million speeches to more than 300 million people may have been excessive, but the CPI's efforts clearly brought the war home to vast numbers of Americans.

Essential as the Creel Committee's work was to the war effort, it often undermined Wilson's political values. The CPI sold the war to citizens exactly the same way that businesses sold their products to customers. It bathed the Allies in an unblinkingly favorable light, as defenders of truth, virtue, freedom, ideals, and all that was good, pure, and noble in the world. The CPI did not shrink from dropping an occasional hint that God was on the Allied side, too. It portrayed the Germans and the other Central Powers as agents of the devil, evil barbarians, and brutal autocrats. The CPI's renditions of the enemy fell short of lurid British visions of the "Hun" and rapacious French depictions of the "Boche," but the CPI's productions were a far cry from the president's complex justification of intervention. Wilson was failing at the task that he valued most and had once practiced best as a political leader: education of the public. Rather than communicate to the American people his sophisticated, far-reaching but limited purposes in waging war, he smiled upon the antics of the CPI and lauded Creel for his contribution to victory in 1918.

The war could be sold at home in ways that were at odds with and ultimately corrosive of Wilson's own objectives because the president delegated authority in home-front management almost as much as in military affairs. He gave Baruch, Garfield, Hoover, and Creel free hands in their respective spheres. He likewise let Postmaster General Albert Burleson, and the successive Attorneys General Thomas W. Gregory and A. Mitchell Palmer, operate with little presidential oversight in matters involving freedom of speech and rights to dissent. Wilson's lack of control did not stem from presidential overwork. Throughout the war, the president stuck to his habits of strictly regulated hours at his desk, tightly rationed meetings and speaking engagements, frequent breaks for golf and rides in the White House limousine, and quiet evenings with family and a few close friends. Not until 1919, at the peace conference in Paris, did the president succumb to the constant strain and unrelenting demands on his time that soon undermined his less than robust health. During the war, Wilson delegated control over mobilization on the home front in order to focus on foreign policy. Wilson ran a largely lone-handed diplomatic show, which came to absorb his energy and attention to the exclusion of nearly every other concern.

Wilson also felt a need to act, and he was not inclined to impede the strong actions of others in his administration. In part this need compensated for his worry that he tended to over-intellectualize, to delay action by endlessly weighing the options. "An intellectual—such as you and I," Wilson once reportedly told Lincoln Steffens, "—an intellectual is inexecutive. In an executive job we are dangerous, unless we are aware of our limitations and take measures to stop our everlasting disposition to think, to listen to—not act." For himself, he had resolved "the day when my mind felt like deciding, to shut it up and act." This need to stop reflecting and second guessing in order to take action also underlay Wilson's decisions to unleash domestic propaganda and to trample on critics and opponents of the war.

Violations of civil liberties from 1917 through 1919 constituted a great failure for Wilson as a war leader, and they left the ugliest blot on his record as president. Some form of official repression was perhaps inescapable in 1917 and 1918 as a corollary to employing an aroused public opinion in waging war. Civil liberties in any nation at war present delicate problems, and even the most democratic of the European belligerents trampled on them during World War I. The British and French governments had summarily interned enemy aliens, executed suspected spies and traitors without trial and often in secret, imposed heavy censorship on the press and public speakers, and permitted private depredations against their own citizens.

In the United States repressions rarely went that far. The Wilson administration showed some sensitivity to constitutional and libertarian questions by heading off more extreme measures. Theodore Roosevelt, for example, wanted all publications subjected to military censorship and the whole country put under marital law. From Capitol Hill came the criticism that the administration did not deal harshly enough with dissidents. Senators and congressmen, at least rhetorically, urged hanging "traitors" from the nearest lampposts and called for widespread use of firing squads. The administration responded temperately with four laws enacted in 1917 and 1918 to restrict domestic exercises of speech and opinion. The first was the Espionage Act, passed in May 1917. It prohibited not only spying and sabotage but also more vaguely defined acts, including public criticism that could be construed as detrimental to the military, and it levied stiff fines and long prison terms as penalties. The second was the Trading with the Enemy Act, which was also passed in 1917. It forbade commerce with Germany and later with Austria-Hungary, and gave the postmaster general broad authority to suspend the mailing privileges of publications that he found objectionable. The Alien Act, passed in 1918, conferred on the commissioner of immigration broad powers to deport non-naturalized persons suspected of hostile actions and beliefs, including anarchism and advocacy of violent revolution. The Sedition Act, also passed in 1918, contained a sweeping ban on "uttering, printing, writing, or publishing any disloyal, profane, scurrilous, or abusive language" against the government or the armed forces, and it likewise imposed strong penalties.

These harsh laws were vigorously executed. Postmaster General Burleson used his powers under the Trading with the Enemy Act like a shotgun against dissident opinion. Few German-language publications fell under his ban, because they generally toed a patriotic line or went out of business. Instead, a variety of native-born critics of the war became Burleson's principal objects of attack. Publications banned from the mails included anti-interventionist books by former Representative Charles A. Lindbergh of Minnesota, and Tom Watson's racist magazine, *The Jeffersonian.* Lindbergh denounced intervention as a plot by Wall Street, while Watson charged that *"no king that ever lived wielded more autocratic control than President Wilson,"* who was trying to "systematize universal-goose-stepping." The postmaster general's favorite targets, however, were socialist newspapers and magazines. These included the *New York Call, American Socialist, Milwaukee Leader,* and *The Masses.* The *Leader*'s editor, former Socialist Congressman Victor Berger, was also convicted of violating the Espionage Act and denied his seat in Congress after being reelected in 1918.

Still harsher acts flowed from the Justice Department, where the attorney general assigned prosecution of dissenters to Solicitor General William H. Lamar. Over 2,000 people were prosecuted under the Espionage Act, and about half that number were convicted under the Sedition Act. The most famous violator of the Espionage Act was Eugene Debs, who was convicted for statements he made in a speech in Canton, Ohio, on June 16, 1918. Debs was at his intensely eloquent best in the speech. In ridiculing Wilson's claims to be fighting for democracy, Debs countered, "They tell us that we live in a great free republic: that our institutions are democratic; that we are a free and self-governing people. This is too much even for a joke." Arrested soon afterward and tried in September 1918, Debs refused to let his lawyers contest the charge. Instead, he proudly proclaimed his opposition to the war and avowed his socialist beliefs. When he was convicted of violating the Espionage Act and sentenced to ten years in prison, Debs answered with the most moving and widely quoted utterance of his long career: "Your honor, years ago I recognized my kinship with all living beings, and I made up my mind that I was not one whit better than the meanest on Earth. I said then, and I say now, that while there is a lower class I am in it, while there is a criminal element I am of it, and while there is a soul in prison I am not free."

Eugene Debs, candidate for president in 1920, pictured here outside his cell where he was serving a ten-year sentence for wartime sedition.

Debs and Victor Berger were the most visible of those Americans whose civil liberties were abridged during the war, but in their cases and others there were the ambiguities that arose when individual rights clashed with the needs of a nation at war. Some of Berger's utterances verged on praise for the enemy, and Debs deliberately violated the Espionage and Sedition Acts in a series of inflammatory statements. Wilson sought some accommodation with Debs but could find none: Debs considered civil liberties to be inviolable, whereas Wilson believed the war effort took precedence.

The laws limiting free speech passed during the First World War created the first institutional mechanisms by which the federal government could regulate freedom of expression. As a response to what one historian has called "the surveillance state," dissenters and concerned citizens formed organizations to defend those freedoms against government intrusions. Roger Baldwin, a young social worker and conscientious objector who was later convicted for refusing to register for the draft, founded the National Civil Liberties Union in 1917. Subsequently renamed the American Civil Liberties Union (ACLU), Baldwin's organization made the defense of free speech and opinion against all public and private attempts to abridge it a lasting concern in public life.

The courts moved gingerly in grappling with issues of civil liberties. The Supreme Court reversed Berger's conviction under the Espionage Act on procedural grounds, but in March 1919, in a majority opinion written by Justice Holmes, it upheld Debs's conviction on the ground that "if a part of the manifest intent of the more general utterances was to encourage those present to obstruct the recruiting service" then the government's war powers overrode protections of free speech under the First Amendment. Also in March 1919, Justice Holmes made one of his most famous and controversial contributions to the jurisprudence of free speech. In *Schenck v. United States,* another case involving a radical convicted under the Sedition Act, he wrote a broad majority opinion that laid down a test of freedom of expression. True to his long-held relativism, Holmes found that the scope of freedom of speech depended upon circumstances. To illustrate its contingency, he used the analogy of shouting "fire" in a crowded theater. Authorities could and must restrict speech under such conditions of "clear and present danger." True to his equally long-held nationalism, Holmes also reiterated the principle that he had asserted in the *Debs* case: "When a nation is at war, many things that might be said in times of peace are such a hindrance to its effort that their utterance will not be endured so long as men still fight."

President Wilson never commented on this opinion, but it expressed his own attitude toward civil liberties in wartime and helps to explain his acquiescence in official repression. Although Wilson did not take an active part in the wartime crackdown on dissent, he seldom opposed the actions of his more zealous subordinates. When complaints reached his ear, the president sometimes asked Attorney General Gregory and Postmaster General Burleson for explanations, but they rarely had to say much in their defense to satisfy him.

Ironically, Holmes himself soon reversed course on the civil-liberties issue. Under criticism from his one-time protégé, Judge Learned Hand, and Harvard Law School professor Zechariah Chafee, Holmes rethought his position on guarantees under the First Amendment. Starting in November 1919, he joined Brandeis in a series of dissents in free-speech cases that extended over the next decade. The first of these celebrated dissents came in the conviction under the Espionage Act of a group of foreign-born radicals who in August 1918 had distributed a leaflet protesting the dispatch of American troops to Russia, which they called an imperialist effort to quash the Bolshevik Revolution. In his opinion in *Abrams v. United States*, Holmes declared that "free trade in ideas . . . the power of the thought to get itself accepted in the competition of the market" lay at the heart of the Constitution. "It is an experiment, as all life is an experiment," and nothing but "the emergency that makes it immediately dangerous to leave the correction of evil counsels to time warrants making any exception to the sweeping command" of the First Amendment not to abridge the freedom of speech.

The federal government's repressions of civil liberties offered an unfortunate example that state and local governments emulated. Most of the official discrimination against German-Americans took place at these levels. During the war Nebraska passed a law forbidding the teaching of the German language in public schools at all grade levels. Although similar attempts failed in other states, most notably Wisconsin, a number of city and county school boards banned instruction in German. Local bodies also forbade the playing of music by German composers, including Bach, Mozart, and Beethoven. Some communities stripped library shelves of books in German and by German authors, including Goethe, Kant, and Nietzsche. State and local authorities came down hard on radicals, particularly Socialists who opposed the war and members of the IWW in the West. Several states adopted versions of the Sedition Act by enacting statutes that made it a crime to express anarchist or revolutionary beliefs. State legislatures also emulated Congress in refusing to seat duly elected Socialists.

Official actions stimulated private individuals and groups to commit much worse violations of civil liberties. Governmental discrimination spawned acts of repression that ranged from the comic to the tragically violent. German-American conductors and musicians were fired from the nation's leading symphony orchestras. Sauerkraut was briefly rechristened "liberty cabbage," and dachshunds were stoned in the streets. As one historian later noted, during World War I Americans sacrificed not only their liberties but also their sense of humor. German-Americans felt the sting of social disapproval. Many stopped speaking their native language at home, while others anglicized their names, including members of the family that owned the *New York Times*. The German-language press, already in decline because of assimilation by the second generation and the diminished flow of newcomers, emerged from the war with a fraction of its previous circulation and number of papers.

German-Americans now displaced southern and eastern European immigrants as the main targets of discrimination and restrictionist agitation. Italian- and Greek-Americans were now more acceptable because their home countries fought on the side of the Allies. Czechs, Croats, Poles, and others were welcome because they were subject peoples of the Austro-Hungarian Empire, and sought independence through the defeat of the Central Powers. For the year-and-a-half of America's belligerency, the brunt of popular hostility was lifted from these groups and shifted to the Germans. But the respite was short-lived: "Nordic" biases, augmented by fears of a flood of immigrants from war-ravaged Europe, quickly revived previous patterns of prejudice after the armistice.

Radicals too came under increasing attack from private groups and officials. These attacks worsened after the Russian Bolsheviks made their separate peace with Germany in March 1918, and called upon workers everywhere to rise up and end their capitalist-imperialist oppressors' war. Conservative elements in the United States seized upon the opportunity to tar all labor, socialist, and reformist groups with the brush of disloyalty. Nor were some American Socialists merely hapless victims in the revulsion against bolshevism. Many radicals openly sympathized with the new regime in Russia, and in 1918 the Harvard graduate and former Greenwich Village habitué John Reed published his laudatory eyewitness account of the Bolshevik Revolution, *Ten Days that Shook the World.* "Not by compromise with the propertied classes, or with the other political leaders," wrote Reed, ". . . did the Bolsheviks conquer the power." Rather, the Bolsheviks triumphed by "accomplishing the vast desires of the most profound strata of the people, calling them to the work of tearing down and destroying the old, and afterwards, in the smoke of falling ruins, cooperating with them to erect the framework of the new."

Reed returned home early in 1919 to join other left-wing Socialists in founding the American Communist Party, which advocated violent revolution and pledged obedience to the newly formed Communist International in Moscow. "Big Bill" Haywood of the IWW, who had been convicted for violation of the Espionage Act, likewise joined the party and then jumped bail and fled to Russia. Communist predictions of imminent uprisings in Europe turned out to be pipedreams, but the specter of revolution in Russia and the applause of American radicals were genuinely disturbing to the Wilson administration and others. A. Mitchell Palmer, who was appointed attorney general early in 1919, recalled that at the end of 1918, revolution had seemed like a prairie fire, "and that its sharp tongues of revolutionary heat were licking at the altars of the churches, leaping into the belfry of the school bell, crawling into the sacred corners of American homes, . . . burning up the foundations of society."

The IWW furnished a special target for private and official wrath. Vigilante actions during the war crippled the union in many locales. In the summer of 1917, the sheriff of Bisbee, Arizona, deputized 2,000 men, who rounded up 1,200 Wobblies and "deported" them to a remote desert area, where they were left without food and water. Lynchings, shootings, and tarrings and featherings of IWW members occurred regularly in the West during 1917 and 1918. In September 1917, the new Bureau of Investigation demonstrated its prowess by leading state and local police forces in a coordinated series of raids on IWW offices throughout the West. In often violent sweeps, the agents arrested over 200 Wobbly leaders, confiscated their files, and effectively closed down the organization. The ensuing prosecutions under the Espionage Act ended the IWW's role as anything more than a legal defense committee. The anti-Wobbly campaign drew support from employers and other businessmen with old scores to settle against them. Gompers and AFL union leaders were equally eager to purge the labor movement of radicalism and strengthen their own control, and they applauded and assisted in the raids and trials.

War critics closer to the political mainstream likewise suffered. On

*"THE IWW AND THE
OTHER FEATURES THAT
GO WITH IT." A* New York
Globe *cartoon depicting the
IWW as treasonous, 1917.*

the Great Plains and in the Mississippi Valley, the Nonpartisan League
remained cool to "war profiteers" and the Allied cause. President Wilson tried to find grounds for accommodation with the NPL, even conferring with its leader, Arthur Townley, at the White House in November
1917. In March 1918, however, Senator La Follette delivered an allegedly inflammatory speech to the NPL convention in St. Paul, Minnesota, in which he asserted, in response to hecklers, that Germany "had
interfered with the right of American citizens to travel on the high
seas—on ships loaded with munitions for Great Britain." Local conservatives seized upon the incident to move against the organization.
Townley and ex-Congressman Lindbergh, whom the NPL was backing for governor of Minnesota, were arrested and tried for violations of
state conspiracy laws. Both were acquitted, but Lindbergh was stoned,
burned in effigy, and run out of towns as he campaigned for and eventually lost the Republican primary for the governorship.

In Wisconsin, La Follette's foes pushed a resolution through the legislature condemning his St. Paul speech and demanding his resignation from the Senate. Faculty and students at his alma mater, the
University of Wisconsin, passed similar resolutions. The senator's effigy
was hanged and burned on the campus and in several towns. Some of

La Follette's followers in Congress and the state legislature were defeated in 1918, smeared by opponents as pro-German and disloyal. It was a political irony that, despite his opposition to prohibition and American intervention in the war, La Follette had never been close to the state's German-Americans, and their strongest enclaves had consistently opposed him and his reform movement.

The worst domestic strife during the war years took place in the West, the Plains, Minnesota, and Wisconsin. These areas had been scorched by social, political, and economic brushfires long before the United States entered the war; belligerency and the issues it raised worsened those conflicts. Old foes of the IWW, the NPL, and La Follette often deliberately manipulated wartime issues in an effort to destroy them. The effect on these domestic conflicts of America's intervention in the war was akin to throwing gasoline on a raging fire: the war transformed the fire into an explosion that quickly absorbed and exhausted its elements.

Change within Continuity

In 1935 the historian George Dangerfield made a celebrated assessment of the effects of World War I on Britain: "The War hastened everything—in politics, in economics, in behavior, but it started nothing." The assessment applies equally well to the United States. Intervention in World War I shoved Americans faster and further down a road they were already traveling.

Belligerency bolstered the American economy by stepping up the pace of industrial growth, technological advance, labor organization, and agricultural expansion. Few shortages occurred during the war, and consumer goods remained plentiful. Even the diversion of trucks and cars to the army failed to slow the growth of private automobile ownership. By some reckonings, 1918 marked the year by which a majority of American families, at least outside the South, acquired their first car. As was true during the Civil War, military procurement encouraged the standardization of products, particularly clothing and shoe sizes. The war also spurred technological development, especially in the electrical and chemical industries. The need of arms and explosives plants for greater electrical generating capacity stimulated development of hydroelectric power sites at, among other places, the government facility on the Tennessee River at Muscle Shoals, Alabama. American chemical producers welcomed the elimination of

Germany, hitherto the world's leader, as competition in their markets, so that they could develop their own production capacities. Cheaper equipment for radio transmission was an offshoot of developments in naval and military communications. Civil aviation took off immediately after the war's end, partly as an outgrowth of the experience with flying and maintaining aircraft that such Americans as Eddie Rickenbacker had gained as military aviators.

No groups profited more directly from the war than farmers and labor unions. Even before intervention, overseas demand for corn, pork, beef, and cotton had brought prosperity to American agriculture. Food Administrator Herbert Hoover's incentives for greater output through better cultivation and more extensive acreage boosted farm income further. But this stimulation revived the chronic problem of American agriculture: overproduction. By 1920, when war orders ceased and European croplands were returned to cultivation, prices sagged in anticipation of an agricultural depression that would plague farmers for the next two decades. Organized labor reaped a comparable wartime bonanza. AFL head Samuel Gompers served on several civilian boards, and he traded wage restraint and no-strike pledges for government approval of AFL organizing. Gompers also ostentatiously wrapped his unions in the flag. AFL officials spoke at Liberty Loan rallies and as Four-Minute Men, and contributed to CPI publications. As a result, AFL membership rose from three million in 1917 to five million by

Samuel Gompers in a patriotic pose during World War I.

1920. The Wilson administration also experimented with government management of labor relations through establishment of the National War Labor Board, headed by ex-President Taft, who proved surprisingly sympathetic to workers. Taft led the board in affirming employees' rights to collective bargaining, outlining minimum-wage and maximum-hour standards, and requiring equal pay for female workers.

America's intervention in World War I also helped bring to fruition three of the most important social developments of the previous two decades. Advocates of prohibition and woman suffrage were determined to turn the war to the advantage of their causes. The prohibitionists succeeded faster and more easily. The need to conserve grain for consumption by soldiers and for overseas shipment to the Allies enlisted previous opponents of prohibition, most notably Wilson and Roosevelt, behind a temporary ban on brewing and distilling. This wartime measure passed easily in both houses of Congress during the summer of 1917 and went into effect in September. The ease of passage emboldened prohibitionists to strike for their ultimate goal, a constitutional amendment to forbid permanently the manufacture, sale, and consumption of alcoholic beverages. Intense, skillful lobbying on Capitol Hill by the Anti-Saloon League and the Women's Christian Temperance Union, coupled with well-packaged appeals to patriotic idealism, racked up the necessary two-thirds votes for the amendment in December 1917. Further lobbying in the states garnered the three-quarters approval needed to ratify the Eighteenth Amendment in January 1919. Only one setback briefly slowed the onset of prohibition. In October 1919, President Wilson vetoed its enforcement legislation, the Volstead Act, because he opposed efforts to enforce moral values on individuals through laws, and because he regarded prohibition as a distraction from more pressing concerns at home and abroad. Congress overrode the veto, and the Volstead Act took effect on January 15, 1920. Nationwide prohibition, which became one of the best remembered symbols of the 1920s, took effect almost exactly at the beginning of the decade.

The suffragists had a harder time, but they reached their goal just a few months afterward. Like the labor unions and the prohibitionists, woman suffrage crusaders wrapped themselves in the flag. They played down Representative Jeannette Rankin's vote against the declaration of war and the opposition to intervention mounted by Jane Addams and some prominent feminists. The suffrage organizations instead followed the precedent of British suffragists, who gained the vote in 1918, by emphasizing women's support for the war. Other leading feminists clambered aboard the patriotic bandwagon. They appeared at Liberty Loan rallies, spoke as Four-Minute Women, and contributed to CPI publications for female readers.

On January 10, 1918, the suffragists won their first victory on Capitol Hill when the House narrowly approved a constitutional amendment to grant women the vote. When Senate approval proved tougher to win, leading suffrage advocates put pressure on President Wilson to redeem his 1916 campaign pledges, and the president delivered. He privately lobbied Democrats through the summer of 1918, and he addressed the Senate on September 30. "We have made women partners in the war," Wilson argued; "shall we admit them only to a partnership of suffering and sacrifice and toil and not to a partnership of privilege and right?" On October 1, the amendment fell two votes short of the necessary two-thirds in the Senate. Suffrage organizations immediately targeted four opponents, two Democrats and two Republicans, for defeat in November. Three of those senators lost, and the fourth barely squeaked in. A political message had been sent and received. When the next Congress convened in May 1919, both parties vied for the credit of passing a new amendment. On May 21, the House supplied more than forty votes over the required margin, and on June 4, the Senate passed the amendment with two votes to spare. More lobbying with governors and state legislatures followed to secure state ratifications, which reached the required three-quarters mark in August 1920. With the Nineteenth Amendment in place, women could vote throughout the nation for the first time in the 1920 presidential election.

On women's private lives, the war had a lesser effect. Women filled only some of the gaps in the labor force left by men who entered the armed forces. Few women became workers in heavy industry during World War I, but many women did drive trucks and buses and maintained farms. In offices the last barriers to female secretaries crumbled. "At last, after centuries of disabilities and discrimination, women are coming into the labor and festival of life on equal terms with men," announced one female trade unionist in 1917. Her enthusiasm was unfortunately premature. The AFL continued to resist the recruitment of women for industrial jobs, and except in the secretarial field, almost all of the jobs opened to women during the war reverted to men afterward. Over 20,000 women served in the armed forces during World War I, including some 5,000 in France as army nurses. They were the only women in uniform in the army, and they did not hold military

A woman mail carrier, 1918.

ranks. The navy and marines enlisted women on the same basis as men, and between 1917 and 1919, 13,000 joined and served mostly as clerks and secretaries.

The already swift current of black migration from the South accelerated during the war. To replace white factory workers lost to the armed forces, Northern employers sent out agents to recruit blacks, who eagerly answered the call. White Southerners displayed mixed sentiments about their departure. Some expressed delight at having fewer blacks living alongside them, but others, particularly planters and businessmen, worried about the loss of low-paid labor. Like their predecessors, these waves of black newcomers to the North found work that was low in pay and unskilled, often menial; housing that was shabby and squalid, usually in segregated neighborhoods; and scant welcome from whites. Racial violence continued its spread northward. A major race riot broke out in East St. Louis, Illinois, in July 1917, leaving nine whites and a much larger but uncounted number of blacks dead. Still, migration to the North brought blacks the promise of improvement in income and in the basic conditions of life. Moreover, military service instilled a new pride and sense of possibilities in black soldiers.

A striking political transformation wrought by the war was the res-

urrection of Theodore Roosevelt. Before intervention, his bellicosity
had made him a liability to Progressives and Republicans alike; with
America in the war, his views acquired respectability again almost
overnight. In April 1917, acting on the advice of Secretary of War Baker
and his generals, President Wilson refused Roosevelt's request to raise
and lead a division of volunteers. The generals doubted the value of
the ex-president's previous military experience, as well as the state of
his health. They also feared the effect his recruitment effort might have
on the orderly raising of armies, especially since nearly every able,
ambitious officer down to the rank of lieutenant was clamoring to get
into Roosevelt's division. Whatever its soundness on military grounds,
the refusal carried a cost. Nothing would have done more to whip up
popular enthusiasm and bolster solidarity with the Allies than the dispatch of the old Rough Rider to France. One Democratic senator
reportedly shook his head at the decision and sighed, "It doesn't seem
like a war without Roosevelt." Further, keeping the ex-president at
home gave him complete freedom to attack administration policies on
industrial mobilization, civil liberties, inter-allied diplomacy, and the
conduct of the war. Partly as a result of the fervor and effectiveness of
Roosevelt's criticisms, many Republicans, including some of his formerly implacable foes, started to tout him as the party's presidential
nominee in 1920.

Congressional critics of Wilson's conduct of the war mainly echoed
Roosevelt's charges. They asserted that the president was half-hearted
about fighting the Germans, and that his administration was ineffi-
cient in mobilizing troops and procuring weapons. Senator Lodge
teamed up with one of his few like-minded Democratic colleagues,
George Chamberlain of Oregon, to plan ways to give Congress a larger
role in the war. They tried to set up an oversight committee, but improved
performance on the homefront blunted their criticisms. Wilson's
appointment of a five-man Committee on National Defense, which
was in effect an inner war cabinet, offered additional reassurance about
the efficiency of the war effort. The president finally spiked the Lodge-
Chamberlain effort by going before Congress in May 1918 to appeal
for nonpartisan cooperation and to make his pledge, "Politics is
adjourned." Those assurances did not satisfy Lodge and Roosevelt, but
they were unable to mount any further efforts to intrude on Wilson's
war leadership. After the spring of 1918, congressional criticism shifted
its focus to excessive zeal in the administration's wartime efforts,
including the repression of dissent. Republican progressives, such as
Senators William E. Borah and Hiram Johnson, opposed passage of

*Senators Hiram Johnson (left) and
William E. Borah.*

the Sedition Act and denounced government violations of civil liberties. Unfortunately, they rallied few supporters at the time.

In one way, Wilson succeeded too well in fending off domestic political opposition. The trouble that a congressional oversight committee
would have caused might have been outweighed by the advantage of
allowing senators and congressmen a greater sense of participation in
the war. As it was, Republicans and some restive Democrats on Capitol
Hill could only fume impotently and lash out verbally at perceived mistakes and abuses. Republicans were in a nasty partisan mood anyway.
Their hairbreadth loss in 1916 had relegated the party for the first time
in history to longer than four years outside the White House, and that
loss came on top of their first taste of more than two years without
controlling at least one house of Congress. By not doing enough to give
the opposition party a stake in the war effort, Wilson displayed another
great failure in his war leadership. Considering the venom that Roosevelt and Lodge felt toward him, it might have seemed futile to reach
out to Republicans, but those men did not make up the whole of the
Republican party. Taft remained, as before, a fair-minded critic who
was in tune with much of Wilson's foreign policy. Others, most notably

Elihu Root and Charles Evans Hughes, were similarly inclined to cooperate with the administration.

What was lacking was bipartisanship. As a student of parliamentary coalitions and an observer of Britain's and France's multi-party war governments, Wilson understood the problem intellectually, and he did make an occasional stab at bipartisanship. In 1917 he sent Root to Russia as head of a diplomatic mission, and a year later he appointed Taft to chair the War Labor Board. He also departed from tradition by refraining from a partisan war effort. But these efforts fell far short of a genuine bipartisan approach. Some of Wilson's advisors urged him to bring leading Republicans on board, particularly as he began to consider possible representatives to the postwar peace negotiations. But after initially appearing receptive to these suggestions, Wilson petulantly brushed them aside in the summer of 1918.

Wilson had always been a party man. As an academic political scientist, governor, and president, he had always concentrated on party responsibility and party leadership, and this had contributed greatly to his earlier success in politics. No matter how much he eschewed partisanship after 1917 and tipped his hat toward coalition politics, Wilson did not abandon his reliance on his party. Two presidential actions in 1918 made it clear that politics, and especially party politics, had not been adjourned. First, during that summer, he conducted a party purge. To avoid the appearance of a power play from the White House, Wilson helped create situations in which local Democrats solicited his opinions of certain senators and congressmen, all of whom were Bryanites and several of whom had voted against the declaration of war. Their requests allowed the president to declare his opposition publicly to those Democrats, thereby complementing quiet uses of patronage against them. By and large the strategy worked. Senators James K. Vardaman of Mississippi and Thomas W. Hardwick of Georgia, an erstwhile ally of Tom Watson, and several Southern congressmen all lost their bids for renomination.

The other notably partisan action that Wilson took in 1918 came at the end of October, just ten days before the November elections. Bowing to importunings from the Democratic National Committee, he issued a statement to the press asking voters to elect Democratic majorities in the House and Senate as evidence that the American people "wish me to continue as their unembarrassed spokesman in affairs at home and abroad." No other single action of Wilson's received such near-unanimous condemnation. Roosevelt and other Republicans at once denounced the statement as a cheap partisan trick which gave the lie to claims that "politics is adjourned." Wilson's staunchest defenders later deplored the appeal as a lapse of judgment and a gesture of ingratitude toward Republicans who had supported his war policies. But Wilson's action, though perhaps unwise in the immediate circumstances, flowed naturally from his basic ideas about leadership. Now that he had rid the Democrats of a number of dissenters and lukewarm supporters, he believed that he could honestly urge voters to elect Democrats as a sign of support for himself. If nothing else, Wilson's party purge and appeal for a Democratic Congress in 1918 showed how far away from bipartisanship his thinking remained.

But the president's actions had little effect: the Democrats lost their majorities in both houses of Congress. Roosevelt and other Republican spokesmen gloried in the outcome as a repudiation of Wilson, but the voters' message in 1918 was not that clear. The Democrats lost twenty-five seats in the House, to give the Republicans a fairly comfortable margin, and four in the Senate, which gave the Republicans a one-vote majority there. But normal midterm attrition accounted for most of the shifts, while sectional issues played a role again in many contests. As in 1914 and 1916, Republicans had lambasted administration tax measures as raids on the hard-earned, well-deserved prosperity of the Northeast and Midwest. Wheat farmers' resentment at apparent government favoritism toward Southern cotton growers in price fixing also hurt the Democrats on the Great Plains.

Despite these setbacks, there were some bright spots for the Democrats in 1918. Two upset victories by Democrats in the Northeast offered the party its first real hopes of a competitive position there since before 1896. These wins were especially gratifying because they owed much to the party's rising strength among new voting groups. In Massachusetts, David I. Walsh unexpectedly unseated John W. Weeks, a well-entrenched conservative and one of the four senators targeted for defeat by the suffragists. In New York, Alfred E. Smith beat the incumbent Republican governor, Charles W. Whitman, a well-publicized former prosecutor and likely presidential contender. Both winners were Irish-American Catholics who drew big votes from their ethnic and religious compatriots in cities. Al Smith's emergence gave the party's urban wing a dynamic new leader and the Democrats their freshest face on the national scene during the next decade. For all its narrowness and ambiguity, the outcome of the 1918 elections had major consequences. Republican control of the Senate meant that Henry Cabot Lodge would become both majority leader and chairman of the Foreign Relations Committee. Those positions promised to give him and Roosevelt a large part in shaping the peace settlement and the postwar American role in world affairs.

TO THE FOURTEEN POINTS

Any Republican role in foreign affairs was bound to stir conflict because Wilson had already advanced his own ideas about international order. As he had proclaimed in his war address, he was seeking "peace without victory," and in pursuit of this during the war, he maintained arm's length relations with the Allies and an emphasis on liberal, non-punitive war aims.

To the chagrin of the British, the French, and pro-Allied enthusiasts at home, Wilson insisted on calling the United States an associated power rather than an ally. The administration conducted cool, controlled relations with its co-belligerents and maintained diplomatic ties with all the Central Powers except Germany. In February and March 1917, Wilson tried to induce Austria-Hungary, Germany's faltering war partner, to make a separate peace. Though the Austrians severed relations with the United States in April 1917, America did not declare war against them until December. Wilson finally decided to go to war against Austria-Hungary to buttress Italy's flagging war effort and to encourage nationalist movements in Central and Eastern Europe. The United States never did enter the war against the remaining two Central Powers, Bulgaria and Turkey, despite cries from Roosevelt for all-out common cause with the Allies. These actions sprang from Wilson's doubts, as he told Taft in December 1917, about "the desirability of drawing the two countries [Britain and the United States] too closely together" because of "divergences of purpose." Wilson was referring to his suspicions about Britain's objectives in the war, especially regarding colonies in Africa and Asia, and postwar control of the seas. His suspicions went double for the French, especially regarding their colonial designs, and their desires to dominate the postwar European continent. The president's lack of warmth was not lost on the British and French. King George V once reputedly snapped, "Do we have a co-belligerent or an umpire?"

The Allies had both in Wilson, especially in regard to war aims. Wilson was not alone in his search for a middle course. In Europe left-wing parties and trade unions on both sides of the fight were critical of the war and reluctant in their support, insisting upon non-imperialistic purposes behind belligerency. And by 1917, bowing to war-weariness, the British government had begun to pay lip service to a non-punitive peace. The restiveness of the European left gave Wilson the opening that he sought for promoting his vision of a new world order. In 1917 he allowed Colonel House to form the Inquiry, a band of bright young men who included Walter Lippmann of the *New Republic* and the future presidents of Yale and Johns Hopkins. They were to study war aims, plan for peace negotiations, and cultivate sympathetic contacts on the other side of the Atlantic. In August 1917 Wilson stole a march on the Allies when he made a public reply to an appeal for an end to the fighting by Pope Benedict XV. The United States and the Allies, he avowed, "believe that peace should rest upon the rights of peoples . . . great or small, weak or powerful,—their equal right to freedom and security and self-government and to participation upon fair terms in the economic opportunities of the world,—the German people of course included, if they will accept equality and not seek domination."

After November 1917, as it started to move toward a separate peace with Germany, the Bolshevik government of Russia published the secret Allied treaties that had promised spoils of the war to Czarist Russia. The emergence of the Bolshevik challenge to the war aims of the Allies placed Wilson for the first time in a centrist role on the international stage, where he had to distinguish his positions on war aims from opponents on the right and left. Socialists, labor groups, and others on the left in Allied countries might prove receptive to calls from Russia to lay down their arms, in the belief that their governments fought only for imperialistic ends. On the right, traditional nationalists considered the war a fight for military, naval, territorial, colonial, and economic gains for their respective countries.

Wilson set out his middle course in his most celebrated and powerful foreign-policy declaration: a speech to a joint session of Congress on January 8, 1918, in which he proposed a numbered set of peace terms that were at once dubbed the "Fourteen Points." Those points included "open covenants of peace, openly arrived at"; free use of the seas; removal of trade barriers; reduction of armaments; fairness to Russia on territorial and economic issues as "the acid test" of a peace settlement; evacuation and indemnification of Belgium; restoration to France of the Alsace and Lorraine, which had been lost to Germany in 1871, new frontiers for Italy, territorial adjustments and national autonomy for peoples in the Austro-Hungarian and Turkish empires, and independence for Poland. The final point was: "A general association of nations must be formed under specific covenants for the purpose of affording mutual guarantees of political independence and territorial integrity to great and small states alike."

The Fourteen Points speech was a diplomatic masterstroke. The Allied governments were grateful for Wilson's answer to Bolshevik attacks and to their own critics on the left. They muffled their reservations over naval and territorial questions and applauded the statement of war aims. Wilson had avoided commitments either to make peace with Germany on the basis of the Fourteen Points or to break up the Austro-Hungarian and Turkish empires, but he had clearly implied that those provisions might be essential parts of a post-war peace settlement. Wilson had also hoped to induce Russia not to leave the war, but in that effort, the Fourteen Points failed. Published on March 3, 1918, the Treaty of Brest-Litovsk, in which the Bolsheviks submitted to humiliating peace terms, seemed an act of betrayal in Allied quarters, and it heightened already rampant anti-radical sentiment in the United States. Wilson himself momentarily succumbed to the mood of bitterness. "There is," he declared in April 1918, ". . . but one response possible for us: Force, Force to the utmost, Force without stint or limit, the righteous and triumphant Force which shall make right the law of the world and cast every selfish dominion down in the dust."

Such Roosevelt-like fervor did not last long. Wilson did not let anger at the Bolsheviks guide his policy toward Russia. Throughout 1918 British and French leaders, particularly Winston Churchill and Marshal Foch, strove to mount a joint intervention to aid counterrevolutionary forces in Russia in efforts to overthrow the new Bolshevik regime. Wilson would have no part in those ventures. He reluctantly permitted small-scale participation by 14,000 American troops alongside the European Allies at the Russian towns of Murmansk and Archangel, and with the Japanese at Vladivostok, but the commanders were under strict orders to limit their activities to guarding Allied property and to stay out of internal Russian affairs. Wilson believed that these moves might help marginally in winning the war by preventing supplies from falling into German hands, and perhaps by allowing pro-Allied Czech forces in Russia to be transported to the Western Front. At no time did he express sympathy with any plans for outside intervention to bring down the Bolsheviks. His attempts to intervene in Mexico had taught Wilson the hard way not to butt in on revolutions. "In my opinion," he observed about Russia in 1919, "trying to stop a revolutionary movement by troops in the field is like using a broom to hold back a great ocean."

Having stated the Fourteen Points, Wilson began to lobby for their acceptance as a basis for peace. Quiet, informal contacts with liberal elements in Germany, and the CPI's distribution of the Fourteen Points in translated leaflets, played a big part in undermining the Central Powers' will to resist. Bulgaria, Turkey, and Austria-Hungary dropped out of the war in September and October 1918. After the successes of the Allied counteroffensives in the summer and early fall, especially the American onslaughts at St. Mihiel and at the Argonne Forest, Germany's military leaders privately admitted that they could not hold out much longer. Instead of bearing the onus of defeat themselves, however, they stepped aside in October and let a new civilian government open negotiations for an armistice on the basis of the Fourteen Points. A tense, complicated set of exchanges followed. Wilson forced the Germans to accept terms that would prevent them from resuming offensive operations. He used Colonel House, who was already in Europe, to cajole the British and French into agreeing to an armistice based on the Fourteen Points.

Wilson also tried to keep the Allies from achieving, as he told House, "too much success and security" under the military terms of the armistice. Too strong an Allied position would, he believed, "make a genuine peace settlement exceedingly difficult, if not impossible." Yet at the final armistice negotiations, held in a railroad car in the forest of

Celebrating the Armistice.

Compiègne in France, no American representatives were invited, and Marshal Foch imposed harsh terms which ended any possibility of even defensive German resistance. The elimination of a credible threat from the other side was already weakening Wilson's leverage over the Allies.

At an hour before noon on November 11, 1918, the Armistice took effect. A wave of euphoria sprang up among victors and vanquished alike. As the AEF newspaper *Stars and Stripes* reported, "At the eleventh hour on the eleventh day of the eleventh month hostilities came to an end from Switzerland to the sea. . . . There followed then a strange unbelievable silence as though the world had died. It lasted but a moment, lasted for the space that a breath is held. Then came such an uproar of relief and jubilance, such a tooting of hours, shrieking of whistles, such an overture from the bands and trains and church bells, such a shouting as the world is not likely to see again in our day and generation."

11

1919

During the first three-quarters of the twentieth century, as huge areas of Europe, Asia, and Africa suffered periods of vastly destructive warfare, the United States stood as the envy of much of the rest of the world, for not since the Civil War have fighting armies clashed within its borders. Although over 300,000 Americans had been killed or wounded in World War I, those casualties were minuscule when compared to the nine million Russian casualties, the more than six million suffered by Germany, the nearly five million of France, and over two million each of Britain and Italy. Moreover, no American civilians had died in combat, and no homes, farms, factories, churches, bridges, roads, towns, or cities in the United States had suffered damage, whereas wastelands now covered great expanses of France, Belgium, Italy, Poland, and Russia.

Economically, the United States had profited from the war. America's gross national product had risen from $62.5 billion in 1916 to $73.6 billion in 1919. Also during those years, the balance of debt had shifted to make America a creditor nation for the first time in its history. By 1919, America's $7 billion of private investment abroad was more than double foreign investment in the United States, almost exactly the reverse of the figures at the outbreak of the war. In addition, Allied governments owed the United States Treasury over $10 billion. The United States had become the world's leading creditor.

A Sea of Troubles

On December 3, 1918, Woodrow Wilson sailed for Europe as head of the American delegation to the peace conference at Paris. Except for a few days' return in March 1919, he would remain abroad for the whole first half of the year. Although some critics deplored the president's long absence, he received much more applause at home for his decision to go to Paris. Abroad, his tour of the Allied capitals in December 1918 drew frenzied adulation. In Rome, school children spread flowers at the president's feet, and in Paris, bigger throngs cheered him than had greeted France's own victorious armies.

The first weeks after the Armistice were a heady time, which one historian has dubbed "America's moment." It was an interval when the United States and its leader appeared to hold in their hands the promise of a new, better world. Unfortunately, the moment was fleeting and deceptive. The year that dawned with such promise would become one of the worst years in American history. Troubles erupted in almost every aspect of national life in 1919, from health to labor relations, from prices and jobs to race relations, from civil liberties to sports. The worst problems involved reactions at home to the peace settlement, and played a part in the eventual physical collapse of the president.

One cloud had already formed in the fall of 1918 to shadow the jubilation after the Armistice. A gigantic epidemic of influenza gripped Europe and the United States. Often called "Spanish influenza" because the king of Spain was an early sufferer, the disease spread rapidly among civilian and military populations on both sides of the Atlantic. More doughboys fell to the flu than to enemy bullets, and thousands of the wounded died because they were weakened by the disease. At home the epidemic touched every corner of the nation and all social and economic groups. About twenty million Americans fell ill; over 500,000 died from the flu and its complications during the winter of 1918–19. Cities were particularly hard hit. In Philadelphia, 650 flu deaths were recorded on a single day. Urban dwellers took to wearing surgical masks over their noses and mouths in the mistaken hope that they would lessen risks of infection. No effective prevention existed. The medical advances necessary to isolate the virus and develop a vaccine would not occur for another fifteen years. The flu epidemic at the end of 1918 seemed a devastating throwback to the plagues of the Middle Ages and a frightening prelude to 1919.

Getting soldiers home, finding them jobs, and paying bills likewise strained the country as the year began. The war's unexpected end caught the Wilson administration with no plans for demobilizing the armed forces and transporting men, women, and equipment back across the Atlantic. Soldiers and their families clamored for their immediate discharge, but decisions had to be made about whom to release at what time. Since there was no administrative machinery set up to discharge individuals, the army demobilized whole divisions at a time. Chance governed who got out of uniform when. Most stateside units were disbanded within three months of the war's end. The first overseas contingents arrived home in April 1919, and the spring and summer featured repeated parades in New York and other cities. By August 1919, the speedy demobilization had returned most American soldiers home. Only 40,000 American troops, all regulars, remained in Europe for occupation duty. The last American units, stationed in Germany on the banks of the Rhine, would not leave until 1923.

The key to the formidable task of bringing back the doughboys and their weapons, horses, and machines was the wartime "bridge of ships" to Europe. Running in high gear by the time the war ended in 1918, it was put in reverse to pull the armies out. The reversal created foul-ups and grumbling among impatient doughboys, but few of them had to wait overly long to get home. The return of military equipment was not as easy. Some horses, cars, and trucks were shipped back, but many were sold off at a loss to save the cost and trouble of transporting them. Profiteering in surplus equipment began almost as soon as the guns fell silent, and it would continue for years to come. Secretary of War Newton D. Baker and Secretary of the Navy Josephus Daniels prevented flagrant abuses under the Wilson administration, but under their Republican successors in the early 1920s, surplus matériel, especially medical supplies, and confiscated enemy property became prolific sources of corruption. Frustration, confusion, and unfairness were unavoidable in this, as in any, demobilization. Considering the lack of advance planning, luck played the biggest part in making the process as smooth as it was.

The luck ran out when returning doughboys tried to find work and joined civilians in confronting price inflation. As soon as the war ended, Wilson ordered all price controls and profit restraints lifted. Prices shot up as consumer demand competed with continuing war orders, the contracts for which ran for over a year after the Armistice. In 1919 the consumer price index rose by 77 percent over the 1916 level, and in 1920 by 105 percent over 1916. When military production contracts expired in late 1920, the lapse triggered a severe recession that began early in 1921.

Reconversion of the economy to a peacetime basis, or reconstruction as it was called at the time, became a battleground of conflicting interests. Representing the interests of veterans was a new organization, the American Legion. The Legion lobbied for economic benefits and health care, and it kept up wartime patriotic rhetoric that was marked by a strong bias against pacifists and leftists. Business, labor, and reform leaders also meant to make the most of reconstruction in 1919. Management in major industries was bent on rolling back the wartime gains in union membership and on resisting union efforts to bargain for recognition and higher wages. Business and conservative publicists had already capitalized on anti-radical sentiment to mount a propaganda campaign promoting the open shop as "the American way." They insinuated that all unions were subversive of the nation's most cherished values. How persuasive those arguments were at the time cannot be determined, but they did play a part in a more generalized narrowing of the American political spectrum. The kinds of criticism of private enterprise and property rights that Roosevelt, La Follette, and other progressives had mounted before 1917 now diminished in respectability and attractiveness.

The labor movement was equally eager to push its agenda in 1919. Both the AFL and the more radical unions believed, for different reasons, that the time was ripe for big gains. Now released from no-strike pledges and wage restraints, Gompers and his followers pushed for tangible results. Rank-and-file workers felt the pinch of the high cost of living as much as everyone else, and they demanded action by their unions. As a result, 1919 witnessed the largest number of strikes before or since in American history. Two thousand six hundred work stoppages occurred, involving over four million men and women, or 20 percent of the industrial workforce. Some strikers won wage increases, but unions seldom gained recognition as bargaining agents.

Two major strikes in 1919 harmed the reputation of unions with the general public. In November the United Mine Workers staged a walkout in the nation's coal mines. Management quickly met the miners' wage demands, and the strike ended just before New Year's day. But with inflation running at more than 75 percent over pre-war levels, and with much of the press portraying them as abettors of inflation, the miners evoked little public sympathy. The UMW's militant though decidedly mainstream leader, the bushy-browed, oratorical John L. Lewis, used this strike to begin his long career as one of the most

John L. Lewis.

powerful forces in American labor. He also began to emerge as a symbol of supposedly arrogant, irresponsible union power, a reputation
that he would retain for the rest of his long life.

The other major industrial strike of 1919 contributed even more to
the worsening reputation of unions. In September the newly formed
United Steel Workers led a walkout of more than 250,000 workers in
the nation's steel mills. The strikers accounted for more than half the
steel industry's workforce nationwide and higher proportions in and
around its center in Pittsburgh. The main issue was union recognition
rather than wages, but the union's message was compromised somewhat by its leadership, which included outspoken radicals who advocated government ownership of the industry. Management's leader and
spokesman, Elbert H. Gary, had prepared for the strike by stockpiling
iron ore and coal, and he later pressed the coal operators to settle with
the striking UMW in order to keep the steel mills running. The steel
companies hired 30,000 strikebreakers and exploited interunion rivalries to get railroad workers to continue making deliveries. Management also played up the union leadership's radicalism to discredit the
workers' cause. The union's cause was hurt above all when several
riots, possibly fomented by strikebreakers, erupted in October outside
steel mills in Gary, Indiana. The strike collapsed in January 1920, and
one of its leaders, William Z. Foster, left the union soon afterward to

become a member of the Communist party and later its candidate for president.

Two other highly publicized strikes during 1919, though far less significant economically, added still more to public fear of radicalism. In February the IWW-dominated Central Labor Council of Seattle seized upon a walkout by shipyard workers to proclaim a general strike. Over 60,000 workers stayed away from their jobs, paralyzing the city. Seattle's mayor, Ole Hansen, a former Progressive, denounced the general strike as an attempt "to duplicate the anarchy of Russia," and he asked for federal troops to augment his police force. Between the show of force and the refusal by AFL unions to join, the general strike collapsed in nine days. "The rebellion is quelled," exulted Hansen, "the test came and was met by Seattle." There had been little chance of an armed uprising, however, even though some newspapers depicted Seattle as teetering on the brink of revolution. "The strike is Marxian," warned the *Los Angeles Times*, while the *Chicago Tribune* declared, "it is only a middling step from Petrograd to Seattle." For smashing the strike, Hansen was widely hailed as the "man of the hour" and touted as a potential candidate for higher office. The mayor preferred, however, to earn lucrative fees by giving public lectures during the rest of 1919 about the threat of "bolshevism."

Public fear of radical disorder flashed again in September 1919 when three quarters of Boston's 1500 policemen went out on strike in a dispute over wages and their union's effort to affiliate with the AFL. Since neither city nor state officials had made any preparations for the strike, downtown areas and rough neighborhoods exploded in a two-night orgy of looting, rioting, and vandalism. Boston's newspapers branded the striking policemen as "agents of Lenin" and depicted the city as in the throes of a "Bolshevist nightmare." A number of citizens, including several hundred Harvard students, turned out as volunteer constables, but the disorder did not end until the governor responded to the mayor's plea to send in state militiamen. Curiously, although he had originally refused to bestir himself, it was Governor Calvin Coolidge who emerged as the hero of the affair. To suggestions to reinstate the strikers, who had been fired by the mayor when they walked out, Coolidge made a one-sentence reply: "There is no right to strike against the public safety by anybody, anywhere, any time." The press across the nation hailed the statement and the man who made it for having, as one observer avowed, "struck fire from the Americanism of the entire country." That one sentence transformed a newly elected, close-mouthed party hack into a promising new name in Republican national politics.

Boston's Scollay Square during the police strike, 1919.

These labor disputes occurred against the backdrop of a series of radical incidents in Europe. In Paris in February 1919, a would-be assassin identified as a "Bolshevik agent" made an attempt on the life of France's premier, Georges Clemenceau. From March to June of that year, a Bolshevik regime ruled Hungary, until it was toppled by right-wing forces aided by the Allies. Twice during those months revolutionary socialist revolts occurred in Germany, first the abortive "Spartacist" coup in Berlin and later a short-lived "Soviet republic" in Bavaria. Radical violence came home to Americans in a series of bombings at the end of April and beginning of May. Thirty-six bombs disguised as packages were delivered to unsuspecting targets through the mails. One that was sent to Seattle's Mayor Hansen fortunately did not explode, but another that went to former Senator Thomas Hardwick of Georgia injured his wife and maid. A bomb delivered to the home of Attorney General Palmer blew up on the front porch. It killed the bearer, who was later identified as an Italian immigrant with alleged radical connections.

These incidents at home and abroad lent weight to the calls for revolt emanating from Bolsheviks and American radicals, creating genuine public apprehension. Apprehension exploded into hysteria as the outbursts of 1919 fed upon emotions fanned by the propaganda of the war years. During the war Americans had been admonished to think and

A. Mitchell Palmer.

act patriotically, and the armistice did not break the grip of this war-time psychology. In 1919 it provided the atmosphere for the explosion of a Red Scare in America.

If overheated emotions permeated the United States in 1919 like a room filled with gasoline fumes, it only took someone reckless enough to strike a metaphorical match to create an explosion. The forty-seven-year-old A. Mitchell Palmer was a former congressman and a Democratic senatorial candidate from Pennsylvania with impeccable reformist, pro-labor credentials. He had been raised in a devout Quaker family, and he had privately opposed much of the wartime repression of civil liberties. This opposition had played a part in Wilson's appointment of Palmer as attorney general in March 1919. But Palmer harbored a genuine fear of Bolshevism, and the bombings of April and May 1919 shook him, especially the explosion on his own doorstep, which had endangered the lives of his family.

The attorney general's other motive in sparking the Red Scare was almost certainly political ambition. According to his friend and cabinet colleague, Josephus Daniels, the brief consideration of Palmer as a dark-horse compromise choice at the 1912 Democratic convention had left him with a desire to run for president. Ironically, his Quaker origins and his disdain for what he regarded as a lesser office had led Palmer to decline Wilson's offer in 1913 to become secretary of war, an office that might have provided an excellent springboard for a leap toward the White House. The instant fame heaped on Mayor Hansen and Governor Coolidge for their anti-radical actions in 1919 did not escape Palmer's notice. Moreover, as head of the Justice Department he became the target of demands for federal action against "reds." By mid-1919 this erstwhile friend of labor and defender of civil liberties was changing his tune. In June, President Wilson cabled back from the peace conference, ". . . it is my desire to grant complete amnesty and pardon to all American citizens in prison or under arrest on account of anything they have said in speech or print . . . during the period of the war." Palmer's strong objections persuaded Wilson to defer amnesty, and the attorney general's later opposition served to harden the president against all pleas to pardon Eugene Debs. In the fall of 1919, Palmer took a tough line against the steel and coal strikes, and he evidently persuaded Wilson not to sanction any government efforts at mediation.

Starting in November 1919, Palmer made a series of moves to suppress the threat of radicalism. On November 7, Justice Department agents raided offices of radical organizations in twelve cities. They seized files, broke up furniture and machines, and arrested about 250 suspects. The attorney general then pressed for deportation of 199 of those detainees, together with 50 other people previously convicted under

"WHOSE COUNTRY IS THIS, ANYHOW?" A New York World *cartoon commenting approvingly on the mass arrest and deportation of radicals.*

WHOSE COUNTRY IS THIS, ANYHOW?

the wartime Alien Act. On December 21, 1919, the steamer *Buford*, previously a troopship, sailed for Russia with 249 of these deportees as passengers, including the veteran anarchist Emma Goldman. This much-publicized dispatch of the "Soviet Ark" only added to the choruses of praise lavished upon the "Fighting Quaker." Next, on January 2, 1920, Palmer topped his earlier feat with a much bigger nationwide raid in thirty-three cities, which closed every known Communist party headquarters and rounded up over 4,000 people. Led by its young assistant director, J. Edgar Hoover, the new Bureau of Investigation displayed great efficiency in coordinating what were approvingly dubbed the "Palmer Raids." State and local police, who made most of the arrests, often apprehended suspects at home in the middle of the night. Federal officers detained prisoners in filthy, overcrowded prisons and permitted them no communication with their families and attorneys.

As had happened during the war, states, cities and even private citizens took their cue from federal actions. In New York, a state legislative investigating committee had begun confiscating files and shutting down radical organizations in June 1919. In November, the day after the first of the Palmer Raids, the committee enlisted 700 policemen to swoop down on seventy-three offices of radical groups and arrest over 500 people. In Illinois, Washington, and California, authorities cracked down on Socialists and IWW members, and twenty-four states passed "Red Flag" laws, which forbade display of Communist banners or any other allegedly revolutionary symbols. Also in January 1920, the New York State legislature expelled five duly elected Socialist members. Vigilante violence once more predominated in the West, where the worst incident occurred in Centralia, Washington, on November 11, 1919, the first anniversary of the armistice. Four members of the American Legion tried to storm the IWW headquarters in Centralia and were killed by gunfire. Ten Wobbly leaders were jailed and later indicted for murder, and one who fled was chased and caught by a mob that tortured and lynched him. Two days later, in Oakland, California, a mob inspired by the citizens of Centralia demolished the offices and meeting halls of several radical organizations.

Like a fire that exhausts the conditions that fed it, the Red Scare was short-lived. Its excesses bred resistance that soon brought Palmer and his imitators to a halt. If anything, the attorney general and his young deputy, J. Edgar Hoover, demonstrated too much efficiency in their raids. Their massive violations of legal procedures aroused protest from liberal Protestant clergymen and law school faculty members. Coincidentally, on January 26, 1920, the Supreme Court handed down a decision that barred illegally seized papers from being used in subsequent indictments. Federal judges immediately started to apply this rule in order to dismiss proceedings against detainees from the Palmer Raids. The jury in the trial of the Centralia Wobblies acquitted two of them, found another not guilty by reason of insanity, and convicted the remaining seven for second-degree murder, which did not carry the death penalty.

Palmer also met resistance within the Wilson administration. Secretary of Labor William L. Wilson and Commissioner of Immigration Louis F. Post obstructed the Justice Department's further efforts to deport aliens seized in the raids. Acting on their own, Secretary Wilson and Commissioner Post refused to supply information to Palmer or cooperate with him in his raids, and either delayed or refused to initiate deportation proceedings against aliens seized in the raids.

President Wilson evidently allowed the Red Scare to proceed in part because he shared the prevailing fear of bolshevism. Wilson also liked and respected Palmer, who had been an early backer of his in 1912 and was an enthusiastic supporter of his foreign policy in 1919. Most important Wilson was incapacitated when Palmer began his raids in November. He had suffered a major, crippling stroke at the end of September, which left him bedridden and secluded from nearly all contact with anyone but his wife and physician for several months. It is unlikely that the ailing president ever knew the full extent of the attorney general's rampage. Yet elements of mystery remain about Wilson's conduct. Fearful of the effects on public opinion, Wilson reportedly warned several times, "Palmer, do not let this country see red." In his annual message to Congress, in December 1919, which his stroke prevented him from delivering in person, the president declared, "The seed of revolution is repression. The remedy must not be negative in character. It must be constructive." In light of these views, Wilson's failure to stop Palmer or rein him in is not fully explicable even by the severity of his illness or the distraction of other events.

Nothing aroused more opposition to the Red Scare than the New York State legislature's expulsion of its Socialist members. Theodore Roosevelt's son led the opposition to the move in the legislature, and Governor Al Smith publicly deplored it. The most potent attack came from the former Republican presidential candidate, Charles Evans Hughes, who declared that the expulsions were not "in my judgment, American government." Hughes also enlisted the New York Bar Association to defend the expelled legislators against criminal charges. "We have passed beyond the stage in political development when heresy-hunting is a permitted sport," declared Hughes and other leading New York lawyers in a public protest to the legislature.

By mid-1920, A. Mitchell Palmer's political star had fallen. In April the attorney general scrambled to revive his crusade when he warned of a new series of radical actions planned for May Day 1920, the anniversary of the 1919 mail bombings. But May 1, 1920, passed without incident and left Palmer looking ridiculous. Some newspapers compared him to Little Red Riding hood crying "wolf"; others likened him to Chicken Little screaming that the sky was falling. At his party's convention in June some Democrats derided him as the "Quaking Fighter" and the "Faking Fighter," and Palmer eventually withdrew his name from consideration for the presidency. That was the end of his political career. He stayed on as attorney general until the Wilson administration left office in March 1921. In September 1920 Palmer made a last stab at reviving the Red Scare after a bomb exploded on Wall Street, killing forty-three people, injuring two hundred others, and demolishing the offices of J. P. Morgan's firm. This time only derision greeted Palmer's warnings of a Bolshevik uprising.

Palmer's antics were not the only blots that marred the Wilson administration's performance during 1919. The president washed his hands of concern for domestic reconstruction. In his annual address to Congress in December 1918, delivered just before he left for Europe, Wilson brushed aside the "problem of economic and industrial readjustment. . . . Our people . . . do not want to be coached and led. They know their own business, are quick and resourceful at every readjustment, definite in purpose, and self-reliant in action." Wilson eschewed "any leading strings" or "any general scheme of 'reconstruction,'" and he declined to involve himself in debates during 1919 over economic reform, labor conflict, race relations, prohibition, or civil liberties. By the beginning of the year, the War Industries Board and other wartime agencies were closing down, though the nation's trains continued to be run by the Railroad Administration. Railway workers' unions pushed for a permanent government takeover, while the companies demanded the immediate return of the train system to private ownership. Support for continued government operation was initially widespread, but anti-labor sentiment sparked by the major strikes of 1919, and the railroad unions' undisguised grabs for big wage increases, eroded that support even among many progressives. The collision between labor and management set off a bitter, protracted debate on Capitol Hill. Finally, in a mood of weary resignation, Congress passed an act in March 1920 that restored the railroads to their previous owners.

The railroad wrangle furnished the major issue of economic reform in 1919, but the White House steadfastly refused to take part. Nor did the administration speak or act on matters of racial conflict, even when there were ugly incidents in the government's own backyard. Black migration sparked two major race riots in northern cities during the summer of 1919. At the end of June, several days of street fighting broke out in Washington, leaving a large but uncounted number of blacks dead. A month later, when a black youth who had wandered onto a segregated beach on Lake Michigan was stoned and drowned, Chicago exploded into five days of gang fights, gunfire, and burnings. These disorders left thirty-eight people dead—twenty-three blacks and fifteen whites—more than five hundred injured, and several million dollars in property destroyed. National guardsmen were stationed on rooftops and curfews were imposed to restore order. In all, twenty-five incidents of racial violence erupted in American cities during the summer of 1919. Neither those outbreaks nor the large number of lynchings of black people in the South elicited any reaction from federal authorities. This was all the more tragic since many of the victims were veterans of the war.

Race riots and lynchings, strikes and inflation, the crackdown on "reds," wrangling over the railroads—these occurrences made the summer and fall of 1919 a tense, anxious time for many Americans. In September, scandal tainted even the national pastime, baseball. Soon

"THE THINKER—NOW."
A Richmond Planet *cartoon of 1919 depicts the harsh paradoxes facing American blacks after World War I.*

after the favored Chicago White Sox lost the World Series to the Cincinnati Reds, rumors began to circulate that eight Chicago players, including star center fielder "Shoeless Joe" Jackson, had conspired to throw the deciding game. They had taken payoffs from professional gamblers, so the stories went, and secretly bet against their own team. Finally in September 1920, a persistent sportswriter corroborated the rumors with hard evidence, and a grand jury in Chicago indicted the eight accused players. A trial jury acquitted seven of them, while charges against the eighth were thrown out for lack of evidence. Still, wrongdoing had almost certainly taken place in what became known as the Black Sox scandal. White Sox owner Charles Comiskey was an autocratic skinflint who was cordially hated by his players, nearly all of whom had financial problems. Several of the accused men had previously consorted with gamblers, and in a somewhat legendary encounter with a youthful fan who pleaded, "Say it ain't so, Joe," Jackson sadly replied, "Yes, kid, I'm afraid it is." The commissioner of baseball banned the eight from the game for the rest of their lives. The press warned of irreparable damage and the demise of the sport, but baseball recovered. At the end of 1919, however, even some of the least

"Shoeless Joe" Jackson.

politically and socially concerned Americans worried about what their country was coming to.

PEACEMAKING AT PARIS

By the end of 1919, Americans had far weightier causes for doubt about the state of the nation, for the matter of greatest importance to the administration was faring badly. President Wilson's overriding concern from the moment he committed the United States to war in 1917 had been peacemaking. By 1919 his concern with the shape of the peace had grown to the point of obsession. Wilson spent the entire first half of that year at the peace conference in Paris, and he devoted the rest of his presidency to an effort to get the United States to uphold the settlement by joining the League of Nations.

Wilson's troubles began before he left for Europe in December 1918. Theodore Roosevelt had attacked the Fourteen Points and the president's liberal peace program during the fall congressional campaign. When the Republicans won majorities in both houses, the ex-president and Massachusetts Senator Henry Cabot Lodge began privately communicating with British and French leaders, assuring them that Wilson did not speak for the American people and admonishing them to impose harsh terms on Germany. At the same time, Roosevelt started to moderate his long-standing rejection of a league of nations. He may have anticipated making a league the centerpiece of his own foreign policy if he ran again for president in 1920, as many Republicans wanted him to do. What might have come of his thinking would never be known, though, because the sixty-year-old Roosevelt, who had been in poor health for several months, died in his sleep early on the morning of January 6, 1919.

Roosevelt's death was a setback to those Republicans who pressed the United States to pursue an activist role in international affairs. Without the prospect of Roosevelt as their next president, Lodge and most of the other Republican senators had little incentive to do much besides hamper and obstruct Wilson's projects. All was not lost for the president, however, for ex-President Taft remained as stout an internationalist as ever, as did a number of other leading Republicans. Wilson could have aided his cause by showing a more cooperative, compromising spirit toward the opposition party, but the president seemed uninterested either in bipartisanship or even in appointing a strong American delegation to the peace conference. In addition to his

Georges Clemenceau (standing) presides at Versailles; Wilson sits to his right, and Secretary of State Lansing on Wilson's right; David Lloyd George sits to Clemenceau's left.

aide Colonel House and Secretary of State Lansing, Wilson appointed General Tasker S. Bliss, a military expert, and Henry White, a veteran diplomat and nominal Republican. None of the delegates, not even House or Lansing, enjoyed the president's full confidence, which meant that he relied almost entirely on his own judgment and energy during the negotiations at Paris. Wilson's intention essentially to keep his own counsel at the peace conference put him at a disadvantage in dealing with the other Allied leaders, who could lean on able, trusted lieutenants. His habitual lonehandedness in foreign affairs levied a heavy toll on his emotional reserves and health.

The peace settlement emerged as the Treaty of Versailles after six and a half months of trying, tedious negotiations. Wilson had to struggle against many of the war aims of the Allies in order to secure the Fourteen Points as a framework for peace. Often he was forced to concede elements of his peace proposal in order to win support at the conference for his most precious goal: the League of Nations. Whether he conceded too much to the national aims of the Allies in order to win their approval of the League remains an open question.

The Allies sought to strengthen their positions within the balance of power. The French, led by the crafty, obdurate seventy-seven-year-old Georges Clemenceau, sought revenge for past humiliations at the hands of Germany and guarantees against future aggression. To accomplish those aims they advocated breaking Germany up into several smaller nations with weakened or no armed forces. The French also wished to restore their nation to its former glory as the dominant power on the European continent. The British, led by the occasionally devious Prime Minister David Lloyd George, sympathized to an extent with Wilson's plans for a new international order, but they desired above all to see Germany rendered impotent as a naval power. They also wanted to strip the Germans of their colonies in Africa and the Pacific, and to make them pay much, if not all, of the financial cost of the war. Those policies would have the effect of maintaining Britain's position as the world's leading naval and imperial power and, it was hoped, recouping some of the losses that had demoted them from global financial leadership. For its part, Italy harbored grandiose visions of extending its borders at the expense of Austria and of dominating the Balkans. The new nations that had sprung up as a result of nationalist movements in central and eastern Europe—Yugoslavia, Czechoslovakia, and Poland—also sought security guarantees. The fourth major ally, Japan, pressed claims to German colonies in the Pacific and sought to expand its own power in the Far East.

Against these self-interested, conservative objectives, backed by uncertain support at home, and in fragile health, Wilson struggled virtually alone as the champion of a new, liberal approach to international order and peace. He supported the League of Nations as a world forum in which nations could come together and peacefully resolve their differences. Wilson believed that the awarding of territory or colonies at the peace conference mattered less than the establishment of an international body to consider such questions and decide them according to changing conditions. Likewise, he proposed that economic claims arising out of the war be weighed and decided after care-

" 'Curious! I seem to hear a child weeping!' " Will Dyson's Daily Herald *cartoon of 1919 proved startlingly prophetic. Expressing doubts about the Versailles treaty, it shows Clemenceau commenting to Wilson and Lloyd George about the generation of 1940.*

ful deliberations by expert commissions set up by the League. Perhaps
most of all, Wilson wanted the League to become the means by which
nations would begin to limit armaments on land and sea, eliminate
trade barriers, and establish new rules of international conduct. In all
these matters, the United States, as the most detached and relatively
disinterested of the great powers, would play the part of honest broker
and inspirational leader. This was a far nobler and more commanding
role than America could play if there were a postwar retreat to traditional power politics.

The Allies battled over a limited ground, since much of the settlement occasioned little disagreement. The boundaries and rights of
Europe's new nations remained largely outside the scope of the peacemakers' labors. So did the fate of Russia. Neither Russia's future role
nor the specter of international revolution loomed large in the minds
of the negotiators at Paris. Although there were attempts by some French
and British leaders, most notably Foch and Churchill, to mount an
anti-Bolshevik crusade, Wilson fought them off. The historian A. J. P.
Taylor has pointed out that, had the Allies really feared the Bolsheviks,
they would have treated Germany more leniently in order to create a
strong bulwark between themselves and the red tide to the east. The
main concerns of the Allied leaders and the main issues in contention
at the conference involved Germany and settling scores from the war.

Five issues dominated the struggle to shape the peace at Paris: first,
the fate of postwar Germany; second, the financial burden left by the
war; third, the mediation of colonial claims; fourth, Japanese expansion in China; and fifth, Italy's boundaries. On the first and toughest
of these issues, Wilson stood firm against French demands to dismem-
ber Germany and establish long-term foreign occupation, because he
opposed a return to the old-style balance of power. He outwaited and
faced down the sharp-tongued Clemenceau, who sneered behind Wilson's back about God having needed only Ten Commandments compared with the American president's Fourteen Points. The British favored
Wilson's position because they did not want the French to dominate
the continent of Europe, but they stood aside and let him fight their
battle for them. At a critical moment, the president ordered his ship
readied to sail home, and his threat to walk out brought the French
around. For their part, the French did win a short-term occupation
along the Rhine, permanent demilitarization of the Rhineland, strict
limits on future German military strength, and a separate security pact
for themselves with Britain and the United States. Otherwise, Germany remained intact and potentially strong, though within dimin-

ished borders that gave Alsace and Lorraine to France, Schleswig to Denmark, and western Prussia to Poland.

On the issue of who would bear the war's huge financial burden, the British and French together pressed exorbitant claims for monetary compensation from Germany, including payment for civilian damages and widows' and orphans' pensions. Wilson resisted these claims as unjust, injurious to Germany, and dangerous to future peace in Europe. After protracted, unproductive discussions, Wilson fell ill for several days early in April 1919. At the time his doctor said that the president had the flu, but it seems more likely that he suffered from something else, possibly a circulatory disorder. After a quick recovery, Wilson gave in on the question of which categories of financial damages would be included in the peace treaty. This retreat ensured that Germany would have to pay a huge sum in reparations. In response, the brilliant young economist, John Maynard Keynes, resigned in protest from the British delegation. Keynes then dashed off a scathing book, *The Economic Consequences of Peace*, in which he denounced the financial clauses of the treaty for damaging the international economic structure of Europe and for imposing ruinously high reparations payments on Germany. Keynes condemned the settlement in general and heaped the greatest blame on Wilson, whom he dubbed "a blind and deaf Don Quixote."

Wilson succeeded, however, in having the actual fixing of reparations delegated to a commission that would be established under the League of Nations. In 1920, the Reparations Commission set the figure at $33 billion, a huge sum, but about $20 billion less than the damages originally demanded from Germany by the British and French. Whether it was feasible, or even justifiable, for the Germans to shoulder that burden would fuel heated debate for the next twenty-five years.

On the issue of apportioning Germany's colonies, Wilson and other advocates of an international order wanted to organize former German possessions in Africa and the Pacific as mandates under the League of Nations, to be administered by smaller, non-colonial European nations. But Britain, France, Japan, and especially the British Dominions of Australia and South Africa demanded that those former German possessions, which they had seized during the war, become their own colonies. Inasmuch as these powers were already in possession of the territories, Wilson had little leverage against them, but he did persuade them to take on the former German possessions as League mandates rather than as colonies. Under this system the League exercised rights of inspection, and the nations in charge assumed, at least on paper, obligations to provide their mandates with health care, education, economic aid, and the groundwork for eventual independence. The commitment to eventual independence for territories under the mandate system marked a momentous step. It represented the first promise of self-government for the African and Asian possessions of European powers. The United States itself had not yet made such a pledge for the Philippines, but Wilson had wrung from the European powers the first formal acknowledgment of the impending end of colonialism.

The fourth dispute involved Japanese expansion in China, which the United States had already opposed under the Taft and Wilson administrations. Fighting on the side of the Allies, the Japanese had conquered the German concessionary area in China, the province of Shantung, and once it was in their possession the Japanese refused to evacuate. The Chinese argued that on the principle of self-determination the province should revert to them. Bowing once more to the fact of territorial possession, Wilson arranged a compromise under which the Japanese would stay in Shantung as an occupying power until 1922. This arrangement came under fire in the United States as a "sellout" to the Japanese. Two of Roosevelt's former Progressive cohorts from the West Coast, where anti-Japanese prejudice ran high—Senators Hiram Johnson of California and Miles Poindexter of Washington— made the Japanese possession of Shantung a principal ground for their opposition to the peace treaty and American membership in the League of Nations.

The issue of Italy's boundaries caused further dissension among the European Allies. Half a century earlier the German Chancellor Otto von Bismarck had quipped of Italy's desire for imperial conquest, "The Italians have such a big appetite and such poor teeth." The Italians had never displayed their territorial hunger more brazenly than during World War I. They had entered the war in 1915 only after making both sides bid for their allegiance, and at Paris in 1919 they expected the victorious Allies to pay off. The British and French resented the Italians' grasping, but they shifted the onus of opposing Italy's demands onto Wilson's shoulders. The president acceded to the Italians' pleas for a defensible frontier by accepting their claim to the South Tyrol up to the Brenner Pass in the Alps between Austria and Italy. This concession, which put over 200,000 German-speaking Austrians under Italian rule, raised an outcry from advocates of self-determination in Britain and the United States. "If Wilson could swallow the Brenner, he would swallow anything," recalled Harold Nicolson, another young member of the British delegation. "The moral effect of this discovery can scarcely be exaggerated." The concession turned many young idealists at the conference, Americans as well as Britons, against the final treaty.

Wilson stood firm against further Italian demands for territory along the Adriatic coast. He opposed their claim to the city of Fiume on the grounds that a majority of its population was non-Italian and that the new nation of Yugoslavia needed a seaport. When the Italian delegation ostentatiously stormed out of the conference on April 23, 1919, the president resorted to his practice of appealing directly to the people, in this case the Italians. His appeal brought no immediate reversal on Fiume, and critics scoffed at his apparent failure. But trade unions and leftist elements in Italy applauded Wilson's stand and opposed their government on the question. Early in May, the Italian delegation slunk back to the peace table. Wilson refused to budge on Fiume, and the issue was shelved for direct negotiations between Italy and Yugoslavia. Even Harold Nicolson later conceded that on the issue of Italy's boundaries as a whole, Wilson "did in truth maintain his principles intact. Such was not, however, the impression which spread through the hot saloons of Paris."

These key elements in the peace settlement obviously entailed com-

promises on the Fourteen Points. Liberal critics at the time and later lambasted Wilson for having sold out his principles. They accused him of allowing the Europeans to impose a harsh, or carthaginian, peace on Germany and to rebuild the old-style imperialistic balance of power. Those charges contained much truth. Wilson had found himself forced repeatedly to abandon the high ground of the Fourteen Points, and it had been foolish of him and others to believe that he would not have to do so. Wilson labored under many disadvantages besides his own lonehandedness and the pressure of domestic opposition. Not only had the United States entered the war later than any of the Allies and made much smaller sacrifices of blood and treasure, but the main issues at the conference involved interests of the European and Asian nations far more vitally and directly than those of the United States. Moreover, the Allied government with views and positions closest to the Americans, the British, frequently held back from offering vigorous support, particularly because they wanted to keep the issue of naval power off the table. In the end what was remarkable, as Winston Churchill later observed, was not how little but how much of the Fourteen Points Wilson succeeded in incorporating in the final settlement.

In Wilson's view, the creation of the League of Nations was the keystone of a new international order, and well worth the concessions he made elsewhere. The main draft of the League Covenant was the work of the British diplomat Lord Robert Cecil and the South African foreign minister Jan Christiaan Smuts. Their draft combined universal representation of nations on an equal footing with an inner directorate of great powers, which controlled the exercise of collective force against aggression. The critical provision of the League Covenant, Article X, governed invocation of diplomatic, economic, and military sanctions against nations that broke the peace. All members of the League Council, both the great powers that would be permanent members—the United States, Britain, France, and Italy—and the smaller powers that would be elected on a rotating basis, would have to agree in order to impose sanctions. Only the Allies, the United States, and neutral nations were to be members of the League; the defeated Central Powers—Germany, Austria, Hungary, Bulgaria, and Turkey—and Bolshevik Russia were originally excluded, although they all joined the League at one time or another over the next twenty years. The self-governing dominions of the British Empire—Australia, Canada, New Zealand, and South Africa—as well as India, which was not self-governing, became members, as did the Latin American republics, including those that were in fact protectorates of the United States.

With great effort, Wilson persuaded the Allied leaders to accept Cecil's and Smuts's draft early in the conference. He succeeded mainly through force of argument, compromise, and collegial consultations, reminiscent of his cabinet deliberations at home. Wilson then presented the draft covenant to a public session of all the delegates to the peace conference on February 14, 1919. "Armed force is in the background of this program," the president told them, "but it *is* in the background, . . . [as] the last resort, because this is intended as a constitution of peace, not as a league of war." Wilson called the covenant "a practical document and a humane document. There is a pulse of sympathy in it. There is a compulsion of conscience throughout it."

Having achieved acceptance of a draft covenant at the peace conference, the president still faced two great obstacles to building his new international order upon the League. One was looming opposition to the League at home, and the other was the postwar designs of the European Allies. The domestic opposition reared its head when Wilson made a brief voyage back to the United States at the end of February and beginning of March 1919. On March 3 Henry Cabot Lodge unveiled a "round robin" signed by thirty-nine Republican senators and senators-elect, in which they announced that they found the League

"THE PRESCRIPTION THAT WENT ASTRAY." J. N. "Ding" Darling's cartoon depicts a Wilsonian article of faith, self-determination, coming back to haunt the president in the Senate's opposition to the League.

Covenant unacceptable "in the form now proposed." They specifically cited the Covenant's failure to exempt from League jurisdiction the hallowed American expression of paramount interest and influence in the Western Hemisphere—the Monroe Doctrine—as well as such sensitive domestic policies as tariff protection and immigration restriction. Those senators, in addition to other critics such as La Follette, who did not sign the round robin, constituted more than the one-third of the Senate necessary to deny consent to a treaty. Wilson had no choice but to try to mollify them. Upon his return to Paris he reopened negotiations on the League, and got the Covenant amended to exclude tariff issues, immigration restriction, regional security pacts, and expressions of influence; the Monroe Doctrine, which no other nation had ever acknowledged, was cited by name.

The Senate's round robin exposed Wilson's weak domestic support, and made him a supplicant toward the Allied leaders. These leaders remembered both his weakness at home and his debt to them when the other major issues of the conference came up for resolution. Wilson had to compromise as much as he did on these other issues because he staked so much on the League of Nations.

The work of the peacemakers at Paris in 1919 became the subject of obsessive scrutiny and furious argument for years to come because the peace they arranged ultimately failed. Many critics would argue that Wilson had wrought a settlement that was neither fish nor fowl. It was, so the argument went, neither punitive enough to crush Germany, as the French and such Americans as Roosevelt and Lodge wanted to do, nor was it liberal enough to mollify Germany, as Wilson had originally sought to do with the Fourteen Points.

The Treaty of Versailles collapsed, however, not because its provisions were ill-conceived, but because all of the victorious powers, including Wilson's United States, later lost the will to uphold it. Even a carthaginian peace could not have prevented Germany's resurgence without lasting commitments to enforce it. And even a peace based solely on the Fourteen Points could not have satisfied the nationalistic, vengeful elements in Germany. Their real grievances were not the military and financial penalties of the Versailles treaty: they resented having lost the war. Unless the victors were determined to make the Germans accept their defeat and live with the consequences, no settlement, harsh or mild, was going to last.

The Struggle over the League of Nations

Wilson's effort to win acceptance of the Versailles treaty in the United States began to falter with a serious mistake at the conference itself. To Wilson the essence of political leadership was education of the public, but at the conference he failed in this role. His relations with the press covering the Paris conference grew strained despite the efforts of Ray Stannard Baker, the one-time muckraker whom Wilson had appointed as chief information officer of the peace delegation. The time-consuming negotiations and the president's reclusive habits kept him from having much contact with reporters, who, starved for information, seized upon rumors and leaks that flowed from sources disgruntled over the peacemakers' decisions. As a result the American public gained little overall sense of what to expect as the final product of the deliberations at Paris. Critics of the settlement, especially of America's membership in the League of Nations, had the field largely to themselves at home.

In his lonehanded pursuit of the peace settlement the president also neglected the political contacts that would be necessary to gain the Senate's consent to the treaty. This was where his refusal to include senators or leading Republicans in the peace delegation hurt badly. Perhaps if he had taken his secretary, Joe Tumulty, with him to Paris, some of the damage might have been avoided. Tumulty had always supplied much of the attention to detail and day-to-day personal contact that the reclusive president had scanted in his relations with Congress. But Tumulty no longer enjoyed Wilson's full confidence, and his advice about keeping senators informed and soliciting their views went unheeded. When Wilson returned to Washington early in July 1919, he faced a tough situation on Capitol Hill. In his formal presentation of the treaty to the Senate on July 10, the president did not dwell on specific terms; instead he argued that the League of Nations had become "the practical statesman's hope of success. . . . The united power of free nations must put a stop to aggression and the world must be given peace." America's duty to play a leading part in this enterprise was plain. "Shall we or any other free people hesitate to accept this great duty? Dare we reject it and break the heart of the world?"

Those brave words opened the hardest and most momentous struggle of Woodrow Wilson's career. The president took up the battle with considerable political strength, despite the many months in which he neglected to cultivate that support. Taft and a number of leading Republicans continued to advocate League membership, as did the overwhelming majority of Democrats. Polls of newspaper editors found support for the League running between three and four times as strong as opposition, although the support did not run deep. With some conspicuous exceptions, few spokesmen criticized or commented much on the provisions of the Treaty of Versailles other than the League of Nations.

By the time of Wilson's return to Washington in mid-1919, supporters and opponents of League membership had aligned themselves into firm groups in the Senate. Party loyalty weighed most heavily with Democratic senators, all but a handful of whom had come out for virtually unrestricted American participation in the League. Those Democrats, who numbered about thirty-five, made up the bedrock of Wilson's support. Some of them were convinced internationalists, but most were simply following their party's president, regardless of where he led them. They added little persuasive argument to subsequent debates over the treaty.

Republicans reacted differently. Despite Taft's continued leadership of the League to Enforce Peace, Republican newspapers did not endorse membership in the League of Nations with the near unanimity of their

"THE LEAGUE OF NATIONS ARGUMENT IN A NUTSHELL." "Ding" Darling's summation of the debate over the League.

Democratic counterparts. Many widely read Republican journals, such as the *New York Tribune* and the *Los Angeles Times*, criticized the collective security commitment under the League Covenant and demanded safeguards for American independence through "reservations" to be attached by Senate consent to the treaty. A sizable minority of Republican papers, including the influential *Chicago Tribune*, opposed League membership under all circumstances. As the round robin had shown earlier, Republican senators harbored much skepticism about joining the new international organization. Some signers of the round robin were outright opponents, but most of them followed Henry Cabot Lodge and expressed willingness to accept League membership if it were hedged with what came to be called "strong reservations."

Reservations became the crux of the Senate's debate over acceptance of the Versailles treaty and membership in the League of Nations. Under Lodge's leadership, the Republican majority, joined by a handful of Democrats, adopted reservations to define and limit the role of the United States under the terms of the treaty. Some of the reservations condemned specific parts of the settlement, such as the cession of China's Shantung province to Japan, and others castigated its omissions, such as a failure to grant Ireland independence from Britain. But the critical reservations concerned the collective security clause of the Covenant of the League of Nations, Article X. Lodge's reservations would have required majority approval by both houses of Congress in order to participate in actions voted by the League Council, especially economic sanctions and the use of military force. The Republicans who followed Lodge on Article X numbered about forty, and they were joined by a few Democrats; together, they constituted the largest bloc in the Senate. Another handful of Republican senators supported League membership with fewer restrictions, or "mild reservations"; when added to the bloc supporting stricter reservations, those who sought some restrictions on the League fell just short of a majority.

Finally sixteen senators—fourteen Republicans and two Democrats—totally rejected American participation in the League of Nations. These men, who earned the nicknames of "irreconcilables" and "bitter enders," included veteran Republican insurgents such as Robert La Follette of Wisconsin, George Norris of Nebraska, and William E. Borah of Idaho, as well as three former Progressives, Hiram Johnson of California, Miles Poindexter of Washington, and Medill McCormick of Illinois. Another irreconcilable was Senator Philander C. Knox of Pennsylvania, who had served as attorney general under Roosevelt and secretary of state under Taft. Most of these senators had come out against

League membership soon after the Covenant was published. Their opposition rested on two principal grounds. One was American autonomy, or as Borah expressed it, "the unembarrassed and unentangled freedom of a great Nation to determine for itself in its own way where duty lies and where wisdom calls." Many of these criticisms echoed Roosevelt's earlier attacks on the League to Enforce Peace, and it was fitting that several of these senators had once followed Roosevelt as Republican insurgents and Progressives. Roosevelt's daughter Alice applauded the irreconcilables, while his one-time imperialist cohort Albert Beveridge spoke out often to denounce the League Covenant as a "net that would entangle the American Nation in a European-Asiatic balance of power."

The irreconcilables' other ground of criticism stressed such ideals as peace and freedom. Several of them denounced the League as a mechanism to enforce an imperialistic settlement and as a source of future wars. These criticisms recalled Bryan's earlier attacks on the League to Enforce Peace as an instrument of war, and it was likewise fitting that such opponents of intervention as La Follette and Norris rejected the League along with the other fruits of victory in the war. These irreconcilables voiced the few criticisms heard in the Senate of other provisions of the Versailles treaty. They attacked the treaty's harsh treatment of Germany, and the dispersal of Germany's colonies to Britain, France, and Japan. As La Follette put it, Wilson had "cut and slashed the map of the Old World . . . in mockery of that sanctified formula of 14 points, and made it our Nation's shame." Outside the Senate some Irish-Americans attacked the treaty's inaction toward Ireland, and reformers such as the editors of *New Republic* backed the irreconcilables in dismay at what they saw as a punitive, unjust settlement. Though few in number, these liberal critics deprived the pro-League forces of eloquent support at a crucial time.

In the contest over ratification of the treaty, Senator Lodge and President Wilson faced each other as leaders of rival political followings with competing strategies. The Massachusetts senator's role in the debates over the Versailles treaty marked the high point of his long public career. As leader of the Senate Republicans and spokesman for those who would accept League membership with "strong reservations," Henry Cabot Lodge drew upon a wealth of intellectual and political resources. He had honed his legislative skills in more than three decades on Capitol Hill. He had engaged in scholarly study and writing about American history and international affairs. He possessed deep familiarity with the foreign policies of previous administrations,

Henry Cabot Lodge.

which he had gained particularly through his intimate friendship with
Theodore Roosevelt. Despite his reserved, aloof manner, Lodge harbored strong feelings about carrying on for his fallen comrade, and
these feelings included a deep repugnance toward Woodrow Wilson,
which added personal animus to his conduct during the debates over
the treaty.

Personalities aside, two goals ranked uppermost with the senator.
The first was to maintain Republican unity. The spectrum of Republican stands on League membership stretched from Taft's warm championship to Borah's and Beveridge's bitter opposition, so that keeping
the party together posed a formidable task. Lodge managed this by
assembling a package of reservations that satisfied the majority of
Republicans inside and outside the Senate. Lodge persuaded the irreconcilables first to support the reservations, despite their intention later
to vote against consent to the treaty, on the ground that the reservations would make the treaty and League membership less obnoxious
if they did pass. He mollified Taft and Republican internationalists
with the argument that these reservations put their party's stamp on
the treaty and that they were the minimum price required for Senate

consent. The "mild reservationists" likewise found the limitations on Article X acceptable. In the end, only one Republican senator broke ranks to vote for the treaty without reservations. This party solidarity was a triumph for Lodge.

Lodge's second goal was to assure American participation in international affairs on what he regarded as the sound basis of national interests. Although some observers suspected that Lodge covertly connived with the irreconcilables to defeat the treaty and League membership, Lodge in fact still desired to see the United States play an active role among the world's great powers. He continued to favor some security pacts with nations outside the Western Hemisphere, especially arrangements with Britain in Europe and the Far East. In 1919 Lodge supported the subsidiary treaty with Britain to defend France, which Wilson had agreed to as the price for France's abandonment of harsher territorial terms against Germany. He also favored extending wartime cooperation with the Allies to create, as he asserted in 1920, "a new agreement, or association, or league—whatever you call it—with all the nations of Europe under the leadership of the United States itself." Lodge professed to believe that his reservations could transform the treaty and membership in "Wilson's league" into a proper basis for a committed, responsible American role in world politics.

On his side, President Wilson pursued essentially similar goals of maintaining party unity and pursuing his own design for American foreign policy. Wilson's success in the White House and undisputed leadership of his party enabled him to count on Democratic support for the treaty, although that support was not unanimous. Two Democratic senators joined the irreconcilables, and in Georgia, Tom Watson was staging a startling political comeback based upon equal measures of racism and denunciation of the Versailles settlement as an imperialistic power grab. A few other Democratic senators also voted for some of Lodge's reservations, while many members of the party's Irish-American contingent denounced the treaty's allegedly pro-British bent. Those defections and criticisms boded ill for the Democrats' fortunes in 1920, but they did not cause Wilson many problems during the Senate debates. The president likewise wanted the United States to play a leading role in world affairs based on what he regarded as the proper grounds, which meant membership in the League of Nations with the fewest possible restrictions, reservations, or hesitations.

Wilson adopted a familiar strategy in seeking approval of the Versailles treaty and League membership. It was the approach that he had used three years earlier when he had battled Bryan and congressional

"GOING TO TALK TO THE BOSS." A Chicago Daily News *cartoon showing Wilson taking his case for the League to the people.*

opponents over military preparedness. Once more the president focused the differences on a central question, in this case obligations under Article X of the Covenant, and he again went out on a speaking tour to take his case directly to the people. Some observers doubted the wisdom of his strategy. Republican internationalists criticized him for not making early concessions to mild reservationist senators, although Wilson did keep lines open to those senators, and he did not rule out some possible accommodation on the basis of reservations regarding Article X of the League Covenant. Foes scoffed at his decision to take to the hustings. "There is no way the people can vote on the treaty," one senator reportedly sniffed. "Only the Senate can do that." In fact, the large, enthusiastic crowds that greeted the president caused several of Lodge's followers to waver.

Wilson's three-week speaking tour in September 1919 marked the supreme oratorical effort of his life. Only during his first presidential campaign had he made more speeches, and never in so short a time. Wilson traveled 10,000 miles and delivered thirty-two major addresses, together with eight shorter talks. He fumbled a bit at the outset, but he soon recovered his wonted clarity and force. At long last Wilson was mounting a campaign to educate the public about his aims in war and peace. Most of his speeches consisted of sober explanations of the country's potential obligations under Article X. The president scoffed at charges that American soldiers would be constantly sent to far-flung trouble spots. Military force was a last resort, he repeatedly explained. After following careful procedures the League would first lay down financial and commercial blockades against aggressors. If force ultimately proved necessary the United States would probably not be asked to join in actions outside the Western Hemisphere. "If you want to put out a fire in Utah," the president observed, "you do not send to Oklahoma for a fire engine."

Wilson also reassured his audience that League membership would not compromise American independence. Wilson tried to refute the charge made by Lodge and others that Article X abrogated Congress's constitutional power to declare war. Wilson argued that Lodge's main reservation, which called for separate congressional approval of any League request for collective action, was superfluous. Congress still had the power to appropriate the money needed to support such actions. Wilson also asserted that Article X imposed "a moral not a legal obligation" on the United States. "It is binding only in conscience, not in law." Wilson never fully developed what he meant by that distinction, but he may have been laying the groundwork for a compromise position on the reservations on Article X. Finally Wilson stressed that the League would stand as a bulwark against future world wars. "Ah, my fellow citizens, do not forget the aching hearts that are behind discussions like this," he pleaded. "Do not forget the forlorn homes from which those boys went out." He urged Americans to see that without a new foundation for peace, "this terrible task will have to be done once more." In the next world war, he avowed, "the very existence of civilization would be in the balance. . . . Ask any soldier if he wants to go through a hell like that again. The soldiers know what the next war would be."

COLLAPSE

Woodrow Wilson's eloquence in September 1919 was like the brilliant flash of a dying star. The grueling pace of the speaking tour exhausted the sixty-two-year-old Wilson, who had been warned by his physician that the trip might injure his health. As he began his speech on September 25, at Pueblo, Colorado, Wilson faltered and seemed about to collapse. He rallied to deliver one of his best messages. "We have accepted the truth and we are going to be led by it," he closed, "and it is going to lead us, and through us the world, out into the pastures of quietness and peace such as the world has never dreamed of before." Those words ended the last speech that Wilson ever delivered as president. That night he complained of blinding headaches and numbness on his left side. Tumulty, Mrs. Wilson, and his doctor, Admiral Cary T. Grayson, insisted on an immediate return to Washington. Back at the White House, on October 2, 1919, the president suffered a massive stroke that almost killed him.

Wilson hovered near death for several days. Within a month he began to stage a remarkable recovery, given his age and the severity of the stroke. Still, he sustained permanent partial paralysis on his left side, some loss of vision, diminished concentration, shortened attention span, and weakened emotional control. His intellectual powers were unaffected, but his capacity for judgment was impaired. Wilson was reduced to a shadow of his formerly masterful, dynamic self, and he never again functioned at anywhere near his accustomed level of activity. Partly because of his undeniable impairment and partly because of the way that Mrs. Wilson and Admiral Grayson handled his illness, public confidence in him and his administration withered. His wife and doctor allowed little official information to reach the press, and rumors filled the vacuum. Some stories insinuated that the president had died and that Mrs. Wilson was deceitfully exercising his powers. Other stories hinted that he had gone insane and that his wife and Grayson were keeping him locked up. Bars that had been put up years before to protect windows from the Roosevelt boys' baseballs were cited as evidence that the White House was harboring a lunatic.

Four weeks passed before the president received any visitors from outside. Only European royalty and an official two-man committee from the Senate were allowed to see him. When the senators came, the Wilsons made elaborate arrangements to conceal the president's paralysis and make it appear that he was attending to business. One of the senators, Albert Fall of New Mexico, a Republican irreconcilable, greeted him by saying, "Well, Mr. President, we have all been praying for you." Wilson quipped back, "Which way, Senator?" Even after these visitors reported publicly that the president was alive and in command of his mental faculties, gossip persisted about who was actually running the government. The nastiest versions insisted that Mrs. Wilson was really in charge. By early 1920 sneers were circulating about a "female President" and "government by petticoat." Edith Wilson in fact acted only to safeguard her husband's fragile health, but by controlling access of people and information to him she probably did function to an extent as a surrogate president. Because Wilson had shared his deepest thoughts with her and had made her his closest advisor

Wilson and his wife, Edith, in their
first public appearance after his stroke.

even before their marriage in 1915, she was well prepared for the job. Yet these allegations helped undermine public confidence in the president.

The most serious immediate consequence of Wilson's stroke was to produce a stalemate over the issue of America's membership in the League. In November 1919, Lodge scheduled votes in the Senate on the Versailles treaty. In a brief interview with the Democratic minority leader, Senator Gilbert M. Hitchcock of Nebraska, the president ruled out any accommodation on Article X. He scorned the critical reservation that would require congressional approval for each enforcement action. "That cuts out the heart of the treaty," he declared; "I could not stand for those changes for a moment because it would humiliate the United States before all of the Allied countries." When Hitchcock suggested that compromise was necessary, Wilson snapped, "Let Lodge compromise." The denouement came swiftly. On November 19, the Senate took two votes on consent to the Versailles treaty. First, with the Lodge reservations, the treaty failed, thirty-nine in favor and fifty-five opposed. A coalition of Democrats loyal to Wilson and irreconcilables blocked consent. Then, without reservations, the treaty fell short by almost exactly the same margin, thirty-eight for and fifty-three against. This time, Republicans and a few Democrats who favored reservations joined the irreconcilables in opposition.

The standoff stunned many people, particularly members of pro-League groups. Taft and the League to Enforce Peace lobbied extensively for reconsideration of the treaty, and a number of prominent Democrats urged Wilson to compromise. Finally, Lodge grudgingly bowed to the importunings and scheduled another vote in March 1920. But Wilson refused to budge. In his earlier interview with Hitchcock, the president had threatened to make senators "answer to the country for their acts. They must answer to the people." In January Wilson issued a public declaration in which he called upon Democrats "to give the next election the form of a great and solemn referendum, a referendum as to the part the United States is to play in completing the settlement of the war and in the prevention of such future outrages as Germany attempted to perpetrate." Although Wilson probably did not recall it, he was seizing upon the same tactic that Bryan had mistakenly used two decades earlier when he had urged Democratic senators to approve the peace treaty with Spain in order to make the 1900 election a referendum on retention of the Philippines.

The tactic backfired even worse in 1920. On March 19, the Senate voted a second time on the treaty with the Lodge reservations. The margin was much closer, forty-nine in favor and thirty-five against, with twenty-one Democrats defying Wilson and voting for consent. The remainder of their party brethren joined the irreconcilables in opposing the treaty, thereby holding the margin seven votes short of the required two-thirds. The vote was not such a great missed opportunity as it seemed, for Wilson had vowed that he would not ratify the treaty if the Senate voted for consent with the Lodge reservations. As matters turned out, this was the last chance for the United States to approve the Versailles treaty and join the League. This defeat also ruled out

"REFUSING TO GIVE THE LADY A SEAT." A comment on the defeat of the League in the Senate.

any consideration of the security pact with Britain and France that Lodge favored.

Over the years, it has tempted many to assign blame for an outcome that no one except the irreconcilables wanted. Wilson's and Lodge's personalities gave the deadlock the look of a collision between an unbending, self-righteous idealist and a proud, vengeful nationalist. But their conflict went deeper, involving philosophical differences over foreign policy. Wilson and Lodge disagreed less about the desirability or extent of America's overseas commitments than about the aims behind such commitments. In his reservation to Article X, Lodge sought to secure for the United States the right to act in its own interests, as any nation would in an alliance. Wilson's idea of a "moral commitment" under Article X entailed a pledge from the United States to make its own peace and security indivisible from a new world order.

To both men the critical consideration was the spirit in which America undertook these commitments. Activism and leadership in traditional power politics were what Lodge wanted for the United States; activism and leadership in building an international structure of peace and justice were what Wilson wanted for his country. Ironically, it was not at all clear which man was the greater idealist or the sounder realist. For all his stress on practical national interests, Lodge prized power politics mainly for the same reason that his friend Roosevelt had: both believed that military service and war promoted the noblest traits of character in men and nations. For all his appeals to moral values and lofty principles, Wilson wanted to build a new international order in which all nations, but especially the United States, could pursue their own interests without the waste and suffering of modern technological war. In a sense, Lodge and Wilson in 1919 were extending to foreign affairs the great domestic debate that Roosevelt and Wilson had conducted in 1912. Once more, the nationalist was the deeper idealist about human nature, inasmuch as Lodge sought to preserve power politics as the arena for exhibiting the finest traits of individual and national character. Once more, the liberal was the greater realist, inasmuch as Wilson sought to weave individual and national interests into a community of peace and happiness.

Insofar as these philosophical differences counted most with them, Wilson and Lodge did right not to meet each other halfway. Insofar as they operated as practical politicians, they were wrong not to seek mutual accommodation. It is hard to judge which man lost more in the outcome, but it is clear which one could have done more to prevent it. Wilson had greater latitude for compromise, and at the crucial moments he held the outcome in his hands. Why Wilson refused to relent has intrigued three generations of historians. His defenders have argued that the overriding goal of preventing another world war demanded an all-or-nothing approach. Limited, hesitant American participation in the League, so they have contended, would have done no more to preserve the peace than such participation by the Allied powers later did. Wilson's critics have maintained that his warped personality prevented him from exercising elementary good sense. League membership even under stringent reservations, so they have asserted, was a worthy half loaf which would have ensured a more active American role in world affairs. These critics have frequently resorted to psychological explanations to account for Wilson's behavior.

Wilson's defenders and critics have fallen short on three counts. First, the main defense of Wilson's actions overlooks the fact that an unstinting participation in the League was impossible for the United States. No matter how necessary it might have been for the United States or Britain or France to embrace a new role in world affairs—one which would broaden the pursuit of immediate national security and advantage—that kind of metamorphosis was not about to occur, and was unrealistic to expect. People behave in limited, self-interested ways, and nations cannot abandon the pursuit of advantage. Second, the primarily psychological criticisms of Wilson's behavior in 1919 overlook how uncharacteristic it was. He had succeeded so well in politics up to then largely because he had shown great flexibility and ready adaptability to circumstances, especially in his New Freedom programs at home and his redirection of the Democrats in foreign policy. Third, both lines of argument miss the critical impact of Wilson's stroke. This catastrophic illness, with its indisputable psychological effects, played a major, probably decisive part in his behavior.

The closest and best qualified students of Wilson's health have concluded that his stroke intensified his customary denial of obstacles and determination to wage heroic struggle against difficulties. The stroke left Wilson physically unable to explore possible grounds for compromise with senators, and it rendered him neurologically incapable of sharp judgments. One of the strongest effects of a stroke is to make the victim, in the words of an expert neurologist, "a caricature of himself." In Wilson's case, the stroke made him even more solitary, radically self-reliant, and impervious to unwelcome advice than he had already become in foreign affairs. Wilson's stroke was much more than a personal misfortune: it contributed to a national and international tragedy. It almost certainly ruined a better—more wholesome, more hopeful, more constructive—outcome to the foreign policy conflict of 1919.

The timing of the president's collapse and the deadlock over the peace treaty worsened the national malaise of 1919. The flu epidemic had come and gone, while the baseball scandal was still breaking. The sizable, at times violent, strikes were still going on. Prices seemed to be rising inexorably. Race riots had rocked cities during the summer, and lynchings continued. Outcries against "reds" had just culminated in the first Palmer raid, and the "Soviet ark" was about to sail. Now the national government appeared to have collapsed, leaving the country rudderless. "I have been in Washington a good bit," a veteran reporter privately commented, "and the situation there is as bad as it can be— no government—no policies . . . Congress is adrift. There is no leadership worthy of the name." That seemed the most unsettling aspect of all in this terrible year—the absence of leadership.

12

The Twenties Begin

The 1920s mark a decade as readily categorized as any in American history. In contrast to the two decades that preceded it, conservatism replaced reform, materialism eclipsed idealism, and retreat toward isolation succeeded international activism. Yet despite those changes, there were strong continuities between the twenties and the two earlier decades. Political concerns about private economic power and government responsibility continued to occupy center stage. A powerful though ideologically divided Supreme Court persisted in playing a large, controversial role in defining and deciding constitutional questions that involved basic freedoms and private versus public economic spheres. Racial and ethnic divisions and conflicts did not disappear but intensified, as did cultural clashes between moderns and traditionalists. The world outside America's borders and especially beyond the seas did not cease to intrude upon people's consciousness, despite widespread efforts to give foreign affairs short shrift. In all, the twenties offered an often odd, sometimes unexpected aftermath to the developments of the period before 1920, but they were the recognizable outcome of those pivotal decades

Politics—A Golden Age No Longer

Of all the changes that appeared on the American scene in 1920, none was more striking than the altered condition of national politics. Gone were the twin commanding presences of the last two decades. Theodore Roosevelt's death a year earlier and Woodrow Wilson's collapse the preceding October had left a vacuum at the top in both parties. Nearly all politicians were now calculating ways to fill the void those men had left. Wilson's disability was doubly damaging because it triggered a hostile public response rather than the wave of sympathy and remorse his death would have brought. The fallen president still inspired a diminishing band of devotees, but in most circles he bore the blame for just about everything. Contradictory criticisms abounded. Conservatives and progressives condemned his administration respectively for too much or too little government intervention in the economy, and too much or too little support for labor unions. Liberals such as the editors of the *New Republic* heaped scorn on Wilson for having abandoned the Fourteen Points and imposed a "carthaginian peace" on Germany, while Republican nationalists such as Henry Cabot Lodge believed that the president had dealt too softly with the defeated foe. Irish- and Italian-Americans criticized his dealings with the claims of their ancestral homelands, and the cession of Shantung fanned anti-Japanese sentiment on the West Coast. But the swelling popular revulsion toward Wilson contained more than the sum of specific grievances. There was a much broader, more diffuse, but palpable sense of contempt. For centuries political theorists had maintained that the swiftest path to oblivion for a leader lay through demonstrable weakness. Wilson's stroke supplied classic proof of that contention.

The president made a partial recovery from his stroke in the spring of 1920, which allowed him to call an occasional, brief Cabinet meeting, to receive some visitors, and to make a few policy decisions. But these sporadic intrusions into public affairs did not help Wilson politically. His call in January 1920 for a "great and solemn referendum" on the peace treaty in the November presidential election, and his unbending refusal to reconsider the Lodge reservations, drew strong, deserved criticism from pro-League stalwarts such as Taft and from leading Democrats such as Bryan. In his weakened state Wilson now ran into more trouble from an old source: Mexico.

After the withdrawal of John J. Pershing's expedition in February 1917, internecine warfare had continued among the revolutionary elements in Mexico. Pancho Villa and other leaders had fallen in the fighting, and some factions began to advance radical proposals for expropriating foreign-owned property. Wilson's always excitable secretary of state, Robert Lansing, who had never sympathized with the president's hands-off policy toward the Mexican revolutionaries, took alarm at reports of violence and radicalism, and tried to create a dip-

"LITTLE GOLDILOCKS." A comment in the Chicago Daily News *on Wilson's dismissal of Lansing.*

lomatic pretext for intervention. In February 1920 Wilson dismissed Lansing, who had also openly criticized the peace treaty as too mild in its treatment of Germany and too dependent on the League of Nations. His dismissal not only rid Wilson of an unreliable, frequently disloyal lieutenant, but it also preserved the policy toward Mexico that the president had established through severe trials.

But the Wilson administration made little effort to explain the reasons for Lansing's dismissal, stating only that he had called unauthorized meetings of the cabinet. To many the president's action seemed spiteful retaliation against a responsible official whose only sin had been to try to keep the government running. It was a case of popular perceptions prevailing over the reality of the situation, thanks mainly to inept handling of the press and public relations by the White House. Wilson was suffering the same fate that had earlier overtaken Taft, only more swiftly and spectacularly. His plummeting popular regard provided unmistakable evidence of how much the public dimension of politics had continued to grow since 1900. These two decades had opened with the first great political career to rise primarily on those new public dimensions—Roosevelt's; now they were closing with the second great career to fall at least in part because of those dimensions—Wilson's.

The president's pervasive unpopularity led many Democrats to regard him as an albatross around the party's neck. Yet he still inspired a small, fervent following. Some League advocates viewed Wilson as a martyr, while some white Southerners enshrined him and his programs alongside the Confederacy as their second Lost Cause. Obsessed as he was with the peace settlement, the stricken Wilson occasionally entertained fantasies about a third-term candidacy as a vehicle for his "referendum." His secretary, Joe Tumulty, his doctor, Admiral Grayson, and Secretary of the Navy Daniels, with Mrs. Wilson's backing, mercifully smothered the notion.

But Wilson made his party's task in 1920 more difficult by refusing to anoint a successor. Palmer's witchhunt disqualified the attorney general in the president's eyes. Many observers thought that Wilson privately favored William Gibbs McAdoo, who was not only his former secretary of the treasury and administrator of the railroads but also, since 1914, his son-in-law. McAdoo's skill as an organizer and appeal to the old Bryanite following, principally through his ardent support for prohibition, made him the leading contender for the Democratic nomination. Discreet backing from the White House might have secured McAdoo's nomination, but the president actually regarded McAdoo as a schemer who was less than a totally faithful supporter of the League. Against McAdoo, in addition, stood equally committed critics of the Eighteenth Amendment and the Volstead Act. These "wets" divided their support between two governors, James M. Cox of Ohio and Al Smith of New York.

With the party leader out of the picture, the 1920 Democratic convention at San Francisco revived the division and deadlock that had

The Democratic National Convention in San Francisco, 1920.

threatened in 1912. Domestic issues, particularly prohibition and immigration restriction, dominated the debates. Bryan again intruded repeatedly in the proceedings, just as he had done in 1912. The Commoner was only sixty in 1920, but he already seemed a figure from a distant past. It was twenty-four years since he had made his first race as the Democrats' presidential nominee, and twelve years since he had made his last run. During the five years since his resignation as secretary of state, he had lost the leadership of the party to Wilson, and he had begun to devote less attention to domestic economic reform and international peace and more to the cultural issues associated with prohibition, immigration, and Protestant fundamentalism. Bryan would soon join the crusade to forbid the teaching of evolution in the schools. One incident above all epitomized how out of step with his party Bryan had become. The 1920 party conventions were the first to use microphones and electric amplifiers, but the old orator shoved the devices aside to harangue the multitude as always in his unamplified voice. The Commoner demanded that the Democrats stand for prohibition and immigration restriction, and that they finish the job of peacemaking as soon as possible through compromise. "Wet" delegates hooted and jeered as he spoke.

The 1920 Democratic convention split along the party's fault lines of Northeast and Midwest versus South and West, wet versus dry, city versus country, and to a less openly acknowledged extent, Catholic versus Protestant. It took three difficult days and forty-four ballots before enough deals could be struck to nominate James Cox. As a Protestant and three-term governor, the Ohioan was more acceptable to the party than Al Smith. As one who had made a point of dissociating himself from Wilson, Cox had fewer drawbacks than McAdoo. But the absent chief still made his presence felt. The biggest demonstration at the convention occurred when a portrait of the president was unexpectedly unveiled. The big Tammany-dominated New York delegation sat sullenly while other delegates marched around waving state placards until the thirty-eight-year-old assistant secretary of the navy, Franklin Roosevelt, grabbed the New York placard and joined the parade. Roosevelt's conspicuous display of loyalty to Wilson, together with the attractiveness of his surname and kinship by marriage to the former Republican president, played a large part in his winning the vice-presidential nomination. In all, the 1920 convention was a bruising experience for Democrats, and an all too accurate preview of coming tribulations.

The Republicans had to fill the void left by Theodore Roosevelt's

The Democratic ticket in 1920: James Cox (left) and Franklin Delano Roosevelt.

death. The closeness of the 1916 result and their victories in the 1918 congressional contests had aroused hopes of improved fortunes even before Wilson's collapse. The Republicans' good chance to win in 1920 brought forth a trio of strong contenders for the nomination, two of whom vied for Roosevelt's mantle. One was General Leonard Wood, the former Army Chief of Staff and long-time critic of Wilson administration military policies. As a close friend of Roosevelt's since the 1890s and his superior officer during the Spanish-American War, Wood fit comfortably into the former president's legacy of assertive nationalism. Moreover, Wood enjoyed the nearest equivalent to a deathbed blessing from his fallen comrade. Not long before his death, Roosevelt had remarked to reporters that if he did not run again himself in 1920 Wood was the kind of man whom he would like to see in the White House. The general played heavily on that quasi-endorsement in his unabashedly jingoistic campaign, which vied with Attorney General Palmer's in execrating radicals. Wood declared, "Kill it [communism] as you would a rattlesnake, and smash those who follow it, speak for it, or support it."

The other Rooseveltian contender sprang from his domestic reformist legacy. This was Senator Hiram Johnson, who, as governor of California, had led the strongest state Progressive party, and had run as the vice-presidential nominee on the Progressive ticket in 1912. A fiery orator, Johnson initially campaigned for tighter regulation of big business, higher taxes for the rich, and more extensive governmental social services. The Californian's candidacy drew support from erstwhile Republican insurgents and former Progressives, but they discovered to their dismay that reform issues no longer struck sparks with audiences or editors. Johnson soon switched to foreign policy. By the time of the Republican convention, he was running primarily on his opposition to League membership and denunciations of the Japanese.

The third main contender was Illinois Governor Frank Lowden, who fitted the mold of McKinley and other nineteenth-century Republican presidents. He was a humbly born Midwesterner, a folksy campaigner, and a popular governor. Some observers judged Lowden the most broadly appealing of the main contenders. None of the three swept the primaries or secured enough endorsements from party leaders to sew up the nomination in advance of the convention. Wood and Lowden each garnered about a third of the delegates, while Johnson ran a distant third. Various state bosses put up favorite-son candidates in order to hold on to their delegations for bargaining at the convention. Senator Warren Harding of Ohio also came to the convention with fairly widespread support as an alternative choice, if the front-runners should falter.

When the Republican convention met in Chicago in June 1920, the stage seemed to be set for a trade that would eventually favor one of the front-runners, either Wood or Lowden. But several factors intervened to forestall the expected outcome. One stumbling block, evidently, was Wood's self-righteousness and political naiveté. At one point during the convention, Senator Boies Penrose reportedly offered to deliver Pennsylvania's votes and other support to Wood in return for a voice in picking cabinet members. "I will not make promises," Wood declared. "I will not be bound to any man." Penrose replied, "I'm sorry, but we plan to elect a Republican president in the fall and we wish to have a certain influence in naming members of the cabinet." Lowden's chief liability was financial malfeasance in his campaign organization, which made uncommitted leaders reluctant to endorse him. Furthermore, Wood and Lowden had said too many nasty things about each other in their campaigns for either one to switch easily to his rival, while Johnson's progressivism made him unacceptable to conservatives. Nor did any of the candidates have resourceful managers who could bring the party's factions together.

The beneficiary of the stalemate was the dark horse, Warren Gamaliel Harding. Later legends about a "smoke-filled room" at Chicago made his nomination appear the product of nefarious machinations by such bosses as Penrose. In fact, Harding's campaign manager, Harry Daugherty, had uncannily predicted his man's route to victory. "I think we can afford to take chances," Daugherty had said in February 1920, "that at about eleven minutes after two Friday morning of the convention when fifteen or twenty weary men are sitting around a table someone will ask whom shall we nominate? At the decisive time the friends of Harding will suggest him and can well afford to abide by the result." Harding finally won the nomination on the tenth ballot because no more acceptable alternative had surfaced. Like his Democratic opponent, he came from the big swing state of Ohio, which had been the key to Wilson's 1916 victory. He was known and liked among Republican leaders, especially fellow senators. Those assets made Harding, in the description of one of his biographers, "the available man."

Familiarity and availability did not translate, however, into respect for Harding's abilities. Senator Penrose supposedly chuckled about his nomination, saying, "The times do not require a first-rater." Harding was the least inspiring choice of any substantial party, major or minor, since Alton Parker in 1904. By picking a man who was neither well known to the public nor well respected among his peers, the Republicans were unmistakably breaking with past political patterns. They were turning their backs on the able, articulate, attractive, sometimes heroic candidates whom the parties had almost always chosen since 1900. The 1920 Republican convention gave further proof of its break with the past in its vice-presidential choice. Because Harding was a conservative, party leaders planned to balance the ticket with a reformer, Senator Irvine L. Lenroot of Wisconsin, a former associate of Robert La Follette's. When the balloting began, however, delegates shouting "We want Coolidge" began a stampede on the floor that upset the arrangement to nominate Lenroot and gave the vice-presidential nod to the Massachusetts governor. Coolidge was actually better known to the public than Harding, although his reputation rested entirely on his stand during the Boston police strike.

"Normalcy"

The nomination of Warren Harding and Calvin Coolidge signaled the end of the second golden age of American political leadership, which had flourished during the preceding two decades. Even at the time of the 1920 convention there were hints of a decline. When Coolidge received the news of his unexpected vice-presidential nomination by telephone, he listened in silence, hung up, turned to his wife, and said just one word, "Nominated." It would later become clear that Harding fit perfectly the mold that the novelist Sinclair Lewis had already begun to make familiar in 1920 with his best-selling caricature of narrow-mindedness, cant, and sham in small-town America, *Main Street.* Harding was such an embodiment of small-town sin and hypocrisy that he could have been one of Lewis's best characters. In 1920 Harding's worst flaws were unknown to all but a few intimates. Republican senatorial colleagues regarded him as an amiable, shallow, handsome fellow who made a nice figurehead at the top of their ticket. They and other Republicans found, to the joy of conservatives and the horror of reformers, that they had gotten a lot more than they had bargained for.

In a speech delivered shortly before the convention, Harding had stated his basic campaign theme and added a new word to English usage. "America's greatest need," he avowed, "is not heroics, but healing; not nostrums, but normalcy; not revolution, but restoration; . . . not surgery; but serenity." In his speeches Harding often called for "normalcy," which prompted H. L. Mencken, in a pun on Harding's middle name, to dub his oratory "gamalielese." William Allen White later referred to "Harding's clarion voice, as impersonal and mechanically controllable as a phonograph," and dismissed him as "a mere bass drum, beating the time of the hour, carrying no tune, making no music, promoting no deep harmony; just a strident, rhythmic noise."

But Harding was no simpleton, especially when it came to politics. His rhetoric dramatized the alternative he offered to the politics of his predecessor. As one historian subsequently put it, Harding presented himself as the "antithesis of Wilson: modest mediocrity, rather than arrogant genius; . . . warm humanity rather than austere intellectualism; genial realism, rather than strenuous idealism." When Harding offered "not heroics, but healing," he was repudiating Theodore Roosevelt as well as Woodrow Wilson. When he promised "not revolution, but restoration," he was turning his back on the previous quarter cen-

Warren Gamaliel Harding.

tury of agitation, uplift, and reform. When he held out the prospect of
a return to "normalcy," he implied the restoration of pre-war quiescence and detachment in foreign policy, and of calmer times at home.
In his Ohio background and his tone Harding recalled William
McKinley, whose memory he often explicitly invoked. Yet "normalcy"
carried the McKinley theme one better by implicitly signalling what an
ordinary, undemanding person Harding was. Nothing he ever said or
did served better to brand on the public mind what a total break Harding offered with the previous twenty years of political idealism, heroism, and striving. "Normalcy" forged the bond between the man and
the moment in 1920.

Harding and the Republicans dominated the campaign from the start.
Cox and Franklin Roosevelt put up a game fight, but they never doubted
what long odds they faced. Whereas Harding intentionally recalled
William McKinley, Cox reached back in spite of himself to the evan-
gelical style and personal touch of the campaigns of William Jennings
Bryan. Strapped for money, the Democrats could not mount an up-to-

date campaign with widespread advertising and large staffs of publicity agents. They fell back instead on Bryan's technique of marathon whistle-stop railroad tours. When he hit his stride, Cox matched the Commoner's sturdy performance, with sixteen to eighteen hours on the stump and as many as twenty-five speeches a day. Franklin Roosevelt's youthful ebullience and jaunty platform manner inescapably reminded his audiences of his distant kinsman. Roosevelt's appeal bothered Republicans so much that they sent Theodore Roosevelt, Jr., out on the campaign trail to assert that this Democratic maverick did not speak for their family. But Cox's and Roosevelt's exertions availed them little. Their press coverage was so limited that when a railroad mishap derailed Cox's train on his western swing, the nominee quipped, "It took a train wreck to get me on the front pages in California."

When it did reach voters, the Democratic message proved unpersuasive. Their party platform in 1920 continued to advocate economic and social reform and to praise the Wilson administration's accomplishments in labor, antitrust, and tax legislation. On the campaign trail, however, the candidates encountered the same indifference to these domestic issues that had already bedeviled Hiram Johnson and his Republican supporters. Still worse for the Democrats, dissension over prohibition continued after the convention. Cox's record as a "wet" and the platform's clumsy attempt to straddle differences over interpretation and enforcement of the Volstead Act alienated many prohibitionist Southerners and Westerners. Bryan left the convention so disgruntled that he lent Cox only perfunctory support in the fall campaign. Getting nowhere with domestic issues, the Democrats reversed field and began to emphasize foreign policy. A visit to Wilson at the White House reinforced this new emphasis for Cox and Roosevelt. The sight of the stricken president moved Cox to tears. "Mr. President," he vowed, "we're going to be a million per cent with you and your administration, and that means the League of Nations." Wilson whispered back, "I am very grateful." Whether it was primarily a noble gesture or a stratagem of convenience, campaigning on the League issue was risky business for the Democrats.

That issue also appeared to carry potential risk for the Republicans. On domestic matters their platform called for higher tariffs, heaped scorn on socialism, and promised to lower taxes—standard party fare even during Roosevelt's heyday. On League membership and the peace treaty, the Republicans fell back on verbal gimmickry concocted by Henry Cabot Lodge. Ever since the Versailles treaty had failed to gain Senate consent with and without the Lodge reservations, pressures had

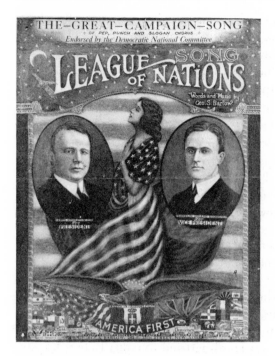

"The Great Campaign Song" showing Cox and Roosevelt as supporters of the League.

mounted on the Republicans to take a clear-cut stand. Taft and the party's internationalists wanted an unequivocal commitment to League membership under Republican auspices. The party's isolationists wanted an equally unequivocal rejection of League membership under any circumstances. With such deep divisions in the party, Lodge understandably strove to keep the platform ambiguous on the point: the 1920 Republican platform condemned the League but kept the door open to membership in an "association of nations."

That plank did not mollify such irreconcilables as William E. Borah and Hiram Johnson, who made private threats to bolt if Harding committed himself to League membership. They had nothing to fear. Despite a long friendship with Taft, Harding appeared to have been an irreconcilable at heart. Once during the Senate debates he had told Borah, "Bill, I'd like to get into the fight against this League of Nations, but the people of my state are all for it I'm afraid." In October 1920, Harding found the partial courage of his convictions. Over the objections of his campaign managers, he insisted on making two brief trips to give major speeches. In Des Moines, Iowa, Harding announced that regarding "this particular League proposed by Wilson, I do not want to clarify the obligations. I want to turn my back on them. It is not interpretation but rejection that I am seeking." It was one of the clearest stands that Harding took during the whole campaign.

The nominee's declaration threw Republican internationalists into a tizzy. Their painful choice between a cherished goal in foreign policy and party loyalty recalled the choice that had confronted Republican anti-imperialists twenty years earlier. A few of them bolted to support Cox after Harding's speech, but most of them followed their predecessors' example and remained loyal to the party.

Except for that one flap, Harding's pursuit of the presidency proceeded swimmingly. He conducted a front-porch campaign in openly acknowledged imitation of McKinley. Carefully selected delegations representing such groups as Italian-Americans or industrial workers visited his home in Marion, where the candidate made remarks calculated to appeal to their particular concerns. Most of Harding's statements dwelled on Democratic misdeeds and how bad everything had gotten under Wilson. Aside from promising to raise the tariff and give tax breaks to business, Harding took few firm stands on domestic issues. Although his record was unequivocally conservative, he made efforts to woo insurgents and former Progressives with promises to listen to their views and advice. When Harding tried to enlist Robert La Follette's support, the Wisconsin senator rebuffed the overtures, but he did not endorse anyone else. Harding conducted an extensive correspondence with the ex-Progressive journalist William Allen White, who eventually came aboard the bandwagon but did so, he confessed privately, "with all the enthusiasm of an usher at his best girl's wedding." Some ex-Progressives proved less tractable. A few of them backed Cox because they found the Democrats' domestic stands far more to their liking. Others supported minor party candidates, including Eugene Debs, who was making another run on the Socialist ticket.

Those defections made only slight ripples on the smooth surface of Harding's campaign. Not even prohibition disturbed his march toward the White House. Neither wet nor dry, Harding had voted in the Senate for the Eighteenth Amendment and the Volstead Act, but he had also expressed doubts about the ultimate success of the anti-alcohol experiment. Those Senate votes, together with Cox's apparent transgressions, made Harding acceptable to drys without evidently alienating the wets. The strongest sign of his appeal was the failure of racial bigotry to hurt him. For years, untrue stories had circulated in Ohio that one of Harding's great-great grandparents had been a Negro. Shortly after his nomination, a pamphlet charging that Harding was "colored" began to circulate in the Midwest and South. Republicans went to great lengths and spent much money to suppress the pamphlet, but a whispering campaign continued through the election, often with covert Democratic encouragement. The only apparent effect of these racial charges was to reinforce already strong inclinations among blacks in the North to vote Republican.

Harding emulated McKinley's use of skilled campaign managers and political advertising. The candidate retained Will Hays as Republican national chairman and put him in overall charge of the presidential drive. Hays once more demonstrated the abilities that had helped bring Charles Evans Hughes within a whisker of winning four years before. With a united party behind him and virtually unlimited funds at his disposal, Hays ran a well-coordinated, efficient, frugal organization. One of his smartest moves was to pick Albert Lasker as publicity director. A Chicago advertising man and self-made millionaire, Lasker was what one admirer called "the genius of the commonplace." Before and after his campaign service in 1920, Lasker specialized in coming up with catchy slogans and jingles for brands of soap, toothpaste, and cigarettes, and in adapting advertising to movies and radio. Those talents proved equally serviceable in politics. It was Lasker who seized upon normalcy as the centerpiece of the campaign, making "Back to Normalcy" its most widely circulated slogan.

Lasker's magic touch lay in recognizing the potential appeal of Harding and what he stood for. The upshot was an ingenious blend of old and new. The message behind normalcy was unabashedly backward-looking, yet Harding uttered no criticisms of material progress and raised no questions about those who profited most from technological and economic advance. Moreover, his front-porch campaign employed the newest methods designed to penetrate public consciousness. His managers drew on the popularity of sports stars not only by seeking endorsements but also by staging a major league baseball game in Marion, with the candidate throwing out the first pitch. In addition to soliciting testimonials from entertainment figures, the Harding campaign staged performances by the singer Al Jolson and popular jazz bands, and sponsored parades by Broadway and Hollywood stars. Photographers swarmed around the candidate's home, recording these events for newspapers, magazines, and newsreels. Harding's running mate got into the publicity act, too. Widely circulated photographs and newsreels showed Coolidge pitching hay on his father's Vermont farm, attired in new, unwrinkled overalls over a starched white shirt, necktie, and polished city shoes. In the fall of 1920, Harding became the first presidential candidate to give a speech over the radio, and in November, station KDKA in Pittsburgh became the first to broadcast election returns.

One other aspect of the presidential campaign blended the old and the new. Eugene Debs was back on the ballot for his fourth and last run as the Socialist candidate. But Debs was not back on the campaign trail. Gone were the flag-draped "Red Special" train and the slender, intense man's appealing figure and fiery eloquence. Debs languished in the federal penitentiary in Atlanta, Georgia, and his campaign buttons and literature featured his inmate's number. The Socialist campaign in 1920 once more assailed big business and condemned both intervention in the world war and the Versailles treaty, but the greatest attention by far went to the condemnation of wartime repression of civil liberties and the Red Scare. With his prison number and photographs in his prison uniform, Debs offered living proof of the violation of cherished liberties.

The outcome of the 1920 election was never in doubt, but the full magnitude of Harding's margin of victory was a surprise. He scored one of the biggest electoral triumphs in American history. His popular vote was just over sixteen million, or 60 percent of the total, to Cox's nine million and 34 percent. Harding captured thirty-seven states with 404 electoral votes, the largest count garnered yet for any presidential candidate. Cox carried only ten Southern states and one Border state;

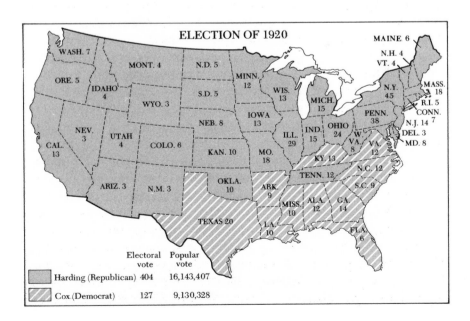

Harding swept the rest of the Border states and cracked the Solid South by winning Tennessee.

Democratic bastions fell all over the country. Harding became the first Republican to carry New York City and Boston. Racial rumors apparently carried little weight among white Southerners, because Harding bettered previous Republican showings in all but one of the Southern and Border states that he lost. His coattails proved long and strong. Governor Al Smith went down to defeat in New York, while former Speaker of the House Champ Clark lost in his normally safe Missouri district. The Republicans picked up 61 House seats, to give them a total of 301 representatives, 10 more than the Democrats had won in their big sweep in 1912. In the senate the Republicans added another 10 seats, for 59 in all, the widest margin that any party had enjoyed in that chamber in a century. Wilson's secretary, Joe Tumulty, summed up the results when he said, "It wasn't a landslide. It was an earthquake."

Voter turnout in 1920 was the lowest yet, at just over 49 percent, making the 1920 election the first presidential contest in which less than a majority of eligibles voted. Drop offs in Democratic and, in less significant numbers, Socialist votes underlay most of the Republicans' wide margins. Apparently most of the defectors simply stayed away from the polls, although some probably voted Republican. Ironically, Debs racked up the largest number of votes, 920,000 ever given to a Socialist candidate, as he attracted thousands of protest votes. Even so, Debs improved on the number of votes in his 1912 showing by only 8,000. More significantly, his and the party's share of the total was less than half of what it had been eight years before. The Socialists also did poorly in other contests. Despite having won two previous elections in his congressional district in Milwaukee, Victor Berger lost to a Republican in 1920. Most of the mayors and legislators elected during the war had long since been voted out. The Socialists had passed their peak.

In 1920, foreign policy played an appreciable role for the first time in a twentieth-century election, and ironically it hurt the party that had embraced the issue. Many of the Democrats' big losses in the Northeast and Midwest came from ethnic groups that resented Wilson's policies during the war and at the peace conference. German-Americans deserted the party in droves, as did Irish- and Italian-Americans. The Democrats' losses among Irish and Italian voters were short-lived, but Germans remained disaffected for the next generation in several states, particularly in the Midwest. If many voters switched to the Democrats out of support for League membership, their numbers were too small and scattered to be noticeable. The party did register less marked declines and occasional small gains among Czech, Polish, and Slavic voters— ethnic groups grateful to Wilson for helping their homelands achieve independence.

For all their decisiveness, the 1920 returns did not mark a lasting political realignment. They did, however, confirm longer running political trends and the ideological appeal of normalcy. The 1920 results bore out in exaggerated fashion the trends revealed in congressional and presidential elections since 1914. Harding and his party achieved their widest margins once more in the Northeast and Midwest, their traditional strongholds. Outside those regions, Republican support fell off decidedly, as was traditional. Their sweep of the West in 1920 was deceptive, since their majorities were much narrower in states west of the Mississippi. Overall, the voting patterns in 1920 revealed much more continuity than change from the preceding two decades.

The sense of resignation expressed in the 1920 election seemed a sad conclusion to the glamor, gusto, idealism, and zeal of the preceding two decades of political reform at home and intervention abroad. Yet the letdown was understandable. Many observers at the time talked about "tired reformers" and the need for a respite from crusading fervor. Some historians would later write about a "slump in idealism" as an inevitable aftermath to great wars fought for noble ends, such as the Civil War and World War I. Perhaps something of the sort did take place in 1920, when the tone of fatigue on all sides was unmistakable.

If 1920 initiated a decline from the excellence of leadership and seriousness of debate that had marked the two previous decades, it marked a lesser change in the prevailing concerns of the American people. The greatest puzzle about these years from 1900 to 1920 to insightful contemporaries and to later historians would be how reform had flourished so spectacularly in an age of political dominance by a conservative party. Others would ask why the United States had repeatedly embarked on major ventures in Europe and Asia at a time when the vast majority of people and politicians were indifferent or hostile to involvement in world affairs. Still others would wonder how the United States could sustain leaders of high idealism and noble purpose during an era when religious and ethnic groups, business and labor, men and women, and blacks and whites were not only in conflict but sometimes literally at each others' throats. It was a tribute to the breadth of concern over the appropriate role of big business in politics, the economy, and society, to the tolerance and broadmindedness many middle-class people showed toward seemingly radical ideas, and to the moving example of great political leaders that these decades would be best remembered not as a time of civil strife but, in the phrase of the historian Richard Hofstadter, as an "age of reform."

As an age of reform these had been pivotal decades. The leaders and thinkers of this era—not only Roosevelt, Wilson, and Bryan but also Robert La Follette, William Howard Taft, W. E. B. Du Bois, Jane Addams, Herbert Croly, Walter Lippmann, Oliver Wendell Holmes, Jr., and Louis Brandeis—had advanced what became the most important ideas in every sphere of American life for the next three-quarters of a century, whether the issues involved government, diplomacy, economics, race, gender, ethnicity, or culture. Public affairs for the rest of the twentieth century would remain in the shadow of this golden age. In a democracy, leadership that can induce citizens to rise above narrow interests and prejudices is always exceptional, and indeed with Harding's election came the return of normalcy. The year 1919 had witnessed the removal of both Theodore Roosevelt and Woodrow Wilson. William Jennings Bryan and Robert La Follette were still on the scene, but their roles were changing. The Commoner was opening the last sad chapter of his career, which would leave him branded on

Woodrow Wilson, pictured here shortly before his death in 1924.

Americans' memories as an apologist for the Ku Klux Klan and the persecutor of teachers of evolution. Although Wisconsin's "Little Giant" had already begun an impressive comeback, he would remain a lone wolf rather than a central figure in his party and in national politics for the rest of his life. Bryan and La Follette would die within a few weeks of each other in 1925, at a time when, in their choice of Coolidge, the voters had just again endorsed the less elevated, less demanding approach to public life that Harding had inaugurated in 1920.

Normalcy forged a significant but partly misleading political mandate for that decade. Its meaning was clearest in foreign affairs, where it ruled out both Wilsonian proposals for membership in the League of Nations and Rooseveltian ideas about military pacts and great power leadership. But normalcy in foreign affairs did not imply any commitment to the equally active, self-conscious isolationism preached by the irreconcilables. Instead, it meant reversion to the easygoing unconcern about world politics that people and politicians had felt before World War I. Americans were assured that they could still accept and reject involvement in foreign affairs, especially outside the western hemisphere, whenever and wherever they pleased.

In domestic affairs, normalcy had a more ambiguous meaning. It rationalized the resumption of power by Republican conservatives who promoted material prosperity through friendly relations with big business. Outwardly, therefore, normalcy resurrected the pro-business orientation that had existed under McKinley and, despite challenges by Bryanites, Democrats, and insurgents, under Roosevelt and Taft. The Wilsonian interregnum, with its temporary tilt in favor of disadvantaged sections and groups, was over. However, one sign that normalcy meant less than a wholehearted embrace of pro-business conservatism was that local Republican insurgency was on the rise again. In Wisconsin, La Follette's Progressives recaptured control of the party and inaugurated a new reform administration in 1920. In Montana, ex-Progressives took over the party that same year and installed Joseph Dixon, an old ally of Roosevelt's, in the governor's chair. During the rest of the decade, more insurgencies and third-party movements would rumble through the Midwest and West.

Still, the Republican party's conservative leaders had every reason to feel vibrant and confident in 1920. Soon they would pin a label on their programs and policies. In unconscious imitation of Roosevelt's New Nationalism and Wilson's New Freedom, they would adopt as their slogan the "New Era." The phrase indicated how much their old adversaries, whom they had apparently obliterated, still affected them.

Like Roosevelt and Wilson before them, these Republican conservatives believed that history was on their side, and that they could find
ways to combine the values of the past with the benefits of the future.
America had changed markedly since the new century began, at home
and in its power abroad. Yet, for all the continuing industrial and technological growth, and for all the horrors and dislocations of the war,
so much remained the same in the attitudes and outlooks of Americans. Optimism still reigned supreme. "Normalcy" was just its latest
incarnation.

Further Reading

All students of this period of American history, from beginners to veteran scholars, have available to them an extraordinary richness of written and printed material. Between 1900 and 1920, the United States, in common with other advanced industrial nations, stood at a special moment in cultural development. The combined impact of technology and education made literacy available to vast numbers of people, over 90 percent among native-born whites and more than 60 percent among even the most disadvantaged group, Afro-Americans. Typewriters and telegraphs made written personal communication easier and faster than ever before in history. Higher speed printing steadily lowered the cost of newspapers and magazines. Books also became more plentiful and more affordable, while the proliferation of public libraries made them the "poor people's colleges" for residents of cities and small towns.

At the same time, the written and printed word reigned virtually unchallenged by any other media of information and entertainment. Because the long-distance telephone was always expensive, often difficult, and sometimes unreliable, it had made only the smallest dent in the primacy of the letter and the telegram for personal, business, and official correspondence. Although improved photoengraving processes increased the number of photographs and illustrations in books and periodicals, their proliferation did not challenge the primacy of reading matter. Most periodicals simply expanded their size to accommodate larger pictorial dimensions. Moreover, since high-speed transmission and reproduction of photographs would not be perfected until the 1920s, the advent of "photojournalism" still lay in the future. Non-printed media remained embryonic. Only motion pictures, still in their "silent" era, became a big business before 1920, although they would not assume an overwhelming place in American popular culture until after the coming of the "talkies" at the end of the 1920s. Radio remained the "wireless telegraph" until 1919, and television was no more than the figment of daydreams.

As a result, people in America and Western Europe had more to read and read more during the years between 1900 and 1920 than at any time in history before or since. The major consequence of this apogee of literacy was twofold. First, the enormous proliferation of the private written word and the public printed word meant both that people at the time wrote and read more in going about their lives and that now students of this era must read more in their efforts at historical understanding. Second, unlike students of later eras, students of this era must read as attentively as possible, because these written and printed words retain as much value as the laborious copying of medieval monks or the scratchings of previous centuries' quill pens. This combination of greater availability and undiminished value makes studying the written and printed records of this era both challenging and daunting.

I. PRIMARY MATERIAL

A. Manuscripts and Published Editions of Letters, Diaries, and Speeches

One type of raw material for historical research in this era abounds in millions of pages of manuscripts of letters, diaries, and drafts of speeches and other writings, which have been collected in repositories throughout the United States. Many of the most important of these collections have been reproduced on microfilm, which can be either purchased or borrowed on interlibrary loan. In addition, some of these collections have been and continue to be published in expertly edited printed volumes.

The complete papers of the four presidents between 1900 and 1920—William McKinley, Theodore Roosevelt, William Howard Taft, and Woodrow Wilson—are available from the Library of Congress in thoroughly indexed microfilm editions. Roosevelt materials are further accessible through two large published collections. Elting E. Morison, ed., *The Letters of Theodore Roosevelt* (8 vols., Cambridge, Mass., 1951–54), gathers his letters from many sources and contains helpful annotations and incisive interpretative essays by Morison, John M. Blum, and Alfred D. Chandler. Hermann Hagedorn, ed., *The Works of Theodore Roosevelt* (29 vols., New York, 1926), includes much of his published writing and some of his speeches, together with introductory essays by friends and associates, among them Albert J. Beveridge, Henry Cabot Lodge, Elihu Root, and William Allen White. For Roosevelt's presidential speeches, see Albert Shaw, ed., *Presidential Addresses and State Papers by Theodore Roosevelt* (8 vols., New York, 1910). Also important are *The New Nationalism* (New York, 1911), a compilation of Roosevelt's speeches in the 1910 campaign, and Ralph Stout, ed., *Roosevelt in the Kansas City Star* (Boston, 1921), a complete run of his newspaper columns during the last two years of his life.

Woodrow Wilson's materials are more readily accessible still, thanks to three decades of unrivaled editorial work by Arthur S. Link and his associates. Link, ed., *The Papers of Woodrow Wilson* (60 volumes, Princeton, N. J., 1966–)brings together his important correspondence from every source and deciphers and reproduces his shorthand notes for writings and speeches. This edition also includes accounts of meetings with Wilson from contemporary diaries, letters, and journals, and it contributes a variety of editorial and interpretative notes on topics that range from influences on Wilson's childhood through his education and academic career to speculative medical diagnoses of his physical condition during and after the Paris Peace Conference in 1919. Future volumes will cover the remainder of Wilson's life. Thanks to the editors' excellent work, *The Papers of Woodrow Wilson* make their subject's life and thought as much of an open book as any figure of this era can probably ever be. This edition supersedes Ray Stannard Baker and William E. Dodd, eds., *The Public Papers of Woodrow Wilson* (6 vols., New York, 1925–27).

Manuscript material about aspects of this era can be found in every state historical society in the country, in most city and county historical societies, and in a large number of college and university libraries. Usually these materials relate to local and regional figures and activities, and they tend to be particularly useful for studying grassroots social and economic history. They provide rich and, as yet, generally untapped sources for this period. Larger repositories contain both regional and national manuscript materials on these decades.

Appropriately, each of the four most extensive sets of manuscript collections is located in a different region of the United States. The Library of Congress houses the greatest number and largest collections, with heaviest emphasis on national political leaders but also including such organizations as the National Association for the Advancement of Colored People and journalists such as William Allen White. The State Historical Society of Wisconsin in Madison ranks next in both number and extent of materials, many of which relate to Robert M. La Follette and the Wisconsin Progressives but also include archives of labor unions and motion picture studios. The Southern Historical Collection at the University of North Carolina-Chapel Hill holds important papers of Southern figures. The Bancroft Library at the University of California-Berkeley contains collections on all aspects of western history, particularly the papers of Hiram Johnson and most of the leaders of California Progressives.

Many important collections from these and other depositories are available in microfilm editions produced by the National Historical Publications and Records Commission. The microfilm editions for individuals and organizations from the period 1900–1920 include the following: Jane Addams, American Federation of Labor, Richard A. Ballinger, Louis D. Brandeis, Eugene V. Debs, Detroit Urban League, W. E. B. Du Bois, Washington Gladden, D. W. Griffith, Warren G. Harding, Morris Hillquit, Frank B. Kellogg, Claude Kitchin, Robert M. La Follette (Wisconsin period), John Muir, National Non-Partisan League, Socialist Labor Party, Socialist Party of America, Henry L. Stimson, Willard Straight, M. Carey Thomas, Wisconsin Progressives, Women's Trade Union League. An annotated microfiche edition makes available the most important diary of the Wilson administration, the one kept from 1913 onward by the president's confidant and special diplomatic envoy, Colonel Edward M. House. A number of collections at the Library of Congress have also been microfilmed, with copies available on interlibrary loan. Two significant sets of microfilmed papers from this period are those of Charles Evans Hughes and Robert Lansing, including his diaries. Many depositories either are currently microfilming some of their collections or will film them at cost, upon request.

Comprehensively edited, well annotated, recently published editions of papers of important figures from this period include Melvin I. Urofsky and David W. Levy, eds., *The Papers of Louis D. Brandeis* (5 vols., Albany, N. Y., 1971–1978) and Louis R. Harlan and Raymond W. Smock, eds., *The Booker T. Washington Papers* (14 vols., Urbana, Ill., 1972–1988). A nicely edited diary of a western senator during the 1910s is George F. Sparks, ed., *A Many Colored Tioga: The Diary of Henry Fountain Ashurst* (Tucson, Ariz., 1972). Older, more selective, and less satisfactorily edited published collections of diaries and letters are also available. The three most important of these collections must be used with great caution, because they contain errors, omissions, and misleading implications. These are Charles Seymour, ed., *The Intimate Papers of Colonel House* (4 vols., Boston, 1926–28); Burton J. Hendrick, *The Life and Letters of Walter Hines Page* (3 vols., Garden City, N. Y., 1922–25), and Henry Cabot Lodge, ed., *Selections from the Correspondence of Theodore Roosevelt and Henry Cabot Lodge* (2 vols., New York, 1925). Other useful published collections for this period include, Worthington C. Ford, ed., *The Letters of Henry Adams, 1892–1918* (Boston, 1938); Anne W. Lane and Louise H. Wall, eds., *The Letters of Franklin K. Lane* (Boston, 1922); John M. Blum, ed., *Public Philosopher: Selected Letters of Walter Lippmann* (Boston, 1985); Ella Winter and Granville Hicks, eds., *The*

Letters of Lincoln Steffens (2 vols., New York, 1938); Walter Johnson, ed., *Selected Letters of William Allen White* (New York, 1947); Allan Nevins, ed., *The Letters and Journal of Brand Whitlock* (2 vols., New York, 1936); and Elena Wilson, ed., *Edmund Wilson: Letters on Literature and Politics, 1912–1972* (New York, 1977).

B. Newspapers and Magazines

The periodical press in America stood at its apex between 1900 and 1920. Excellent newspapers and magazines had flourished earlier and would flourish again later. But at no other time have so many high-quality periodicals reached such a large proportion of the population and with so much influence. Newspapers and begun to emancipate themselves from the shackles of patronage by political parties and factions. Higher speed printing, cheaper paper production, and speedier delivery over broader areas allowed metropolitan and smaller city newspapers to support themselves through subscriptions, newsstand sales, and advertising without needing the financial cushion provided by official printing contracts awarded for political service. Although most newspapers in this period retained their partisan editorial leanings, overwhelmingly Democratic in the South and largely Republican elsewhere, reporting improved greatly in scope and quality, and editorial pages displayed increasing independence and sophistication. Most newspapers from this period are readily available on microfilm.

The two best papers in the United States between 1900 and 1920 were the *New York Times* and *New York World.* The *New York Times* did more extensive and thorough reporting, whereas the *World* ran more searching editorials and columns and maintained more incisive political coverage. The *World* also featured the most talented editorial cartoonist of the time, Rollin Kirby. For students, the *New York Times* has the advantage of a complex index.

Each region of the country likewise enjoyed several first-class newspapers. In the Northeast outside New York, the *Springfield Republican* (Mass.) stood out, along with the *Boston Transcript, Hartford Courant* (Conn.) and the *Philadelphia Public Ledger.* The Border States supported the *Baltimore Sun, Louisville Courier Journal,* and *St. Louis Post-Dispatch.* The South's best newspaper was the *Atlanta Constitution,* while the *Raleigh News and Observer* (N. C.) gained importance because its editor, Josephus Daniels, was an intimate advisor of William Jennings Bryan and Woodrow Wilson's secretary of the navy. In the Midwest, the most widely read paper was the *Chicago Tribune,* and other excellent large-circulation dailies included the *Kansas City Star, Minneapolis Tribune,* and *Des Moines Register,* where J. N. "Ding" Darling was a rising star among editorial cartoonists. One small-town Midwestern paper that rose above the limitations of its surroundings and readership, thanks to the talent of its editor, William Allen White, was the *Emporia Gazette* (Kans). In the West, the most influential papers were the *San Francisco Examiner,* owned by William Randolph Hearst, whose publishing empire also included the *New York American* and *Chicago American* and the *Los Angeles Times.*

Every sizable ethnic group in the United States also had its own lively, widely circulated newspapers. European immigrants in cities read daily or weekly papers in their native languages. First in the South and later in Northern cities, black communities founded their own newspapers. The most militant and one of the two best of these was the *Boston Guardian,* edited and largely written by William Monroe Trotter. The other of the best and the most influential of all black journals was the NAACP's organ, *The*

Crisis, begun in 1910, edited by W. E. B. Du Bois, and featuring some of Du Bois's finest writing.

Major economic interest groups and political factions likewise supported their own newspapers. Labor unions published national, regional, and sometimes local weeklies, while the AFL maintained the *American Federationist,* which served as Samuel Gompers's mouthpiece. Interestingly, the most widely read radical periodical in the country was the *Appeal to Reason,* published in Girard, Kansas. The largest circulation urban Socialist paper was the *New York Call,* and the *Milwaukee Leader* was influential because its editor was Victor Berger. Farmers read a number of agricultural papers, often with regional emphases. Three of the most important were the *Progressive Farmer* (Raleigh, N. C.), *Wallace's Farmer* (Des Moines, Iowa), and *Capper's Weekly* (Topeka, Kans.). Political leaders with well-defined followings also turned out their own weekly newspapers, which often later became monthly magazines. The three most significant such periodicals were Bryan's *The Commoner* (Lincoln, Neb.), *La Follette's Weekly* (Madison, Wis.), and Tom Watson's *Weekly Jeffersonian* (Thomson, Ga.), which was banned from the nails and suppressed in 1917. Watson also published a monthly successively entitled *Watson's Jeffersonian Magazine* and *Watson's Magazine,* which suffered the same fate during World War I.

Excellent as American newspapers were between 1900 and 1920, by far the best medium of communication and entertainment was the magazine. The first truly national medium, magazines achieved a stature and influence that had been unequaled previously and that began to wane soon afterward. *McClure's Magazine,* started in 1893, had already established itself by 1900 as the pioneer low-priced periodical combining popular fiction with informative articles. When S. S. McClure launched the muckraking movement in 1902, his magazine dominated the field for the next five years. McClure and his magazine are the subjects of two informative books, Peter Lyon, *Success Story: The Life and Times of S. S. McClure* (New York, 1963) and Harold S. Wilson, *McClure's Magazine and the Muckrakers* (Princeton, N. J., 1970).

A magazine that resembled *McClure's* in liveliness and investigative doggedness but differed in political viewpoint was *The Masses.* Founded in 1911, this magazine really established itself as the the voice of youthful political and cultural radicalism when Max Eastman became its editor the following year. Under Eastman's editorship, *The Masses* spoke equally through his writings and John Reed's for the original Greenwich Village radicals, and through the drawings and lithographs of Art Young, who ranked as another of the best editorial cartoonists of the time. *The Masses* likewise fell under official repression in 1917. It was later revived in name only as the *New Masses,* a Communist party organ. Fortunately, in addition to microfilm, much of the written and graphic material of *The Masses* is available in two beautifully produced collections, William L. O'Neill, ed., *Echoes of Revolt* (Chicago, 1966) and Rebecca Zurier, *Art for the Masses: A Radical Magazine and Its Graphics* (Philadelphia, 1988). See also, O'Neill, *The Last Romantic: A Life of Max Eastman* (New York, 1978).

The best magazine of all in this era, and probably in all of American history, was *The New Republic,* which George F. Kennan has placed "in the foremost ranks of English-language journalism of all time." Begun in 1914, with a subsidy from Willard and Dorothy Straight, the *New Republic* featured Herbert Croly as editor, assisted by Walter Weyl and Walter Lippmann. Besides the unsigned editorials and signed articles of the three editors, the magazine carried contributions by a galaxy of writers, who included

Charles A. Beard, Randolph Bourne, Louis Brandeis, Robert Frost, Harold Laski, Roscoe Pound, Josiah Royce, George Santayana, H. G. Wells, and Rebecca West. Published collections do not convey a sense of how the *New Republic* each week demonstrated how superb a magazine could be. Three fine books do, however, illuminate the inner workings of the magazine and the lives of its founding editors: Charles Forcey, *The Crossroads of Liberalism: Croly, Weyl, Lippmann and the Progressive Era, 1900–1925* (New York, 1961); Ronald Steel, *Walter Lippmann and the American Century* (Boston, 1980); and David W. Levy, *Herbert Croly of the New Republic* (Princeton, N. J., 1985).

Other important magazines from this period, which are widely available in libraries and on microfilm, include *The American Magazine,* founded in 1907 by the secession of McClure's star reporters; *Collier's,* a popular weekly with reformist leanings; *Everybody's,* a sensationalist imitator in the muckraking movement; *Harper's Weekly,* a high-toned alternately conservative and progressive journal that closed in 1916; *Metropolitan,* which was founded in 1911 and served as an editorial platform for Roosevelt from 1915 to 1918; *The Nation,* which underwent a rebirth as a critically liberal weekly when Oswald Garrison Villard became editor in 1917; *Outlook,* a thoughtful progressive weekly that served as Roosevelt's outlet from 1909 to 1915; *Saturday Evening Post,* the leading purveyor of popular fiction and voice of conservative middle-class views, and *World's Work,* an innovative monthly new magazine founded in 1900 and edited until 1913 by Walter Hines Page.

C. Contemporary Books, Autobiographies, and Memoirs

Both fiction and non-fiction made lively reading between 1900 and 1920 and furnish excellent fields for study. Most of these books are available in libraries and in reprint editions. In the flood of novels that appeared every year during those decades some of the most interesting and enduring are those of Frank Norris, especially *The Octopus* (New York, 1901) and *The Pit* (New York, 1903); Jack London, such as *The Iron Heel* (New York, 1907) and *Martin Eden* (New York, 1909); Theodore Dreiser, particularly *Sister Carrie* (New York, 1900) and *The Financier* (New York, 1912); Sherwood Anderson, most notably *Winesburg, Ohio* (New York, 1919). Two novels of the time remain noteworthy because of their social and political impact. Upton Sinclair, *The Jungle* (New York, 1906) played a big role in muckraking and still illuminates socialist attitudes. Thomas Dixon, *The Clansman* (New York, 1905) is a lurid racist tale that expresses the prejudices that Southern white demagogues then espoused. *The Clansman* furnished the script for D. W. Griffith's classic film, "The Birth of a Nation" (1915), which in turn kicked off the refounding of the Ku Klux Klan.

Important non-fiction books addressed most of the important social and political problems between 1900 and 1920. Herbert Croly, *The Promise of American Life* (New York, 1909) brilliantly analyzed political ideas and itself played a role in the development of Roosevelt's progressivism. Other significant books in the same vein were Croly, *Progressive Democracy* (New York, 1914); Walter Weyl, *The New Democracy* (New York, 1912); and Walter Lippmann, *A Preface of Politics* (New York, 1913), *Drift and Mastery* (New York, 1914), and *The Stakes of Diplomacy* (New York, 1915). For a different vein of progressivism, with an economic thrust, see Louis D. Brandeis, *Other People's Money and How the Bankers Use It* (New York, 1914). The three most important books on race relations are one by a white man, the muckraker Ray Stannard Baker, *Following the Color Line* (New York, 1908), and two by the greatest of black American intellectuals,

W. E. B. Du Bois, *The Souls of Black Folk* (New York, 1902) and *Darkwater* (New York, 1920). The best book of general observation of the time is Henry James, *The American Scene* (New York, 1907).

Many leading figures of these years wrote autobiographies or memoirs. Theodore Roosevelt, *Autobiography* (New York, 1913) must be read with caution, but it is surprisingly revealing for a book by a practicing politician. The same observation applies to Robert M. La Follette, *Autobiography* (Madison, Wis., 1911). More candid among the memoirs of public figures are George W. Norris, *Fighting Liberal* (New York, 1944); Henry L. Stimson, *On Active Service in Peace and War* (New York, 1948); Nicholas Murray Butler, *Across the Busy Years* (2 vols., New York, 1939–40), and Gifford Pinchot, *Breaking New Ground* (New York, 1947). Woodrow Wilson wrote no first-hand account of his life and career, but three memoirs by members of his family are Edith Bolling Wilson, *My Memoir* (Indianapolis, 1939); Eleanor Wilson McAdoo, *The Woodrow Wilsons* (New York, 1937), and Maude Axson Elliott, *My Aunt Louisa and Woodrow Wilson* (Chapel Hill, N. C., 1944). A comparably intimate family view of Roosevelt comes from Alice Roosevelt Longworth, *Crowded Hours* (New York, 1933). Intimate, insightful views of Roosevelt and Wilson by friends can be found in Owen Wister, *Roosevelt: The Story of a Friendship* (New York, 1930); Lewis Einstein, *Roosevelt: His Mind in Action* (Boston, 1930), and Edith Gittings Reid, *Woodrow Wilson* (New York, 1934). For the Wilson administration and World War I, nearly every cabinet member and civilian and military leader left an account of his role in major events. They vary in readability and reliability, but all are useful.

The best autobiographies of the era are, not surprisingly, those of writers and journalists. *The Education of Henry Adams* (Boston, 1918) stands apart as a classic of American literature, and it contains arresting interpretations of Roosevelt. *The Autobiography of Lincoln Steffens* (New York, 1931) likewise enjoys special status, but it must be used with caution as an account of events and people. More reliable and more useful for public affairs and middle-class attitudes is *The Autobiography of William Allen White* (New York, 1944), which matches Steffens's in literary quality. Other fine journalists' autobiographies are Ida M. Tarbell, *All in a Day's Work* (New York, 1939); Ray Stannard Baker, *American Chronicle* (New York, 1945); Mark Sullivan, *The Education of an American* (New York, 1938); and Oswald Garrison Villard, *Fighting Years* (New York, 1939). The best autobiography by a woman of these years is Jane Addams, *Twenty Years at Hull House* (New York, 1910). Samuel Gompers, *Seventy Years of Life and Labor* (New York, 1925) is useful for the mainstream of the labor movement, while Morris Hillquit, *Loose Leaves from a Busy Life* (New York, 1934) gives a leading Socialist's viewpoint. Two superb but different autobiographies of Afro-Americans are Booker T. Washington, *Up from Slavery* (New York, 1901), and W. E. B. DuBois, *Dusk of Dawn* (New York, 1940). For an unusual Wall Street financier's autobiography, see Thomas W. Lamont, *Across World Frontiers* (New York, 1951).

II. Interpretative Works

The significance and excitement of events in the United States between 1900 and 1920 have drawn some of the best historical minds to recount and interpret them. Historians and other writers have viewed these decades at all levels, from the grandest sweep of political and social movements to the doings of individuals and small groups at particular moments. Controversies have raged and continue to burn over the meaning and value of ideas, programs, and decisions from this era. Appropriately, the two biggest events have attracted the greatest attention and argument—the reform movements called progressivism and intervention in and peacemaking after World War I.

Three fine essays that examine interpretative controversies surrounding those events are David M. Kennedy, "Overview: The Progressive Era," *Historian* 37 (1975), 453–68; Daniel T. Rodgers, "In Search of Progressivism," *Reviews in American History*, 10 (1982), 113–32; and Daniel M. Smith, "National Interest and American Intervention, 1917: An Historiographical Appraisal," *Journal of American History*, 52 (June 1965), 5–24. These essays contain abundant citations to books and articles about progressivism and World War I. Another good place to begin examining historical writing is with bibliographies and historiographical essays. Some of the most comprehensive of these are Arthur S. Link and William M. Leary, *The Progressive Era and the Great War, 1896–1920* (New York, 1969); Link and Richard L. McCormick, *Progressivism* (Arlington Heights, Ill., 1983); John Milton Cooper, Jr., ed., *The Causes and Consequences of World War I* (New York, 1971); and David R. Woodward and Robert F. Maddox, *America and World War I: A Selected Annotated Bibliography of English Language Sources* (New York, 1985).

A. General Works and Interpretations

Some of the most incisive historical writing done on any period of American history covers the two decades between 1900 and 1920. Three excellent narratives based upon extensive primary research by the leading experts on the subjects are George E. Mowry, *The Era of Theodore Roosevelt and the Birth of Modern America* (New York, 1958); Arthur S. Link, *Woodrow Wilson and the Progressive Era, 1910–1917* (New York, 1954); and Robert H. Ferrell, *Woodrow Wilson and World War I, 1917–1921* (New York, 1985). The Mowry and Link volumes are especially authoritative and insightful on national politics, and the Link and Ferrell volumes are masterful on diplomacy.

Two outstanding interpretative syntheses treat these years as part of a broader focus: Richard Hofstadter, *The Age of Reform: From Bryan to FDR* (New York, 1955) and Robert H. Wiebe, *The Search for Order, 1877–1920* (New York, 1967). Some of Hofstadter's interpretations have come in for sharp attack, especially his "status revolution" view of progressivism, but the *Age of Reform* remains his greatest work and the most penetrating and encompassing depiction of this era. Wiebe's viewpoint emphasizes social forces more than politics and is open to question about the relation between the two areas, but the *Search for Order* stands as an outstanding achievement in illuminating complex developments.

Other works that treat this entire period with various emphases are Mark Sullivan, *Our Times, 1900–1925* (6 vols., New York, 1926–35), which is particularly good for middle-class culture and attitudes; Eric F. Goldman, *Rendezvous with Destiny* (New York, 1952), whose scope, liveliness, and attention to social and political thought have never been equaled; Lewis L. Gould, *Reform and Regulation* (New York, 1978), which gives much needed attention to organizational and conservative politics; James MacGregor Burns, *The Workshop of Democracy* (New York, 1985), which depicts the entire spectrum of politics and government; Michael E. McGerr, *The Decline of Popular Politics* (New York, 1986), which stresses voter turnout and methods of campaigning; and Neil I. Painter, *Standing at Armageddon* (New York, 1987), which corrects earlier inattention to radical, feminist, and Afro-American groups in this era. Two interpretations of reform politics after 1900 from radical perspectives are Gabriel Kolko, *The Triumph of Conservatism*

(New York, 1963) and James Weinstein, *The Corporate Ideal in the Liberal State* (Boston, 1968).

For intellectual and cultural histories of this period see Alfred Kazin, *On Native Grounds* (New York, 1942); Henry F. May, *The End of American Innocence* (New York, 1959); Christopher Lasch, *The New Radicalism in America* (New York, 1965); T. J. Jackson Lears, *No Place of Grace* (New York, 1981); and Robert M. Crunden, *Ministers of Reform* (New York, 1982). Other fascinating aspects of American thought and attitudes in these decades are brilliantly treated in Richard Hofstadter, *Anti-Intellectualism in American Life* (New York, 1961) and *The Progressive Historians* (New York, 1968) and Daniel T. Rodgers, *The Work Ethic in Industrial America, 1850–1920* (Chicago, 1978). American education in this period is the subject of two books by the foremost historian of the subject, Lawrence A. Cremin, *The Triumph of the School* (New York, 1961) and *American Education: The Metropolitan Experience* (New York, 1987).

The growth of the American economy and business in these decades is ably examined in W. Elliott Brownlee, *The Dynamics of Ascent* (New York, 1974); and in two notable books by Alfred D. Chandler, *Strategy and Structure* (Cambridge, Mass., 1982) and *The Visible Hand: The Managerial Revolution in American Business* (Cambridge, Mass., 1977). For conflicting views of the impact of reforms on the biggest and most important industry in this era, see Gabriel Kolko, *Railroads and Regulation, 1877–1916* (Princeton, N. J., 1965) and Albro Martin, *Enterprise Denied: Origins of the Decline of American Railroads* (New York, 1971). On the conflicting wings of organized labor, see Philip Taft, *The A.F. of L. in the Time of Gompers* (New York, 1957) and Melvyn Dubofsky, *We Shall Be All: A History of the Industrial Workers of the World* (Chicago, 1969).

B. Biographies and Studies of Individuals

Given the importance and color of leading personalities between 1900 and 1920, it is no surprise that some of the best biographies of Americans depict their lives. Because Theodore Roosevelt and Woodrow Wilson loomed so large in public affairs, treatments of them stand out in number and quality. None of the most recent works on Roosevelt has yet reached his presidency, but Edmund Morris, *The Rise of Theodore Roosevelt* (New York, 1979) and David McCullough, *Mornings on Horseback* (New York, 1981) shed fresh light on his early years. The best single volume biography remains William H. Harbaugh, *Power and Responsibility: The Life and Times of Theodore Roosevelt* (New York, 1961). By far the most penetrating studies of his political career are still George E. Mowry, *Theodore Roosevelt and the Progressive Movement* (Madison, Wis., 1946) and John M. Blum, *The Republican Roosevelt* (Cambridge, Mass., 1954). Two good studies of his foreign policies are Howard K. Beale, *Theodore Roosevelt and the Rise of America to World Power* (Baltimore, 1956) and Frederick W. Marks III, *Velvet on Iron: The Diplomacy of Theodore Roosevelt* (Lincoln, Neb., 1979).

Wilson has attracted even more study. The fullest and easily finest biography is Arthur S. Link, *Wilson* (5 vols., Princeton, N. J., 1947–65). Link's volumes contain not only accounts and analyses of Wilson's thought and actions, but they also chronicle the politics and diplomacy of the period from 1910 to 1917. No one who wishes to study those years in real depth can afford not to read these volumes. The most recent and generally satisfactory single-volume life of Wilson is Kendrick A. Clements, *Woodrow Wilson* (Boston, 1987). In a special category is Edwin A. Weinstein, *Woodrow Wilson: A Medical and Psychological Biography* (Princeton, N. J., 1981), which is a pioneering venture in this type of biography. The most complete and incisive studies of Wilson's foreign policies are Arthur S. Link, *Wilson the Diplomatist* (Baltimore, 1957) and its considerably revised successor, *Woodrow Wilson: Revolution, War, and Peace* (Arlington Heights, Ill., 1979) and N. Gordon Levin, *Woodrow Wilson and World Politics* (New York, 1967). Another masterful work is Patrick Devlin, *Too Proud to Fight: Woodrow Wilson's Neutrality* (New York, 1975). One work that examines Wilson and Roosevelt in comparative perspective is John Milton Cooper, Jr., *The Warrior and the Priest* (Cambridge, Mass., 1983).

Among other political leaders, the middle president of the period gets fair but critical treatment in Henry F. Pringle, *The Life and Times of William Howard Taft* (2 vols., New York, 1939) and James R. Anderson, *William Howard Taft: A Conservative's Conception of the Presidency* (Ithaca, N. Y., 1973). The fullest biography of Bryan is Paolo E. Coletta, *William Jennings Bryan* (3 vols., Lincoln, Neb., 1964–69), but the best and most readable biography is Le Roy Ashby, *William Jennings Bryan* (Boston, 1987). Other incisive studies are Paul W. Glad, *The Trumpet Soundeth: William Jennings Bryan and his Democracy, 1896–1912* (Lincoln, Neb., 1960); Lawrence W. Levine, *Defender of the Faith: Bryan, the Last Decade, 1915–1925* (New York, 1965); and Kendrick A. Clements, *William Jennings Bryan, Missionary Isolationist* (Knoxville, Tenn., 1983).

On the Republican side, leading conservatives receive excellent treatment in Philip C. Jessup, *Elihu Root* (2 vols., New York, 1938); Richard W. Leopold, *Elihu Root and the Conservative Tradition* (Boston, 1954); John A. Garraty, *Henry Cabot Lodge* (New York, 1954); and William C. Widenor, *Henry Cabot Lodge and the Search for an American Foreign Policy* (Berkeley, Calif., 1980). Moderate leaders are ably depicted in Merlo J. Pusey, *Charles Evans Hughes* (2 vols., New York, 1951); Dexter Perkins, *Charles Evans Hughes and American Democratic Statesmanship* (Boston, 1956); and Elting E. Morison, *Turmoil and Tradition: A Study of the Life and Times of Henry L. Stimson* (Boston, 1960). The fullest biography of the leading insurgent-progressive Republican is Belle Case La Follette and Fola La Follette, *Robert M. La Follette* (2 vols., New York, 1952), but equally useful and more incisive are Patrick T. Maney, *"Young Bob" La Follette* (Columbia, Mo., 1978) and Herbert F. Margulies, *Senator Lenroot of Wisconsin* (Columbia, Mo., 1977). Another full biography of an insurgent is Richard W. Lowitt, *George W. Norris* (3 vols., Syracuse, N. Y., and Urbana, Ill., 1963–78). On a leading insurgent who became a Progressive, Claude G. Bowers, *Beveridge and the Progressive Era* (Boston, 1930) is lively and good on his personality, while John Braeman, *Albert J. Beveridge: American Nationalist* (Chicago, 1971) is useful on party politics.

Aside from Wilson and Bryan, few major Democrats have attracted good biographers. Exceptions are John M. Blum, *Joe Tumulty and the Wilson Era* (Boston, 1951); John Milton Cooper, Jr., *Walter Hines Page* (Chapel Hill, N. C., 1977); and Jordan A. Schwartz, *The Speculator: Bernard M. Baruch in Washington* (Chapel Hill, N. C., 1981). Ironically, three of the best biographies of Democrats of this era examine the lives of virulent racist Southern demagogues, C. Vann Woodward, *Tom Watson: Agrarian Rebel* (New York, 1938); Francis B. Simkins, *Pitchfork Ben Tillman, South Carolinian* (Baton Rouge, La., 1944); and William F. Holmes, *The White Chief: James Kimble Vardaman* (Baton Rouge, La., 1970).

Judicial leaders have also received good biographical treatments. In addition to the works on Hughes, biographies of Oliver Wendell Holmes and Louis D. Brandeis have illuminated the careers of the most significant justices of the Supreme Court. Mark DeWolfe Howe, *Oliver Wendell Holmes* (2 vols., Cambridge, Mass., 1957–63) unfortunately covers only his early life and career, but Gary M. Aichele *Oliver Wendell Holmes*

(Boston, 1988) is an insightful brief biography which spans his entire career. Alpheus T. Mason, *Brandeis: A Free Man's Life* (New York, 1946) is the most detailed biography, but the best interpretation of his thought and character is Philippa M. Strum, *Louis D. Brandeis: Justice for the People* (Cambridge, Mass., 1984).

Other figures from the period in many fields have likewise received good biographical treatments. For leading black Americans, the best biographies are Louis R. Harlan, *Booker T. Washington* (2 vols., New York, 1972–83); Stephen R. Fox, *The Guardian of Boston: William Monroe Trotter* (New York, 1970); and W. Manning Marable, *W. E. B. Du Bois* (Boston, 1986). Prominent women of these years are not yet adequately represented in the biographical literature. The best lives of women reformers are Allen F. Davis, *American Heroine: The Life and Legend of Jane Addams* (New York, 1973) and David M. Kennedy, *Birth Control in America: The Career of Margaret Sanger* (New Haven, Conn., 1971). The only really good work on a suffrage leader treats a figure of the preceding era, Elisabeth Griffith, *In Her Own Right: The Life of Elizabeth Cady Stanton* (New York, 1984). Because he was so colorful and so effective, Eugene Debs has attracted more attention than any other radical of this era. Ray Ginger, *The Bending Cross* (New Brunswick, N. J., 1949) captures Debs's personal appeal, while Nick Salvatore, *Eugene Victor Debs, Citizen and Socialist* (Urbana, Ill., 1982) conveys a sense of the working-class culture in which he operated. The best biographies of journalists are those of McClure, Croly, and Lippmann mentioned earlier. See also W. A. Swanberg, *Citizen Hearst* (New York, 1961). On American military commanders in World War I, the fullest biography is Frank W. Vandiver, *Black Jack: The Life and Times of John J. Pershing* (2 vols., College Station, Tex., 1977), but the best are Elting E. Morison, *Admiral Sims and the Modern American Navy* (Boston, 1943) and Edward M. Coffman, *The Hilt of the Sword: The Career of Peyton C. March* (Madison, Wis., 1966).

C. Progressivism and Other Reforms

Progressivism has dominated the literature on domestic American history between 1900 and 1920. The general and interpretative works and the studies of Roosevelt and Wilson previously cited address the rise and decline of reform at the national level. The deepest delving and most thought-provoking interpretations are in the works of Hofstadter, Link, Mowry, Blum, and Wiebe. For congressional reformers, two useful studies are Kenneth W. Hechler, *Insurgency* (New York, 1940) and James L. Holt, *Congressional Insurgents and the Party System, 1909–1916* (Cambridge, Mass., 1967). For the other side, see Horace S. Merrill and Marian C. Merrill, *The Republican Command, 1897–1913* (Lexington, Ky., 1971). The best party study is David Sarasohn, *The Party of Reform: The Democrats in the Progressive Era* (Jackson, Miss., 1989). Regional studies of progressivism include Russell B. Nye, *Midwestern Progressive Politics* (East Lansing, Mich., 1951); C. Vann Woodward, *Origins of the New South, 1877–1913* (Baton Rouge, La., 1951); George B. Tindall, *The Emergence of the New South* (Baton Rouge, La., 1967); Jack Temple Kirby, *Darkness at the Dawning: Race and Reform in the Progressive South* (Philadelphia, 1972); and Dewey W. Grantham, Jr., *Southern Progressivism* (Knoxville, Tenn., 1983).

Some of the best studies of progressivism examine reform at the state and municipal levels. Because they spawned the strongest progressive movements, Wisconsin and California have drawn the greatest attention. In addition to works on La Follette, his state's reform movements are best examined in David P. Thelen, *The New Citizenship: Origins of Progressivism in Wisconsin* (Columbia, Mo., 1972) and Herbert F. Margulies, *The*

Decline of Progressivism in Wisconsin (Madison, Wis., 1968). On California, see George E. Mowry, *The California Progressives* (Berkeley, Calif. 1951); Spencer W. Olin, Jr., *California's Prodigal Sons: Hiram Johnson and the Progressives* (Berkeley, Calif., 1968); and Michael Paul Rogin and John L. Shover, *Political Change in California* (Westport, Conn., 1970). Studies of northeastern states include Richard M. Abrams, *Conservatism in a Progressive Era: Massachusetts Politics, 1900–1912* (Cambridge, Mass., 1964); Richard L. McCormick, *From Realignment to Reform: Political Change in New York State* (Ithaca, N. Y., 1981); and James Wright, *The Progressive Yankees: Republican Reformers in New Hampshire, 1900–1916* (Hanover, N. H., 1987). For southern states, see Albert D. Kirwan, *Revolt of the Rednecks: Mississippi Politics, 1876–1925* (Lexington, Ky., 1951); Sheldon Hackney, *Populism to Progressivism in Alabama* (Princeton, N. J., 1969); and Lewis L. Gould, Jr., *Progressives and Prohibitionists: Texas Democrats in the Wilson Era* (Austin, Tex., 1973). Two good studies on municipal reform are Zane L. Miller, *Boss Cox's Cincinnati* (New York, 1968) and James B. Crooks, *Politics and Progress: The Rise of Urban Progressivism in Baltimore* (Baton Rouge, La., 1968). An excellent general discussion of urban progressivism is John D. Buenker, *Urban Liberalism and Progressive Reform* (New York, 1973).

Various aspects of reform in this era receive extended discussion in a number of works. Muckraking journalism is covered in works already cited. The conservation movement comes in for analysis in Samuel P. Hays, *Conservation and the Gospel of Efficiency* (Cambridge, Mass., 1959), while its sharpest controversy is shrewdly examined in James Penick, Jr., *Progressive Politics and Conservation: The Ballinger-Pinchot Affair* (Chicago, 1968). Business reactions and contributions to reform are discussed broadly in Robert Wiebe, *Businessmen and Reform* (Cambridge, Mass., 1962) and in specific instances in Melvin I. Urofsky, *Big Steel and the Wilson Administration* (Columbus, Ohio, 1969) and Stanley P. Caine, *The Myth of a Progressive Reform: Railroad Regulation in Wisconsin, 1903–1910* (Madison, Wis., 1970). A superb study of the Social Gospel is Henry F. May, *Protestant Churches and Industrial America* (New York, 1949). Besides the biographies of Debs, the most useful work on socialism in this era is James Weinstein, *The Decline of Socialism in America, 1912–1925* (New York, 1967).

Social reforms in this era have likewise received extensive and penetrating treatment from historians. Social workers and their allies are examined in Robert C. Bremner, *From the Depths: The Discovery of Poverty in the United States* (Cambridge, Mass., 1956); Roy C. Lubove, *The Professional Altruist* (New York, 1965); and Allen F. Davis, *Spearheads of Reform* (New York, 1967). The woman suffrage movement is treated at various levels and from different perspectives in Eleanor Flexner, *Century of Struggle* (Cambridge, Mass., 1959); Aileen Kraditor, *The Ideas of the Woman Suffrage Movement* (New York, 1965); Allen Grimes, *The Puritan Ethic and Woman Suffrage* (New York, 1967); and William L. O'Neill, *Everyone Was Brave* (Chicago, 1969). Three useful and balanced historical works on the prohibition movement are Joseph R. Gusfield, *Symbolic Crusade* (Urbana, Ill., 1956); James W. Timberlake, *Prohibition and the Progressive Movement* (Cambridge, Mass., 1963), and Norman F. Clark, *Deliver Us from Evil* (New York, 1976). The nascent civil rights movement is examined in Charles Flint Kellogg, *NAACP* (Baltimore, 1967); Nancy J. Weiss, *The National Urban League, 1910–1940* (New York, 1974), and Robert L. Zangrando, *The NAACP Crusade against Lynching, 1909–1950* (Philadelphia, 1980). The best work on immigration restriction is John Higham, *Strangers in the Land* (New Brunswick, N. J., 1955).

D. Race, Ethnicity, and Gender

Perhaps the most eloquent testimony to the domination of American life by white Protestant men between 1900 and 1920 and long afterward is the comparative paucity of historical work on blacks, immigrants, and women. Some of the most exciting and impassioned fields of historical research during the last quarter of a century have been Afro-American and women's history. The results of this research are only now beginning to correct the imbalances in previous historical attention.

Afro-American history is the best developed of these new fields for this era. In addition to the biographies of Washington, Trotter, and Du Bois, and works on civil rights, excellent studies illuminate facets of black life in America between 1900 and 1920. The exodus from the South is treated in Florette Henri, *Black Migration: The Movement North, 1900–1920* (New York, 1975). Gilbert Osofsky, *Harlem: The Making of a Ghetto* (New York, 1965), and Allen Spear, *Black Chicago* (New York, 1965) describe and analyze black experience in building communities in northern cities. The unhappiest side of black migration is recounted in Robert V. Haynes, *A Night of Violence: The Houston Race Riot of 1917* (Baton Rouge, La., 1976) and William M. Tuttle, *Race Riot: Chicago in the Red Summer of 1919* (New York, 1970). On the immigrant experience in broad perspective, Thomas J. Archdeacon, *Becoming American* (New York, 1983) is an able recent treatment, although much can still be gained from Oscar Handlin, *The Uprooted* (New York, 1952).

E. Foreign Policy, World War I, and the Post-war Period

Two contrasting general treatments of American foreign policy between 1900 and 1920 are George F. Kennan, *American Diplomacy, 1900–1950* (Chicago, 1951) and Robert E. Osgood, *Ideals and Self-Interest in America's Foreign Relations* (Chicago, 1953). Roosevelt's and Wilson's foreign policies are treated best in the works already cited. The most comprehensive study of American diplomacy leading to intervention in World War I is Ernest R. May, *The World War and American Isolation, 1914–1917* (Cambridge, Mass., 1959); see also Ross Gregory, *The Origins of American Intervention in the First World War* (New York, 1971). On war-time diplomacy, W. B. Fowler, *British-American Relations, 1917–1918: The Role of Sir William Wiseman* (Princeton, N. J., 1970) is incisive. Recent treatments of peacemaking and the controversy over joining the League of Nations are Arthur Walworth, *Woodrow Wilson and His Peacemakers* (New York, 1983) and Lloyd G. Ambrosius, *Woodrow Wilson and the American Diplomatic Tradition: The Treaty Fight in Perspective* (New York, 1988).

The best military history of the United States in World War I is Edward M. Coffman, *The War to End All Wars* (New York, 1968). The draft is chronicled in John Whiteclay Chambers II, *To Raise an Army* (New York, 1987). Financial, industrial, and labor aspects of mobilization are treated in Charles Gilbert, *American Financing of World War I* (Westport, Conn., 1970); Robert D. Cuff, *The War Industries Board* (Baltimore, 1973); and Valerie Jean Conner, *The National War Labor Board* (Chapel Hill, N. C., 1983). The Wilson administration's propaganda efforts are ably covered in Stephen L. Vaughn, *Holding Fast to Inner Lines: Democracy, Nationalism, and the Committee on Public Information* (Chapel Hill, N. C., 1980), while grass-roots mobilization is treated in William J. Breen, *Uncle Sam at Home: Civilian Mobilization, Wartime Federalism and the Com-*

mittee for National Defense (Westport, Conn., 1984). The impact of the war on fighting men and succeeding generations comes in for a brilliant discussion in a British context in Paul Fussell, *The Great War and Modern Memory* (New York, 1975)—a book that every student of World War I should read.

The effects of the war on the United States have received much attention from historians. The fullest treatment remains Frederic L. Paxson, *American Democracy and the World War, 1914–1920* (3 vols., Boston and Berkeley, Calif., 1936–48), while the volumes of Link, *Wilson*, superbly cover the period up to April 1917. For aspects of the war's effects on public affairs before intervention, see John Milton Cooper, Jr., *The Vanity of Power: American Isolationism and the First World War* (Westport, Conn., 1969); John Garry Clifford, *Citizen Soldiers: The Plattsburg Training Camp Movement* (Lexington, Ky., 1972); and John P. Finnegan, *Against the Specter of the Dragon: The Campaign for American Military Preparedness* (Westport, Conn., 1974).

A good study of the war's impact after intervention is David M. Kennedy, *Over Here: The First World War and American Society* (New York, 1980). On political developments, see Seward W. Livermore, *Politics Is Adjourned: Woodrow Wilson and the War Congress* (Middletown, Conn., 1966). The ways in which the war affected German-Americans are analyzed in Frederick C. Luebke, *Bonds of Loyalty* (DeKalb, Ill., 1974), and some of its effects on women are treated in Maureen W. Greenwald, *Women, War, and Work: The Impact of World War I on Women Workers in the United States* (Westport, Conn., 1980). The experiences of blacks in military service are examined in Floretta Henri, *The Unknown Soldiers: Black American Troops in World War I* (Philadelphia, 1974) and Gerald W. Patton, *War and Race: The Black Officer in the American Military* (Westport, Conn., 1981).

War-time and post-war repression of civil liberties have also attracted a lot of attention from historians. In addition to the works on Debs and the Socialists, see also William Preston, Jr., *Aliens and Dissenters: Federal Suppression of Radicals, 1903–1933* (Cambridge, Mass., 1963); Harry N. Scheiber, *The Wilson Administration and Civil Liberties, 1917–1921* (Ithaca, N. Y., 1960); Donald B. Johnson, *The Challenge to American Freedoms: World War I and the Origins of the American Civil Liberties Union* (Lexington, Ky., 1963); and Paul L. Murphy, *World War I and the Origin of Civil Liberties* (New York, 1970). The post-war hysteria is treated in Robert K. Murray, *Red Scare* (Minneapolis, 1955) and Stanley Coben, *A. Mitchell Palmer* (New York, 1962). See also Francis Russell, *A City in Terror: The 1919 Boston Police Strike* (New York, 1975). The judicial response to infringements of civil rights is the subject of Richard Polenberg, *Fighting Faiths: The Abrams Case, the Supreme Court and Free Speech* (New York, 1988).

The political controversies over the Treaty of Versailles and membership in the League of Nations receive exhaustive, usually contentious treatment in works on Wilson, Lodge, and the diplomacy of the war. An excellent study of the diehard opponents of joining the League is Ralph A. Stone, *The Irreconcilables* (Lexington, Ky., 1970). On disenchantment with the war and Wilson, see Warren I. Cohen, *The American Revisionists: The Lessons of Intervention in World War I* (Chicago, 1967) and Stuart D. Rochester, *American Liberal Disillusionment in the Wake of World War I* (University Park, Pa., 1977). On changes during the immediate post-war period, see David Burner, *The Politics of Provincialism: The Democratic Party in Transition, 1918–1932* (New York, 1968) and Burl Noggle, *Into the Twenties: The United States from the Armistice to Normalcy* (Urbana, Ill., 1974). An excellent study of the last election of these decades is Wesley M. Bagby,

The Road to Normalcy: The Presidential Campaign and Election of 1920 (Baltimore, 1962). Of the many biographies of the man who rang down the curtain on the second golden age of American politics, the best is Francis Russell, *The Shadow of Blooming Grove: Warren G. Harding in His Times* (New York,1968).

Illustration Credits

Page 1, Library of Congress; p. 4, The Kansas State Historical Society, Topeka; p. 7, The Bettmann Archive; p. 9, Jacob A. Riis Collection, Museum of the City of New York; p. 10, Museum of the City of New York; p. 12, Courtesy of the Rockefeller Archive Center; p. 13, The Pierpont Morgan Library; p. 14, The Bettmann Archive; p. 15, H. V. Allison Galleries, New York; p. 17, Library of Congress; p. 19, Missouri Historical Society; p. 21, Library of Congress; p. 22, Historical Pictures Service, Chicago; p. 27, Historical Pictures Service, Chicago; p. 29, Library of Congress; p. 32, PACH / Bettmann Archive; p. 34, Courtesy, Frederic Remington Art Museum, Ogdensburg, N.Y.; p. 35, The New York Public Library; p. 37, Library of Congress; p. 41, Library of Congress; p. 43, The Warder Collection; p. 45, Historical Pictures Service, Chicago; p. 47, Library of Congress; p. 49, Forest Service Collection, National Agricultural Library; p. 50, Culver Pictures, Inc.; p. 54, Library of Congress; p. 55, Theodore Roosevelt Collection, Harvard College Library; p. 57, The Warder Collection; p. 60, Library of Congress; p. 64, Historical Pictures Service, Chicago; p. 67, The New York Public Library; p. 69, Library of Congress; p. 70, Historical Pictures Service, Chicago; p. 72, The Warder Collection; p. 74, Courtesy, South Caroliniana Library, University of South Carolina; p. 75, Library of Congress; p. 76, Harvard University Archives; p. 77, Library of Congress; p. 79, *New York Times*; p. 80, Historical Pictures Service, Chicago; p. 81, Archives of Labor and Urban Affairs, Wayne State University; p. 83, Brown Brothers; p. 85, Culver Pictures; p. 88, Brown Brothers; p. 86, Courtesy, Indiana University; p. 87, The Bettmann Archive; p. 91, State Historical Society of Wisconsin; p. 94, State Historical Society of Iowa; p. 96, Library of Congress; p. 98, Brown Brothers; p. 102, The Warder Collection; p. 103, Culver Pictures, Inc.; p. 105, Library of Congress; p. 107, Historical Pictures Service, Chicago; p. 108, The Metropolitan Museum of Art, Fletcher Fund, 1942 (42. 13. 11); p. 110, California State Library; p. 112, Forest Service Collection, National Agricultural Library; p. 116, Library of Congress; p. 118, Library of Congress; p. 124, The Warder Collection; p. 126, Schlesinger Library, Radcliffe College; p. 130, Historical Pictures Service, Chicago; p. 132, Illinois State Historical Library; p. 133, Courtesy, Ford Motor Company; p. 134, Culver Pictures, Inc.; p. 135, National Archives; p. 136, Smithsonian Institution; p. 138, Culver Pictures, Inc.; p. 139, Library of Congress; p. 141, Ohio Historical Society; p. 142, Library of Congress; p. 144, Library of Congress; p. 146, Brown Brothers; p. 148, Library of Congress; p. 150, Brown Brothers; p. 152, The Warder

Collection; p. 156, Historical Pictures Service, Chicago; p. 160, Brown Brothers; p. 165, The Bettmann Archive; p. 167, The Bettmann Archive; p. 173, The Warder Collection; p. 177, Library of Congress; p. 180, Library of Congress; p. 184, The Warder Collection; p. 191, Historical Pictures Service, Chicago; p. 192, Historical Pictures Service, Chicago; p. 193, State Historical Society of Wisconsin; p. 194, Library of Congress; p. 196, Library of Congress; p. 198, Historical Pictures Service, Chicago; p. 199, Historical Pictures Service, Chicago; p. 204, The Warder Collection; p. 205, UPI / Bettmann Newsphotos; p. 206, Library of Congress; p. 209, Library of Congress; p. 211, Archives of Labor and Urban Affairs, Wayne State University; p. 215, Courtesy, Brandeis University; p. 222, Library of Congress; p. 224, Library of Congress; p. 226, Library of Congress; p. 229, Historical Pictures Service, Chicago; p. 234, *New York Times;* p. 235, National Portrait Gallery, Smithsonian Institution, Washington, D.C.; p. 239, The Warder Collection; p. 240, Brown Brothers; p. 245, Library of Congress; p. 248, Historical Pictures Service, Chicago; p. 250, UPI / Bettmann Archive; p. 257, The Bettmann Archive; p. 262, Historical Pictures Service, Chicago; p. 263, State Historical Society of Wisconsin; p. 265, UPI /Bettmann Archive; p. 269, National Archives; p. 270, The Warder Collection; p. 272, Brown Brothers; p. 274, National Archives; p. 275, National Archives; p. 279, National Archives; p. 280, National Archives; p. 282, National Archives; p. 283, Brown Brothers; p. 284, The Warder Collection; p. 285, National Archives; p. 286, National Archives; p. 288, Historical Pictures Service, Chicago; p. 290, Library of Congress; p. 293, The Warder Collection; p. 294, National Archives; p. 295, National Archives; p. 299, The Bettmann Archive; p. 304, Library of Congress; p. 306, National Archives; p. 309, National Archives; p. 311, Library of Congress; p. 317, National Archives; p. 323, State Historical Society of Wisconsin; p. 325, Boston Public Library; p. 326, Library of Congress; p. 327, The Warder Collection; p. 331, Historical Pictures Service, Chicago; p. 332, The Bettmann Archive; p. 334, Brown Brothers; p. 335, The Warder Collection; p. 341, The Warder Collection; p. 344, The Warder Collection; p. 347, Library of Congress; p. 349, The Warder Collection; p. 352, Library of Congress; p. 353, Library of Congress; p. 359, Historical Pictures Service, Chicago; p. 360, Reuters / Bettmann Newsphotos; p. 362, Library of Congress; p. 366, Courtesy, Ohio Historical Society Library; p. 368, The Bettmann Archive; p. 374, Library of Congress.

Index

italicized page numbers refer to illustrations